Ben Ammi Ben Israel

Bloomsbury Studies in Black Religion and Cultures

Series Editors: Anthony B. Pinn and Monica R. Miller

Bloomsbury Studies in Black Religion and Cultures advances innovative scholarship that reimagines and animates the global study of Black religions, culture and identity across space and time. The series publishes scholarship that addresses the mutually constitutive nature of race and religion and the social, cultural, intellectual and material effects of religio-racial formations and identities. The series welcomes projects that address and foreground the intersectional and constitutive nature of Black religions and cultures and privileges work that is inter/transdisciplinary and methodologically intersectional in nature.

African Spirituality, Politics and Knowledge Systems
Toyin Falola

Black Transhuman Liberation Theology
Philip Butler

Innovation and Competition in Zimbabwean Pentecostalism
Edited by Ezra Chitando

Religion and Inequality in Africa
Edited by Ezra Chitando, Loreen Maseno and Joram Tarusarira

Speculations on Black Life
Edited by Darrell Jones, Monifa Love and Anthony Pinn

Ben Ammi Ben Israel

*Black Theology, Theodicy and Judaism
in the Thought of the African Hebrew
Israelite Messiah*

Michael T. Miller

BLOOMSBURY ACADEMIC
LONDON • NEW YORK • OXFORD • NEW DELHI • SYDNEY

BLOOMSBURY ACADEMIC
Bloomsbury Publishing Plc
50 Bedford Square, London, WC1B 3DP, UK
1385 Broadway, New York, NY 10018, USA
29 Earlsfort Terrace, Dublin 2, Ireland

BLOOMSBURY, BLOOMSBURY ACADEMIC and the Diana logo are
trademarks of Bloomsbury Publishing Plc

First published in Great Britain 2023

Series design: Maria Rajka
Cover image © African Hebrew Israelites of Jerusalem

A catalogue record for this book is available from the British Library.

Library of Congress Control Number: 2023933710

ISBN: HB: 978-1-3502-9513-1
         ePDF: 978-1-3502-9514-8
         eBook: 978-1-3502-9515-5

Series: Bloomsbury Studies in Black Religion and Cultures

Typeset by Integra Software Services Pvt. Ltd.

To find out more about our authors and books visit www.bloomsbury.com
and sign up for our newsletters.

Contents

Acknowledgements

This book has been more than ten years in the making, ever since I first sat down in the library of the African Hebrew Israelite community in Dimona. It was planned and written between 2020 and 2022 as part of a Fellowship at the Polish Institute of Advanced Studies (PIASt), funded by the Gerda Henkel Stiftung and The Spalding Trust. At PIASt I benefited from the conversations held with other fellows from across the range of human sciences, but also from the kindness and warmth of my hosts, Marta Walenta and Prof Przemysław Urbańczyk.

Two chapters incorporate research I carried out for previous articles.[1] I am grateful to Alastair Lockhart (of the Centre for the Critical Study of Apocalyptic and Millenarian Movements) and Gerard Hödl, Hannah Blackenwegner and Helmut Deibl of the *Interdisciplinary Journal of Religion and Transformation* for allowing me to republish extracts of my research with them.

I would like to thank the editors at Bloomsbury, Lily McMahon and Lalle Pursglove, as well as the series editors, Anthony Pinn and Monica Miller, for their enthusiasm and help with making the book available. Thank you also to Sudhagaran Thandapani and Integra for their work in typesetting and graciousness in accepting my last minute revisions.

I also wish to extend my thanks to Fran Markowitz, Jacob Ari Labendz, John L. Jackson, Simon Podmore and Andrew Esensten who have at various times read or commented on elements contained herein, as well as to John Bracey for his advice. During the final stage of production of this book, word reached me that John Bracey and Bruce Rosenstock, two professors who kindly provided advice and support to me while writing, had passed away. May their memories be for a blessing. Yvonne Gillie-Wallace and Tziona Yisrael provided important clarifications and details. Archivists at numerous institutions have been instrumental in providing scans of material. Particular thanks go to the staff at Schomburg. Finally, Ahmalyah Elyashuv and Sar Ahmadiel Ben Yehuda of the AHIJ have provided immense help in answering my questions and providing material for me.

The text would have been impossible without the support and encouragement of my wife, Katarzyna Wierzbicka-Miller, our daughter Zosia and my parents. I dedicate this book to them, to everyone striving for a better world, and to the memory of Esmie.

Abbreviations

AHIJ	African Hebrew Israelites of Jerusalem
HI	Hebrew Israelites
NOI	Nation of Islam

Ben Ammi's texts

Each of these has undergone several printed editions and subsequent electronic editions, in which the pagination is slightly different. The versions used herein for reference are the original paperback publications, with the exception of GBMT, where the first printing of the second revised edition is used.

Euro-gentile	Ben Ammi's portmanteau indicating all peoples of European descent.
GBMT. 1990	*God, the Black Man, and Truth,* Second Revised edn. First published 1982; first revised edn 1986. Washington, DC: Communicators Press.
GLR. 1991a	*God and the Law of Relativity.* Washington, DC: Communicators Press.
MEW. 1991b	*The Messiah and the End of This World.* Washington, DC: Communicators Press.
EL. 1994	*Everlasting Life: From Thought to Reality.* Washington, DC: Communicators Press.
YHM. 1996a	*Yeshua the Hebrew Messiah or Jesus the Christian Christ?* Washington, DC: Communicators Press.
P. 1996b	'The Prophecy'. *Essence* 26.10, p.54
IL. 1999	*An Imitation of Life: Redefining What Constitutes True Life and Living in the New World.* Washington, DC: Communicators Press.
2YHM. 2002	*Yeshua the Hebrew Messiah or Jesus the Christian Christ? Part 2: The Final Confrontation.* Washington, DC: Communicators Press.
RHS. 2004	*Revival of the Holy Spirit.* Washington, DC: Communicators Press.

RJPJ. 2005   *The Resurrection: From Judgement to Post-Judgement.*
                    Washington, DC: Communicators Press.

RV. 2008   *The Restoration Village: The Restoration of Heaven on Earth*
                    through the Revitalization of the African Village Concept.
                    Washington, DC: Communicators Press (e-text only)

ANA. 2009   *The Ascension of the New Adam* (e-text only)

PI. 2010   *Physical Immortality: Conquering Death.* Washington,
                    DC: Communicators Press.

DAI. 2011   *Dehumanization: Artificial Intelligence, Technology and the*
                    Final Onslaught of the Dominion of Deception. Washington,
                    DC: Communicators Press.

In addition to these published texts, Ben Ammi gave many lectures which were
recorded by the AHIJ. I was given access to these recordings (some of which are also
viewable on YouTube).

Introduction

The African Hebrew Israelites of Jerusalem

The African Hebrew Israelites of Jerusalem (AHIJ) are an expatriate African American community, who since 1969 have lived in Israel, claiming to be authentic descendants of the ancient Israelites. They are one community within the broader movement known as Hebrew Israelism, designating African Americans who believe that they are descended from the Israelites and for this reason adopt (or reclaim) the practices of biblical religion or modern Judaism. Ben Ammi Ben Israel (1939–2014) was the AHIJ's spiritual leader, Messiah and principal theologian. He had taken them from Chicago's South Side, where he co-founded the A-Beta Hebrew Culture Center, first to Liberia in 1967, and from there to the Holy Land in 1969–70. Through decades of struggle with the Israeli state, the group evolved from a couple of hundred members to three thousand in Israel, with large communities in America, the UK, the Caribbean and several African states, totalling perhaps ten thousand affiliates. They reached an agreement with Israel in the 1990s which resulted in their being granted legal status as permanent residents with the option of citizenship.

While not the sole leader at the outset, Ben Ammi was the driving force and quickly became the focus of the group, displaying a combination of pronounced drive, sophisticated communication skills and a vision of the group's role in the modern world which has solidified them into a potent aggregation of African American belief and whose influence belies their size.

While other groups from similar backgrounds – the Nation of Islam, the Temple of Yahweh, the Nuwaubian Nation (Ansaaru Allah) – have achieved international recognition and infamy, the AHIJ have pursued a distinct path. They are not necessarily the most well-known Hebrew Israelite group, and are certainly not the largest, but their history demonstrates that they could be the most significant, indicating the future potential of Hebrew Israelism as a New Religious Movement. The AHIJ currently have branches in the United States, UK, the Caribbean, France and several African states. They are engaged in community development projects in Ghana, Kenya and Liberia, as well as promoting ecology, preventative healthcare and non-violent conflict resolution around the globe. Their vision has gone beyond merely the African American community and is attempting to improve the world for everyone.

The Black Hebrew Israelites

(Black) Hebrew Israelism is a movement stretching back at least to the end of the nineteenth century, when two rural southern preachers and Freemasons, William Christian and William S. Crowdy, independently received visions instructing them to take on a new message: that Black Americans were the Israelites. The movement spread quickly across the United States, with further congregations appearing in Philadelphia and New York, especially the latter's Harlem in the 1920s. Scholars are still untangling some of the historical details, but it should be noted that the movement is broad and diverse; the AHIJ have a very specific history and set of doctrines which separate them from other groups, groups which run the gamut from the para-rabbinic Beth Shalom B'nai Zaken Ethiopian Hebrew Congregation, run by Rabbi Capers Funnye in Chicago, to the aggressive (and frequently antisemitic) street preachers of Harlem's One West Camp and its many offshoots.[1]

An important caveat should be noted that Hebrew Israelism is largely unrelated to the Judaizing movements in the African continent which have gradually gained traction and publicity in the last few decades. The Lemba of Zimbabwe and South Africa, the Igbo of Nigeria, the Abayudaya of Uganda, the House of Israel (Sefwi) of Ghana and several other groups each have their own story and traditions of how they found their way to or rediscovered their tribal connection with Judaism.[2] Demonstrating what Edith Bruder terms 'Black Philo-Semitism',[3] these African communities have largely pursued rabbinic Judaism as the goal, attempting to integrate with the norms and rites of the modern Jewish community, sometimes even converting. However, the existence of these groups is often utilized by Hebrew Israelites to argue for their own narrative of the Israelite identity of African Americans, and as the movement grows connections are beginning to be made. Complicating matters, the AHIJ's own presence in several African states has encouraged some, including some of prior Jewish identification, to join them. In the other direction, the Rusape, Zimbabwe branch of William S. Crowdy's Church has evolved towards a more normative rabbinic practice.

These African communities constitute only part of a global trend towards Judaizing movements, one which is especially present in the developing world. Hebrew Israelism itself stands as unique in emerging from within the developed world, albeit within that world's underclass. There is much that could be said about the historical appeal of Abrahamic religion generally for oppressed and marginalized groups, Judaism itself having evolved within a marginalized and powerless people, but more important for our purposes is the opinion voiced by several scholars that the growing reality of 'self-defining' or 'emerging' Jewish communities will present a demographic challenge to the established Jewish world, potentially outnumbering them already.

Nathan Devir writes:

> In this digital era of globalized interconnectedness, emerging Jewish communities from developing nations are redefining what it means to be Jewish vis-à-vis their coreligionists elsewhere in the world [...] ideas are like a contagion: one can never know who will get the bug. Seeing cellular modems used to access proper Sabbath

liturgy from a mud hut in the savannah has convinced me of this. The prophecy of
Is.11:12, according to which God will 'assemble the dispersed of Israel, and gather
together the scattered of Judah from the four corners of the earth,' is a prediction
taken seriously by many more people than some of us in the West might ever
imagine.[4]

Devir suggests that the 'unprecedented wave of self-defining Jews from the developing
world' could form the pivotal event of the twenty-first century, on a par with the
Shoah (Holocaust) and the establishment of Israel in the twentieth. In this case, Ben
Ammi's African Hebrew Israelites present an important case study of a self-defining
Jewish/Israelite community who have successfully negotiated their place in relation to
the Jewish world.

It is not the aim of this text to assess the validity of Hebrew Israelite claims of
Israelite identity, for either Ben Ammi himself, his community or African Americans
overall. The investigation herein is one of theology, philosophy and intellectual history.
For those interested in objective truths and genealogy, there is a slowly growing body
of literature which would be of interest; however, they will still have to reach their own
conclusion from it. First, the pathbreaking work of Tudor Parfitt and his students into
African identifications with Israelites and Jews, including of course the Ethiopian Beta
Israel.[5] These scholars have likewise made little attempt to determine the truth of the
assertions, though it is fair to say there are stronger and weaker claims, and much depends
on the weight one places on various methods of research (genetic, cultural, linguistic,
etc). The work of Howard Brotz, Ruth Landes, Graenum Berger, James Landing, Jacob
Dorman and Bruce Haynes, among others, on American Black Jewish congregations is
also very important.[6] Several of these researchers have explicitly answered the question
of Jewish, if not more distantly Israelite, heritage with a firm no. This firm no is now
being challenged from two directions: First, scholars such as Walter Isaac have argued
that the presumption of Black Christianness conceals the many enslaved who lived
within Jewish communities or households and who thus absorbed Judaism organically,
as well as becoming halakhically Jewish upon manumission.[7] (The term 'many' here
indicates a large number rather than a high proportion; the vast majority of slaves were
held by Christians.[8]) Second, highly significant research has been carried out recently
on mixed race Black-Jewish communities and individuals emerging from the Atlantic
world, especially in the Caribbean.[9] The legacy of the Caribbean has been suggested
as the most likely explanation for New York's Hebrew Israelite groups since research
began, most of the groups and membership having initially Caribbean origin. To this
author's mind it is this which still presents the most fruitful area for concrete answers,
and there is still much work herein to be done.

At this stage it is difficult to know the precise evolution of Hebrew Israelite theology
and biblical interpretation simply because most of the thought of the leaders has not
been preserved, in either written, aural or oral form. However, it is my hope that
this text will serve as an opening for the subject, a first attempt at taking seriously
the theological and intellectual workings of a movement growing in presence and
importance.

How different is Hebrew Israelite theology from African American Christian theology? The answer, I believe as demonstrated herein, will be that it is significantly different: the priorities, the worldview, the biblical interpretation – all of these evidence that HI is a movement with its own traditions and its own character. Many of the principal characteristics of HI thought – a very specific theodicy grounded in a unique historical narrative, a millenarian outlook, an emphasis on repatriation – are distinct and indicate a very different worldview than the Black Christian. Hebrew Israelite theology centres Blackness in a way that is arguably impossible for Christianity.[10] However, there are still underlying similarities: an emphasis on the African American role in the world; a recognition that the Transatlantic slave trade must be accounted for within the theology; and the correlation of Israelite and Black, in terms of both experience and skin tone (in Christian Black Theology the latter is most notable in the ascription of Blackness to Christ). On the other hand, this text will demonstrate that Ben Ammi's thought displays at least as much similarity with Elijah Muhammad's Black Muslim thought as it does with Black Christianity. In part, therefore, this book will help to show that, while Black Theology is usually presumed to be Christian theology, there is a broader school of African American theology from which Black Christianity, Black Islam and Black Judaism all draw.

Anthony Pinn has defined African American religion as follows:

> Black religion [...] is not a transhistorical mode of reality but, rather, a creative and bold wrestling with history in order to place black bodies in healthier spaces, with a greater range of possibilities. What are the implications of this statement? For example, does it mean the gods and their stories are illusions, figments of our imagination? No. The language used by the oppressed in developing their stories has a materiality of its own that renders the gods true. In pragmatic terms, they are real and present to believers [...] gods are mythic – as opposed to fictitious – figures whose stories and rites explain something about the core feelings revolving around subjectivity and provide examples of how to extend agency.[11]

In Ben Ammi's Hebrew Israelite thought we find one potent way of creating a new mythical reality which describes the phenomenological world Black Americans found themselves in. Pushing the identification of enslaved Africana peoples with the Israelites and in particular the story of the Exodus to a new level, Ben Ammi took some 300 people to Africa and then to Israel as the vanguard of a newly liberated and reinstated iteration of the biblical Israelites.

Ben Ammi

The intention of this study is to outline, and to critically engage with, the thought and theology of Ben Ammi. Ben Ammi was the Messiah[12] and spiritual leader of the African Hebrew Israelites, and author of eleven texts and countless speeches, setting forth a vision of renewal for the African American people and for humanity generally. He led a group of Black Hebrew Israelites from Chicago to Liberia in 1967, and then to Israel in 1969, and after decades of standoff reached an agreement with Israel; his 3,000 strong community now reside there legally, where they live by the Mosaic Law and participate in the life of the state: they perform military service, study and work in Israel, and represent the state internationally. He was of the generation of Martin Luther King and Malcolm X, the major political representatives of Black Christianity and Black Islam respectively, and while he is less well-known, his legacy as the representative of the Black form of Judaism is still unfolding.

Ben Ammi was known to many Black revolutionaries during and after the Black Power period, and to many Jewish leaders since then. Since the 1990s he was a privileged point of contact for Israeli leaders who paid him and his community great respect. As a pacifist and vegan who was committed to the Hebrew Bible and the God of Israel, he managed to work behind the scenes in ways the significance of which has yet to become fully obvious. While many other revolutionaries were killed, imprisoned or silenced in other ways, Ben Ammi saw the futility of fighting for a future within America and strove to build a new world elsewhere. He and the movement he led are significant figures in African American religion, pan-Africanism and in modern iterations of Judaism, broadly defined.

In centring his thought, as expressed in his literature and speeches (what we will consider his body of work), we are stabilizing the centrality of Ben Ammi and of his beliefs about the community, about history, about theology and human nature. Ben Ammi has not been the only thinker of the community – far from it – and he constantly engaged with and learnt from others as they entered the community and shared their wisdom, their learning, and their interpretations. Any thinker is undeniably formed by the intellectual community they engage with, especially those who are in immediate proximity, for conversation. Indeed, it was Shaleak Ben Yehuda who penned the community's first published book, and placing the two side by side (as well as Shaleak's earlier work under his previous name LA Bryant) the influence of his ideas on Ben Ammi's is obvious. Much the same thought flows through both, and several important concepts appear in *nuce* in Ben Yehuda that would become fully developed by Ammi. Ben Ammi is a more forward-facing thinker, less concerned with the events of the past and more with how we progress into the future, but we can be sure that all of these ideas which he shares in his books and talks were hammered out in conversation with those around him.

Furthermore, all philosophers and theologians draw upon prior generations, thinkers and writers and speakers whom they have known and read, who have been absorbed into contemporary culture and formed the paradigms that are impossible to escape or ignore. No intellectual can operate in a vacuum, and all are located necessarily at a particular point in the history of thought which admits the influence of one group of thinkers while not yet being privy to that of others. We 'stand on the shoulders of giants' and our worldview is shaped by those who have come before us, by the ideas they have had, the problems they solved, and the world they had to engage with. In terms of biblical interpretation we need only look so far as the central HI dependence on chapter 28 of Deuteronomy, which is held to prophesy the American enslavement; if we recognize that Ben acquired this exegesis from his elders, how much else did he? This volume will show that many aspects of his thought, including his approach to health and diet, his belief in immortality, his eschatological and messianic views, and his immanent, this-worldly, emphasis, can likely be traced back to earlier figures in the Hebrew Israelite movement and in some cases to other leaders in African American religion. In particular, the influence of Wentworth Matthew, founder of the Commandment Keepers, the most famous and prolific Hebrew Israelite congregation, can be discerned, as can that of the Nation of Islam's Elijah Muhammad, and Albert Cleage of the Shrine of the Black Madonna and Child. However, it will also be shown that Ben Ammi drew upon African American thinkers of all stripes, including secular revolutionaries like the Black Panthers and even the pan-African *Negritude* movement of the 1920s. Mark Chapman has claimed that it was a combination of the Nation of Islam's 'relentless critique' of Christianity along with the emergence of Black Power in 1966 that provoked questioning of Christianity on a previously unimaginable scale in Black America.[13] We will see that these two movements, along with the revolutionary Black Christianity of Albert Cleage, form equally powerful pillars in the thought of Ben Ammi.

One certain influence is the scholar and one-time president of the Association of Black and White Jews, Rudolph R. Windsor. This Hebrew Israelite researcher and author studied under noted Afrocentric historian and prolific author Yosef A.A. Ben-Jochanan[14] and penned several books detailing his findings. The first of these, *From Babylon to Timbuktu*, was published in 1969 and was certainly read by members of the community. He spoke out about their plight in Israel in 1971, as well as in his second text.[15] Windsor held a rich base of historical knowledge and was more nuanced than many of his contemporaries. Some of his ideas can be seen repeated in Ben Ammi's books.

Another author who must be figured as influential upon Ben Ammi's thought in this respect is Ishakamusa Barashango. This little-known thinker authored several texts as well as lecturing extensively from the 1960s to the 2000s. His writing is very much in the polemical style of Cleage, and in particular his 1970 text *God, the Bible and the Black Liberation Struggle*[16] has much in common with Ben Ammi's outlook, while admitting the influence of Cleage's *Black Messiah* (as well as citing Windsor, Ben-Yochannon, Elijah Muhammad and Jamaican-American historian Joel Augustus Rogers). This particular text was present in the AHIJ library when this author visited in 2010. Ultimately it is more radical than either Ben Ammi or Cleage, in that he rejects any kind of cooperation with whites or white society.

Indeed, not only African American religion but African American culture generally informed Ammi's outlook – this study will show that Ben Ammi inherits the perspectives of Black Power and other cultural movements.[17] Ammi creatively reinterprets many tropes present within Black culture, blending them into a systematic, holistic theology which explains history, the future, human nature and racial division, the existence of evil, the possibility of immortality, social structure and relations, and, yes, God.

It should be made clear that, while it is impossible to separate the AHIJ and Hebrew Israelites generally from African American religion, we must also contextualize them in the general field of American religion. White American organizations such as the Texan group House of Yahweh share a surprising amount of details with Hebrew

Israelite groups (they refer to God by Name, follow the commandments and even changed their own names to biblical ones),[18] and the milieu from which the Black Israelite movement emerged was peculiarly American, incorporating at the earliest point American cultural influences which existed in the air of the time.[19] Albert Ehrman in 1971 remarked that there was likely some relationship between the Black Jewish groups and 'a most pervasive' trend of Judaization within the more extreme forms of Protestantism, especially those that manifested in the Anglophone world.[20] We witness this in the Seventh Day Adventists, among others, who see in the Hebrew Bible a clear guide for living which holds divine and scriptural authority, and has in no way been rendered obsolete by the New Testament. Adventism ever since its early nineteenth-century inauguration with the Millerites has formed a potent ground for American religion, and its influence through various progeny such as Charles Taze Russell's International Bible Students Association (Jehovah's Witnesses) is palpable within various forms of Black American religion. The focus on imminent apocalypticism and a return to practices described in the Hebrew Bible present repeated irruptions which typify the American religious paradigm.

Ever since Luther and Calvin et al. demanded the right to read the scriptures in vernacular, the Protestant churches have demanded a greater individualism of religion, one that expected that scripture could be read by anyone, and the meaning would show itself. Tradition did not need to be the guide to meaning; in fact, the tradition was usually what masked the actual, self-evident meaning of the text from being grasped. This of course is a double-edged sword: while traditions of interpretation accrete to every text, they can also be indicators of the context of its creation, cues which are no longer self-evident. What the stripping of such commentary from scripture does is allow the reader to locate the text in *their own* context. That is, the presumptions, priorities, values and interests of each individual reader become the interpretative framework for the text, bringing it firmly into the present moment and creating the possibility of startling relevance – many people will be familiar with the experience of reading a passage, whether in a religious text, literature or poetry, and thinking 'this could be talking about me'. The reading of scripture outside the frameworks of previous interpreters makes that possibility much more real. Here, we can cite one of the fathers of African American religious studies, Albert Raboteau, who wrote:

> As [enslaved Africans] reflected upon the evil that had befallen them and their parents, they increasingly turned to the language, symbols, and world view of the Christian Holy Book. There they found a theology of history that helped them to make sense out of their enslavement. One story in particular caught their attention and fascinated them with its implications and potential applications to their own situation. That story was the story of the Exodus.[21]

Bracketing the question of historical Jewish descent of some African Americans, the power of the Exodus narrative, brought into the present of those enslaved, was undeniable.

Ben et al. have created a systematic framework, within which individuals can understand the rest of reality and life. They are excitedly exploring the world and recreating it in terms of this viewpoint, as outgoing adherents of new religions do. They hungrily incorporate new ideas and integrate them, educating themselves in agriculture, biology, politics and religious history. The system offers an inherent and easy way of locating experiences and knowledge, and so is very satisfying.

Ben Ammi's is a total system – everything is explained and there is no room for anything else; everything one does, thinks, says, has to be correctly attuned, and there are guidelines, correct expectations, for everything. One cannot just like a kind of music – it has to be the right music. One cannot go into a career for oneself, one must be doing it for God. This is satisfying; it plays on the need for order and intense meaning that informs all religions, especially legalistic ones. And the members will mostly find happiness easily within these limited horizons; the stress of choice is taken away from them, and certain options are simply not possible. Not many will attempt to think outside that and wonder about the other options; those who do will leave the community. But it also means the horizons are limited; Ben et al. would claim they are limited to only the righteous options. Thankfully Ben and his followers are not as radical or as angry as some other New Religious Movements; they are sensible, a sensibility having been bred into them by the decades of attrition and final resolution of their struggle with Israel. This aspect of evolutionary progress is critical to the present text: we will show that what constituted the prominent features of the AHIJ in their first decades drew most heavily upon the tropes present in Black American religion of the twentieth century. But equally important is what came after, because as Ben's community became accepted within Israel and on the broader stage, they evolved in a way that other Hebrew Israelite groups and thinkers have not: largely, the early 'paranoid' features of apocalypticism, messianism, conspiratorial worldview and binary thought were de-emphasized in later decades. Ben Ammi's own understanding shows the hallmarks of an individual whose horizons broadened immensely during his lifetime, progressing from oppressed underclass to accepted model minority.

This means that Ben Ammi's theology has evolved beyond being simply African American; it incorporates experiences and positionality in the world which other Black American NRMs, Hebrew Israelite or otherwise have not accessed. But still it is relevant to the field of African American religion, having shown how these doctrines can progress when removed from the urban American life. Stephen Finley described NOI theology as:

> [A] theodicean response to the abject horror of African American life in the context of the violence of white supremacy and capitalism (in which their bodies were commodified for profit, pleasure, and violence) that must be taken seriously in order to apprehend the meaning and function of the narrative for the NOI and its broader appeal to African Americans.[22]

Ben Ammi's narrative comes from the same source, even if it subsequently evolved beyond those parameters.

There have been many radical Black thinkers who discussed history, theology and society from an Afrocentric perspective; many will be discussed in these pages.[23] What sets Ben Ammi apart is that he developed a systematic theology which encompassed creation, history, theology, biblical exegesis and eschatology in a holistic system which then provided a way of life. This singularly rich and holistic outlook was what fascinated me from the first time I opened one of Ben Ammi's books, and what has motivated me to write this text.

As Lewis Gordon writes, there is a paradox in that 'African Americans are, *as blacks*, indigenous to the modern world that rejects them'. That is, there is no African American people prior to the modern period, only the diverse African peoples they came from. And because of this rejection, 'blacks are homeless in the epoch to which they belong'.[24] Ben Ammi has succeeded in forging an identity and home, through the innovation of a bold narrative and the successful struggle and overcoming of significant hurdles which solidified the community. These shared experiences of relocation and struggle within Israel, and the victory they finally achieved, have created a people with a unique bond and sense of community, and indeed of mission.

The life of Ben Ammi, the city of Chicago and the Black Revolution

Ben Carter[25] was born to Rena and Levi Carter near Southwest Side Chicago, Illinois, on the 12th of October 1939, six weeks after the Nazi invasion of Poland instigated the Second World War. He was the youngest of six siblings and the first to be born outside of Arkansas: John Henry (b.1933), Hester Lee (1934), Helen (1935), Everett (1936) and Ollie Mae (1937). Rena and Levi had been born (*c.*1919) and raised in the small city of Philadelphia, Mississippi, but moved to Hot Springs, Arkansas, when they married, before joining the Great Migration northward, to Chicago, along with many other family members, in 1938–9. They were a large but close-knit family, with many aunts, uncles and cousins living nearby in South Side, who would vacation together, as well as congregating for Sunday dinner at the patriarch's home, after the Baptist Church service. Rena was a gospel singer, even taking singing lessons from Mahalia Jackson at one point. Ben's cousin Penny was ten years younger than him, but she grew up under his wing and he was protective of her as his siblings were of him.[26]

Even during his childhood Ben was known for his way with words and his powerful personality: his lifelong friend William Henry Butler (nicknamed Archie at the time, and who would later take the name Gavriel haGadol) was three years older than Ben but shy by nature. He recalls, 'Ben seemed to always know just how to verbally activate people. His thinking ability was keen and his articulation sharp, always "on the ball". His ability to talk his way into, or out of, whatever he encountered was extraordinary.'[27] Ben was always inquisitive, especially about religion: often he would challenge his father on concepts that didn't make sense to him, pushing for further explanations. He was also a deep thinker, Penny recalling him spending long periods reading or in quiet contemplation.

Ben studied at Washburn Trade School but dropped out before graduating. He finished his high school education during his army service at the missile base, for one year, during the Vietnam War. On the 15th of October 1959, after completing his military service, he married Patricia Price, who would become known as Adinah

Carter. She was nineteen, and he was twenty-one. Patricia was the maternal half-sister of Chicago Mayor Harold Washington,[28] and trained as a radio/TV mechanic. Through the 1960s Ben worked as a metallurgist at Howard Foundry, and it was here in 1961 that he met Landar (or Leonard, later Eliyahu) Buie – a fateful meeting that, according to legend, took place at a water fountain, where Buie asked Ben if he'd ever heard about Black Hebrew Israelites. Ben recounted later in his life that he remembered being told by his parents that they were Jews,[29] but it was only while listening to Buie that he realized what this had meant: that African Americans were the people of the Bible. He began attending meetings with Buie, and by 1964 he had become convinced and emotionally invested in the concept enough to help found the Abeta Hebrew Culture Center – an initiative intended to unify the many Black Jewish/Hebrew Israelite groups inhabiting Chicago at the time.

Ben's teachers in Abeta were the elders Levi Israel and Avihu Reuben (1902–91). Reuben had been born in Jackson, Tennessee, originally named Henry Brown, and moved to Chicago in 1919 before adopting Judaism in 1925 apparently as a reaction to Christian racism. In Chicago he worked closely with Joseph Lazarus (aka Edward Witty and David Lazarus),[30] a fellow member of Marcus Garvey's UNIA[31]: they founded together the True Ethiopian Foundation, later renamed as the Congregation of Ethiopian Hebrews – one of a growing number of 'Ethiopian' organizations in the city during the 1930s,[32] but with the distinction of affiliation with one of the most famous Black Jewish/Hebrew Israelite organizations of the time, Harlem's Commandment Keepers – or Commandment Keepers Ethiopian Hebrew Congregation of the Living God Pillar and Ground of Truth, to give them their full title. In the late 1940s Reuben moved to New York to study with the founder, Rabbi Wentworth Matthew (d.1973), who ordained him (Matthew also apparently ordained Lazarus, at least according to one source), before returning to Chicago to serve the Congregation in 1951.[33] The congregation they founded still exists, having merged with Rabbi Capers Funnye's Congregation Beth Shalom to become Beth Shalom Ethiopian Hebrew Congregation. Since Reuben's death in 1991 it is run solely by Funnye (b.1952). Reuben, like several older and more conservative members, left A-Beta because of his opposition to emigration, which quickly became a core point of A-Beta's platform. Another notable leader who left not because he opposed emigration but because he thought the time had not yet come was Rabbi Robert (Ahzrael Dahniel ben Israel) Devine (1926–2019). Devine was born in Port Gibson, Mississippi, and lived in Memphis Tennessee for six years before arriving in Chicago, where he began to restore the Hebrew roots his parents and grandparents told him of. He was also ordained in Matthew's Commandment Keepers, and had founded the House of Israel Hebrew Culture Center in Chicago in the late 1950s, also officiating a congregation in Gary, Indiana. He was a prolific teacher, including of Capers Funnye.[34] Hebrew lessons at A-Beta were provided by Rabbi Naphtali Israel, leader of the Royal Order of the Essenes; he was also a member of CEH in 1963. Indicating one approach to diet taken by members, Naphtali had adopted vegetarianism in order to fulfil kashrut regulations.[35]

But it was Landar/Leonard (Eliyahu) Buie who was his first introduction to the Hebrew Israelite movement. Buie was a follower of Lucius Casey (1903–78), the (self-proclaimed) leader of Chicago Black Jews, but he and his family also ran the

Righteous Branch of African Hebrews on Chicago's West Side from the early 1960s. Casey himself had been an occasional attender of Reuben and Lazarus's Congregation of Ethiopian Hebrews and from 1943 was preaching on the streets of South Side, earning the title of Prophet. Eventually he formed the Negro Israelite Bible Class, holding a doctrine of separatism as well as of imminent apocalypticism. From 1951 they began acquiring land in southern Illinois, which they would develop into a self-sufficient farm residence where they planned to live through the coming 'tribulation'.[36] These motifs of separatism and self-sufficiency would manifest again when the members of A-Beta made the journey to Liberia to begin their agricultural lifestyle, but it was also prefigured by the Nation of Islam who developed a similar farmland to produce food for their members. Ben had attended Casey's classes with Buie, but they disagreed with his belief that the Israelites would be able to keep the biblical law while remaining in America. For them, remaining in America was not viable.

Ben introduced the rest of his family to the Hebrew Israelite movement, and although a few joined him, for most it represented too much of a break with their own family tradition. In particular, their intention to leave the United States was too much for the family, and some saw his insistence on this plan as defying the family's morals and ideals. A rift began which took decades to fully heal, and the rejection by his family was difficult for Ben. He had the drive and vision of a natural leader, but he was also stubborn, and he seems to have reacted by drawing further into his beliefs. It is possible to speculate that it was this very rejection that solidified Ben's resolve, his urge to prove to his family that he would not fail serving to propel him through the numerous difficult times that the community faced in the coming years.

It was in 1966 that Ben had a spiritual experience that convinced him that emigration from the United States was imminently necessary. Termed the '45 seconds' by the AHIJ, this vision solidified for Ben the exegetical calculation that one A-Beta member, James (Yaacov) Greer, had produced from the Bible – that in 1967 there would be a mass exodus of Israelites. The signs were perceptible for many: the seething racial and political tensions during the 1960s indicated that there was not much time left for the 'land of captivity', but a series of unusual weather events that year also precipitated belief that the end was nigh. Some preferred to wait for divine intervention, but Ben believed he had received personal confirmation of the Divine plan. So, on Pesach (Passover, 24 April) 1967 members of A-Beta congregated in their meeting hall, performed the biblical rites and waited to be transported. However, no angelic assistance was forthcoming, leading the group to question what had gone wrong – it was decided that they must make the arrangements for travel themselves. The initial expectation was that they were destined for Ethiopia, but this was not viable, and Liberia was selected as the next best option. Thus, Ben Ammi spent an initial month scouting out the land, with James (Yaacov) Greer and Willie Butler (Gabriel haGadol), before helping to lead altogether some 300 African Americans into the Liberian desert where they purchased land and began creating their camp.

While many of the original emigrees left, they were replaced by figures who would go on to become pivotal members of the AHIJ in Israel. One was Asiel Ben Israel (Warren Brown, 1941–2022), who would go on to become the group's American Ambassador. Asiel had been a member of the Camp of the Lost and Found Sheep of the House of Israel on the South Side, but he joined the community in Israel in 1971. A friend of Asiel's was Louis A Bryant (b. Indianapolis, 1927–2003), who had lived in Chicago since 1957, having shifted from his earlier Baptist preaching in the Church of God in Christ to an Israelite outlook. He ran a print store/publisher called One, Inc., through which he published several of his own texts. He and Ben knew each other since 1964, but he believed in direct migration to Israel; he formally joined the community in late 1970, once they were all in Israel, and took the name Shaleak Ben Yehuda. He was later to found the School of the Prophets, the AHIJ's higher education academy, and would be Ben Ammi's right-hand man until his death in 2003.

In 1969, Ben travelled to Israel with Hezkiyahu Blackwell, leaving the latter at a kibbutz, where he would become fluent in modern Hebrew, learn the culture and pave the way for the rest of the community. Ben relocated with the final group, in March 1970, joining the existing members in Dimona, where he lived until he died in December 2014 (with only a few brief visits to the United States). Ben and Adinah would have seven children, four of whom were born in the United States: Ben Zione and Avinadav; Yocheved and Rivkah; their fifth, Yonah, was born in Liberia. Adinah and their five children had travelled to Dimona before Ben, as part of the second group, and Kavah (Eve) Carter was born in Beer Sheba on 6 March 1971. But Adinah soon left with the children and divorced him in 1972 in Rockville, Maryland. Even when she left, she was pregnant with their seventh child, Timothy, who was born in the United States. Ben had taken his second wife, Tikvah, two years before moving to Liberia and at the time of his death had four wives – Tikvah, Yoninah, Baht Zion and Baht Ammi, as well as twenty-five children, forty-five grandchildren and fifteen great-grandchildren.

Many sources mention Ben's looks – chiselled and handsome, with hazel-green eyes. He made a captivating speaker and was also noted for his diplomacy, a skill that must have served him well in the many negotiations with the Israeli government. In comparing the community's first publication, by Shaleak Ben Yehuda, Ben Ammi's public voice is markedly calmer and more soothing though with no less passion.

The subsequent history of the AHIJ has been given in a number of sources (although there is need of a definitive account).[37] Ben Ammi achieved his goal of legal status for the community and permanent settlement in the Holy Land in 2003, and became a citizen of Israel, along with a number of his followers in 2013, one year before his death. By this point he had gone from being the leader of a small, combative and apocalyptic 'cult' to a nationally respected figure who met with Israeli leaders and had the ear of local government. His community had grown from around 100 at the lowest ebb to around 3,000 in Israel alone. When he died, local and national politicians joined the community in mourning his passing and celebrating his life.

***

One of the arguments of this text is that it is impossible to separate Ben Ammi's project from where it began, in 1960s Black America. Ben spent more time eventually in Israel, but he lived and matured in Chicago's South Side, and that legacy is present in his thought until the end. Ben was born at the end of the Great Depression, and like the 43,000 other Black Americans who entered the city in the 1930s, his family moved to Chicago at the tail end of the first Great Migration (1915–40) to escape the economic plight in the south, and were just in time for the upturn during the war years, although widespread discrimination across the country was creating a palpable tension, sometimes exploding into riots in other cities. Chicago was a symbolic and actual goal for very many migrants, who were not only fleeing the violence, oppression and economic strife of the south but also *running to* the north with its promise of unprecedented liberty, dignity and opportunity. Many of the migrants referred to their movement in terms of the biblical exodus to the Promised Land, Chicago being optimistically dubbed as Canaan (and in fact Ben was the only child of his family not to directly experience this significant relocation, a fact which may subtly have informed his desire to make his own redemptive exodus). The influx led to radical change in the city's demographics during the twentieth century: the Black population went from 40,000 in 1910 to 278,000 in 1940, and then up to 813,000 by 1960, a growth of more than 2000 per cent in fifty years. During much of this time, Black Chicagoans were living under an unofficial segregation, restrictive housing covenants, meaning that Black and white lived almost completely separate existences. But unlike other cities, Black Chicago underwent a 'dynamically prolific' cultural renaissance from the 1930s until the 1950s, which during Ben's formative years demonstrated 'an urgency to create music, literature, paintings, radio programs, magazines, photography, comic strips, and films that expressed black humanity, beauty, self-possession, and black people's essential contributions to not only the local geographical community but also to the development of global communities.'[38] The Black Chicago Renaissance rivalled, or even topped, the cultural flowering of the Harlem Renaissance, which had been cut short by the Great Depression.

Chicago could be one of the first cities to boast a Hebrew Israelite or 'Black Jewish' presence: William Saunders Crowdy established a congregation of his Church of God and Saints of Christ there in 1898, although he had visited and preached on the streets two years prior, even before formally establishing his Church. By 1900 the Church of the Living God also had a branch in the city, and before long several individuals would make themselves known as Black Jews claiming to be born in Africa or Palestine.[39] But Black religion in Chicago would undergo significant changes as a result of the influx of southern migrants: The decades after the First World War saw an explosion of religious/spiritual creativity, with new movements and churches drawing many people away from traditional Baptist, and especially African Methodist Episcopal churches.[40] Southern migrants expected a more charismatic and emotional, and less refined, performance of Christianity – one long abandoned by northern Blacks as it held associations with enslavement and African practices now left behind. While establishments such as the centrally controlled AME could not adapt, the Baptist churches could; the established churches were soon joined by new congregations including the boom in storefront and Community Churches, which by the late 1940s numbered in the hundreds. The storefront churches were idiosyncratic, often independent of any denominational oversight and borrowed iconography, liturgy, hierarchy and doctrine freely from different denominations. These developments 'stimulated new urban religious practices and traditions among the black Protestant churches of Chicago that [...] launched a new sacred order in the city'.[41] A large part of this was a new emphasis on the 'social gospel': the focus on lived experience and the present-day struggles of Black people. They also destabilized the previous class divide of the city churches, and the push to meet the needs of the growing population created a total presence of the church in all areas of life. Wallace Best notes that amongst the moves and expansions intended to house growing congregations, there were 'several cases where a former Jewish worship space became an African American worship space, melding in a unique way Jewish and Christian iconography and architecture'.[42] Many were actively exploring fresher religious pastures, however. Judith Weisenfeld tells that many of the new arrivals 'began to establish and participate in movements outside of Protestantism, and many turned for spiritual sustenance to theologies that provided new ways of thinking about history, racial identity, ritual and community life, and collective future'.[43] Chicago was also the home of Noble Drew Ali's Moorish Science Temple from 1925 and would soon become a centre for the Nation of Islam after Elijah Muhammad took charge of the second branch, Temple No. 2, there; once Muhammad took control of the NOI in 1934, Chicago became their base.[44] In addition, the Africa-focused movements of Garveyism and Ethiopianism were popular in Chicago.[45] It is fitting that this city, first settled by a Black man – Jean Baptiste Point de Saible – and with a phenomenal growth in Black population during the twentieth century who would create a city-within-the-city which two sociologists would name the Black Metropolis,[46] would produce the most vital and revolutionary Hebrew Israelite group. The atmosphere of maverick religiosity, of doctrinal and practical liberty and innovation, with a necessarily pragmatic, worldly orientation, was the religious culture surrounding Ben Ammi and his associates as they matured in the 1940s and 1950s.

The A-Beta Center existed at a pivotal point in Black American history, at the peak of the Civil Rights movement and the birth of its more radical sibling, Black Power. It is difficult to overstate the number and significance of events taking place in the mid-to-late 1960s in America, as the nation's fault lines deepened considerably, disturbing the society's foundations. In the decade up to 1965, the Civil Rights movement had made significant ground in challenging the legal restrictions on Black rights. Despite these gains, most Blacks were still subject to discrimination in many fields – jobs, education, housing – as well as institutional and civil violence, and were becoming disillusioned with the legitimacy of peaceful protest to effect real change in the nation, as well as integration into a world designed by and for whites as the goal.[47] From 1964 a series of protests and riots shook the inner cities of America. The Voting Rights Act removed all *legal* obstacles to Blacks voting in 1965, but a counter-mobilization was swift as some whites set out to prevent the progress of equality. The 'Black Revolution' was gaining momentum, and although its greatest proponent Malcolm X had been shot and killed at the peak of his influence, in February of 1965, his agitation for Black pride and separatism was continued and diversified by many others. Malcolm X, who had been the principal spokesperson for the Nation of Islam until he parted with them in March 1964, argued that any people wishing to survive must have a firm grounding in history, a sense of self and culture which would sustain them. For Malcolm, this was found through the Nation of Islam, led by Elijah Muhammad's narrative of the teleological subjugation of the original Black people by the artificially created 'white devils' and of an imminent eschatological reckoning in the United States. Others found their historical roots in identification with Africa, or with Christianity; in any case, establishing a self-knowledge independent of the imposed American identity and history had been a central platform of Black America for many decades. Yet others believed that the revolution must be military and total (eradicating all oppressions: class, gender and sexuality, and with them capitalism). In all cases, there was a burgeoning sense of pride in Black identity and culture, a flowering of art, literature, music, religion and politics that was informed by racial consciousness and a determination to, in Elijah Muhammad's oft-repeated words, 'do for self'. It was in 1966 that the term Black Power gained prominence, when three events came in quick succession: Stokely Carmichael of SNCC used the rallying cry at Greenwood, Bobby Seale and Huey P Newton founded the Black Panther Party in California, and the incoming leader the Congress Of Racial Equality (CORE), Floyd McKissick, proclaimed, '1966 shall be remembered as the year we left our imposed status of Negroes and became Black Men.' This was also the year that Ben Ammi received the forty-five-second vision which led him to Liberia and finally to the Promised Land, Israel.

African Americans had long thought in terms of returning to Africa, Marcus Garvey being the first to make the concept of large-scale emigration from the United States seem plausible.[48] But it was with the emergence of Black Power that young Blacks began to adopt a truly nationalist framework: they would work for themselves, solve their problems outside of the political system which was designed by and for the oppressors; they did not need help or acceptance from whites; whites merely had to get out of the way and stop *preventing* the Black community's assertions of pride, autonomy and self-mastery. However, emigration had largely fallen out of fashion by the 1960s, and it is notably absent from the Black Power movement – Ben Ammi and A-Beta represent one of the only proponents of the time. Even those who preached separatism believed that Blacks should build their own state on American land, which they had farmed and developed for centuries.[49]

An emphasis on the importance of one's people expressing their separate identity, history and interests through socio-political autonomy was keenly felt during the 1960s, at a time when the flaws of the integrationist model for solving minority oppression were obvious to all. However, any group committed to living within the United States would have to acknowledge some of the values of that society: Floyd McKissick argued that CORE had to recognize capitalism as a 'fact of life' and work within it. Elijah Muhammad's Nation of Islam developed a business empire worth millions of dollars; meanwhile, the AHIJ took a more radical step of removing themselves from the United States in order to create a thoroughly new lifestyle which did not recognize capitalism as inescapable, because they had succeeded in escaping it. The AHIJ from 1967 lived communally, pooling their resources and distributing goods, housing and responsibilities according to need. Some of the community's more disreputable adventures in the past – credit card fraud, airline ticket theft, identity fraud, etc., for which several members have been tried and imprisoned – are best viewed as attempts to get by in a world that required money, as well as the taking-seriously of the claim that most of white America's wealth had been created by the free labour of enslaved Blacks. In the absence of voluntary reparations, it was deemed ethically acceptable to take what was owed.

Ben Ammi took seriously the Black Panthers' critique of capitalism, viewing this as inseparable from Eurocentric Christianity, but he also viewed with disdain the European socialism which inspired the global revolutionary perspective of the Panthers. Ben Ammi believed firmly that God had to be present for the revolution to succeed; and not just any God, but the God of Israel. Despite holding a supreme respect for Martin Luther King Jr., Ben was of the opinion that the Black Revolution of the 1960s had failed because they had allowed their goal – true liberation – to be replaced by one which centred the secular priorities of white society: jobs and income.[50] These tokens of integration into a fundamentally degraded culture were not the way to true liberation for Black people, or for anyone. The Black must return to their true nature; in this way, Ben Ammi fits into the 'Cultural Nationalist' faction of Black Power, which views with disdain the 'Revolutionary Nationalism' of the Black Panthers et al, with their dependence on white European political theories; first must come the recognition of Black culture and identity as uniquely powerful in the lives of Black Americans; and the expression of this through food, hair, clothing, language, arts, music and lifestyle. The difference is that for Ben Ammi *everything* must ultimately be subordinated to God, and the worship of God was primarily manifested through righteousness.[51] For Ben Ammi, culture manifests values, and the cultural norms of America manifest the worst excesses of wickedness in the world.

While Black Power as a movement stalled in the mid-1970s, Ben Ammi's community also entered its most difficult period – concerted persecution by Israel, deportations of members and the refusal of citizen rights meant the group struggled to survive. The non-fulfilment of apocalyptic predictions for 1977 led to a number of defections, but despite this the community continued attracting new members. Especially the last half of the 1980s, when significant sources of funding from the United States were closed down, must have created a desperate state. However, it was from this point that earnest negotiations were begun, and from 1990 a long process of normalizing and regulating their position in Israel began, along with assurances that their antisemitic and anti-Zionist rhetoric would be discontinued, and no further members would join from outside Israel. The ensuing twenty-four years would see a blossoming of goodwill and the eventual incorporation of the community such that Shimon Peres and Benjamin Netanyahu lauded the community, describing them as an integral part of the nation.

Bobby Rush – who went from the Black Panther leadership to Chicago local government – remarked in 1983 that 'militancy is an important part of the maturation process'.[52] Certainly we would be wrong to impute the rhetoric of 32-year-old Ben Ammi in 1971 to 62-year-old Ben Ammi in 2001. He too matured through these struggles, and his initial radical worldview became tempered as he grew. His thought became broader, deeper, but his roots and his prime concerns – the future of humanity, the world and our relationship with the divine, and the central role of Black Americans in shaping those – remained firm.

Religion has never been far from the African American struggle. It was central to many pivotal figures, including both Martin Luther King Jr and Malcolm X, the two most famous leaders of the 1960s. If we can think of King and X as representing the African American perspectives on Christianity and Islam respectively, and the Black Panthers (along with CORE and SNCC) as the secular angle, Ben Ammi's AHIJ represents the African American take on Judaism. This is admittedly a problematic claim, and one which needs substantial unpacking. For a long time the AHIJ, like other Hebrew Israelites, claimed to be not Jews but Israelites. They claimed that the established Jewish community was made up of European converts who had followed a version of the religion without being descended from the biblical people of Israel. They did not recognize the Talmud or any rabbinic writings, but they did read the New Testament and held Jesus to be a prophet of Israel. For many, this indicated the movement as, at most, a Judaizing development of American Christianity, and fundamentally one still more Christian then Jewish. Even the Karaites, the Jewish sect originating in the Arab world at the beginning of the Islamic period who refused all rabbinic interpretation and authority, paid no heed to the Christian (or Muslim) texts. But Ben Ammi and his community have now existed longer within the Jewish world of Israel than in the Christian one of America. Their integration into the state, while not conferring the status of Jews, was in accordance with their public disavowal of separatist genealogy; since 1990 they have publicly stated a new view (which may in fact be a return to an older view, or at least one held by some in the community according to early interviews) that while some Israelites travelled into Africa, some went into Europe. Their perception of themselves as part of the family which includes all Israelite peoples, even if not fully reflected by most Jews, speaks to the new outlook wherein they and the Jewish people are inseparable. For forty-five years (two-thirds of his life) Ben Ammi lived in the Jewish state, conversed with Jews and absorbed the cultural and religious practices of Jews. While the AHIJ defined themselves in opposition to this to a greater or lesser degree for the first two decades, subsequent years have seen them grow closer in cooperation and integration into Israel, as well as gradually becoming more accepted and accepting of the Jewish world generally. Crucially, at the same time, they have lost none of their African American identity, remaining wedded to a thoroughly pan-African self-perception.

I hope to show herein that the thought of Ben Ammi also reflects in significant ways the thought of the rabbinic Jewish world. This is to say that his exegesis of the Hebrew Bible often (though not always) ends with similar conclusions to those of rabbis, rather than those of Christians. In this sense then, Ben Ammi stands as a unique thinker in melding together African American and Jewish traditions. In many ways he is unique to both worlds, but we can still trace and discover the roots of many of his beliefs. Ultimately, these come down to two factors: the African American theological tradition and interpretation of the Hebrew Bible taken as the sole revelation of the God of Israel.

It would be remiss to gloss over the political implications of the AHIJ's integration into Israel. The AHIJ have faced some critique from Black America for their acceptance of Israeli citizenship with all that entails such as military service.[53] Support for the Palestinian struggle has been a part of African American radical politics since Black Power (in fact it was one of the key shifts in outlook that characterized the transition from the Civil Rights generation[54]), and many have seen Israel as an outpost of European colonialism combined with an overwhelming support from the United States, which permits it to carry out regular offensives against a (phenotypically darker) population already brutalized by oppression and lack of self-determination. Ben Ammi did not take a position on the Israel-Palestinian conflict (although he believed that the establishment of Israel – i.e. the broader Arab-Israeli conflict – was divinely sanctioned as a prerequisite for the establishment of the AHIJ in the Holy Land).[55] He publicly supported the annexation of the West Bank into Israel, and although his reasons for wanting a united Israel were spiritual, not political, this would do little to satisfy Palestinian residents of the West Bank (and the diaspora) who desire their own state independent of Israel. He spoke little about the political issues surrounding the existence and nature of Israel and nothing about the plight of the Palestinians (although he was clear that the establishing of Israel in 1948 was providential, a necessary step towards the establishment of the AHIJ in that land).

This was not oversight on his part. It was an expression of his belief in the centrality of his own people's struggle, the necessity of their showing the world that not only was violence never the answer, but that any achievement of worth was to be found through building a society based on holistic ethical and biblical principles. The AHIJ did not perceive the Israeli-Palestinian conflict as paralleling the racial situation of the United States, which is to say they did not reduce it to binary terms of dominance and oppression. Their attempts to help Israelis and Palestinians negotiate and find peace (unfortunately) formed the less successful part of their work in conflict resolution which helped Chicago street gangs and American Black and Jewish communities resolve their differences. While the AHIJ have maintained friendships and partnerships with Palestinians in the Occupied Territories, as well as Arab/Palestinian Israelis, and refused to allow the murder of one member, Aharon Ben-Yisrael Ellis, by a Palestinian terrorist in 2002 to invoke bigotry, they were also clear in their initial narrative that, just like Ashkenazi and Sephardi Jews are largely Europeans who adopted a religion, so were Muslim and Christian Arabs simply descendants of European Crusaders who, as Europeans do, conquered, massacred and repopulated a region, passing themselves off as the original, darker inhabitants. These claims may invoke a reaction of bemusement if not ridicule in most readers; they are the same kind of hopeful, religiously based claim as those of Palestinian non-existence or Jewish descent from Khazars, when they are advocated respectively by Jews or Arabs, and their supporters. But in the case of the AHIJ they have never been intended to be actioned in the removal or subjugation of people, rather they have been a statement of *their own* right to settle also in that land, alongside all of the existing parties.

Critically, Ben Ammi and the AHIJ believe that the (deep and tragic) problems of the region are only the same in nature as those of the rest of the world: manifestations of human beings not pursuing righteousness. They have taken the step of setting an example of how people can live, and the benefits that generates, in order for people to gain from that. Their concern is more with the continent of Africa, and the lives of Africans, who (in their narrative) have been subject to harsher oppression and abuse in the modern period than anyone else. In general they do not advocate for or against governments, and they have no record of speaking out against atrocities, for the reason that they see any human-made government as flawed, and energy better spent on improving lives than campaigning against the evils of humanity. It also must be recognized that if the community had taken steps to side with the Palestinians, their ultimate goal of establishing their autonomous community in the region would have become immeasurably harder.

In short, they have taken pains to ensure that they have no quarrel with either side, while building alliances where they could. Hopefully it will be recognized even by those who fully support the Palestinian struggle that, in the difficult position they found themselves, Ben Ammi and the AHIJ made choices that were essential for their survival.

Having mentioned the term 'myth', Ben Ammi's particular metaphysical conception of Truth will be discussed in Chapter 1. Myth here should be understood as simply the non-literal function by which we understand reality. It complements but does not intrude onto the territory of literal thinking. Of course, this is not to say that Hebrew Israelites, nor Ben Ammi, do not believe in the literal truth of these doctrines – they do – but to the outsider we can see that they function in a different way to propositional assertions. Rather they are axiomatic truths which form the context through which phenomenal experience and information is interpreted.

In fact, in terms of literalism, it is worth noting that from the outset the community has demonstrated a favourable proximity to conspiracy-theorizing; they mention often the 'Great International Religious Conspiracy' through which the global establishment concealed the identity of the Israelites and covered up inconvenient evidence. It is sometimes challenging for the reader to dissect Ben Ammi when he indulges in such thinking, especially after utilizing, without question, modern research on biblical history and scientific findings which aid his case. He condemns without hesitation the institutions of Higher Education as corrupt, except when they agree with him or when what they discover is useful in his narrative. Ben Ammi would find a way of resolving this, probably arguing that it was the changing spirit of the time brought about by the messianic Kingdom of Yah which prompted these realizations although even the scholars didn't realize the true import of their findings. Such is usually the case with conspiracy-minded thinkers, and my approach has been to ignore all references to scientific research.

This is not to say I will advance his thought without critique. In addition to providing relevant context from his peers among Hebrew Israelite, rabbinic Jewish and non-Jewish Afro-American thinkers, I will engage directly with Ben Ammi's thought in terms of its value, its internal consistency and its (actual and projected) consequences.

Indeed, there are some aspects of Ben Ammi's thought that I find objectionable – most clearly, his belief that homosexuality is intolerable, and that of a clear and role-decisive division of the sexes. In this he earns my critique no more or less than any other religious leader with such views. There are also elements I reject intellectually – aspects of his historical narrative, in particular the most conspiracy-laden aspects of it, which strike me as absurd, although again they are no further from reality than most religious histories – Ben simply brings the mythical aspect closer to the present day, and integrates it into the modern historical period. I will present these clearly, simply, without shying away from them, because they are necessary parts of Ben Ammi's thought. His system makes less sense without them. That is not to say that they could not be removed or revised by the community (or some caveat found that allows working progressive values around them). The community has shown itself to be generous, kind and accepting of difference (at least when it arises from the outside), and they are not concerned with damning those in the outside world; they are concerned with making meaningful changes to peoples' lives for the good of all (although that may not comfort a queer person who is told by them that their nature is morally wrong). Whether they will or not is entirely unknowable. But, as outsiders looking in, the people this book is written for and will largely be read by, you are called to listen and critically engage with all of it, including whatever parts you might find distasteful. Ben Ammi was a deep and sophisticated thinker, a man driven by purpose, who changed the lives of thousands. As an untrained, non-academic 'outsider' theologian, he was able to create a web of meaning and value through which his community weathered extreme difficulties. We as outsiders do not need to agree with everything, but we should recognize the good with the bad, and vice versa, rather than condemning the whole for its flaws. In this sense, I firmly believe we can exercise our own 'Divine Spirit' in following the example of the biblical God who agreed that the lives of twenty good people could be enough to not destroy Sodom.

Ben Ammi undoubtedly had a systematic understanding of the world, but he never explained it systematically. One of the difficulties in reading and understanding Ben Ammi is that, while on the one hand he often repeats concepts and arguments across texts, as if he wrote each book with the assumption that readers had no familiarity with his work, on the other he explains some key concepts only fleetingly. An example is the Adamic Civilization which he refers to repeatedly throughout his corpus, but explains only once, in a minor text.

One last query that may be best dealt with before it becomes unavoidable is the question of Islam. This text will show that Ben Ammi draws more than any thinker from the work, writing and approach of Elijah Muhammad. However, while Christianity and its relationship with its ostensible subject, the historical Jesus/Yeshua, is constantly critiqued, talked about and discussed, Ben Ammi mentions Islam and the Prophet Mohammed very sparingly. He asserts that along with Moses and Jesus, Mohammed was a Black African, but he was not a Hebrew. Nevertheless, he was inspired by the Hebrew tradition and upon realizing that the Hebrews had lost their role as the *spiritual* leaders of mankind, so he chose to (try to) take it up. In this he was no different than some gentile Christian converts, who 'understood the same opportunity existed for them that through the adherence to the teachings of Jesus, they could establish that nation which would *spiritually* be Israel and thus become the light of the world' (GBMT29-30).

Finally, the question of reliability should be addressed. Wentworth Matthew was known to present a somewhat different rhetoric when addressing white or mixed audiences than when all Black.[56] It is certainly possible that Ben Ammi did likewise, and that certain aspects of his teaching were reserved only for Blacks or only for members. In this case it is difficult to be sure that we have a complete picture of Ben Ammi's thought, although given the significance of his books and recorded lectures for the AHIJ and their outreach it is difficult to imagine much being radically different. The one aspect that could have been concealed is the retention of his original outlook that the AHIJ alone are descendants and heirs of the Israelites; while many individuals from the AHIJ have echoed Ben Ammi's public statements that they are now engaged in a universal task, a close analysis of Ben Ammi's words shows that both the intended audience and the subject matter are largely African American. The community is still endogenous and they do not permit marriage with non-members, but whites have been accepted when they have joined. Indeed, the reception of myself and many other white, Jewish and non-Black researchers and guests makes it difficult to imagine that they hold any kind of ideological prejudice.

A note on reflexivity

It may strike some as strange that the present text is written by a white, non-Jewish author. To what extent do I have the authority, or the right, to be the one to present this thinker, this subject matter and the many sensitive elements it contains? My own background is one of relative privilege (with an emphasis on relative). I grew up in a family comprising working- and middle-class white English Brits, in the industrial and racially diverse Midlands of the UK. Three things fascinated me during my teenage years in the early 1990s, and informed my adult passions: music (initially and especially Black American underground music, whose political agenda, intellectual depth and passionate execution informed my consciousness); vegetarian/veganism (with an emphasis on animal rights); and Jewish religion (initially and especially the esoteric and mystical aspects). My parents gave me no religion in my upbringing, but my dad's family were Methodist and my mum's vaguely Anglican. I felt no attachment whatsoever to the lifeless, soulless expressions of religion that I saw around me, although my parents inculcated a strong belief in politics, protest and old-Labour values.

While my academic training and prior expertise are in Philosophy and Jewish thought, it is only in recent years that I have turned my attention to the Hebrew Israelite movement, although it has long been a source of intrigue for me. I visited the AHIJ in Dimona, Israel, in 2009–10, during which time I lived with them, shared food, taught at their school, attended the annual Writers Conference and Sacred Visitation tour of Israel and the West Bank, as well as several social events. I spent a lot of time in their library, fascinated by what I could learn about their history and their beliefs, and interviewed several members, probing their personal histories, beliefs and expectations. Since then I have maintained contact with some members, visiting whenever I was in Israel for a conference. My personal appreciation of Jewish, Middle Eastern and Black American culture and history, as well as my long-term involvement with antiracist and antifascist movements and long-term commitment to veganism all contributed to a fascination with the AHIJ, who to me seemed to capture something genuinely new and powerful.

Since 2010, the Hebrew Israelite movement has grown in prominence, although often it has been the most antagonistic groups who have captured the limelight. The necessity of a detailed examination of the theology that underpins the AHIJ and of Ben Ammi as a theologian and philosopher was clear to me, and this gap has not since been filled by anyone else. The world has changed significantly since 2010, and the relevance of Ben Ammi's thought is as great as, if not greater than, the importance of presenting African American and pan-African thought in the context of both historical and contemporary developments. Lastly, it should be noted that Ben Ammi, more than most Hebrew Israelite leaders, spoke of a vision that was truly universal, and saw his mission as one that embraced all of humanity. As already mentioned, the AHIJ have supported to the fullest my project.

Chapter breakdown

One of the central features of Ben Ammi's, and Hebrew Israelites', exegetical project is the reading of the Bible through the lens of slavery. Really, one could say 'slavery and the Black experience in America', because much of Ben's ink is allotted to the present time. But the present state in America is consistently understood as merely a continuation of the true nature of American enslavement, which was to punish the Israelites, disconnect them from God and indoctrinate them into ways of unrighteousness. In this way, there is no redemption within America, any more than there could have been within Egypt or Babylon – the Israelites are called to return home. So, everything is referred to this concept, to what led up to it and to the way out of it. And of course, like many devoutly scriptural religious thinkers, he collapses all of history into the biblical narrative: there is nothing worthwhile to be found outside it, everything in the present order can be explained with reference to the Bible. The first chapter of this book examines the historical narrative that Ben Ammi weaves and the implications that are drawn from it, as well as setting out his conception of race, as articulated into the concepts of Black, white and Israelite. The narrative covers six thousand years of history since the Edenic 'beginning', and a further stretch before that.

The second chapter takes a broad lens to Ben Ammi's apocalyptic predictions and theory. I show that this draws upon the long tradition of African American jeremiad and apocalyptic, wherein the inevitable end of America and the Gentile Age has been imminent for a century and a half. The morally depraved modern world indicated, and deserved, the coming destruction, especially in retribution for the Transatlantic Slave Trade. Ben Ammi is unique in claiming that the apocalypse has already happened, displaying an ability to reinterpret old predictions and maintain them within the framework of his mature thought. A critical element of Ben Ammi's apocalypse is the new Exodus, of Black Israelites from America. However, Ammi is not exclusive in his assertion of who will be saved: based on select biblical passages he argues consistently that redemption is open for all who desire it.

With Chapter 3, we enter the Messianic Age – first examining African American concepts of the Black Messiah, seeing how these formed the context in which Ben Ammi created his doctrine of prophetic-messianic lineage, his concept and story of the messiah Yeshuah, and of the messianic people who repeatedly produce these messianic individuals anointed by God. We will then explicate Ben's take on a famous Black exegetical passage: the Valley of Dry Bones and their resurrection in Ezekiel. This prophecy has long been interpreted as representing the plight of Black America, and Ben demonstrates his immersion in the tradition, while adding his own unique spin to it.

These three initial chapters wrap up the components of Ben Ammi's early thought which can be largely seen as the inheritance of the Black American theological tradition. Chapter 4 begins the theological core of this book, wherein Ammi's own contributions, thought and exegesis which are uniquely his emerge. We begin with a rigorous appraisal of the systematic structure of Ben Ammi's ontology, his God-concept and the centrality of biblical law, all of which contribute to what I name an 'immanent vitalist pneumatology'. Herein, we unpack a divinity who is Spirit, who is immanent in the world and engages the world through human beings, and who is the source of all life. We will move on to see how the manifestation of the Holy Spirit through human actions is expressed in Ben Ammi's commitment to the Mosaic Law, in a form similar to that of various rabbinic thinkers, most especially the Medieval kabbalists. We conclude with a brief explanation of Heaven and Hell as worldly states, completing Ben Ammi's immanent doctrine, and showing how it too draws upon twentieth century Black American tradition. The last section of this chapter will present some possible precursors and sources for Ben Ammi's theology in general.

Chapter 5 offers a similarly rigorous investigation of his theodicy, examining his explanation for evil generally and the Transatlantic slave trade specifically. A specific approach to explaining the American enslavement, as divine retribution, has been a core doctrine of Hebrew Israelite thought for one hundred years. Beginning with an explication of the concept of Black Chosenness and the deeply held relationship between suffering and chosenness, we will show that Ben Ammi stands in a Black American tradition that predates the more recent development of Black Theology as an academic discipline. Black Theology's assertion that Black suffering cannot in any way be explained as part of God's greater good, or as punishment, has become a core part of the discipline, reflecting a similar conviction in Jewish post-Holocaust theology. However, Ben Ammi's particular biblical-based concept of theodicy undercuts these, connecting instead with Haredi (Ultra-Orthodox) Jewish thinkers, who refuse to budge from the plain sense of God's words in the Bible, even if they are counter to twentieth- and twenty-first-century humanitarian ideals. Contextualizing this in terms of Black Theology and Jewish Post-Holocaust Theology will demonstrate the radical nature of Ammi's approach, while arguing that it provides a grounded and concrete attempt to maintain divine justice, the plain sense of scripture and human agency. Emphasizing these elements, I title Ben Ammi's theodicy one of 'Divine Justice and Deserved Liberation'. Like most contemporary Hebrew Israelites, Ammi flies in the face of decades of academic theology by recognizing that, according to the Bible, suffering is the result of punishment. However, I will argue that Ammi's theodicy is dependent upon, even emerging naturally from, his theology. Chapters 4 and 5 taken together form an argument for a highly sophisticated, semi-kabbalistic, mechanization of divine agency which arguably removes personalist identity from God. Fully drawing out the thought and the implications of this challenging aspect of Ben Ammi's theology will allow us to see the potent new possibilities that reframing suffering and agency creates.

Developing some of the themes described in Ben Ammi's theology, the sixth chapter will cover aspects of selfhood: the body, soul and spirit of the individual and how they relate to and even act to manifest Divinity, specifically showing how diet as one part of Ben Ammi's concern for living in accordance with divine principle links to other aspects of health, holistic living and the eventual immortality of humans. This chapter will also contemplate Ben Ammi's ecological beliefs and his belief in future global harmony.

Chapter 7 will look at Ben Ammi's concepts of language, scripture and exegesis, beginning with his central notion of the Power to Define. We will demonstrate how this draws on ideas developed by more secular Black American thinkers and activists, while showing still that Ammi's emphasis on names and (re-)naming in particular continues the traditions of his forefathers.

Chapter 8 is where I discuss what I call Ben Ammi's 'revolutionary conservatism', his ability to combine a programme of overthrowing the world order, to replace it with a return to what are often quite conservative social values. Ben Ammi, drawing his pivotal influence from the Hebrew Bible, accepts that text's designation of family, male and female natures, and the hierarchical ordering of society, as fundamental; and his rejection of individualism is a central pillar in the reformation of society in a way that foregrounds the whole over its parts. However, I will argue that he also incorporates some modern conservative concepts that are not supported by the text, and suggest that even where his conservatism is supported, there is perhaps more to consider.

The Conclusion will provide some final contextualization of the findings, in particular demonstrating the clear dependence of Ben Ammi upon Elijah Muhammad, while also arguing that Ammi shares the fundamentally Gnostic character of the Nation of Islam, as noted by previous scholars. Finally, I will offer an analysis of some particularly curious correspondences with Lurianic Kabbalah, along with a suggestion for future research based on this.

The book is structured so as to illustrate that some elements of Ammi's thought played a larger role at the outset than they did by the end of his life. The initial chapters on history, apocalypse and the Messiah all constitute the former. It should be evident that these are also the most intense, and in a sense the most paranoid aspects; they bear the most in common with the thought of the Nation of Islam and other Hebrew Israelite factions, weaving a new metaphysical narrative that hinges upon a global and racially articulated battle between good and evil forces, that is on the brink of resolution. These elements were still present in Ben Ammi's thought when he started authoring his books in the 1980s and 1990s, but they fade from view in the 2000s. It is likely that, with the growing acceptance and integration into Israel, the constricting powers of poverty and oppression, particularly the oppression of urban American ghetto life, relented; allowing for a more free and positive sense of the world and their place in it. This becomes apparent in later chapters, which present his views on God, Law, ontology, theodicy, diet, the self, immortality and the ideal structuring of society. These later chapters cover topics that, while persisting from his earliest writings, came to be of greater significance for him and the community as they began to thrive in a society that accepted them.

1

By means of a beginning: History, race and truth

[T]he Bible from Genesis to Malachi is a recorded history of Africa and Africans, Black men and women in transition after their fall from God's graces.

(MEWix-x)

And I will hide my face from them, and they shall be devoured, and many evils and troubles shall befall them; so that they will say in that day, Are not these evils come upon us, because our God is not among us?

(Deut.31.17)

This chapter will provide a description and analysis of Ben Ammi's approach to history and the narrative that he developed. I will offer a critical engagement which aims to show not only how Ben Ammi understood the events of history which found African Americans in the United States, but also of how this narrative provides a base for his broader theology, and to attempt an explanation of why this has succeeded in sustaining the community over the initial period of their existence.

The historical narrative is front and centre to Ben Ammi's theology, and as with all Black theologies the principal thinking point, the first question that must be answered, concerns the captivity, transporting, bondage and suffering of Africans in America. As with all HI thinkers since the second generation of preachers emerged in the 1920s, Ben Ammi understands American slavery as a divinely ordained punishment. Drawing on the Hebrew Bible's long and tortuous enumeration of punishments which God promised to Israel should they stray from his commandments, HI thinkers make an axiomatic point of understanding America as the threatened second-Egypt of Deut.28, and the actual fulfilment of God's claim to Abraham that his descendants would serve 430 years in a foreign land (as opposed to the Egyptian enslavement which does not total 430 years).[1] In this way, their experiences and suffering are explained as part of salvation history; these were not simply accidental meaningless pain, but form a crucial part of the plan for national redemption of African Americans.

In attempting to explain the transformation of Africans (free people, part of large communities rooted in their home regions, with unique traditions, and long, often glorious, histories) into Blacks (a people without history, interred in another's land

and culture, speaking a language and living a lifestyle not their own, persecuted by the majority), Ben Ammi weaves many strands together. His 'Black Midrash' (to use Walter Isaac's term) takes biblical history and prophecy, and adds into them African history, conspiracy theory, Elijah Muhammad's ethico-racial binary, European religious history and American history. In the end he weaves an impressively comprehensive web that provides ethical meaning to suffering, innate values, and a sense of direction to history and potent personal agency to those who accept it.

Ben Ammi's historical narrative

Ben Ammi's basic historical narrative, which is centred always on the Israelites, follows the Hebrew Bible and recognized history up until the first century CE (except for the assertion that the Israelites and all other peoples native to the region were Black Africans). It is at this point – essentially with the Roman sacking of Jerusalem – that his story diverges from the accepted version. It was upon the Roman army's invasion and destruction of the Jerusalem Temple in 70CE that the Israelites fled, heading south and west into Africa. As they migrated through the huge continent they lost their faith, their fealty to God, most of their traditions, and were largely lost to history for 1500 years, before being captured and taken as slaves to the Americas. This is the simple narrative shared by virtually all Hebrew Israelites, but Ben Ammi has filled in significantly more details than many others.[2]

Ben Ammi concentrates largely on the emergence of Christianity and the Roman context at the time. One of the key factors in Ben Ammi's narrative construction is that the Greek and Roman incursions into the Land of Israel were a deliberate attempt on the part of European civilization to 'force our people to turn aside from the laws', in order to subjugate them (YHM24). Europe is seen even at this point as singular in its nature and its focus: the destabilization of the Israelites, and the theft of their power is the central goal. As such, the emergence of Pauline Christianity – already a semi-Hellenized version of Israelite belief which many Israelites had been drawn to – presented a potent opportunity to explicitly create a new idol to substitute for Yah; a new religion which would later be forced upon the Israelites in their enslavement, which would captivate them and prevent them from being able to call out to the only God that could save them. In the early centuries of the Common Era, the European scholars – those behind the creation of Christianity – began the process of refining and concealing the real person of Yeshua (Jesus), a genuine Hebrew prophet, manipulating (1) his message, so that the Torah, with its instructions regarding worship, life and the true nature of the Israelites could be replaced and superseded by the New Testament, with its apparent moral of 'turn the other cheek, believe in Jesus, it doesn't matter what you do'; and (2) his image so that a white European with a Latin/Greek name ('Jesus Christ') would be worshipped instead of the God of Israel.[3] The infusion of many pagan elements into Christianity – its festivals, all of which were redefined pagan celebrations; its sense of time, with days named after pagan deities and worship separated from daily life, into one day of the week: the day of the Sun; worship of images; etc – served to defuse all that was still left of value in the new faith. The spiritual centre of the faith was even relocated from Jerusalem to Rome (i.e. within Europe). This pseudo-Israelite religion gained many new converts, pagans who sensed something familiar yet imbued with a more powerful force, one drawn from the Hebrew scriptures – indeed, many of these converts were supposedly sincere, as 'the gentile adherents to Christianity understood … that through the adherence to the teachings of Jesus, they could establish that nation which would *spiritually* be Israel and thus become the light of the world' (GBMT30).[4] Some Israelites also joined the new faith – including those who remained within the Roman Empire after the expulsion from Jerusalem. These were members of those groups amenable to Hellenization to a greater or lesser degree; the most Hellenized Jews largely became Christians and were absorbed into the Roman Empire, led by the arch-Hellenizer Paul. Indeed, as the Gospels tell, the (Hellenizing) Judean religious elites conspired with Rome to persecute Yeshua, sensing in him a threat to their hegemony (2YHM25-6).

By the fifteenth century, the Israelites had largely settled in west Africa (although presumably leaving some remnants behind, in the various tribal groups who claim descent from Israelites, whom Hebrew Israelites commonly highlight as evidence of their claims – the Beta Israel, the Lemba, Yoruba, etc.[5]). From here, they formed the large bulk of those taken in slavery by Europeans, and settled in the Americas. This preordained journey was Divine punishment for their forgetting of their God, language and scripture: as prophesied in Deut.28 and Gen.15.13, the Israelites were taken in ships by a foreign nation, and served in the new Egypt for 400 years, under the most brutal form of slavery ever practised. The Europeans were determined that they would not redeem themselves from it, so they implanted the new Christian religion as a means of concealing any way back to God. Now, every spiritual urge would go towards a pagan, Europeanized god-man, Jesus, who instructed his followers to simply accept their lot, believe in him and wait for death, whereupon they would be rewarded. The sufferings of the present life were to simply be endured, not fought against, and after the world became convinced that righteousness brought no reward, materialistic gods appeared – cars, sneakers, smartphones – that people would work, kill and die for. Finally, in the twentieth century even Christianity appears to be too close to God and so any mention of religion is being stripped from society – marketized, because religion as a choice from options on a list means you can choose the one that suits you instead of suiting yourself to the one God who can authentically offer salvation.[6] While the whole world, indeed the whole of creation, is suffering under this paradigm, it is the African diaspora who are victimized to the point of losing all self-respect and agency. And so, 'During the Euro-gentile reign, the African Hebrews (Children of Israel) underwent a chastisement (oppression) that caused them to descend to the lowest ebb of existence ever witnessed by the people of the world' (GBMT108). This oppression saw them deracinated, stripped of history and identity, brutalized by the system of slavery, before in the ironic *coup-de-gras*, they were legally emancipated only in order to be integrated into a system that was fundamentally evil; having completely lost their bearings and sense of right and wrong they would now do their best to imitate the ways of the Europeans who had treated them so inhumanly. 'The transfiguration of the African Hebrews (Sons of God) into a non-people (negroes) exemplifies the epitome of soul transformation. The people who were once rulers of advanced civilizations like

Songhai, Egypt and Mali have descended into the pits of the most barbaric societies' (GBMT152). They are now 'the laughingstock of the world, disrespected by all people' (ibid.) The African American had been indoctrinated into Godless European culture and taught to walk, talk and act like a European; the Israelites were still in mental slavery, having accepted the thought patterns, priorities and interests of their masters, and were ultimately still working for the good of those rather than themselves: 'The Euro-gentile changed our God and manner of worship. (...) Love and true worship were redefined and shifted from Yah, the God of Creation, to gods made in the image of our captors' (IL26). However, 'at his very best, the negro is only an imitation, a carbon copy' of them. Here, while emphasizing the persisting second-class status of Blacks, Ben Ammi uses the antiquated and faintly derogatory term 'negro' to signify the broken African, who has adopted the name given to them by Europeans, symbolically accepting the definition of their identity from outside.

This conspiracy to confuse and disorient the Israelites has operated on many levels. Not only were they spiritually led astray by the familiar-but-misguiding Christian religion, but much historical evidence was covered up and falsified in order to disguise the identity of the Israelites. Ancient depictions such as the Black Madonnas which still exist around Europe point to an earlier knowledge that Yeshua and the Israelites were dark-skinned, a suggestive image which was replaced by the silky haired, blue-eyed Christ. The Hebrew canon was initially rejected entirely by the Church, removed from the possibility of personal study, and when it was translated into vernacular languages it was distorted to conceal its true meaning and value, with terms such as Cush being left untranslated so as not to show the Bible's close relationship with Africa. In order to *literally* disconnect the Holy Land from its continent, Africa, the Suez Canal was dug out. The enslavers deliberately broke up families and communities in order to prevent language and what knowledge of their heritage still remained from being passed between generations. Thus, 'The history of Black people in America prior to slavery was not accidentally lost; it was purposely destroyed in order to teach Africans in America to be slaves' (GBMT151).

However, some subtle reminders continued: memories that were embedded in the songs of the slaves, which emphasized Israelite heroes and narrative in the spirituals that the enslaved sang: *Go Down Moses, By the Rivers of Babylon,* etc. From the end of the nineteenth century a few spiritually attuned individuals began to preach and find their way back to the real God and the biblical commandments – the return to which were the only thing that could save them. These preachers, individuals such as William Crowdy, Wentworth Matthew, et al., formed a growing movement through the twentieth century, culminating – according to Ben Ammi – in the emigration of he and his followers out of America, and into the Promised Land. Now, 'The return of the Children of Israel and the subsequent establishing of the Kingdom of God signalled the end of Euro-gentile dominion over God's creation and people. [...] The Word of God and the entire planetary force have combined forces to bring about instability, hostility, anxiety and fear in all countries of the world' (GBMT56).

Although Yeshua was an ordained prophet – and so *an* anointed rather than *the* Messiah (see Chapter 3) – his time and his life signified a pivotal point in salvation history. Unlike anything that has gone before, the last two thousand years defined a decline of God's people, and of God's word, out of the limelight and into the shadows. It was here, with the creation of the pseudo-Messiah Jesus Christ and the new religion of Christianity, and the Israelites' near-complete forgetting of their identity that the Torah – and with it, in some sense, even God – went into occultation:

> The crucifixion was actually the attempt to crucify the Word of God, to remove its presence from among the falling Sons of God, and to spiritually destroy God Himself. [...] Jesus was to be the manifestation of the entire prophetic Plan of God; his coming symbolized truth before the people, whose rejection caused darkness or death to befall them. God's chosen servant, Israel, and the Romans (the world), united to betray Jesus in the Passover plot, and by doing so killed the active, living Word of God.

(GBMT94)

This was 'The Era of the Great Deception', when holy scripture entered Europe and became perverted, leading to a spiritual famine – as prophesied in Am.8.11 and Dan.12.4-10 (GBMT30). This concealing of the Hebrew scriptures, and the promotion of a falsified image in the shape of the New Testament wherein Yeshua/Jesus is made – despite his own words which are mostly correctly recorded – by Paul to complete and negate all that went before, represents a grand and all-encompassing conspiracy to defeat the Israelites, to remove them from the centre-stage, to prevent them from finding their way back to God, and ultimately to pull the entire world away from its creator and source of life. While the Holy Scriptures could not be destroyed, they could be buried in plain sight: through banning of lay possession of the Hebrew Bible (in the form of the Old Testament) and the presentation of a completely wrong interpretation of its nature, value and spiritual message, its power to save would be defused.[7] It is only with the twentieth century and the waking up of the Israelites in America and the exodus of Ben Ammi's community back to the Holy Land that the connection with God is being renewed and as a result the world is undergoing a profound shift, as the Kingdom of God spreads light and Truth throughout the globe. This era, and Ben Ammi's unique ability to open the texts that have been sealed for 2000 years, represents the fulfilling of the prophecies of Daniel and Revelation.

There are some brief passages in which Ben Ammi discusses another angle to history: before that which is told in Genesis. In *Everlasting Life*, he allows without preference, 'the last six million or six thousand years – whichever is your doctrinal perspective and numerical preference' for human history (EL139). At other points he remarks that there may well have been other humans before Adam, but the Eden narrative is the significant point for the beginning of *our* era. In *Imitation of Life* he accepts the archaeological remains of prehistoric people from one million years ago, but argues they are simply not relevant to the story and figure of Adam, who was created and vivified by God six thousand years ago. So, 'even if there has been a long-running performance, Adam definitely introduces us to the final act and only those on stage now are a part of it' (IL89).[8] In a short text, briefly available to download from the AHIJ website, he claims that the 400-year interment prophesied to Abraham was only 'the final, climactic portion of a fall that was to last a total of six thousand years', (ANA4) that is, a fall that began with the sin of Adam. That Adam, however, was 'in reality a civilization'. Ben uses the phrase 'Adamic civilization' frequently, but it is only in this text that he explains that he does not mean a people descended from, or living like, Adam, but that behind the symbol of Adam is a historical civilization. Ben Ammi suggests here, without filling in the details, that the Eden narrative allegorically tells us about a people, presumably one living in Africa – hence his common equation of 'Adamic civilization' with Black Africa – who disobeyed the purely good way set down for them by God, and strayed into a mixture of good and evil (this is how Ben Ammi interprets Adam and Eve's eating from the Tree of Knowledge of *Good and Evil*). Up until this error they had been steadily growing and ascending in stature, but the subsequent six thousand years –all of recorded history, and all we find recorded or prophesied in the Bible – then constitute the time of the Fall.

We will soon explore some of the deeper symbolic meaning of the Eden narrative, but it is helpful here to understand that Ben Ammi has no intention of viewing the Creation story literally, holding it to be both symbolic and preceded by a pre-history. Rather, 'The Holy One of Israel used a limited number of characters by name to act out His message that, in its entirety, would unfold in the generations to come' (MEW52). The biblical creation is a dramatization that describes *a beginning*, but there may well have been humans and a world for many ages before then; the Genesis account then must be located within that tale as signifying a critical beginning in *our* history. Ben is here giving space for scientific views which provide a much longer history than a literal reading of Genesis, while maintaining the critical value of the Eden story for understanding our current world.

Equally importantly, Ben Ammi's claim that Genesis' 'beginning' is not *the* but only *a* beginning evokes rabbinic interpretation, which has frequently sought to extrapolate a richer and much longer prehistory from the simplistic narrative of Genesis.[9] It has not been problematic for rabbis to claim that the Creation account is not the *terminus a quo* (at the most, what came before Creation was judged to be too potentially dangerous to discuss openly). Indeed, the creative re-reading, filling in of gaps and picking apart of the biblical text, is essential rabbinic tradition, known as *midrash*. If we consider the frequency of new texts created throughout the Second Temple Period, each offering new details and perspectives on the biblical narrative, the midrashic tradition is pre-rabbinic. Simply put, the creation story has always been seen as one which required explanation, and was in no way to be taken literally.

One element of Ammi's argument is not possible for the rabbis: he claims that the command that Adam 're-plenish' the earth signifies that he was to 're-populate the earth', which therefore must have previously been inhabited (ANA5). However, the Hebrew verb *mala* here simply means fill; it has no connotation of repetition other than in the King James translation. Nonetheless, Ben Ammi's method of interpreting the creation story as a non-literal myth which in no way constitutes *the* beginning of reality (and might even be preceded by a long series of events which were simply not relevant for the purpose of the biblical text) sits unproblematically within the rabbinic tradition of exegesis.

Recognizing that Ammi understands the Eden narrative in part to be allegory for a civilization helps us to understand other passages where he describes the fall of the 'Sons of God'. Prior to their fall, he claims they were blessed with spiritual vision and 'they could see all things' and even perform what we now consider miracles, before satan blinded them (GBMT224ff). Echoes of this power can be seen in Noah's bringing of the flood, and Moses' parting of the waters to escape Egypt, acts which were performed by humans not by God. Such power is still within reach: 'These were not always isolated occurrences, nor miracles; these were the ordinary powers of the Sons of God [...] They became rare manifestations only because the people turned away from God, His authority and power' (GBMT227).

The general historical narrative, spread piecemeal through Ben Ammi's writings, will have been developed in conversation with his colleagues, by reading and meditating on biblical literature, and by reading other historical and pseudo-historical texts by African Americans and others. Parts of the narrative display a similarity which surely belies an influence from other groups and thinkers, and in the overall picture it is identical with other HI literature of the time. The inscription of a new identity along with a highly significant past (whether this is as Israelites, Moors, Ethiopians, Muslims or Egyptians) has usually been interpreted by scholars as part of a psychological mechanism to reclaim a sense of pride and self-assertiveness which was destroyed in the Middle Passage.[10] It was manifest too in Black Power's identification with Africa generally, William L. Van DeBurg writing that by the late 1960s, Blacks felt a need 'to develop a new appreciation of their past – a rich historical pageant that had been obscured by Hollywood images ... They needed to write their own histories and to create their own myths and legends.'[11] Whatever the factual status of the histories utilized by different groups, the creation of a new story which presented Blacks in positive terms to replace the negative caricatures provided by white society was an important step in growing beyond their immediate history in the Americas.

Several important aspects of Ben Ammi's historical narrative are contained also in that of Elijah Muhammad.[12] In brief, Muhammad taught that the world was created some seventy six trillion years ago, and original humanity was Black. It was only when, 6000 years ago, the evil scientist Yakub noticed the ability of magnets to attract their opposite, that he realized he could ensnare and enslave the rest of the population by creating a race opposite to them. This was done over many generations by separating the darker and lighter children, and killing the former. Eventually the fundamentally weak and evil white race was born, who ever since have sought to destroy the original Black humanity. Like Ammi, Muhammad foregrounded the idea that African Americans had a persistent identity: prior to their enslavement they were the Asiatic Tribe of Shabazz, a forgotten identity that they were now reclaiming. The original blackness and righteousness of humanity, from which emerged a white people whose genesis linked them with wickedness, is a further shared motif. Muhammad shared too the doctrine of conspiracy: African Americans were deliberately being kept 'blind, deaf and dumb' to their history, their identity and their calling; that African Americans had been (and were being) brainwashed by white civilization was critical to the NOI, Malcolm X explicitly using that term in his Autobiography.[13] The absurd adoption of white behaviours, interests, even personalities, by Blacks was similarly viewed by Muhammad as part of the dangerous, hypnotizing power of white society – a power manifest most potently in Christianity, which created false concepts of

God and salvation, causing Blacks to passively accept their suffering in this world while waiting for Heaven in the next.[14] The narrative provided by Elijah Muhammad similarly announces that the story of Eden is only the beginning of the terrible events of European history, enabling him to create a wealth of prehistoric myth involving the original and perfect Black civilization.[15] Intriguingly, their reconstructions also pay apparent homage to racist 'polygenist' ideas that Africans were not of the same stock as Adam, although it is unclear whether there was any direct, subterranean influence here.[16] Finally, they share the notion of a fall of the Black nation during their time in Africa, which primed them for their captivity. It is worth noting that, if we do not accept Ammi's assertion that Israel is part of Africa, then they also share the notion that African Americans originated in Asia, only migrating through Africa during their descent. While Ben Ammi developed a sophisticated theology of the all-encompassing lie that pervaded the modern condition of African Americans, Muhammad was not as rigid;[17] indeed, his explanations ascend frequently into the realms of fantasy or science fiction, creating a surreal world of aliens and spaceships.

These similarities cannot be coincidental. The Nation of Islam was, by the 1960s, an established and powerful arena for radical Black thought; it predated (and influenced) Black Power by several decades, promoting the particular interests of African Americans and providing a sense of dignity and pride to many. It was one of the first such organizations to focus on the needs of Black America, without preaching simply assimilation. The AHIJ comprised some ex-Muslims, and even for those who had never joined the Nation Elijah Muhammad was a respected and pivotal Black leader whose ideas circulated widely, especially in Chicago. The influence is therefore to be expected. However, there are other authorities who surely contributed to Ammi's narrative construction.

A few key points resonate strongly with positions outlined by Ishakamusa Barashango. He discusses the consequences of Israelite failure to 'carry out the work entrusted to them',[18] the serpent as the manifestation of humanity's choice to break 'with the laws of nature', thereby ending their intended immortality,[19] and the blackness of Muhammad.[20] Barashango, as noted, took a more radical stance than Ammi on the ethico-racial divide, casting whites as fundamentally compromised.

Several aspects can ultimately be sourced in Wentworth Matthew, the teacher of Ben Ammi's teachers, among many others. He was recorded as saying that '[Blacks] are descended from kings and the white man know it. It is his purpose to keep you ignorant of your past so that he can exploit you. That is why he has falsified the history of the world.'[21] He also stated that 'Christianity violates the Ten Commandments, keeps the Sabbath on the wrong day, and is full of idolatry. It was with Israel that God made the covenant and it is Israel who will be resurrected when the Messiah comes. [...] This is the Gentile age and it is coming to an end as did all other ages.'[22]

Most famously Matthew insisted that neither members nor journalists use the term 'negro' for the congregation, instead naming themselves Hebrews. Matthew's Harlem contemporary, Bishop A.W. Cook, also refused the term negro, and held that the Commandments must be kept in order to attain salvation and escape from the 'Hell' of America.[23] The concept of a sealing of scripture, preventing its accurate interpretation during the time from the turn of the eras until the end of the 'Gentile era' in the twentieth century is found also in a booklet from the 1940s by a soon-to-be member of the Commandment Keepers, although it is unclear whether Matthew ever taught this.[24] This notion of a 2000-year abeyance of Truth and scripture is also reminiscent of Jehovah's Witness doctrine. The latter line is that by the time of Nicea, Christianity had become largely pagan, and would only be taken back to its original truth by the Witnesses. They claim the Bible lay dead and virtually unread for more than fifteen subsequent centuries.[25] The incorporation of Witness doctrines into African American religion, palpable in the Nation of Islam, Christianity and now Hebrew Israelism, is a curious phenomenon.[26] The next chapter will discuss some clear eschatological inheritance.

While the persistent influence of Albert Cleage upon Ben Ammi will be discussed in Chapter 3, it is worth noting here the many points at which Cleage identified the situation of Black America with that of Israel, often approaching – if not slipping straight into – a literal identification. The frequent references to the first century CE as a time when the 'black nation Israel' was oppressed by the 'white nation Rome', while surely intended polemically to engage a sense of righteousness and a certainty that God was with contemporary Blacks, sometimes require careful analysis to make them not outright identifications. There are after all only two 'black nations' that Cleage ever mentions. At one point he even asserts:

> Perhaps if we could just remember that we are God's chosen people, that we have a covenant with God, then we would know that God will not forsake us. Even in the midst of violence and oppression, we would know that we could look the white man straight in the eye and say, 'There is nothing you can do to destroy us, and you cannot take from us our dignity.'[27]

Here the not-unusual assertion of Black chosenness (see Chapter 5) is joined by that of divine covenant – something surely applicable only to Israel, as there is no record of God making a covenant agreement with any other nation. However, we can recognize Cleage's own polemical agenda when he continues: 'We must believe that our struggle is a revolutionary struggle designed to change the world and to establish us in our rightful position. We must have faith that we are doing the will of God who created us in his own image' (ibid.). Here Cleage seems to subtly admit that he is intending for the audience to read themselves into Judea's struggle with Rome, and to be inspired by it, rather than providing an objective identification.

Eden, the emergence of evil and the binary system: Two spirits, two ways of life and the nature of race

If the above account provides the exoteric aspects of Ben Ammi's historical narrative, there is another, crucial part: a deep-rooted spiritual dualism. Because, just as Israel has been guided by the Spirit of God, so the Euro-gentiles were guided by the spirit of err, the evil urge also known as satan[28]: 'The Greco-Roman world is guided by the great adversary satan whose primary objective was/is and shall always be to paganize the Elect of Yah by causing them to forsake the law and covenant made with the Yah of their fathers' (YHM62). Here, the initial imperial power centres of Greece and Rome stand in for the whole of Europe across the ages; as Ben Ammi repeatedly clarifies, he sees no significant cultural or spiritual rupture in the thousands of years and miles separating ancient Greece and Rome, and modern western civilization in Europe, north America and Australia. Despite the impression of 'superior intelligence and culture', Euro-gentiles are actually 'pagans, still honoring the false gods of their fathers' (GBMT141).

This kind of collapsing can be frequently seen in Ammi's writing, throughout his career. He is fundamentally a reductionist, and just as he sees global society through the lens of twentieth-century America, formed on a fault line between Black and white, he often reduces any complex issue to a binary pair. His worldview is of a dualistic cosmos, wherein the Divine, the good, the Godly, defines all that is as it should be, as it was intended; and all that is not as it was intended to be at the point of creation is considered evil, corrupted, wicked. There is no in-between for Ben Ammi; there is simply right and wrong, good and evil: 'all those who do not war against this evil world hate God' (GLR50).

This dualism is found also in Ben Ammi's reading of the Hebrew Bible, which adds another layer to the historical narrative and his spiritual cosmology. Ben Ammi argues that the early history of humanity as described in the Tanakh evidences an ongoing struggle for influence over humanity between the two spirits – good and evil. The former, the Spirit of God or Holy Spirit represents the correct path, whereby humans follow the spirit breathed into Adam which constituted his 'living soul' (Gen.2.7, and which Ben Ammi interprets, as Maimonides, to be the intellect); the latter is the Spirit of Err, the demonic or satanic influence inaugurated by the serpent – representing a shrewd, rebellious, 'political system' – who encouraged Eve to go astray. The struggle between these two spirits or 'seeds' which entered humanity in Eden, which Eve 'allowed to be impregnated in her mind' (MEW51) – can be seen especially throughout the earliest stories in Genesis, where Cain represents another manifestation of the human urge to follow evil and go against the wishes of God, as do the people of Sodom. It is the divine imposition of enmity between the two seeds which functionally generates the separation of good and evil into two distinct forms.[29]

After Cain's banishment from his family, cursed to be 'a wanderer on the earth' (Gen.4.12), and the rebirth of Abel's spirit as Seth and his fathering of the righteous Enoch, Ben Ammi claims that the encounter between the 'Sons of God' and 'daughters of men' (Gen.6) represents the point when the two cultures met again. It was here that began,

> the hybridization of the seeds of good and evil. It is obvious that the seeds of the two types of characters are crossed contrary to the desire of Yah; that is, the Sons of Yah and the sons of satan, good seed versus evil seed. The offspring born out of this crossbreeding were more evil than Cain himself. Keep in mind the mixture of good and evil seeds equals a more evil and wicked seed. It is totally impossible to get a stronger righteous seed from this unholy union.

(IL89)

These two seeds which set the lineage of Adam/God against that of the serpent are clearly present again in the separation of Isaac and Rebekah's twin sons Esau and Jacob. The former, the firstborn Esau who was tricked of his birthright and blessing by Rebekah's favourite Jacob, would sire a rough and brutal people, the Edomites, who represent a biblical mortal enemy of the Israelites and foe of God.

The terminology of Esau/Edom is commonly used by Hebrew Israelites to refer to white Europeans and especially Jews, indicating the evil and confrontational position of these groups towards the *true* Children of Israel. The tradition of identifying Esau with white and Jacob with Black due to their respective descriptions as red and hairy, and smooth-skinned, goes back at least to Wentworth Matthew. Lucius Casey held Europeans (and white Jews) to be Edomites,[30] while Shaleak Ben Yehuda made Jewish descent from Esau a part of his conspiratorial antisemitic philosophy.[31] Ben Ammi is more nuanced in this regard, and displays a powerful ability to pay homage to this tradition, while effectively defusing it. According to him, the heritage of Esau is spiritual, not biological. In the current age, 'the spirit of Jacob (the African Hebrew) is now resurrected and is contesting the spirit of Esau (Euro-gentile). The return of Jacob denotes the downfall of Esau' (GBMT108). So, while Ammi claims a continuity between Esau, the Edomites and Europeans, he does not ascribe an essential ontological/genealogical association between the paradigm of biblical evil and a modern people. Rather, Europeans now are manifesting the *spirit* of Esau/Err, through their choices and values, but they can always renounce and manifest the spirit of God if they so choose.[32] Connecting Esau and Europe through the Catholic Church, Ammi contrasts the virgin *community* of Israel, the Adamic civilization who were immaculately created from earth, who birth the sons of God (prophets/messiahs) ongoingly, and who restores the accountability of all people to God, with the false virgin Mary who bore a single 'Son of God' who made all people accountable to Rome. Europe is thus heir to Cain's satanic spirit, via a trinity of lies (Mary, Church, Europe) that opposes the Trinity of Truth (Eve, Israel, Eden/Africa) (IL110).[33]

He writes that the duality has continued, despite the mixing of seeds (Gen.6):

Cain, the seed of satan, becomes the prince of the underworld, the world of sin ruled and dominated by sinners, and Abel represents the redemptive (regenerative) seed of Truth. Good and evil versus good and right. Up to this point we have two sons and two fathers. The son, Adam, continues on through Seth, Enoch, Noah, and Shem, etc., and soon we find it noted in the scriptures that the House of Israel becomes the firstborn son of the Most High. Parallel to this, germinating in the imitative world is a very challenging sequence of events as an imitative virgin (Mary) brings forth a son to be called the light of the world, sanctifying the Christian Church of Rome to deliver all men from sin. [...] The apostate church brings forth a competitive Euro-centric redemptive concept and the Popes of Rome become the infallible lineage of "anointed personages" during the spiritual transformation, the Age of Deception. Since the satanic character is dual, anti-Yah and anti-life, his objective is to make all of the human family anti-Yah and to destroy all Adamic life (the living) or flesh.

(IL109-10)[34]

Ben Ammi's stark emphasis on duality may be seen to reflect both the American Evangelical fascination with spiritual warfare and the constant threatening presence of satan,[35] and Elijah Muhammad's racial binary which pitted Black against white in a similarly potent historical-teleological struggle. This kind of racial division along ethico-spiritual lines could be perceived in the thought of Ben Ammi, although this is never stated explicitly. It is entirely plausible to suggest that this was an initial part of the community's thought, but which had been dropped by the time of his writing, leaving only the suggestive traces in the prehistorical reconstruction. One ex-member claimed that Ammi had begun as a hater of white 'devils', and given the overwhelming influence of Muhammad on his thought, a similar conception of Euro-gentiles as the basic articulation of evil in contrast to the African American Israelites as good is not too difficult to a conclusion to reach.[36] Certainly, Ben Ammi does perceive European civilization and culture as fundamentally possessed by evil and satanic in nature, although he never applies this to the fundamental nature of white Europeans as did some of his contemporaries.[37] Indeed, it has apparently not been impossible for the Euro-gentiles to indoctrinate Black Africans (and Israelites) into evil ways, indicating that there is no issue of different racial natures innately linked with good or evil. Since the early days of the community's existence in Israel – and certainly since the end of the 1970s – they demonstrably bore no ill will or fundamental rejection of white Jews, or Europeans; Israeli neighbours and white visitors have routinely been treated with kindness and respect. In fact their first attempts ever since entering Israel were to work *with* the establishment, only resorting to controversial statements and disruptive tactics when they were rejected. Even when Ben Ammi announced his bid for the Israeli elections in 1977, on a ticket of his unique ability to overturn the evil nature of Israeli society, he depended upon the willingness of Israelis to vote for him.[38] We will see in Chapter 2 that Ben Ammi came to see his own community as a 'light to the gentiles', thereby sharing the path to redemption for them also to follow.

Ben Ammi is also clear that humanity is one, and the fall is one that all of humanity has gone through together:

> [T]here has been a universal fall in which men fell out of favour with God or turned aside from the old ways of our/their fathers into a state of corruption, angering God Almighty. Satan took advantage of this break between Israel and God. Satan, however, did not satisfy himself with just the fall of Israel; he has deceived the whole world.
>
> (GBMT68)

However, while all individuals are from Adam, Ben Ammi reserves the term 'Sons of God' for Israel only, because they are the group who are chosen to manifest the Divine Spirit and who exhibit the spiritual lineage of Adam rather than the serpent.[39] Given that the lineage of the seeds, and of Esau, is spiritual and not biological, there may be another explanation for the emergence of white-skinned humanity. Ben Ammi suggests, though he doesn't explicitly state, that whiteness has indeed evolved because of sin, as, when critiquing the infamous 'Curse of Ham', he notes that 'every *curse* spoken of in the Bible dealing with the pigmentation of the skin has stated that the *cursed* ones were turned *white*' (GBMT172, cf. 116). The most famous example is Miriam, Moses' sister who was cursed for mocking his choice of Zipporah, an Ethiopian, as his wife (Num.12.1-10). This kind of explanation is traditional, proffered in several prior Hebrew Israelite sources, all of which may have influenced Ben Ammi.[40] We can also find a direct source of Ben Ammi's spiritual genealogical theory in Wentworth Matthew, who held that: 'From Adam to Noah, there were only two classes of men, known as the sons of God and the sons of men: a Godly and an ungodly group. In other words, a carnal and a spiritual-minded race of the sons of men, both from Adam.'[41]

Nonetheless, humanity seem to be able to fall into one of two categories: Black and white, where Black designates those of sub-Saharan African origin (although they originally inhabited all of Africa and the Middle East), and white indicates European/Caucasian.[42] The latter category contains the peoples who currently inhabit the Middle East and North Africa, who Ben Ammi claims descend from European Crusaders who invaded, slaughtered and displaced the original (Black) inhabitants during the Middle Ages. He is decidedly different to his contemporary thinkers such as Elijah Muhammad, James Cone, Albert Cleage and many other Black radicals of the 1960s who, following Du Bois, draw the colour line so that Black included all the world's darker (i.e. non-white) peoples. For these, blackness was an expansive category that embraced everyone darker than the average European, because all of these were subject to the oppression and imperialism of American and European powers. Ben Ammi, like most Hebrew Israelites, has a very distinct and restrictive conception of blackness, one which identifies it totally with Africa, and the specific oppressions visited upon Black Africans.[43] Ammi does not deny that other peoples have suffered and been oppressed, but this does not bear the same significance as the enslavement of African Americans, which is prophetically described in the Tanakh.

For Ben Ammi, all Israelites are/were Black, although not all Blacks are/were Israelites. Israel was intended to be the 'spiritual head' of Africa, the Holy People who would show the continent and the whole world the righteous way, acting as 'a light to the gentiles' (Is.49.6). His tendency to collapse blackness into *American* blackness means that it is sometimes difficult to tell whether Ben Ammi means to talk about all Blacks or merely Israelites. For example, *God the Black Man and Truth* states up front that 'Blacks are the children of God, the direct descendants of Jesus Christ, Abraham, Moses and David' (GBMT6). His contrasting Blacks with southeast Asians in subsequent paragraphs makes clear that the latter are not included within the category. In fact, not even all African Americans are Israelites, although most are.[44] This is the beginning of a fluidity which is ultimately realized in his universalist outlook (with all the forebears that idea has), and also in the community's growing acceptance of outsiders.

The *spiritual* duality which Ben Ammi adopts also allows him to complicate the alignment of Israelite identity with a contemporary race. In a 1995 interview with Ernest White, he said, 'after the exile it is very complicated to point out the children of Israel just by the hue of their skin but if ye be the children of Abraham you must do the works of Abraham'.[45] This is a secondary, less emphasized aspect to Ben Ammi's theology – that despite the fact that 'Blacks are the children of God', the assuming of the spiritual mantle was not limited to them, as righteousness could in principle be taken on by any people. This is because for Ben Ammi no people are evil by nature, they are only misguided; they are still able to change and choose to do right. And if they do, then they will absorb the blessings due no less than Blacks or Israelites. The fact that he takes this theological step is significant, although we should note that there is a clear biblical imperative towards this conclusion (to be discussed in Chapter 3), and that even Elijah Muhammad held that some whites would, through their righteousness, survive Armageddon.

Ben Ammi's formulation of two warring spirits, fighting over the African American, can be found in two other meditations on Black American identity, one on either side of his life. Jordan Peele's 2017 satirical horror film *Get Out* depicts a white society which hides satanic violence and paradoxical fetishistic objectification of Blacks behind a façade of sophistication; this is a concealed pagan blood-lust which only becomes visible to the protagonist Chris as he is drawn into its web, and witnesses others like him who have lost their souls. Throughout the film he encounters other Black bodies which are controlled by white minds, their original self relegated to the condition of impotent observer to their own actions. The attempt at transplanting a new consciousness into Chris at the film's climax speaks surprisingly to Ben's idea that Blacks have their natural consciousness overwritten with that of white society. Ben Ammi could almost be making a commentary on *Get Out* when he writes,

> From the advent of our captivity, everything that was inherent to the well-being of the African Hebrew slave was uprooted and replaced with a foreign culture and nature. Consequently, the African Hebrew was dead in God; genocide of the mind had been committed. They were disconnected from their African soul. They became a non-people and proceeded to mimic every other race but their own. After their subsequent transformation into slaves, they proceeded with their degrees and diplomas on a path of damnation and ignorance to become Maoists, Marxists, Leninists, British, French, and on St Patrick's Day, Irish. These are the souls that were given to the slaves in place of their own. They were totally de-Africanized, and became disenfranchised taskmasters over themselves.
>
> (GLRxii)[46]

Of course, both of these conceptions of African Americans – asleep, their minds replaced, working for another – also replicate the Haitian concept of the Zombie, itself likely intended as a representation of enslaved humanity. Furthermore the concept of imitation, of Blacks imitating whites and thereby absorbing the evil consciousness, is simply a mythical telling of the Black Power ideal that Blacks need to find their true culture/assert their own identity, not simply assimilate into white society.[47]

Yet both *Get Out* and Ammi's theology could be viewed as careful re-conceptualizations of W.E.B. Du Bois' notion of 'double consciousness': that Blacks in America are always forced to incorporate the perceptions of whites of them as Blacks, and thus are never able to develop their own pure subjectivity. Du Bois' concept is of a subjectivity which also must incorporate awareness of how one is seen by the other, by the social majority. Tellingly, he writes, 'One ever feels his two-ness, –– an American, a

Negro; two souls, two thoughts, two unreconciled strivings; two warring ideals in one dark body, whose dogged strength alone keeps it from being torn asunder.'[48]

We can further see how Ben Ammi recreates these ideas in his myth of the Euro-gentile theft of- and intention-transplant into- the Hebrew scriptures, in the form of European Christianity. It is white fascination with Black Israelites, a fetishistic desire to acquire the kind of *soul* that Blacks have; their religion, their culture, their music, fashion and slang. It is possession: whites want to possess not just Blacks but *Blackness*. In Ben Ammi this paradoxical desire-hatred is presented in spiritual terms, very subtly, where Europeans disenfranchise Black Israelites from their Israeliteness, appropriating their scripture in an attempt to appropriate their holiness and their spiritual power; but after translating it into white-language, and shifting the intention of the scripture to promote pagan European ideals they *sell it back to Blacks*, in a sinister manoeuvre which will place white in control of Black.

Here we can posit a response to one important criticism of Black Theology, voiced by Victor Anderson. Anderson was concerned by the necessity of oppression by whites for defining blackness and Black Theology; for him, this essentializing of blackness in terms of oppression was a negative feature which made blackness nothing but a 'blackness that whiteness created'.[49] Ben Ammi presents a way of defining blackness in positive terms, as the spiritual leaders, those whose deeper connection with God and righteousness enables them to deconstruct the destructive white world and lead humanity back to a more positive path. This would not satisfy Anderson, of course, whose criticism hinges on the attempt to define blackness in any way that doesn't allow for a full berth of self-expression. The problem would be that Ben Ammi's is indeed an 'ontological blackness', one that prescribes narrow limits to identity and the possibilities allowed within (American) blackness, and thus it certainly is not one for everyone; the conception of liberation here is different to what liberal thinkers wish for, because, fundamentally, Ben Ammi's concept of the Good is different. It does not involve personal freedom; it does not pursue the classical liberal ideal of individualism, and places rather more limits on the individual as a means of liberating the group.

The dualistic, Manichean cosmos was one found also in NOI (indeed, Essien-Udom perceived a direct linkage between Black Nationalism, a Manichean worldview and a Messianic leadership model[50]). This kind of cosmic dualism is not a part of rabbinic thought, which locates all authority and agency with God. It may however be possible to suggest a humanistic parallel to Ammi's dualism with regard to the evil and good inclinations discussed in the Talmud and other rabbinic literature (*yetzer ha-ra* and *yetzer ha-tov* respectively). These two 'forces' pull humans in the direction of evil and good respectively, but they are entirely internal to us. The evil inclination is said to rule until the age of thirteen (when children become adults, with responsibility to fulfil the Law), when, thankfully, the good inclination becomes dominant (Avot d-R.Nat.16). The evil inclination also targets Israel specifically and incites their enemies against them (bSukk.52a). One rabbi identifies the evil inclination and Satan, thereby making Satan a mythical depiction of the selfish 'id' of humanity (bBBat16a). However, the two exist in constant interplay, more like Yin and Yang than Ben Ammi's creative and destructive, Life and anti-Life forces. The evil inclination, for instance, is responsible for our sexual desire and so without it there would be no will to procreate (BerR9:7, bYom69b). One midrash even identifies the evil inclination with the sole divine pronouncement of 'very good' during creation, signifying the essential role of the urges in creation. It is therefore best to understand the so-called 'evil inclination' as a selfish, egoistic tendency which is necessary for self-sustenance but must be controlled rather than overindulged. Norman Saul Goodman expresses this essential subsumption of bounded, worldly evil under eternal good as follows: 'Just as there are mythic heroes, there are mythic antiheroes. Yet both exist within the dimensions of the holy because they are aspects of the created reality of our universe and represent the forces at work within the universe and within each of us.'[51] What Ben Ammi's description has more immediate resonance with is the threatening ever-present Satan of American Evangelistic Christianity.

Having discussed the natures and origins of Black and white, another issue must be addressed here. It is one that has been of central importance, although clarity has not often been achieved on the matter. This is, the status of the world's *recognized* (*halakhic*) Jewish communities, and where they fit into the narrative (and the binary). Ben Ammi does not address modern Jews in his books (in fact, he barely mentions them). However, he and the community have made public statements regarding them on many occasions. During the early years of significant tension with Israel, spokespeople for the community (including Ben Ammi) decisively stated that any Jews who are not (sub-Saharan) African in nature are ultimately European, and hence not Israelite. Since the thaw in relations with Israel from the 1990s onward, they have been more accommodating, at times making overtures of acceptance of all who claimed Jewish/Israelite identity, and even adjusting their historical narrative to include a migration of some Judeans north and east out of Palestine, leading to the rabbinic Jewish population.

On the one hand it must be noted that these adjustments never made it into Ben Ammi's written texts or lectures, where he consistently promoted the narrative of conspiracy and concealment. He did not explicitly state in his body of work that Jews were not Israelites, nor did he deny such a claim. Simply, Ben Ammi was concerned with the distinct and unique spiritual role of African Americans, whom he had no doubt were Israelites. Arguably, he saw rabbinic Jews as largely irrelevant in terms of teleology, and their religious teachings and interpretations were judged to have been inauthentic: he implicitly dismisses the traditions of the rabbis, claiming their forerunners, the Pharisees, 'brought their new traditions and placed them on a par with the laws of God' (YHM30). However, Ammi and the community understand their relation to the Jewish people and rabbinic Judaism; it is clear that they have not participated in the fulfilment of prophecy (Deut.28) which African American Israelites have performed, and so the pivotal eschatological and teleological role sits squarely upon the shoulders of the latter. Unlike other members of the community who have published more detailed historical reconstructions, Ammi never explicitly addressed the continuity of the rabbinic movement with the Pharisees, or the ongoing existence of large Jewish populations outside of Israel (in Europe, Mesopotamia, etc). While Shaleak Ben Yehuda explicitly claimed that all the currently surrounding peoples – i.e. Arabs, Kurds, presumably even Samaritans and all the other non-Black Africans – are Europeans,[52] Ben Ammi left space for their authenticity, questioning only the authenticity of 'most' European Jews.

On the other hand, it must be stated without caveat that, ever since the negotiations for beginning a normalization of their residence in Israel took place, the AHIJ increasingly spoke and acted in terms of their unity with the Israeli and Jewish people. For decades since (and since well before Ben Ammi's death) they have explicitly stated that their own objective and agenda now transcend questions of race, being concerned with humanity as a whole. Linked to this, the conferences and conversations which this author has participated in have evidenced a belief in a unifying Hebrew culture which can be articulated into various forms including the rabbinic, the Beta Israel, the Igbo, the Ishmaelite, the Samaritan, etc., but which constitutes a distinct section of humanity tasked with providing a new way of life and thought to bring us all out of the darkness.[53] The willingness to engage with and learn from other traditions both within and without this broad Hebrew coalition is an inspiring fact of the AHIJ outlook.

Conclusions: On conceptions of truth

It goes without saying that there are many holes in Ben Ammi's historical reconstruction, most especially in the passage of the Israelites to America; it is difficult to accept that somehow even a significant percentage of the enslaved would be of Israelite descent, without the belief that the desired end result – *African Americans are Israelites* – would be achieved by divine intervention if necessary. The complete absence during the eighteenth and nineteenth centuries, when the majority of the enslaved were transported, of any records indicating Israelite identity, practice or belief (except in those enslaved within Jewish communities) also can be explained easily if one assumes the truth of the theory, but is more difficult if one does not. This is to say nothing of the explicitly spiritual elements of the narrative, such as the deliberate manipulation of the new Christian religion in the early centuries of the Common Era, and the vanishing of the large European and Middle Eastern Jewish communities, which could not fit into a non-polemical version of history; the attempted (although in reality sorely failed) concealing of the Hebrew Bible, which has never been inaccessible to most people (and openly available to all since the end of the Middle Ages, with the exception of some enslaved people in the British Caribbean who were provided a specially edited 'Slave Bible'). Many other problems can be explained only by a shallow knowledge of history and an overriding desire to collapse history into a supremely and unrealistically neat narrative. We also must note that despite his frequent assertions of an all-encompassing conspiracy with regard to religious history, one which many have been aware of, and still, even including Hollywood media moguls, Ammi relies very often on Euro-American scholars and their published analyses of texts in order to make his arguments. This is particularly the case when he discusses the Dead Sea Scrolls, the majority of which were still under lock and key during his life – the published fragments then would be unlikely to be those which proved his accusations.

Of course, to take the reconstruction literally is to entirely miss the point. This is not a historical assertion, but a religious one: it provides a narrative which explains the present, and which makes meaningful a situation which is otherwise painful and debilitating. It is arguably an attempt to create the 'complex subjectivity' that Anthony

Pinn describes as the essential desiderata of Black religion: by projecting African American history back before the American captivity, it asserts a depth of character and identity, and forges a 'subjectivity premised upon agency and defined by a new consciousness'.[54] It operates through the same method of 'Theological Phenomenology' that Stephen Finley finds in Elijah Muhammad, describing the racial reality as it was experienced; which he argues provides 'new ways of understanding life and experience that kept the dignity and worth of African Americans intact'.[55]

In a different key, it is also indebted to the 'surreality'/'hyperreality of conspiracy theories' which John Jackson perceives in the attempts of African Americans to understand their lives within an America where the vectors of power and influence lead to a hideously unequal existence and 'a frantic and unfulfilling search for answers to horrific questions, [where] the explanations chosen become as harrowing as the questions themselves'.[56] There is certainly a similarity between the 'soultheft' that one Harlemite describes to him, the concealed incorporation of Egyptian symbology in American monuments as a form of metaphysically violent cultural appropriation, with Ammi's description of the theft and rape of Hebrew culture in the form of Christianity. This metaphysical paranoia, Jackson argues, is an understandable response to the complete disempowerment of urban Black America, a bleak psychedelia created by the crushing pressure of a first world civilization which they exist beneath, the operations of which are opaque and inaccessible to them.

However, in this author's view, it goes further than any of these (and this is part of the reason, in this author's opinion, why Hebrew Israelite thought has become so popular over the last one hundred years, and why Ben Ammi's group in particular has managed to be so tenacious and achieve what they have): the narrative places African Americans in a position of cosmic significance and responsibility; it locates them as the protagonist of global (even, universal) significance, and makes their choices the ones upon which the Divine plan of salvation hangs.

This aspect of responsibility, to God, to humanity and to the race, is surely a critical one. Responsibility imbues authority and dignity; it also demands capability. In teaching that African Americans have this innate and ineffaceable responsibility, Ben Ammi and other Hebrew Israelites provide an assurance backed with divine authority that the people are not only capable of living up to it, but that they *must* if they are not to descend once again into the pit of slavery. The manifold pressures of American society, history, culture and politics, which in more and less subtle ways all participate in ingraining the concepts of white supremacy and of Black inferiority and impotence, face in Hebrew Israelite theology a serious *theological* challenge; albeit one which interprets them via a mythical structure of divine forces, of cosmic good versus evil. Furthermore, if the assertion to be argued in Chapter 5 is correct, that in distinction to Christian Black Theology, Hebrew Israelite theology is fundamentally more concrete in resolving rather than leaving unanswered the theological paradox of Black suffering, then it succeeds in offering a more common-sense explanation for the laity who have not the time, energy or cognitive inclination to dwell eternally on the enigma.

This may make Hebrew Israelite theology seem like a purely vernacular theology, one that offers simple but vulgar answers for individuals not attuned to the finer points of intellectual reasoning or to probing the penumbra of the infinite. This is not the case, as this study will hopefully show. There is a great degree of nuance and intelligent reasoning in the movement, especially in Ben Ammi's approach. However, it is worth also considering that theology as a discipline has very often been located within the ivory towers of scholasticism and academia; which is to say, far away from the needs of regular humans. Arguably one of the most important features of Black Theology, along with its sisters Liberation and Womanist Theology, has been that it is engaged in a theology *for* the people, not for abstract thinkers. Given the critical stance that theology's prime goal, when not conducted as a subfield of academic philosophy where reasoning is pursued for its own sake, should always be the mental and social liberation of people, then a theology which prioritizes its comprehension by non-theologians and the effect it has upon them over its own logical consistency or imperviousness to detailed technical arguments, is of superior nature. This text will hopefully show that this is what Ben Ammi has achieved.

To take this reasoning one step further, we may wish to interrogate the specific theory of truth which we bring as a lens, in order to see whether it is the same lens that Ben Ammi was using. Because, if Ben Ammi's historical narrative is not that of a historian, it is for the reason that his mission was not to be a historian. For him, 'truth' is not a dry and dusty description of events – it is a power to change, to enlighten and improve. It is the very structurer of the world (and so cannot be *of* the world), and it is intimately linked to Divinity.

The nature and value of Truth (spelled as he usually does, with a capital) are something he returns to frequently though briefly, offering pithy comments in the midst of discussions in almost every book. 'Truth consists of those words, doctrines, outlooks and visions which keep man in harmony with the processes that sustain life eternal', he proclaims twice with identical words in two texts (EL30; YHM39); the essence of creation and of created things is Truth, because they were created by God (EL42), and Truth is both the Word of God and the energy which is necessary in creation (as well as what was breathed into Adam to animate him) (RHS205). Truth is the essential factor which makes real what is real, by connecting it with God – any non-truth, *falsity* or *lie* functions as a gap which separates what-is from God, beginning a process which, if not healed by means of Truth, will end in the non-existence of that thing, because of its disconnection from God. Truth even has a holistic effect on the physical being of humans: it 'enlivens and sustains the human body and all of its functions', (RJPJn) and so 'As the influence of Truth in your life increases and the influence of lies wanes, you will become less vulnerable to disease' (PI74).

Furthermore, Truth itself is divine, and at points he comes close to identifying Truth with God, claiming in his lectures that truth is the 'most sacred thing' (Perception of Deception), and the only thing with the capacity to redeem (As in the Days of Noah). In one of his last texts he explicitly identifies Truth with the Holy Spirit that is immanent in humans and writes that 'The truth is the spirit and thought that are the invisible creators of matter' (PI20; 77).[57] In contrast to Truth's intimate relationship with divinity, the Euro-gentile domination is built on lies, about both their history and Israel's (and, as well shall see, God). Truth however always unmasks lies as light does darkness: 'Thus, the primary problem [to the Euro-gentile] is not our Black skin, but the Truth, which is the companion of our Black pigmentation' (MEW32).

Truth for Ben Ammi then is metaphysical: it is not correspondence between propositions and observation, it is what stands underneath all that exists, as a foundation: it is the *Divine intention* of how things should be.[58] And if the existing is not adequately connected to Truth, then it is without foundation; it will wither and die. It is always the spirit of vital life which generates and undergirds material substance; if something is disconnected from that source, then it slowly begins to decay, as its existence becomes *untrue*. In order to make life more Truth-centred we must ascertain the Divine intention, of how things should be. This is what will reconnect us with God.

Perhaps the deepest aspect of this explanation may come when he states, 'Only true life or life that is Truth-centered yields reality as it was meant to be. Lies yield an illusion. It is essential to know the Truth, for it is the Tree of Life that produces immortality' (PI77). In these three brief sentences Ben Ammi tells much about his programme and his agenda: he wants to return human beings to Truth, but this is not the Truth of historians, who merely tell us what has happened – which at its best, even if accurate, is merely a collection of facts. Ben Ammi looks around us and sees a world of disconnection from God, a world which is not how it should be. The world has gone off-course, emphasizing the wrong things, the wrong values in life. It has become increasingly distant from its intent and hence increasingly untrue; because of this it is dying. In order to reconnect people (and crucially his people, African Americans) with the right ways of being, Ben Ammi has created a myth which incorporates much that is correct in its basic historical structure, while building into it an epic cosmological battle between good and evil at the centre of which are those he is trying to save.

2

As in the days of Noah: Eschatology and apocalypticism

The end of the world does not imply the total devastation of the earth. It suggests the end of the civilization that controls the minds of men and influences nations; the end of the image or acceptable standard of evil and a return to Genesis and the original plan of creation for a world governed by men governed by God – the end of evil imperialism.

(MEW55)

[T]he magnitude of the evil that has been wrought upon the world was hidden from discernment, allowing the time of the Gentiles to run its course in accordance with the Word of God. Now in this, the Day of the Lord, the revelations of the unending, unbelievable evil that has been perpetrated upon the planet are coming to the light and believe me, they are mind-baffling.

(GBMT81)

African American apocalypticism must first of all be seen in the context of the broader American millenarian trend. Indeed, American Puritans viewed the settling of America in terms of an escape from the new Egypt (Europe), and the opportunity to create a new world free of the corruption of the old. African American tradition has largely inverted this, reading America itself as Egypt, and slavery as the fundamental sin which must be accounted for. By the nineteenth century, several Black thinkers had already presented the racial-ethical challenge to white America in terms of divine punishment, rhetorically announcing that only white repentance and the liberation of Blacks could save America from punitive destruction.[1] The model for these thinkers was typically that of Egypt and the Israelites, and as Egypt had been punished for its refusal to liberate the people so would America. These jeremiad stylings were not yet apocalyptic: they called for reformation, and upon repentance and correction, disaster could and would be averted. America, after all, was itself a uniquely chosen nation.[2]

The idea that repentance, even if forthcoming, could atone for such evil as America had propagated upon Blacks was not universally held, however, and by the end of the nineteenth century the failings of the emancipation proclamation to actually liberate Black people helped to engender a more damning narrative: America was fundamentally evil and soon *would* be destroyed for its sin.[3] This belief was held by American-Haitian Bishop James Theodore Holly, among others. The Nation of Islam was apocalyptic from its inception, and by the 1960s its newspaper *Muhammad Speaks* featured regular exhortations on the coming destruction of the United States and the present world order, and Malcolm X was using similar imagery, forecasting America's 'Divine Destruction'.[4] His 1963 speech titled 'God's Judgment on White America' cited the biblical destructions of wicked lands (Sodom, the Flood, and Egypt) as precursors to the coming destruction.[5] This comparison of America with egregious biblical examples was thus not limited to Hebrew Israelite or Christian thinkers. The mid-1960s in particular were a time of apocalyptic rhetoric, as the Civil Rights movement won its battles and realized that legal equality might not engender the kind of freedom they had imagined and the Black Power movement emerged in its place, offering a more radical vision that suggested America could not be reformed and must be replaced, at least for Black Americans.[6]

The Hebrew Israelite movement grew within this context, absorbing and reinterpreting it, and so has often if not usually been one of an apocalyptic bent. Ben Ammi existed and was educated in this particular flavour of the tradition, as will be shown. He did not shy away from thinking about or talking about a coming end to the present world order, and the emergence of a radically new condition. In fact, he thought that we had already entered the new age and were watching the old order pass away before our eyes. Ben Ammi's apocalyptic thought – present most clearly in his third book, 1991's *The Messiah and the End of This World* – is rich, lucid, surprising in detail, and unlike what many would expect from such a title, penned by someone who was only just making the transition from an apparent radical cult leader to a more respectable figure, one accepted by the Israeli establishment.

The version given in MEW is now the definitive account, but we must see this in the light of what went before. In the early days of A-Beta there had been some suggestion that the apocalypse would occur in 1970 along with the appearance of the Messiah – indeed, the impending destruction of America was one of several reasons given for the urgency of their exodus. At least some in the community seem to have believed that this would be a literal destruction.[7] There is no record of Ben Ammi claiming this, although it is notable that in May 1970, just two months after arriving in Israel, Ben Ammi is reported as saying 'The Messiah will walk the streets of Jerusalem. His visit will be for a period between Pesach and Yom Kippur. this will be the beginning of the end times, and the beginning of war and terrible storms. He who believes will believe and he who doesn't believe will not believe.'[8]

The non-appearance of apocalyptic events in 1970 seems to have passed without comment; the group may have at the time been more concerned with their rapidly deteriorating relations with the state of Israel. They had also recently absorbed the highly influential Shaleak Ben Yehuda (Louis A Bryant) and his followers, who may have been pushing a different agenda – Shaleak was probably a key figure in steering the group towards a more radical messianic (and authoritarian) style.[9] By the time

American sociologist Morris Lounds interviewed them in 1972–3, the date had moved to Yom Kippur (the biblical Day of Atonement festival, where the last year's sins are repented and forgiven), 22 September 1977, the 'year of the Kingdom of God', when Ammi claimed there would be plagues and 'a war like a war that has never been, and never shall be again between almighty God and Satan', involving military machinery against God's power.[10] Then, the current state of Israel would be swept away and 'the Kingdom of God will be in its glory at Jerusalem … recognized by the governments of the world'. Interviewed on the BBC's *Tonight* programme, he announced that on that date, 'the world as we know it will come to an end and I will be summoned to Jerusalem to establish a new order of righteousness'.[11] As it happened, on this day Ammi was anointed in a public ceremony in Dimona as King of Kings and Lord of Lords; and after his coronation he announced that America had temporarily been spared its retribution but the old age of the Euro-gentiles had now ended and the New World Order had begun.[12]

It is not my concern here to discuss the prophecies and their failure; much has been written on such occurrences in other movements, and from what contemporaneous reports we have, it doesn't seem that these predictions were a central focus of the leadership, although it has been claimed that a number of members left following the lack of a world-changing cataclysm in 1977. While Ben Ammi may have believed that such an event would occur, its non-appearance was not treated with any great disappointment; in fact, he seemed prepared for life continuing as usual before the ceremony ended. What is most interesting however is that Ben Ammi did not simply forget these dates as failures, and provide revised predictions, as many would-be prophets of doom do, rather he actively reinterpreted them and wove them into his matured theology, wherein the destruction he had predicted became allegorical and the change political. Therefore, he continued to hold that they had, and were still, occurring. The predictions were in this way still correct, simply not in the manner that most had understood them. After the model of Hebrew Israelite millenarianism, Ben Ammi always believed that the world would continue, only with he and his people lifted up to be rulers and spiritual guides,[13] and so it was not difficult to read the apocalypse as something subtle, and already in effect. In fact the community argue that the many changes of the last few decades confirm that the end of the Euro-gentile era is well under way, although one can still witness that dying world's struggle to survive. Much of this was also stated in *God, the Black Man and Truth*, where he discusses 'the wrath of God and the impending destruction of the Euro-gentile world', holding that only those who understand what is coming, and make the change before it's too late, will be saved: 'one must hear the plane engines roaring and see the bombs falling *before* the actual event takes place' (GBMT238). Here he interprets Rev.18 as predicting the coming nuclear holocaust, after which, 'there will be nothing or no one to save'.

Ben Ammi had already had the experience of having to cope with a disappointed expectation in a miraculous occurrence: the night of Pesach 1967, when their divine transportation which would take them out of America had failed to materialize. At that point there was no viable conclusion except to make the arrangements themselves – i.e. to book flights. It is not recorded who was responsible for that decision, but it is echoed in the reinterpretation that Ben Ammi placed on subsequent prophesied dates: the expected *is* happening, and it *will* be achieved; we just need to have faith, be patient and work towards it ourselves.

In Robert Carroll's study of failed biblical prophecy, he shows that sometimes a belief's disconfirmation can simply not be accepted as disconfirmation: 'The nature of hope for the future is such that it can hardly be falsified by any amount of apparent disconfirmation.'[14] The key term here of course is hope – if people place a high degree of *hope* in something happening then the cognitive dissonance resulting from its disappointment simply isn't acceptable, and it becomes necessary to find a way of convincing oneself that it either has, is or will happen. In Ben Ammi's case, he simply accepted that the winding down of European dominion was to be a longer process than he had expected; yet, everything else still pointed towards that eventuality.

The predictions were re-glossed in *The Messiah and the End of this World*, where the year 1970 was now defined not as the end of America; rather, that year's Yom Kippur (9–10 October) was the date on which the Kingdom of Yah was officially established. By this time the whole Liberian contingent had settled in Israel and had begun their new existence, uncertain as it was. This date heralded the beginning of the 'inevitable decline of Euro-gentile dominion' (MEW148) as the mustard seed kingdom of less than two hundred people was initially set, fulfilling the everlasting Kingdom prophesied in Dan.2. The intentional formation of the Kingdom when they met for April 1967's Pesach signified the entry into 'the prophetic season of time called "the Day of the Lord"' (MEW146) and heralded the reunification of Jerusalem, which took place only six weeks later, in June, at the culmination of the Six Day War:

> Our motion was the spiritual force behind the success of the Six Day War because the unification of Jerusalem was a prerequisite for the establishing of the Kingdom of God and the beginning of the Messianic Process of Deliverance for all men from the yoke of Euro-gentile economic and social strangulation. The fire that was released by our acceptance of our moral responsibility to humanity activated the process of destruction of the satanic forces and the purification of the earth.
>
> (MEW150)

Yom Kippur (22 September) 1977 was now claimed as the date when the Kingdom went public, no longer hidden. This was the point at which the Kingdom began to proclaim its existence and preach its message to the world.

Now:

> The former Heavens and earth are passing away; this world is presently in a period of transition. Many inhabitants of the earth have grown weary of evil societies and evil systems. The yearn for change is stronger than ever before; they are overcoming the fear to speak out against and confute that which is deadly wrong.
>
> (MEW153–54)

Ammi had previously described unprecedented international wars and disaster in the time of America's judgement, which would consume anyone left on the continent as the order of the world was upended. By 1991 he was still invoking 'the mother of all wars' as inevitable (MEW15), but now the old order had been in the process of passing away ever since 1967, and the new one emerging. The world did not and does not face physical destruction by God – in fact, it must now be saved from the ongoing destruction being undertaken by 'greed motivated Euro-gentile science, technology and evil intentions' (MEWvii). Ammi reiterates often that the Euro-gentile political system has led the world to the brink of destruction; in pursuing an unrighteous materialism, the planet has been poisoned, our societies made wicked and satan is in control. Reformation is not a possibility, the existing world must simply be swept away in order to let the new emerge:

> The end of the world does not imply the total devastation of the earth. It suggests the end of the civilization that controls the minds of men and influences nations; the end of the image or acceptable standard of evil and a return to Genesis and the original plan of creation for a world governed by men governed by God.
>
> (MEW55)

And so, as Ammi makes clear in the book's title, the transformation of the world, its reorientation, is synonymous with the end of *this present* world: this world, its values and priorities, its systems and methods, will be brought to an end to be replaced by those of righteousness (i.e. living by biblical principles). Referring again to the Hebrew Israelite theory of Esau as Europe and Jacob/Israel as Black Americans, he cites 2Esdras6:9: 'For Esau is the end of the world, and Jacob is the beginning of it that followeth' (MEW55).

This is to be 'the greatest period of change the world has experienced since the fall of Adam' (MEWvi). There is still to be a war, but this will signal the end of the transformation, not its beginning. This time 'does not begin with atomic weapons and chemical warheads. When those weapons are used at the end of the age, it will be after the end of this, the Euro-American, Euro-gentile world.' In his frequent comparisons of the end of *this* world with the end of Noah's, he argues that the apocalypse of the biblical flood did not destroy the world, because the destruction had already begun: 'The rain was merely washing it all away, it did not in itself cause the end of the world. The rain came after the end of the world' (MEWvii). It was clearing the chaos of the old, dead world, to prepare for the new.

It is logical for Ben Ammi that the Euro-gentile world would destroy itself – as God is creative rather than destructive, it is the destructive negative potency of the Euro-gentile world which will cause its own demise. This will be catalysed by the re-emergence of God's Word – the spiritual Truth which was banished from the world since the crucifixion of the last anointed, Yeshua, and which Ben Ammi's own teachings were bringing back into the world. The friction of this Truth against the untruths of this world will cause growing destruction, as the untrue civilization collapses. God's Word is the Truth which, in contact with evil, forms a fire in which some will be purified, some consumed (MEWX, 141, 144–7). He explained previously that the Divine encounter must be prefaced by proper ritual sanctification in order to prevent madness, and therefore 'every mind not prepared and sanctified unto God at the appointed time will be destroyed' (GBMT241). For this reason he describes the spiritual war that the AHIJ are engaged in as a war of 'Redemption': 'The Sons of God are engaged in the Holy War of Redemption, the war for the salvation of every bird, bee, elephant, pulp tree, the air, the water, and the souls of all men' (GBMT252). In distinction to unrighteous humans, 'The Deliverer is not equipped with carnal weapons of war, but with the weapons of God's Truth, to dissect, reject and bring to an end to all ungodly influence.'

Such claims became less frequent through Ben Ammi's career, and the AHIJ do not seem to still hold such beliefs at all. While it is possible to argue that it was disappointment in these prophecies that led to a more conciliatory approach towards Israel, and in his thought in general, Ammi always publicly claimed that it was a shift in Israel itself towards accepting the AHIJ, combined with their own gradual learning and acceptance of Israel and Israelis, that led to the possibility of reconciliation. The community still believe in the irredeemable status of America, with some holding that soon the American descent into decrepitude will be complete and the AHIJ will no longer be able to save Blacks from it: The chaos and pain there will engulf particularly the Black community who will become re-oppressed, and the AHIJ must now focus on the new communities in Africa.[15] But talk of a catastrophic war is absent from the community, who are focusing their efforts on global improvement – i.e. on building the Kingdom of God which is already replacing the old order.

Mechanism of apocalypse: The moral depravity of America

One of the key components that Ben Ammi returns to throughout his books is the critique of materialism as a negative, damaging and 'unholy' aspect of the Euro-gentile world: 'The materialistic diet never satiates the appetite; it merely creates greater lust (greed). These inanimate objects cause man to always be discontent, and soon he is possessed with greed, the end result of trying to solve a spiritual problem through materialistic attainments' (MEWviii). In this simple but incisive comment, Ammi locates the fundamental problem of materialism: that it promises *material* solutions to what are in fact *spiritual* problems. This is very much in line with his critique of the Civil Rights Movement: that it had failed ultimately because in demanding jobs and equal economic opportunity, the movement had done nothing to solve the more important spiritual problems faced by Black people still living in the land of their captivity.

However, we should also recognize that even if Ben Ammi is here tapping into a fashionable contemporary trope regarding the evils of materialism, that this concept is nevertheless basically correct. To take the latter first, it has become increasingly apparent that the human consumption of raw material extracted from the earth can only go on for so long, before we destroy – if we have not already – the environment that sustains us. Our conversion of ever more of the planet's material into objects which are ultimately discarded, often becoming poisonous polluting junk that still has to be stored somewhere, simply cannot be sustained. But even in principle, the focus on material things rather than on persons or beings, cannot provide for the entire complex needs of human beings. His use of materialism then is quite interesting, because it suggests that materialism is ultimately responsible for the destruction of the material world: our materialism in fact turns ourselves into material; it prevents and overwhelms our subjectivity. We are then consuming as a means of self-annihilation.

Certainly, we need some objects in order to continue living, but the centring of objects in human lives seems to lead to the absence of that which should be provided by human connection. Ben Ammi is no luddite: he sees the value of technology when it is correctly used as a tool for human purposes, but when technology in itself is valued then it destroys the focus on humanity. Therefore, 'Humanity has to now submit and be fashioned again in the image and likeness of God' (MEWix).

Unlike prior Black jeremiad thinkers, Ben Ammi addressed his calls to moral improvement to Black, not white, America. Similarly to Malcolm X, Ammi believed it was Black America which must live up to the calling of God and their status as the Chosen People; white America have been merely tools for God to bring Israel back to the path.

The reformation of the world which Ben Ammi calls for has far-reaching consequences. It means the dismantling of liberal democracy, a system built upon the belief that humans know best rather than God; it means focusing on health and wellbeing in this life instead of lifestyles that bring about poor health and ultimately death; and it means returning to the laws given in scripture to Moses rather than believing them to have been annulled. It means a wholesale reordering of society to focus on God and righteousness instead of personal interests, liberties and appetites. These ideas will all be analysed in later chapters.

Influences and precedents

From a close reading of other sources it is clear that much of the early apocalyptic tradition of Ben Ammi's movement can be traced back to previous generations of Hebrew Israelites. Lucius Casey predicted the apocalypse during the 1960s, and purchased farmland so that they could learn agriculture before they were transported to Israel by God.[16] Wentworth Matthew, interviewed in the 1940s, expressed a number of concepts identical with Ben Ammi's, stating that 'the Gentile age … is coming to an end as did all other ages'; he continued that this time the destruction would be not via flood but fire, as God 'has placed the atomic bomb in the hands of the Gentiles who know only how to make machines and instruments of destruction.' He expressed the view that the atomic war of 2000CE will leave 'no one on earth' except the Israelites, who will be restored to their land as part of the messianic or 'theocratic' age.[17] A similar prophecy was part of Frank Cherry's Church of the Living God in Philadelphia.[18] Bishop A.W. Cook, the Harlemite contemporary of Matthew, predicted a 'great destruction.'[19] The one-time Commandment Keeper who would go on to found the more radical One West Camp, Abba Bivens, had also written that 1914 had marked 'the beginning of the end of the Gentile age.'[20]

It is worth considering the implication of the central Hebrew Israelite idea here: if European civilization has been merely God's rod of correction against the Israelites, then America was discovered, and the United States founded, solely as a vessel for slavery. Stated in these simple terms, it becomes clear that once its use has passed – once the Israelites have begun to awaken from their slumber and reassert their identity and place in the world – then the United States as an institution will crumble from existence. The Assyrian and Babylonian empires vanished soon after their task (of punishment) was completed, and so will America.

However, even prior to the emergence of the Hebrew Israelites, some Black Christians were suggesting that the white Christian nations embodied the spirit of the Antichrist and would destroy themselves during the battle of Armageddon. This was even framed by them as part of the transition of eras, understanding world history as having progressed from the Age of Shem (when the scriptures were revealed to the Semitic Hebrews) to that of Japheth (when Europe adopted and spread Christianity), and now standing on the verge of the Age of Ham – when Africans would show the true way of living by the gospel, in contrast to the warlike ways of European nations.[21] Theophilus Gould Steward argued from the New Testament Greek that 'end of the world' could only mean 'end of the age', to be followed by another; he interpreted the present age to be that of the Gentiles (successors of the Roman Empire: Europe and America), which is soon to end, whereupon the Jews will be returned to their land.[22] James Theodore Holly notes 'the Japhetic character of the Christian Dispensation', which predated the coming Hamitic age. The latter will fulfil the promise of peace and goodwill given at Christ's entry into the world, but the changing of eras would be 'a deluge of blood, shed by those warlike nations in fratricidal combat', as predicted in the Armageddon of the Book of Revelation. That Hamitic Africans will be the elect of the coming age is proven by Ps.68.30's conjunction of the scattering of 'the people that delight in war' with the emergence of royalty and godliness from Egypt and Ethiopia.[23] Both writers utilize the phrase of Luke 21.24, 'the Times of the Gentiles' in describing the present, almost complete, period, as did Ben Ammi, and prior Hebrew Israelites. These predictions are simply biblical interpretation through the creative combining of certain passages, and the transmission of these through the African American religious tradition, from first Christian thinkers, into the next century's Muslim and Jewish thinkers, evidences the linearity of the tradition and the survival of certain interpretative tropes across generations. It is a Black Muslim who presents the most-clear forerunner to Ben Ammi in terms of African American Apocalyptic.

Elijah Muhammad preached an imminent apocalypse, one that would see America destroyed by natural forces, leaving only the righteous who would inherit the land and begin their new civilization there. In the mid-1960s he was predicting that 'the judgment, or doom, of the white man's world' would occur 'before or by 1970',[24] or in one case, 'within a few days'.[25] In 1965 he wrote, 'All signs of the times point to the fact that the day of judgment is not some "far-away" day coming in the distant future – but a day that has already dawned and that the black man in America is caught in its terrible cross-fire'.[26] Martha Lee comments that even at this point, he 'had begun to prepare for the possibility of his prophecy's failure. Most Muslims remained convinced, however, that the Fall of America had already begun'.[27] He shared Ben Ammi's interpretation of Revelation as describing America, with the terms Babylon, Beast and Dragon all indicating the United States. However, Muhammad was decisively literal – the 144,000 of Rev.14.1 are all that would remain of Black America; the remaining 16,856,000 would 'go down with our enemies'.[28] He even described a huge plane concealed beyond the moon that would come to rain destruction on America in the final stages of its punishment, and of a great war between Christianity and Islam.

By 1969 however (after the non-apocalypse of 1966–7), Minister Louis (Farrakhan) stated that there had been two stages: to build Black pride first, and then for Blacks to begin building society for themselves.[29] This reinterpretation is very similar to that which Ben Ammi ultimately provided regarding the public mission of the Kingdom. By 1972 Muhammad was discussing the possibility of white salvation through Islam, and a final war in which Blacks would not use 'carnal weapons' but would be supported by God's power over nature. He claimed that a beautiful future of peace and harmony and Black Islamic power lay ahead, and that white civilization was falling before their eyes, but provided no date and only the timescale of after-his-own-death for the end of white rule. This is exactly the same as expressed by Ben Ammi, and Muhammad even hints at a dispensational providence behind the rise of white people, mentioning a 'divine term' given to that nation as to all others.[30]

Despite the crucial influence of both Muhammad and Hebrew Israelite tradition in his apocalyptic outlook, it is here that we can most clearly see the Christian inheritance of Ben Ammi's group. The predictions are taken straight from the two texts central to Christian apocalypticism: Revelation and Daniel.[31] The former is a Christian New Testament text (although most likely written by a Jewish Christian as it incorporates much Jewish symbolism); the latter is part of the Hebrew Bible although the rabbis treated it with suspicion (its inclusion was debated in the Talmud, demonstrating their uncertainty about its propriety/value); Daniel is not considered a prophet and the text is not often cited in rabbinic Judaism whereas it is highly valued and utilized in Christian texts; its composition in the early second century BCE locates it as one of the closest biblical texts in time to the New Testament. The Kingdom of Yah is interpreted as the eternal kingdom of Dan.7, which will break all others into pieces and supplant them, and which all shall come to serve in the future.

In addition to this however, it is notable that their chronology, their historical narrative, centres upon the life and person of Jesus – it is with the death of Yeshua that the Dominion of Deception began, and it is since that point that the gradual disenfranchisement of the Israelites was solidified, up until their enslavement in the Americas. This locating of Jesus as a pivotal figure – indeed, unprecedented in biblical history, although still not the incarnate Divinity of official Christian belief – places Ben Ammi as someone clearly heavily influenced by the New Testament and Christian thought generally. It is worth remembering that by the time Wentworth Matthew was teaching Ben Ammi's teachers, he had expunged any trace of Christianity from the Commandment Keepers, so this was not imbibed from him, although the Christian influence upon Matthew's millennialism was noted by Landing.[32]

If we can understand the early predictions of a literal apocalypse as part of Ben Ammi's inherited tradition, then his own reinterpretation of the motif after the predictions' failure takes on a new significance: this is his own input into the tradition (or at least, that of he and his advisers). In this we see not simply a charismatic leader instructing his people in their existing tradition, but a thinker applying his own reasoning and creating new concepts. Ben Ammi places the present moment as the nadir of history and civilization: the point where humanity has descended to its lowest point, and only now can we begin to emerge into a new righteousness. Once the apocalypse became read as not a literal nuclear holocaust but a gradual reordering of the global socio-political system, Ben Ammi and his coterie were left to imagine what would come next: as the old world, the Gentile Age, passed away, what would be the nature of the new world they heralded? The next chapter will demonstrate some of the most creative and utopian visionary thinking of the African American tradition.

Exodus and separatism

What is unique and overwhelming in the Hebrew Israelite thinkers as compared to other Black apocalyptic thinkers is repatriation: Blacks would not remain in America, but prior to the destruction would return – or be taken – back to their own land, which some considered to be Africa, some to be Israel. From the end of the First World War (i.e. during the second generation of the movement) some began to think in terms of an imminent time when God would bring God's People out of the land of bondage and to their Promised Land, while America would be destroyed for its sin. It is no coincidence that this was the period when Marcus Garvey's back to Africa movement took hold of great swathes of the African American populace, and the significance of Hebrew Israelite presence in and support for that movement is also apparent. That both movements were centred in Harlem meant that they could not but come into contact. However, where repatriation generally fell from fashion in the following decades, it remained a critical part of Hebrew Israelite thought. In this we must see also the significance of biblical ideas of the ingathering of the exiles and return to the Holy Land.

In addition to Garveyism and the biblical influence, another factor might be accountable. Without wishing to psychologize too much, Merrill Singer has noted that many of those who joined A-Beta in the mid-'60s had themselves relocated North during the Great Migration, while still very young children. It may not be too difficult to imagine the intergenerational stress and alienation caused by 'the loss of familiar social and economic patterns' to have informed that generation's renewed enthusiasm for emigration, as well as their willingness to embrace the new religious form of Black Judaism.[33] The emergence of Black Power with its assertion of Black agency must have contributed, as did surely the social instability of the 1960s. Certainly, something critical changed at this time, and a new decisiveness was born.

Ben Ammi was unwavering in his belief that African Americans had to leave the land of captivity in order to realize themselves. Like Elijah Muhammad, he drew on the biblical call to 'come out of her, my people' (Rev.18.4), and developed from this a decisive separatist social theory wherein the absolute negation of the Euro-gentile

(American) way of life was a prerequisite to redemption, and remaining within the 'beast' was impossible if one desired salvation.[34] There is a biblical precedent to this that cannot be ignored: when Israel was saved from Egypt and Babylon, they removed themselves, they did not seek assimilation, so: 'at every great deliverance there was a *separation* instead of an *integration*' (GBMT186). Accordingly, the community must separate itself initially, both physically and in terms of their objectives; African Americans must not be part of the corrupt world anymore, but must show the way *out* of the current paradigm; they must prove that there is another way entirely outside of the modern Babylon.

Ben Ammi's separatism is not identical with Elijah Muhammad's, but it is worth noting the continuity: while Ammi argued for the emigration of African Americans back to their homeland, the Land of Israel, Muhammad had no real concept of a homeland (according to his narrative the Tribe of Shabazz had lived in several parts of Asia and Africa before being taken into captivity). However, he did discuss repatriation to whence they were taken (Africa), which would require the reparative payment of monies owed for centuries of slave labour. More practically, he sought a territorial separation within America, with several states becoming an autonomous Muslim republic. He was clear that separation was essential: for him, as Ammi, assimilation was the last attempt of satan (whites) to prevent Blacks from attaining anything for themselves. Assimilation presented, for each of them, not the benefit of enhanced rights and status but the *threat* of being consumed by the evil world created by Europeans.

Like Martin Luther King Jr., Ben Ammi suggested that Blacks will always be under threat in America, because they serve to remind whites of their own evil. Being forced to encounter the victims of their 'hideous, scandalous, hellish past' torments whites: 'The presence of those whom they lynched, murdered, slandered, raped, and flagrantly imprisoned without cause' must cause whites 'at least, embarrassment and vexation'. Ironically the Black attempt to mimic the white only creates more hatred. The black 'has become more European than the European. Therefore, every time a European looks into the black face of a negro, the European sees himself, his work, his creation and he loathes it' (GBMT153). This argument, that guilt forces us to further hate the ones we oppress, is an important one, but at this point in history we should also recognize white America's terror at the (now imminent) prospect of losing demographic dominance over a shifting society: the recent rapid transformation of the conservative right into a hotbed of extremists and conspiracy theorists evidences this, in particularly American terms.

Emigrationist approaches to the African American question have fallen almost entirely out of favour since the 1960s; ironically, in the same time that Zionism has become increasingly popular within the Jewish mainstream, to the extent that it is now often seen as an essential component of Jewish self-determination. It is unclear what has changed, but the AHIJ currently stand as the only major advocates of emigration. This trend has been present within the Hebrew Israelite movement since its inception, as it quickly became entangled with Garveyism. Famously, Arnold Ford, musical director of the UNIA and teacher of Wentworth Matthew, emigrated to Ethiopia in 1930 with a small band of followers.[35] It is difficult now to see which might have come first: the

Garveyite influence which shared Harlem with the second generation of Hebrew Israelites in the 1910s and 1920s, or the biblical emphasis on a return to the Promised Land. Either way, these have bonded into an inseparable belief in repatriation to the Land of Israel for many Hebrew Israelites.[36] Ben Ammi's community is one of only two to have made the move, although others attempted it (one seems to have been forced to delay their entirely religiously motivated Aliyah due to the tension between Israel and the AHIJ during the 1970s and 1980s[37]).

3

Black Messiah: Ben Ammi, Yeshua and Messianism

Then he said unto me, Son of man, these bones are the whole house of Israel: behold, they say, Our bones are dried, and our hope is lost: we are cut off for our parts. Therefore prophesy and say unto them, Thus saith the Lord GOD; Behold, O my people, I will open your graves, and cause you to come up out of your graves, and bring you into the land of Israel. And ye shall know that I am the LORD, when I have opened your graves, O my people, and brought you up out of your graves, And shall put my spirit in you, and ye shall live, and I shall place you in your own land: then shall ye know that I the LORD have spoken it, and performed it, saith the LORD.

(Ez.37.11-14)

Only after the regeneration of the Messiah has the ray of light and hope once again been ignited in the hearts and minds of the Holy people. Endowed with the Spiritual Magna Carta revealed to him by the Holy one of Israel he has successfully reopened the Book. He has allowed the Holy Prophets of Israel to guide him through this maze of lies, falsehoods and deceptions to triumphantly establish the long-awaited Kingdom of Yah prophesied by Daniel the prophet at Jerusalem, northeastern Africa (Daniel 2.44).

(MEW92)

The Constantinian adoption of the logos *would by mutual agreement combine various Greco-Roman components to produce an opposing intellectual force. Thereafter, it would strive for the satanic objective of deposing the intellectual reign of the Holy Spirit of the Genesis. The subsequent reign of these Sons of Darkness would be cataclysmic, bringing the earth and all of its forms of life to the brink of certain extinction, this is the time during which the Prophet Daniel saw the Kingdom of God being established. The Kingdom of God would be the source of great regenerating spiritual, psychological and physiological effects, causing the great confrontation between the Sons of Light and the Sons of Darkness alluded to by the Essenes in the Dead Sea Scrolls.*

(RHS59)

As is generally known, and as is not concealed by the title of this book, Ben Ammi was considered the Messiah by his community. However, as is common with the group, they manage to commingle in this a complex blend of Christian tradition, Hebrew biblical exegesis which up-ends (aspects of) Christian tradition, and twentieth-century American new age and African American bricoleur thought.

The most comprehensive description of Ben Ammi's understanding of the Messiah and what Messiahship means can be found in two texts: 1991's *The Messiah and the End of this World* and 1996's *Yeshua the Hebrew Messiah or Jesus the Christian Christ*. In the latter text he is introduced by Prince Immanuel Ben Yehuda as God's 'personal representative on earth', invested with God's authority; and 'Messianic Leader of the Kingdom of God' (YHMa-c). However, it is notable that Ben never refers to himself with that term – even in the former text, he sets out the programme of the Messiah and it is clear to anyone knowledgeable about Ben Ammi and the AHIJ that he is talking of himself, but he leaves enough room in the text for the reader to be unsure. This may be a reflex of humility; however, my own feeling is that it is modelled on the ostentatious absence of any such explicit claim on Jesus' part in the Christian gospels. We find Ben stating, 'The creator has anointed a new Messiah to teach the doctrine of the Kingdom of God,' during his teaching about the doctrine of the Kingdom of God, without ever naming that person; likewise he states that 'the end of this world will come in the lifetime of some of you that are reading these words' just as Jesus did 2000 years prior (MEW16).

However, Ben Ammi is not considered by himself or others as *the* Messiah. Arguing from the Hebrew Bible's term *mashiach*, meaning anointed, Ammi explains that the Messiah is not a single person, and is not necessarily an apocalyptic figure; rather, a Messiah is simply one who is anointed as a leader, sent from God with a mission to bring the people of Israel back to the correct path. These are 'anointed individuals chosen periodically by Yah during set times to accomplish a specific objective'; they are chosen to represent God, God's interests and to be under the direct command of God (IL66).[1] They have appeared throughout Israel's history; Ammi notes that several individuals are described as being 'anointed' in the Tanakh, often with a kind of oil, as was the case with Israelite kings. He suggests that this oil symbolizes the wisdom that shines forth from them, because (as with Moses), '[t]he exposure to God's Truth causes a light to radiate which can be seen in one's way of life and countenance' (MEW18). Ammi does not provide a comprehensive list of messiahs, but he names Noah, Moses, Abraham and of course Yeshua as among them. It is not entirely clear where the distinction between Messiah and prophet lies, but the former certainly represents a more practical form of inspiration and direction.

Multiple messiahs are not unknown to previous biblical interpretation. There is an early rabbinic tradition of twin messiahs – the Messiah ben Joseph and Messiah ben David.[2] According to this tradition, the former would come and be killed in battle before the latter would take the throne and redeem Israel. For Ammi, however, the messianic line is a spiritual inheritance: indeed, each Messiah can be understood to manifest the Holy Spirit of God within their person. While this manifesting is never fully explained, it verges in some way on incarnation, without committing fully to that theological principle. He writes, 'God's message unto us concerning this is thus: when the word of God comes alive in spirit or in the flesh of His messengers, it is God in the midst of the people' (MEW41). The Messiahs, therefore, 'were God within the Messianic nation'. In support of this he cites God's statement to Moses, 'I made you a God' (Ex.7.1), the psalmist's 'I said you are gods' (Ps.82.6) and Jesus' claim that 'before Abraham, I Am'. Furthermore, if John the Baptist could be called Elijah (Matt.11.13-15) 'then someone else could be called Yeshua (Jesus, the Savior)'.

In the quotations above we can see that sometimes Ben Ammi seems to play with the Christian idea of messianic incarnation, knowing that it will strike certain chords with his readers, while not actually stating outright that this is what he intends. Certainly the notion of a Holy Spirit which one can manifest through adherence to righteousness leads to the conclusion that the most righteous humans, the Messiahs, thereby share the same spirit: after claiming that 'the one spirit of a/the chosen anointed messenger(s) that was/were consecrated for a special mission and service unto God throughout the generations', he remarks that the spirit of God that was upon David and Isaiah is the same manifested through himself (MEW6). It has been claimed by some ex-members that Ben Ammi held himself to be the reincarnation of Jesus,[3] and according to one scholar who spent time with them Ammi admonished his followers for considering him to be God when in fact he was merely(!) 'God Junior'.[4] This theology of divine sonship, of an adoptionist kind of stance wherein a human can be a lesser divine being who in some way shares God's divinity, is one certainly not sanctioned by the Hebrew canon, with the possible exception of Dan.7, depending upon interpretation. It was however widespread in the Jewish world around the turn of the Common Era, wherein a number of Second Temple traditions flowed together in the form of an angelic semi-divine human who manifested the *logos* of God, bore God's Name and was God's representative on earth (these are particularly clear in the Enoch literature and other pseudepigrapha of the time). These traditions formed a large part of the foundation of Pauline Christology and, when blended with certain pagan and Greek philosophical ideas, became gentile Christianity, but they remained a part of Jewish thought for some centuries as well – expressed in mythical figures such as the archangel Metatron.[5]

This blending of Jewish and pagan concepts is something Ben Ammi spends much of *Yeshua* discussing, in highly derogatory terms. For him, this was the first stage in the gradual but intentional emergence of a religion with the outward appearance of Hebrew monotheism, claiming its heritage from there and identifying itself as the logical completion of such, but with the internal nature and meaning taken wholesale from European paganism: the worship of a sun God with a Latin-Greek name, the rejection of the biblically mandated commandments and festivals, the absorption instead of existing pagan festivals, the days of the week named after pagan gods and the shifting of the sabbath from Saturday to Sunday.[6] This last in particular was heinous, as it promoted worship on a day dedicated to the pagan god of the sun.

There is of course some truth in the notion that Paul blended concepts popular in Greco-Roman thought into his new form of, what we might call, Judaism for gentiles; although it has also become increasingly clear in recent years that much of what Paul utilized had already become common and popular in Judaism – including the very trends such as incorporating or identifying the Messiah with the Godhead which Ben Ammi picked up on for his own messianic self-understanding. Either way, we can trace a line of influence for some of this thought back through Albert Cleage, who wrote that Paul corrupted Jesus' teachings in order to make them appeal to pagan gentiles.[7] The pagan nature of European Christianity was being talked about by Black Americans even in the nineteenth century,[8] and this is only one of many critical concepts expressed by Cleage that Ben Ammi and the community made heavy use of – as might be expected of someone who had written *The Black Messiah* in 1965, proclaiming that white Jews were converted gentiles and the Israelites were black.[9]

Cleage also claimed, like Ben Ammi, that 'almost everything you have heard about Christianity is essentially a lie', meaning that contemporary Christianity had been radically altered by white Europeans.[10] Here, the influence of Elijah Muhammad's construction of Christianity as a 'tricknology' designed to stupefy and pacify Blacks is obvious, but we should also consider the possible mediating presence of Ishakamusa Barashango's *God, the Bible and the Black Liberation Struggle*, which carried Cleage's convictions of the Black Jesus/Israel and the untrustworthiness of large parts of the New Testament (especially Paul's letters) into a model that holds modern Christianity as essentially a European construct (the grand difference is in Barashango's insistence on the importance of native African traditions, over and above the Hebrew Bible).

However, there is clearly a flattening of history in Ben Ammi's notion that all of this was pointed towards the goal of fashioning a new religion; a deeper reading of history, including of the Jews around the turn of the eras, makes resorting to such simplicities impossible. What we should recognize, if we must reject the literal truth of this doctrine, is how this signifies the place of Christianity in twentieth-century African American life: many, including those noted in this chapter, were rejecting traditional Christianity, even while feeling deeply connected to the spirituality and sense of history it contained. The church's role in the slave trade, and the use of Christianity to humble enslaved persons, cast an extremely negative shadow on the institution. This shadow was not one that was as readily found within the scriptures, which when read minus the traditions of interpretation built up around them in Europe/America, present a narrative of liberation, justice and communal care that is easy to be inspired by.

The crucifixion, the event that has the most pivotal significance for all Christianities, which radically shifted Christian theology into a new realm, is of a crucially different importance to Ben. Jesus himself was only one of many sent to bring Israel back, so was not ontologically significant in himself – and his life and death were not axiological cosmic events which condition soteriology; he was only the latest in a long line of messianic-prophetic messengers who *all* embodied the spirit of God. However, Jesus' death *is* significant, because he was the last Messiah before the Age of the Gentiles began – it was with his assassination that scripture was sealed (became uninterpretable), and the Israelites strayed further from the Divine Spirit than ever before. This was the beginning of the spiritual famine prophesied by Amos:

> The crucifixion was actually the attempt to crucify the Word of God, to remove its presence from among the falling Sons of God, and to spiritually destroy God Himself. [...] Jesus was to be the manifestation of the entire prophetic Plan of God; his coming symbolized truth before the people, whose rejection, caused darkness

or death to befall them. God's chosen servant, Israel, and the Romans (the world), united to betray Jesus in the Passover plot, and by doing so killed the active, living Word of God.

(GBMT94)

Intriguingly, Ben Ammi inverts the traditional Christian understanding of the crucifixion as the culmination of God's plan (as it led to the resurrection and signified the ultimate universal liberation of humanity). For him, it is the culmination of satan's plan, and the crucifixion represents the inauguration of the era of death. The resurrection happens only two millennia later, as the Israelites *en mass* rise from their grave, in fulfilment of Ez.37 (see below).

In the present context it is interesting to note that in 1972 Ben told an interviewer that, not he, but 'we [the whole community] are the anointed, we are the Christ that the world has been waiting for'.[11] It is also worth noting the fascination that the community developed with a somewhat obscure German Jewish thinker, Oskar Goldberg. In January of 1972 a German esotericist Harry Dörfel wrote to them, having read an article about them in the German magazine *Stern*; he informs them that Goldberg predicted their coming, apparently with the phrase 'The coming of Black people from America to the Promised Land will be the vanguard of the Messianic Age'.[12] This quote is still frequently mentioned by the community, along with citations from Isaac Newton, Nostradamus and Jimmy Carter which they interpret as prophetic utterances regarding the End of Days and the Kingdom of Yah.

The Black Messiah

Shortly after A-Beta left for Liberia, the Rev Albert Cleage published *The Black Messiah* (1968), based on sermons given in his Detroit church. The previous year he had renamed the church The Shrine of the Black Madonna and Child. Cleage was attempting to forge a more radical kind of Christianity, one informed by Black Power, with revolution and race consciousness at its core. In some ways, Cleage could be seen as the Black church's answer to the fiery approach of Elijah Muhammad and Malcolm X; adopting and transforming their argument that Christianity was the white supremacist's religion, designed to facilitate enslavement of Africans, in his hands Christianity became the religion of Black struggle against white oppression, one that had been lied about and castrated by Europeans. As Jawanza Eric Clark wrote, 'Both Cleage and Malcolm X essentially argue that the symbol of a White Christ is an idol and an imperial weapon used to perpetuate and legitimize White power and White authority wherever and whenever they encountered African-descended people and sought to control them.'[13] At the critical juncture of the late 1960s, Cleage's work represented an attempt to redefine and reclaim Christianity. As William Van DeBurg wrote in discussing the influence of Cleage, 'Rediscovery of the black Messiah was intimately related to black Americans' rediscovery of themselves. Once freed of the self-hatred fostered by worshipping a white God, they could reclaim their religious heritage by struggling to rebuild the disunited Black Nation just as Jesus had 2,000 years ago.'[14]

Cleage was clear in his assertions that Christ was not white: 'Jesus was the non-white leader of a non-white people struggling for national liberation against the rule of a white nation, Rome [...] Jesus was a revolutionary black leader, a Zealot, seeking to lead a Black Nation to freedom.'[15] However, between these two sentences there is a semantic gap that is seldom bridged in such works: 'non-white' and 'Black' are used almost co-terminously; Cleage in fact provides a convincing argument for the non-whiteness of the Israelites (for anyone who needed it), but immediately folds non-whiteness into blackness. This was a popular practice among African Americans in the 1960s, to identify a binary 'color line' (in the words of DuBois) whereby everyone was on one side (white, with all the privileges that entailed), or the other (Black/dark, peoples who all over the world were oppressed in one way or another by whites). The same is seen frequently in the Nation of Islam who frequently folded everyone that would now be called 'people of colour' into Black.

Just one year after Cleage's text, James Cone published *Black Theology and Black Power*, shortly followed by *A Black Theology of Liberation*, and again made the argument for the blackness of Christ – although here made with principal connection to the symbolism of oppression rather than literalism. Cone argued that if Jesus were to have any relevance to Black Americans then he must be understood as Black; must share in their blackness. The revolutionary and liberatory narrative of the gospels makes clear that Jesus was arguing the side of the oppressed, not the oppressor. In the quest to make Jesus relevant today, Jesus must be understood as Black. While the literal skin colour of Jesus is not relevant to Cone's theological argument here, still Jesus 'certainly was not white in any sense of the word'.[16] and the depth of blackness would make no difference to depth of oppression in the United States.

Cleage was not the first to assert the blackness of Christ – indeed, we can likely trace the lineage back to the first Hebrew Israelite preachers at the end of the nineteenth century (thereby suggesting that it goes even further back, beyond our extant records): William Christian, the Mississippi founder of the Church of the Living God (est. 1889), argued that Jesus was Black because the Israelites were Black.[17] While Christian's arguments, like most of the used by the first generation of Hebrew Israelites, were scriptural passages taken out of context (and often dependent upon quirks of the King James translation), nevertheless it was undeniable that Jesus and the other Israelites were certainly not white Europeans, and would have had a skin tone no different from that of their neighbours in Egypt and Arabia.[18]

As Van DeBurg notes, the literal factuality of the Messiah's blackness was not so important; it was not something to be debated and proved, as previous generations of theologians had the number of angels who could dance on the head of a pin. Rather, for many, it was the usefulness of the concept in signifying that Blacks no longer must worship and be saved by a deity imagined in the form of those responsible for their oppression: white Europeans. This is not to say that many did not also take it literally – they did, including Ben Ammi et al., for whom this was another piece of the puzzle, and the rising tide of such concepts indicated that during the 1960s Black Americans were approaching a critical mass of consciousness which was soon to be realized in the mass emigration from America before its destruction.[19] Sixty years later, it may not be immediately obvious, but for Ben Ammi and his colleagues, who had just awoken to the truth of their Israelite identity and were picking apart a web of lies and distortions that had kept them asleep until that point, witnessing the emergence around them of popular concepts like the Black Messiah utilized across the board – by popular preachers, by religious leaders and by academics like James Cone, such doctrines were obviously true and beyond question. It is in this context that certain statements made slightly after this time, which caused understandable concern, should be understood: that 2 million Black Americans would any day arrive in Israel, ready to drive out the 'white' inhabitants, was a religious statement of faith which was part of a messianic-apocalyptic fervour. This is not to judge the reception of such statements or to justify them (indeed one could argue that much antisemitism and anti-Judaism have shared those characteristics, including the most violent and murderous moments of history), but to understand that the AHIJ were speaking not from a place of hatred, and they at no point expressed hatred or made any step towards violent attack on Israeli (or American) Jews.

So, it may be that Ben Ammi, in reading as literal the African American identification with the Israelites, performs a manoeuvre on the traditional African American tradition, very similar to that which Cleage performs on the concept of the Black Christ – something which is intended as different, deeper, than literal truth, is re-read as literal for an age in which literalism is seen as the default mode of truth, where myth is subsumed under the concrete factuality of science.

The messianic people

In the reforming of the messianic concept into a pagan ideology, a key element that Ammi claims has been removed by Christianity is the notion of a messianic people, from whom the messiahs come. The messianic individuals who arise within Israel preach to the people, refining and returning or evolving their concepts and relationship with God. The anointed only come to Israel, and through Israel (the same is true of prophets, with extremely few notable exceptions – such as Jonah – and as the Bible's narrative progresses it becomes ever clearer that the only real subject of interest is Israel). According to Ben Ammi, it is the responsibility of the people of Israel to then spread these concepts to the rest of the world through their practices, thereby forming a buffer for the transmission of revealed Divine Truth. 'The priority of the Messianic nation is to show forth the Glory of God in their lifestyles and morality, that they may bear witness to the benefits of a people living under the laws (instructions) of God' (MEW30).[20]

Ben Ammi takes this concept wholesale from the Hebrew Bible, but subtly reconfigures it himself; whereas the Israelites were considered a priestly people, who bore within them a number of important roles, developed at different times for largely different purposes – priests (Cohens and Levites), prophets and the messiah – Ben Ammi has largely collapsed these roles into a single, more cohesive concept: the messianic people and the messianic individuals who rise up from within that people as leaders. Ben Ammi does frequently mention the priests, and the community has *Cohenim* (priests who offer spiritual guidance and administering the festival and shabbat services), but there is little place for them in his theology. There is no mention of a High Priest, and the central role of the Israelite priests – within the Temple – is absent because there is to be no Temple again. Ben Ammi, again appearing to draw more upon the presumptions of Christianity than upon the Hebrew Bible itself, argues that now the body is the Temple and there is no need for the reconstruction of God's earthly dwelling place for the Spirit should reside within (the) people. This is a re-reading of the Hebrew Bible which clearly updates certain pivotal concepts, and which could largely only become relevant in the international age; they make perfect sense to the twenty-first century (post-Christian) reader; but of course, this is not what the Bible itself says.

Even Ben Ammi's own adherence to the concept of the Messianic Nation is slippery. At points he states it in the most-firm terms, for example, 'The authenticity of the Messianic individual … can only be confirmed through the Messianic Nation' (MEW9). Here Ammi claims that the messiah can only come from the messianic people, and that anyone outside that cannot be a Messiah. It should be remembered that Ammi holds Israel to be the most authentic inheritors of the Image of God bestowed upon Adam (the rest of humanity having allowed satan to impose his own image upon them). The continued suppression of the true nature of Black America 'deprives the world of the knowledge of God's redemptive plan for the earth and her wretched inhabitants' (MEW17). However, at others he states that other nations will have their own individuals who will show them the way: 'Revelations of God have come to many men of other nations, as evidenced by the similarities of Truths written by many other authors not of the nation of Israel' (MEW68). The same Truth, after all, is accessible to anyone and will be revealed to anyone seeking it earnestly (MEW109).[21]

The resurrection

Despite the insistence on the plurality of messiahs, and even on other cultures having their own teachers and wisdom bringers, Ammi always positions his own time of action as the central one: the *real* end is coming now; the previous prophets had spoken of this age, which comes as the culmination not just of African enslavement, but of the Torah – because the entire Torah points towards this fate of the Israelites; and not just the entire Torah, but of all our history, because the actions of Ben Ammi and the Kingdom of Yah now are undoing the primal sin of Adam and Eve, taking us back to Edenic existence from where we can begin a new life, transcending the narrative of the fall. This then makes Ben Ammi arguably the single most important Messiah – the one who comes at the juncture, sealing the past and inaugurating the correct way of life, the Kingdom of God. It is he of all God's messengers who will succeed in his mission, of bringing Israel back to Truth.

Ammi's early apocalyptic beliefs skilfully wove together several concepts: the 6000-year plan of creation (which was for him an ongoing descent), culminating in the warlike Gentile Age (the past 2000 years, wherein the Word of God was occluded and Torah became opaque), with its nadir in the final 400 years, the Israelite enslavement in

America. According to all of these metrics, the end had been reached and it was time for the concluding act: the coming of the Messianic Age.

In terms of the meaning of the Messianic Age for Ammi and the AHIJ, quite simply it is the passing away of European domination and control. The Israelites were now awakening, having served their prophesied 400 years as punishment for their own forgetting of their nature, their God and the laws, and they would again take the mantle as the light to the gentiles to lead the world out of the abyss we currently inhabit.[22] This role of Israel as global leaders feeds directly into Ben Ammi's clear-eyed universalism. Channelling the prophecies of Zephaniah, he writes: 'There will soon come a time when all men and nations will be referred to as Sons and Daughters of God, Sons and Daughters of Light, one universal family under God, the Holy One of Israel' (MEW71).

Drawing on a tradition persisting since the prophetic books of the Tanakh, that the Messiah will come from the lowest, humblest section of society, Ammi makes clear that it is Black Americans who fulfil this:[23]

> In the days of the Kingdom of God, the heavenly Father will avenge their exploitation by hiding His Truths from the high and mighty and reveal them instead unto babes, the meek and weak (relatively) of the earth that shall confound and dumbfound the power brokers of today. It is the high and mighty that must come down that those considered lowly may take them up into the new world – Heaven and Earth.
>
> (MEW134)

Ben Ammi makes much of the biblical trope of the inversion of social order, using this in service of his argument that it is African Americans, the most mocked and maltreated group, who will inaugurate the new dispensation: 'Salvation will come from the last, not the first, in this world. The momentum has to start at the bottom and carry the outcasts of societies to the top to save this planet earth' (MEW119-20). It is 'the lowly and meek of the people, not the high and mighty' who will carry the Divine Spirit into the world, as Zech.9.9 prophesied; the Deliverer 'will emerge from amongst those considered left out or dropouts – those appearing to be insignificant'. And to make it explicit he concludes, 'the long-awaited Messiah or the Savior will emerge from the midst of those called African Americans in America, the land of their chastisement'. This 'will explain the peculiarity of Black people's "hidden" heritage and more importantly, the special relationship Blacks have with God' (MEW122).

It is here that we can witness Ben Ammi's dependence on one of the most common African American exegetical innovations. Since at least the nineteenth century, Ez.37.1-15's vision of lifeless desiccated bones reforming and becoming revivified, originally a promise that God would remember and redeem the Judeans in Babylon and return them to Israel (although rabbinic tradition interpreted it as referring to physical resurrection in the Messianic Age) had been applied to Black America.[24] In every stream of the African American theological tradition, whether Christian, Muslim or Hebrew Israelite, this passage has appeared with the same interpretation.[25] This is the grand subject of his ninth (and final major) text, *The Resurrection: From Judgment to Post-Judgment* (2005), but it is discussed in most of his others also.

The great plan, which Ammi finds in scripture, is that of the revival of the dead (unknown, unacknowledged) God, and the dead people Israel. Referring to his equation of life with endowment-with-the-Holy-Spirit, where the Spirit is identified with the lived expression of divinity, and of death as the slow death of moving away from God and righteousness (to be discussed in detail in the next chapter),[26] Ammi explains that 'Salvation would come in the revival of the values and moral codes established by God Almighty' (GBMT94). At this point, the Word of God, the living doctrine, 'will suddenly come alive and instil in men the desire to live again under the simple rulership of God' (GBMT86). As Black America first comes to life again, the Truth will radiate out from them, to all other people: 'The resurgence of Black America spells the revival of the light (intelligence) of God, the essential element and prerequisite for the redemption of the world' (GBMT166). The Word of God, identified also as Truth and 'The Universal Corrective Force' (GLR84), is of course the same that was breathed into Adam and made him a Living Soul, that was passed down as the Seed of Holiness through the Sons of God (the righteous patriarchs and then the Israelites).

In addition to Ez.37 Ben Ammi also utilizes the resurrection of Lazarus in Jn.11. His metaphorical analysis reads Lazarus as African Americans, his family as the family of nations, and the Pharisee Nicodemus, who challenged the doctrine of rebirth (Jn.3) as African American leaders who are dead without knowing it, and unable to help their people.

The 'death' of the Children of God, their status prior to resurrection, was thus because they abandoned their living soul – the intellect that God breathed into them – and only when they readopt this, i.e. once again take up the mantle of the Law, will they become once more alive. Ammi here connects Dan.12.2's 'those who sleep in the dust' with the creation of Adam from dust, prior to the imbuing of the Holy Spirit; they have 'died and returned, metaphorically, to the dust' (RHS51). This deathly state, distant from God, is linked to the Hell that they are undergoing in America. In a passage that recalls a rabbinic tradition, he writes: 'The Adamic civilization/House of Israel incurs death by loss of the Holy Spirit and subsequently are subject to the physical infirmities of the "dead" until their final expiration. It was His spirit (not ours for we never owned one!) that departed from us, symbolically returning to heaven after residing in the midst of us, individually and nationally' (RHS62).[27]

However, as the Israelites are resurrected they will be redeemed from their suffering. This requires a complete shift from the old ways; and as in Jewish tradition, the return to the Land of Israel is a necessary component. From this point, creation will effectively reboot: 'The new creation begins with the resurrection/revival of the B'ray-sheet idea of the first-born son, Adam – the House of Israel, the *"highway of the seed"* of the Adamic civilization' (RHS109). The Israelites who served to preserve and transmit the Holy Seed from the Adamic civilization are being resurrected, so there will be a cosmic new beginning, in a return to the original plan of Genesis.

At this point as the Euro-gentile world is ending there will be a new Genesis: Humanity will be recreated in the image of God, as will societies, nations and governments. It is the responsibility of Israel to show the way back to righteousness from the imitation 'religions' that have pulled humanity away from God: 'We (Israel) were chosen not just to provide light or guidance of God for our numerically small selves, but to provide the same light or guidance unto all the nations' (MEW69).

The change in lifestyle, which brings greater health and wellbeing (see Chapter 6), will precipitate also a change in consciousness, and humankind 'will quickly learn the values of love and understanding by living them daily in oneness with others. He will see that the beauty of the brotherhood is better than living in competition and hostility' (GBMT187). Then, people will live in an eternal earthly paradise; 'a world of the original creation,' i.e. as Creation was intended to be (GBMT87).

This utopia, and the struggle leading to it, are not limited to the Israelites, but is universal:

> [W]e understand that we are an organ of a human family; therefore, an enemy of that family is our enemy. The Messianic nation has to share the God intellect, display its positive effects and encourage all men to join hands in the Universal struggle against the forces of evil. [...] The doctrine that He bestows upon the Messianic people will be universal.
>
> (MEW35-6)

Throughout his writings Ben Ammi emphasizes that redemption and the Messianic Age are open to all people who will hear and accept the truth.[28] He makes no distinction with regard to race, nationality or prior religious commitment: Even now, 'there are those of Euro-gentile origin that realize that they have been deceived by their fathers and led into a self-destructive trap. They are opposing their own systems vehemently, standing against all odds. They stand as a truly enlightened minority' (GLR47).

The first stage of the redemption is that of the individual Messiah bringing his teachings to the messianic people Israel; but as Israel are brought back to righteousness, others will naturally be drawn towards the new life. The necessary first stage – the reestablishment of the Israelites in the Holy Land – has already been accomplished; 'Thus, the Messianic plan for the beginning of the new world has begun in the Holy Land' (MEW43). A flyer issued by the community in 1983 mentions their blackness only in passing, claiming that they have 'developed a community with a life-style that we know would be beneficial to all men – but it is not enough to go off into a corner of the world and practice a life-style. You must teach this form of alternative life-style to the world.'[29] This universalistic aspect to Ben Ammi's teaching is clearly counter to that of more publicly visible Hebrew Israelite groups, especially those descending from the notorious One West Camp, who preach that salvation is for the Israelites alone, of whom all other peoples shall become slaves in the Messianic Age.[30] However, Elijah Muhammad taught that some white Americans could survive the apocalypse, if they were of righteous character.[31]

Quite apart from the technical theological aspects, we should recognize in Ben Ammi's reconfiguring of the messianic tradition, a particular application specific to the needs of African Americans. The saviour they needed was a Moses, not a Christ, to help them escape their oppression in 'Egypt,' and return home. This is what Ben Ammi brought them, not a final divine figure, but a human who would save them, return them and allow them to redeem themselves. This second Moses then challenges the foundations of Christian messianism with its singular personification and universal significance: Ben Ammi came as the Messiah for the Israelites alone, serving their needs. We can also see that Ammi emphasizes the biblical and Jewish motif of a *messianic people* as part of Black Chosenness – the people, having suffered and liberated themselves, will have a special role to play in the liberation of all humanity.

In fact, we might suggest a similarity where the time spent in Israel worked on Ben Ammi as did the *hajj* (pilgrimage to Mecca) for Malcolm X: it was only after stepping outside of America and witnessing a society not based around a fundamental racial binary, where race was not the first consideration, that he realized people could actually live together and transcend race.[32] From the late 1970s, his vision became noticeably less antagonistic, and he began to perceive a future for the community within Israel.

The Black Messiah, where that Messiah was Ben Ammi, was a central element of Ben Ammi's thought for some time – referred to in interviews and press releases throughout the 1970s and 1980s, and forming the subject of his second book. But, like the apocalyptic predictions it became arguably less important in the last two decades of his life, as the AHIJ became accepted and integrated into Israel. During this last stage of his thought the Messianic role seems to have matured into a symbolic one, just as the eschatology became a slow cultural shift rather than a cataclysmic war. His later books refer little to the concept, and while the community retained use of the title for him, its meaning softened. From here we will progress to examine some aspects of Ben Ammi's more mature thought.

4

Pneumatic immanence: God, ontology and law

Jesus said that satan was the father of a lie, but what has he been lying about? Since he is the arch enemy of God, we can presume that first and foremost that he has been lying about God, His plan and way of life in righteousness.

(GBMT253)

And I will put My Spirit within you and cause you to walk in My statutes and to carefully observe My ordinances.

(Ez.36.27)

The life of the body is the Spirit of God.

(GBMT90)

The Spirit of God is the invisible force behind the law that is written and unwritten.

(MEW92)

Ben Ammi doesn't explicitly describe God in his works or attempt to construct what might classically be considered a theology. However, from his writings we can form quite a clear picture of what he thought God was and was not. Ben Ammi was a thinker of immanence, rejecting much metaphysical speculation, and disavowing any talk of God as a being or of a non-material heavenly existence in the afterlife. His thought is fundamentally concerned with this-world, and the problems of life as we know it, viewing abstract philosophical and theological questions as irrelevant. This is part of the tradition he inherited from Hebrew Israelism, and indeed Black Theology generally: increasingly throughout the African American theological tradition in the twentieth century, embodiment is figured over and above any rejection of the body, and the earthly life here and now is treated with prime importance. This is true of James Cone, Elijah Muhammad and Albert Cleage, the latter of whom condemns otherworldly religion as false Christianity.[1] Simply, a theology geared to the needs of Black Americans in the second half of the twentieth century was necessarily political, and aimed at improving lives in America, rather than dealing with other realms. The nature of God then is of less concern to Ben Ammi than what God does, what God wants from us and how we should relate to God.[2]

Ben Ammi is damning of any attempt to find God outside of the present world: 'The quest for God is of the utmost practical and temporal significance. It has nothing at all to do with fantasy or mysticism or the so-called "supernatural" world' (GBMT40). The supernatural itself is a problematic concept for Ben Ammi, one which is native to the euro-Gentile (pagan) system of belief; for him there is no 'outside' of nature, no other realm from which beings sit and observe us. This separate world of the Divine is what makes possible the fantastical speculations of Greek and Roman myth about the lives of gods. Ben Ammi is not the first to suggest that the Israelite faith is unique in grounding human beings in their own lives, and making God an intrinsic part of them.

This chapter will show that Ben Ammi pursued something like a vitalist theology, one that placed life and growth (and the possibility of those forces expressing themselves) at the centre of reality. We will look at this in terms of the thought of Black Theologians Albert Cleage and James Cone as well as previous Hebrew Israelite thinkers, showing that Ammi drew on a deep tradition within African American religious thought – and perhaps one which draws upon native African conceptions the enslaved people brought with them to the Americas.

The nature of God

While the AHIJ permit the use of God's Name (the four-letter name YHWH as revealed to Moses, to which like many Hebrew Israelites Ben Ammi ascribes only long-a vowels (YAHWAH), the usual form is Yah. The AHIJ seem to have reasoned that there is no biblical command to avoid pronouncing the Name, only to avoid taking it in vain. On this, Ben Ammi writes,

> [A]ny use of the name of God out of the context of truth (any use of His name in matters that are not in one's heart) will result in a curse instead of a blessing. Thus, the blessed name of God can only be uttered from the *hearts* of men, not their mouths. Whereas, it is easily understood that the name of God is ineffectual when uttered from the mouths of the wicked; from the mouth of the wicked it will bring a curse upon its user.
>
> (GLR115)

Any visitor to the AHIJ will quickly become familiar with the phrase *Yah Khai*. Translatable as 'God lives' or 'God is living', this phrase is emblazoned around the Village of Peace, and is the standard shout of praise or celebration in many situations. Although it does not appear in this form in the Tanakh, it is a paraphrase of several passages wherein God is described as living, usually in the form *Khai-YHWH,* or in invocations of 'the Living God', *Elohim Khaim.*

This is the core of Ben Ammi's concept of God, who is immanent in the world, involved in human life, and an active presence among us. God, as Creator, is the source of life, and all that is vital, growing, living, and thriving has its source in God. Critically, this is what God provides for human beings: to grow, to thrive, to be healthy and productive. What is arguably the first commandment, to go forth and multiply (Gen.1.28), engenders the necessity of this creativity and spreading of life onto humanity. While the appellation of God with connotations of life is most often interpreted in Jewish and Christian thought with the sense of God being personal and relatable, in Ben Ammi's theology 'living' plays a dual role: on one hand it determines that the Spirit of God is present with us as only a living force can be, but on the other that *life* is a primary characteristic and attribute of God, inseparable from God. As the Creator, God is the force that underwrites all of existence, and is the force that allows life to exist. This nourishing, life-centred definition of God is what leads me to characterize Ben Ammi's theology as vitalist.

There are some important consequences of this doctrine, which Ben Ammi developed into a systematic cosmology. First, if God is the source of all life, then everything that is must remain connected to God in order to sustain itself. Anything which moves away from, or weakens the connection with, God, is initiating a process of decay which will ultimately end in non-existence.

Secondly, this subtly relocates agency with humans rather than God: any vitalist theology effectively depersonalizes God, because it locates the *reception* of God's bountiful energy not with choices that God makes, but with choices that humans make. If God's nature is to vivify, then any absence of vitality must be the responsibility of humans.

Third, because of this, there are immediately perceivable resonances with recurring Jewish theological concepts: most noticeably, the mechanistic/theurgic worldview of the Kabbalah wherein divinity is less a person and more a fluid realm of being, which sustains yet is dependent upon human beings for facilitating the transmission of that sustenance into the world. At its most extreme, this could present divinity as more akin to a cosmic fountain than a parent.

Lastly, creation is essential to God: as the causation of all life and reality, this causation is less *willed* by God than an essential corollary of God. Destruction is so antithetical to God that the inevitable defeat of satan and overturning of the present world worder require explanation to show that this is not in fact a destructive outcome: Ammi explains several times that the Truth of God's Word is a *corrective* force, and the destruction which is occurring is a logical consequence of the friction caused between Truth and untruth; the apocalypse is thus a creative event, correcting the world.

Related to these points, Ben Ammi rejects any kind of interventionist deity outright. At no point does he describe God as acting in the world; at most, God only attempts to convince humans to act in certain ways. God does not answer prayers himself, but provides one with the strength to achieve them: 'God instills skill and understanding ... if one prays that a huge mountain be moved, then, after praying, he rolls up his sleeves and takes a pick and shovel and begins moving the mountain' (GBMT135). The miracles of the Bible were not interventions by God but were the actions of Israel, who attained such powers due to their righteousness.[3] This rescripting of agency to humans, albeit ones open to the influence of God, is a radical but important step which conditions much of his approach conceptually and pragmatically. Simply, God's aims are expressed through humans, and one cannot rely simply on God to achieve what is right: our doing it for God *is* God's doing it.

The opposite of God as the force of Life is satan, the anti-Life force. Satan (uncapitalized) appears frequently in Ammi's texts, adamantly opposing and challenging the Truth, Life and Righteousness that is God's. Satan is an important part of Ben Ammi's cosmology, one he spends almost as much time talking about as God. In several places he appears more comfortable making direct statements about satan than about God, and it is through the consideration of the God-satan binary that we can extrapolate much about the former. We get the sense that there is a fundamental dualism to Ben Ammi's thought, one which places God and satan at either sides of the grand stage (the world), engaged in combat against each other. Frequent references to the spiritual warfare ongoing between them can make Ammi's world seem Manichean, expressive of a constant struggle between good and evil. This is to misrepresent the overwhelming righteousness of God, which effectively guarantees the victory; Ben Ammi is not strictly a dualist, though he is binary.[4]

Ben Ammi does not explain satan's existence other than with two sentences in *Eternal Life*: 'an evil force came into existence called satan, the devil. He was made necessary by the law of relativity' (EL144). The reference to the 'law of relativity' here intends his deceptively simple theory (the basis for his second book, 1991's *God and the Law of Relativity*) that everything must be relative (related to in kind and proportion) to all else; in a way this is like the New Age 'Law of Attraction' which designates that one attracts the same kind of energy as one puts out oneself; so, kind acts attract kindness, a distrustful outlook encourages others to distrust you, etc.[5] In this particular case Ben appears to suggest that satan came into existence as a necessary consequence of human disobedience in Eden: once human beings began to prioritize non-Divine ideas and behaviour, a spiritual force which would guide them in those ways was required.

Throughout his work he repeats that neither God nor satan acts in the world, but only effects their aims through the vehicle of human beings, whose minds they are able to affect, convincing them to act in certain ways. In what comes closest to a definition of God, he states: 'In my every dissertation, I acknowledge the existence of an immeasurable, incomprehensible, intellectual force that has used ways, means and men to confirm its involvement in the earthly affairs of men' (IL87). The presence of 'intellect' in this description is significant, and will be returned to soon. Similarly, he states regarding satan: 'The devil was in need of a tangible soul, but this he could not create. To gain a tangible soul to show forth his intellect and to challenge God, he had to tamper with the creations of the people of the eternal, Almighty, Living God' (GBMT247). We must also highlight a dual description given in an early text:

> God ... is the spiritual force representing righteousness, love, peace and all things positive and good as determined by God the Creator. Likewise, satan is the spiritual force behind all things wicked, perverse, deadly and unjust. These two opposing spirits can, and do possess (or are taken on by) men and women, governing their thoughts and actions. Thus, when I refer to satan, know that I am referring to a person or groups of people whose souls and minds are totally in opposition to God and driven by the spirit or force we call "the devil" or "the spirit of err."

(GLR2)

Here, Ben Ammi describes God as a 'force' which represents the qualities usually associated with positivity. Satan meanwhile is the force representing the inverse. The two spirits engage in a battle to influence the minds of humans, and to lead them towards actions which promote their representative qualities in the world. But critically, neither of them can exercise material agency, which is why they require humans to implement actions which will further their interests. Thus:

> Satan … is not the mythical character depicted in horror movies and fairy tales … Satan is a negative spirit, an adversarial force working against the Omnipotent and righteous spirit, and the force of God Almighty. The devil is the force of evil, wickedness, war, death, crime, hatred of God and fellowman – the epitome of all things negative and destructive. These vile characteristics and situations manifest themselves in the actions and thoughts of men.
>
> (MEW66)

It is unclear how satan works against God if God is omnipotent; or why such omnipotence does not extend to acting in the material world. Perhaps God limits Godself from intervening in order to protect human free agency in the world. The key may be in what exactly Ben Ammi means by 'spirit': This word is evocative but deceptively broad in possible meanings. In one text he offers the following clarification:

> In order to deceive the whole world, satan or the spirit of err, a demonic, fiendish force, imbues men and influences their thoughts and behavior. As a spirit, satan is an invisible force (almost like what we consider a ghost to be), but in order to do his evil he must find a vehicle or instrument (human beings) to work through.
>
> (GLR15)

Even in the early 1970s when ethnologist Morris Lounds visited the fledgling community he reported Ben telling him that 'The devil is represented upon this earth by wickedness and wicked people who follow after wicked principles'.[6] Ben Ammi is here describing the impossibility of the direct action in the world by the spiritual power, satan. While he does not explicitly say that God *cannot* act directly upon the physical world, his insistence that both God and satan are spirits, and that satan *because he is a spirit* cannot do this lead this author to conclude that the same may be true of God, but Ben Ammi the theologian did not feel comfortable making such a limiting statement about the Divine.

In the first passage quoted above, Ammi explicitly depersonalizes satan, making this name refer to nothing more than humans acting under a certain inclination. This reduction of satan to human behaviour or mental states implies a corollary reduction to impersonal status of God, because it comes immediately after his creating a direct parallel between the natures of God and satan as spiritual forces which manifest primarily through human action. God might influence humans, as in the case of the Euro-gentiles whom he encouraged to persecute Israel, but that is all.

Finally, 'the devil is a spirit, and is activated by lies. God is a spirit that is motivated by the truth' (MEW47). The way that Ben Ammi describes these 'spirits' as forces that both feed on and encourage particular actions makes it very easy to read his theology in non-personal terms. That is to say that will, intention and consciousness are not at all necessary to this theology, as any will for salvation on God's part can be removed without creating defect: the impetus is with human beings to choose to nourish themselves from the impersonal fountain of life, or not. God seems static, a force who simply emanates life without actively engaging or caring whether humans approach it and benefit or distance themselves and do not. There is an inherently mechanical core to this theology.

There is some support for this when we consider that, of the two poles to reality, the second is not so much a pole as simply the absence of Good; satan itself could not be said to exist, because existence is a good, and satan's opposition to God is total. The Manichean cosmos thus collapses into a singularity of vitalism, where everyone can choose to go with the grain and be nourished, or go against it and be destroyed.[7]

After several years of working with and reading Ben Ammi's texts, there are still frequent moments when I am unsure whether it would be accurate to characterize Ben Ammi as a believer in a personal God. His frequent assertions against the western metaphysical tradition could lead one to deny this, although he does often personify God (and satan), with an intention and a will.[8] However, many who are non-personal believers still resort to personalist terminology as the simplest means of expression. Many of the revisions Ben Ammi makes to God-talk and God-thought seem to move God away from, rather than towards, a personalist conception. It may be that when he says, for instance, 'The Euro-gentile has formulated a doctrine of religious deception to prevent the attainment of salvation and to dissuade men from the true quest for God', (MEW41) he actually intends that the personalized, willing God should be replaced with the more dynamic idea of a spiritual force which can be invoked, can inhabit and guide individuals, and which guarantees growth, life and strength, but has no internal will of its own. If, because of the logical consuming non-existence of satan, we are tempted to read passages such as 'satan deceived himself into believing he could outdo Yah. Throughout all the ages his campaign to supplant Yah has been relentless. Satan's ultimate plan was/is to destroy all Adamic flesh', (IL103) as metaphorical, then there is no problem doing likewise with any personification of God. It is always difficult to separate out in a thinker who is opposed to speculation and phenomenological in outlook, the fields of ontology and epistemology. This is aptly shown when he writes, 'the Holy Spirit is like unto the wind. You don't know the wind by pointing it out as if it has an identity. You know the wind by what you feel and determine is a result of its presence' (EL103). Here he likens the Holy Spirit to the wind and invokes the wind's lack of 'identity' while arguing that this doesn't make the wind any less real to us. It would be easy in such cases to read a similar lack of identity, and the interiority that goes with that, onto God. To do this would not even be a radical step: Albert Cleage's God-concept evolved in the same direction, and we will see at the end of this chapter that pantheistic, immanent and vitalist conceptions of God are well-established in African American religious thought.

One point which must be made, and it is an extremely important one, is that despite applying the adjective omnipotent to God, the non-interventionist concept of God can be shown to thoroughly penetrate Ben Ammi's theology, conceptually linked with his ontology and ethical history narrative. This recalls most of all the 'weak God' of postmodern theologians like John Caputo, and the non-dominating God of feminist and womanist theologians like Melissa Raphael, Delores Williams and Monica Coleman.[9] This is surprising, given Ammi's repeated dismissal of modern theology, of revisionist religious ideas and of feminism generally. That Ben Ammi evinces an integrated concept of a God who does not act upon or dominate the world, but rather who is present within human beings as an ethical calling for self-improvement, illustrates that he is in no way wedded to conservative tradition and is willing to consider and reinterpret ancient doctrines that are obviously out-of-step with the world we exist in. The direct root of this theological motif is not clear, but it is worth considering the deep and rich tradition of African American religious thought, wherein the dominating force with the functionally omnipotent power over life and death was not one for good: the slave master represented that kind of authoritarian power, and therefore in a dialectical movement identical to that of feminist and womanist theology, Ben Ammi's God is not an expression of *power* but of *resilience*. We will see in the next chapter that Ben Ammi's God is indeed one who is in control of history, but divine non-intervention in an immediate capacity could represent the anti-authoritarian rejection of divine might, based surely upon the historical knowledge that might is the tool of oppressors. Simply put, a God who expresses Godself through dominating power places God in the role of slave master. Divine power instead expresses itself in the ongoing sustenance provided to Africans in America by God.[10]

Finally, although Ben Ammi has defined God (as best one can) in terms of life, there is an important other element which he does not ignore: God's anger. Any reader of the Hebrew Bible will know that God sometimes becomes extremely angry with humanity, punishing wickedness with a firm hand. Ben Ammi takes these passages at face value, and affirms that God is not merely concerned to express love and forgiveness towards humanity; this is reserved only for those who follow the path God sets down. The Jewish theologian Eliezer Berkovits agrees that God's 'justice and anger' must be affirmed as equally necessary to theological realism as God's love and mercy; without these, 'there is no basis for a living God of religious relevance.'[11] We will investigate this characteristic in detail in the next chapter.

Embodiment and earthly life

Spirit (Holy) – in Hebrew, *ruahk*, meaning:
1. The inexplicable source of Divine revelation.
2. The wind/breath of life.
3. Vital principles held to give life to physical organisms.
4. Truth (sacred language) that reveals how we are to conceptualize and express an idea (thought).
5. Truth (sacred language) that conveys the essence of how to identify the perceptible form of the Holy Spirit. (RHS43)

Ben Ammi does not engage in mysticism, or in any variety of experiential religious practice. Traditional mystical ideas about the human soul travelling to the divine realm and experiencing or uniting with divinity have no place in his theology, indeed they do not figure in African American religious thought generally. Instead, God comes to humans, visiting them internally and strengthening them; God is expressed through them and their actions. This speaks partly of the deflated, worldly spirituality which views matters of the present world as more important (if indeed there is even talk of a hereafter); Ben Ammi is firmly practical in orientation. In fact, Ammi claims that mystical turning inward is the problem not the solution: We must look outwards and see what is becoming of the world and correct our mode of living, seek a new image to model ourselves after. Ben Ammi thus has no doctrine of *unio mystica*; however, he does hold an esoteric doctrine of the indwelling God. In a somewhat ironic twist, it is also because of this that Ben Ammi does not share the modern Judaic conception of/relation to God as ethical encounter with the other; in an important sense, God is not a transcendent who is in relationship with humanity, but is *part of us*.

Ben Ammi understands God as a spirit, meaning that God is neither a mythical, eternity-dwelling superhuman, nor a manifest physical being. God is non-material, but is present to us in the phenomenal world, experienced almost as part of ourselves.

This is usually expressed through the idea that the Holy Spirit can be manifested in human individuals and communities, guiding their thoughts and actions. It is through the 'God-mind' that was breathed into Adam in Gen.2 that the Holy Spirit is present within humans, and this God-mind is the intellect:

> What did God breathe into Adam? Intellect. We can say that God gave man a mind. Understanding the oneness of God, what mind, then, did he put into Adam except the "God Mind?" It was God intellect or God's intellect; intellect to command your hands to fashion and form as God would have them to fashion and form. We received a mind to instruct our feet to tread on the path of God. It would cause the eyes to see the beauty of God and His Holy Creation, and the tongue to taste and appreciate a Divine diet, eaten from a table prepared by God. The "God Mind" defines according to the oneness of God – one God, one Mind, one Plan. So we see that we are a living, vibrant people if we have the "God Mind" in us, but without it, we are just a lifeless structure. I am sure you don't believe that moving, talking, thinking you are lifeless, but you are. Only by moving in the direction God would have you move in, talking of the things of God and thinking as He would have you think do you have life.
>
> (GLR40)[12]

In this passage Ben identifies the 'breath of life' which made Adam a living soul with the intellect, an intellect which could only be God's own, and therefore Divine both in kind and in responsibility.[13] Adam, when enlivened by this Spirit, represents the earthly manifestation and presence of God: Adam is the 'earthly image, likeness-form of Yah but not the complete heavenly force' (IL97). He interprets Gen.1.27 as 'Yah created Adam *to be* His image and likeness on earth.' So, arguing that Adam was intended as something like an extension, whose role was to continue the process of creation begun by God, he concludes: 'the term *image* implies Adam is to be Yah's creative genius to continue the incessant process of bringing forth that which was not' (IL33). Here, then, the essential generative character of God is inherited too by human beings, who therefore are creative by nature.

From the creation account Ben argues that humanity is the primary location of Divine manifestation: 'Yah reveal[ed] Himself on earth through Adam, who after receiving the breath (spirit) of Yah became a living soul. The life in his physical body was made dependent upon the active mind (spirit) of Yah guiding him in all of his endeavors' (IL88). It is only through the indwelling Divine mind that we are alive rather than dead matter, because through it we participate in the vital nature of God. However, the acceptance of this *God Mind* means carrying out the actions it guides us towards, rather than any others; which is to say, we must actively pursue Divine actions in order to remain the locus of Divine presence in the world. If we do not, then God departs from us and we are no longer in the Divine image.

Thus, it is through the actions of human individuals, when they are guided and informed by God's Spirit, that God is made manifest in the world; The mind is 'a way station that transmits the spirit of God or the devil to the brain, which then forwards that spirit on to the body's members for activation' (GBMT120). God's image is a spirit inherited and expressed by the righteous lineage of the sons of Shem, and therefore 'when you see the Edenic son (a spirit) you see the Heavenly Father (a spirit)' (IL90). Because God is identical with Life, those with the *God Mind* project and sustain life in the world, and those without it are 'dead'. This helps to explain the prefix 'Divine' in the community's endeavours of Divine Health, Divine Marriage, Divine Education, etc.: they are the institutions which promote Godliness and thus further the Spirit of Life in the world.

Not only, however, can human minds be brought into line with the Divine Spirit; as discussed already, there is the Spirit of Err or satan, imbued into humanity by the serpent who taught humans to disobey God. The diverse effects of this are apparent in the world today:

[T]his devastating [nuclear] arsenal is not under the control of world leaders, but an unseen, subtle, Satanic force. The same force causes songwriters to write sexually explicit verses or lyrics that have led many children to commit suicide. This same Satanic force causes seemingly sane people to indulge in drugs, as though it is all right to do so, while knowing that drugs are killing them and their children.

(GLR42)

In the end, satan's 'plan is to destroy all flesh' (GLR42). This is because living existence is divine in nature, and therefore precisely what satan is in opposition to.[14] Satan is to death as God is to life: 'the Creator (Yah) is Himself "life," meaning that one cannot choose life except by choosing obedience to His will. Obviously, to refuse to follow or obey Yah is to choose death by denying the sovereignty of Yah over your soul' (RHS10). By 'obeying the will' of God, Ben Ammi holds that one will draw down and manifest God's Spirit, through oneself; doing this vivifies us, nourishing us by strengthening the connection to the source of life. Just as God is identified with life, he explicitly links satan with death: 'the satanic psyche that men evince, is in fact a personalized representation of death' (IL160). Satan redefined life in terms of materialist accumulation, 'redefined it to conceal the fact that what you were/are experiencing is indicative of the dead'.

> Man's enemy, thusly, has put his mind into the human family, causing it to automatically self-destruct without being consciously aware. As your understanding increases, you will be shocked when you seriously consider just who satan motivates and controls. Remember, we are talking about a force that imprisons men's souls, possesses their minds and destroys their outlook and mode of thinking. Your boss, your father, your wife or child is more than likely "possessed" by the destructive satanic force.
>
> (GLR51)

The use of the word 'possessed' here, even though employed in quotes, is indicative of Ben Ammi's belief that the aligning of one's mind with the good or evil, nurturing or destructive, spirits, can constitute something like possession – where these spiritual forces manifest their own ends through human actions. Here, again, Ben is more comfortable making direct statements about satan than about God, although presumably the same functions would be true for both. In this case there have already been some hints that the same is true of God – as a Spirit and a spiritual force, God can inhabit, 'possess' and guide individuals and societies, and this is synonymous with leading them towards actions that enhance (or in satan's case destroy) divine qualities such as life, health, growth and righteousness. To be 'possessed' by God is to have the Divine Mind. The implications are laid out when he asserts that, just as he previously argued that a thought always precedes manifestation into reality, 'Works are mind (thought) made manifest. Works are energy, and reveal the true source of one's mind: God or the devil. All forms of physical manifestations can be attributed to a mind' (GLR69). The first sentence demonstrates that God is manifest in the world through works done by those who possess God's spirit. For this reason, the Kingdom of Yah constitutes the presence of God on earth just as the Temple in Jerusalem did some three thousand years ago.[15] Likewise, evil actions 'perpetuate [satan's] existence. They are his source of strength' (GLR87). This is the reason for his claim that 'God, the Almighty Spirit, must be seen through a human face', (MEW15) a sentiment made even stronger in his first text, where he writes, 'You are whomever's spirit you possess' (GBMT252). Here, the human can become completely identified with the Spirit it manifests – a logical consequence of the doctrine that God is a Spirit and breathed this Spirit into Adam in order to give him life. The full consequences of this can be witnessed in Ben Ammi's crypto-incarnationist messianism, wherein at times he identified himself with God and Jesus, because he was manifesting the same Holy Spirit that Yeshua had. He writes that this doctrine demonstrates 'the difference between the Hebraic and Greek conceptions of deification [because] you were to be in the image of the Messiah, and in his likeness', (MEW33)[16] meaning that not just one saviour figure should embody the Holy Spirit, but all humans – and certainly all of Israel – should.

The idea of embodying the Divine Spirit not only ties into mystical/messianic notions of incarnating God, however, but also those of the Black Israel as (sons of) God;

we can perceive here a suggestion that Israel are the spiritual font of humanity, in sum they are the manifestation of God on earth. This is very similar to the Five Percenters (Nation of Gods and Earths), the Nation of Islam offshoot created by Clarence 13X whose interpretation of ISLAM as an acrostic signifying *I Self Lord And Master* is part of their doctrine of Black Divinity – that the Black Man is God.[17] Ben Ammi of course never makes such a statement, and I do not wish to impute such to him, but the notion that Black Israel alone carried the full weight of God's Spirit as manifest in themselves, where other humans (gentiles) are typified by the (partial, though growing) lack of it, bears an unmistakable resemblance. As with much of Ben Ammi's thought, it is possible that he and other members of the community held this belief in the past and now it remains only in suggestive hints, as a memory of a discarded doctrine.

Ben's first text demonstrates that God and satan's primary battleground for influence is Israel itself – i.e. Black Americans: 'There is no higher dwelling place than the minds of the Sons of God. This is where satan strives and struggles with the Sons of God, and even with the Almighty Himself, in order that he may eventually sit upon the throne of God Almighty and inherit His Kingdom' (GBMT229). The reason for this is that Israel has the responsibility of leading humanity in righteousness, in showing them the way to God; indeed, Israel are God's primary manifestation on earth. If satan is to nullify humanity's connection to God and the possibility of their redemption, it is Israel who must ultimately be defused.

To this end, satan has implanted an 'image and misconception of God', thereby 'living in their [humans'] minds' (IL38). According to Ammi's interpretation, Is.14.12-14 which famously tells of the 'fallen' 'son of Dawn', the 'shining one' previously translated as Lucifer, who attempted to elevate himself above even God, 'reveals that satan is hidden deep within the image of God, subsequently making his detection a very complex matter' (RHS17). This is to say, that the pagan-Christian concept of *logos* has smuggled satan into the false Godhead that is worshipped by Christians.

This notion, developed at length in 1999's *An Imitation of Life* and 2004's *Revival of the Holy Spirit*, is thoroughly gnostic, but Ben Ammi makes a fantastically lucid argument in demonstrating how Christianity as currently practised in the west effectively ignores or inverts every single important precept of the Hebrew Bible, even while claiming to be in direct continuity of them: the sabbath has been moved from Saturday to Sunday (even the name of the day invokes pagan sun-worship); the Mosaic Law has been annulled; Christ (a human being, rather than Yah) is saviour; the day starts at midnight rather than sunset; the Israelites are now European; judgement and reward come after death rather than in life. Ben Ammi is able to demonstrate how each of the Ten Commandments is constitutionally broken by the United States (IL62): freedom of religion is against the first, icons are against the second, freedom of speech against the third, Sunday sabbath against the fourth. Laws about parental discipline are against the fifth, allowing the sale and consumption of cigarettes and alcohol the sixth, freedom of expression including promotion of adultery the seventh. He notes that legislation banning idolatry would be considered 'religious' and so unenforceable, whereas legislation *allowing* it is not.

All of these things are, for Ben Ammi, intentional moves to discourage the practices which would bring humans, especially Israelites, back to God.

Ben Ammi's use of the term 'spirit', as explored in this section, solves little in terms of the personalization question, as a spirit could mean a disembodied autonomous mental presence, or it could mean a non-personal intellectual tendency ('the spirit of the age' or 'in the spirit of Martin Luther King'). When Ammi argues that humans should manifest the Divine spirit in their actions, and that by doing this we are manifesting God into the world, it seems more the latter; in this case, we can find associations with the thought of post-process theologians such as Mordecai Kaplan who sought to depersonalize religious language while keeping its power; so that, in order to understand the claim 'God is love', we should invert the equation, making it 'Love is divine'. This means that the objects under the purview of God-language are not persons, or even objects at all, but they can still be located in the structures of reality that provide the possibility of outcomes such as redemption, love, peace and religious experience. This is not identical with the proposals that Anthony Pinn makes for an 'African American nontheistic humanist theology', but it is compatible with them.[18]

The continuity between God and human is also found in Jewish thought, most especially in the kabbalists, expressed through the keeping of commandments and the ongoing innovations of Torah interpretation.[19] The dependence of God upon humanity is found in very similar formulation in the Kabbalah and Ben Ammi, where in both God requires the actions of humans to manifest God's will or glory, and thus to sanctify the world. In the words of Gershom Scholem, 'it is not the act of the Messiah as executor of the tikkun [repair], as a person entrusted with the specific function of redemption, that brings Redemption, but your action and mine'.[20] Likewise when Joseph Citron describes kabbalistic causality, he explains: 'God and Man share the same root, so Man's actions directly impact the operation of the cosmos'.[21] The essential unity or continuity of God and human is a kabbalistic axiom traceable to the biblical text, but one directly opposed to exoteric rabbinic doctrine.

Ultimately, we can conclude with certainty only that Ben Ammi was a deflationary thinker: he did not seek to make claims about metaphysics, other than those that are clearly stated in scripture. Ben knew decisively that it is crucial to believe in God, to have faith and to live by the commandments. But whether God is a person, or a force, or something in between, is not the concern of humans. This rejection of metaphysics and resolving of reality as the phenomenal is still, however, an important theological contribution.

Law

All of this brings us to what may be one of the most important features of Ben Ammi's theology, or at least what most clearly distinguishes it from other, *Christian* Black Theologies. His emphasis on biblical law, as delivered by God to Moses and the Israelites in the desert as they walked from Egypt to Canaan, is what makes Ben Ammi a thinker more on the Jewish side than the Christian. While the first generation of Hebrew Israelite leaders and congregations – those before the First World War – taught that some of the Israelite practices must be reabsorbed, such as the biblical festivals and especially the Shabbat, often as well as some dietary laws, many of the rules given in Deuteronomy and Leviticus were presumably seen as too strange or too demanding for life in the modern secular world. The Harlemite congregations of the 1920s and 1930s saw things differently, beginning with Rabbi Wentworth Matthew's Commandment Keepers who, as their name suggests, pursued a more orthodox approach to Judaization. Ben Ammi was always clear that the Law was a key part of returning to the covenant and breaking the curse which had seen the Black Israelites enslaved in America. In no small way, keeping the Law is essential to the AHIJ.

As has been noted, a key scriptural proof for Israelite identity is Deut.28. Herein, God predicts a series of devastating curses, including dispersal among the nations and a second enslavement, if the Israelites fail to keep the covenant. The Hebrew Israelite tradition has long viewed Deut.28 as predicting the American captivity, focusing in particular on verse 68, which tells of a journey in ships to Egypt, where the people would wish to sell themselves as slaves but no one would buy them.[22] Thus, Ben Ammi reasons, if breaking the commandments was the ultimate cause of this tragedy, the only way to overcome it must be to return to keeping the commandments. Indeed, Deut.28 opens with a prediction of blessings which will be gained if this condition is fulfilled.

The performance of commandments, as a fundamental part of living in accord with righteousness, is an integral part of the 'true worship of God'. In a key chapter in his first text Ben Ammi analyses the Hebrew term *ahvad*, which signifies both work and worship, in distinction to *hishtahvut* (to bow down to; this is the biblical term used in regard to worshiping other gods, but never in regard to the God of Israel). He writes, 'It is deceptive and misleading to make worship a temporary action, in place of a continuous and everlasting action.' This deceptive redefinition whereby a single day was set aside for worship, in distinction to the rest of the week which was involved with work, 'was instituted by the devil in order that man would not relate the activities which he performs the other six days in the week as the worship of God'. It is precisely the separation of worship and daily work which has led to the problems of western society; in fact most people, because they believe that worship is only performed in church on Sunday, unconsciously commit their daily work to satan. The human does not even recognize that he [*sic*] has 'disassociate[d] his job, business, eating habits, shopping habits and recreational habits, from the worship of God' (GBMT108-110). In actual fact, however, nothing is disconnected from or irrelevant to God:

> The true worship of God is an entire way of life, a continuous action, from the meal you eat in the morning to the job you work on. It encompasses your every deed and thought pattern. Only when we understand the connection between work and worship will we totally comprehend how to build and live in a world where all of the people love and worship God. [...] this is why the entire fiber of this world has to be destroyed. It is a world of devil worship; a world against God; a world of sin, madness, sickness, disease, ignorance, poverty and death.
>
> (GBMT110)

Such righteous living should not be difficult – it is in fact only following the grain of the universe. It is rather the way humans live now that is difficult and stressful, because it is not how we were designed to function: 'it took tremendous pains, labor and toil for man to create wars and war machinery. He has toiled against great opposition to reverse the eternal cycles of life. He has labored endlessly and tirelessly to DIE!' (GBMT126) In contrast, righteousness will come naturally to us: 'the functioning of the members of our bodies, according to the spirit or Will of God, manifests the true worship of God.' We only need to witness the ease with which the natural world follows its plan: 'Everything created by God was created to perform perfectly.'[23]

In reviewing the routine acts and creations of the modern western world – warfare, weapons of mass destruction, nutrition-less food, alcohol and tobacco use/dependence, and the degradation of the family, community and morality, Ben Ammi asks, 'To whom should these damnable and deplorable acts against God and His Holy creations be attributed, if not the devil? What should they be termed, if not the worship of the devil?' (GBMT107). That these behaviours which fly counter to any good, which actively destroy human beings, are presented as inseparable from a modern, free, society, is incomprehensible to Ben Ammi, who believes strongly that allowing, let alone encouraging one to do wrong, is almost as evil as the act itself. The devil has succeeded in convincing humans that worship is something done at our convenience, slotted in between the rest of our lives, rather than being the continuous activity which guides us. In order to maintain and strengthen our connection with the source of life we must 'worship [our] Maker every day, night, hour, and minute throughout [our] life' (GBMT114). So it is that every action we perform is part of our worship of either God or satan – and if the majority of our productive activity during six sevenths of the week are helping to produce a negative world then we are worshipping satan more than God.[24]

The creation of this mindset was a critical part of the satanic agenda: human beings now believe they can live how they please and still survive, that a degradation in the quality of life will not result directly from unrighteousness. What humanity does not realize is that it 'has only two choices: worship God and live, or worship the devil and die. There is no neutrality' (GBMT112). It is for this reason that 'The worship of God is the very essence of man's life' (GBMT112): if humans wish to continue living in health and fullness, then they must renew their connection with the source of life with each and every action, ensuring that the right motivation guides it, the right intention accompanies it and the right eventual outcome will result from it. For Ben Ammi, this means that 'spiritual love for one's neighbor and relatives' comes above materialistic desires (GBMT113).

Ben doesn't make it explicit but the keeping of biblical commandments is related cosmologically to his emanative conception of Deity and Truth. In performing the commandments, human beings *exoterically* are living according to God's Will, but in *esoteric* terms, they are connecting with the Divine substance of Truth which nourishes reality and sustains life. The Law is *a part* of God, termed by Ben Ammi God's intellect, and so is identical with what God breathed into humanity to bring us to life (MEW100). Living according to the Law then brings us into direct contact with the Divine, from which we gain nourishment. It is precisely because of this that keeping the commandments is a mechanical necessity if we are to remain in good health and grow in vitality.[25]

Hence, Ben Ammi follows the Maimonidean approach to *halakhah* (performance of law): that all commandments were provided for rational reasons; that is, they all have some incremental benefit, even if this is not obvious to us. Prior rabbinic tradition had differentiated between those laws that were reachable by reason and were therefore shared by most cultures, and those that required revelation, and were largely mocked by gentiles, but Maimonides argued that even the commandments which were opaque in their practical import were provided to humans for practical reasons, because they improved us.

However, Ben Ammi continues the logic through to the next step, meaning that his esoteric understanding of the behavioural link between humans and God, expressed as the biblical commandments, is very similar to that of some kabbalists. While the post-Maimonidean rabbinic tradition understood the Law as something given to benefit and refine human beings, the kabbalists held that performing the *mitzvot* enacted a theurgic power, facilitating the transmission of nourishing/healing divine energy into the world and into the individual.[26] The thirteenth-century Catalonian kabbalist R Ezra of Gerona found that all 613 *mitzvot* relate back to the foundational commandments to love and to fear, and the latter folded into the former anyway, meaning that all commandments were derivations of the primal command to love. Because lovingkindness (*Hesed*) is the fourth *sefirah* on the kabbalistic Tree of Life, and the first of the lower seven that constitute manifest reality, all that is finds its root in lovingkindness, and feeds from the energy generated there. Yakov Travis writes that Ezra portrays the commandments 'both as being rooted in the divine realm and as connecting the individual to that dimension', to the extent that the energetic feeding of the soul gained from the higher sefirot could even negate the need for physical food.[27]

In this kabbalistic system, the commandments are essential for maintaining the functioning of reality generally: performance of them maintains the correct flow of divine energy through the *sefirot*, and thus sustains our reality with the correct balance of divine energy to keep it healthy. For the kabbalists generally, our individual deeds have cosmic significance, perhaps to an extent not found in Ben Ammi, who at most allows that our actions, as with our words, do impact others around us by exposing them to the Truth-energy we are manifesting. Related to this is the theurgical potential of human actions which actively influence the Godhead in a way unknown to Ben Ammi's simpler, more unidirectional scheme:[28] The kabbalists imagine human beings effectively going to and *altering* the flow of divine energy, unblocking and lubricating channels, whereas Ben Ammi perceives humans simply moving (metaphorically) closer or further away, and so enjoying more or less of the natural energy emitting from a primarily recondite deity. However, the active nature of the human in performing commandments in order to receive and manifest divine vitality is the same. The responsibility is on humans and the currency is action.[29]

The pneumatic aspect of Ben Ammi's theology is also deeply interwoven with his approach to Law. Because the Holy Spirit is within us, guiding us to act in accordance with righteousness, by performing the commandments we are manifesting God in the world, becoming the vessel whereby divinity sustains creation. Just as the kabbalists argue, correct action is the necessary channel whereby the Holy Spirit sanctifies creation. Not invoking this spirit, as human has increasingly been doing for the last 6000 years, means that creation is gradually – but subtly – disintegrating, as the world becomes more and more obsessed with demonic, anti-divine qualities: death, war and chaos. Ben Ammi's is a pragmatic doctrine, not a mystical one: it is fundamentally one bound up with worldly behaviour (ethics) and is not intended to induce or explain experiential states. Thus, it is not a doctrine of mystical union, but one of vitalist emanation, with humans as the intermediaries whose will is an essential switch: Being inspired by and embodying/transmitting the Holy Spirit is not the same as being controlled by it; agency still rests with humanity. Ben Ammi never talks in Christian terms of the complete hollowing of the self in order for the Spirit to take control, as suggested by the Greek term *Kenosis*; he does not come close to such statements, as his pragmatic, behavioural emphasis makes it crucial that humans have agency even when they are exercising that agency in a way that manifests God's Spirit.

In a particularly interesting passage of 2004's *The Revival of the Holy Spirit*, (repeated on pages 25 and 55) Ben explains that if God is spirit, then those created in God's image are also spirit by nature, and because we must worship God in spirit – i.e. through our shared nature – any inconsistency or inaccuracy in worship will manifest a problem first in our spirits, and then in the physical, social and biological domains. This is a remarkably kabbalistic claim, presenting the human's manner of worship (remembering the breadth of this term encompasses all action) as directly affecting our connection with God and that if flawed will sabotage our own health and happiness, first in the spiritual and then in the mundane planes. Remarkably, he ends the passage with three sentences that will remind every rabbinic student of a famous rabbinic dictum: 'This process is defined as God's judgment. This is the Law and the words of the Prophets. Everything else in this writing is just expanded commentary.' Although he is reflecting Hillel's famous claim, 'That which is hateful to you do not do to another; that is the entire Torah, and the rest is commentary' (b.Shab.31a), he has altered the 'golden rule' from one of 'treat others as you would be treated', to 'live how God commands'. The significance of this could not be overstated: whereas Hillel's rule places responsibility on the individual to guide their own actions in a manner that is fundamentally independent of God, but which he sources back to the Bible, Ben Ammi simply locates God at the centre of everything, overruling even our interpersonal relationships.

However, the repeated attempts of God to bring humans back to God, especially in sharing with them the behaviours and practices that will strengthen the bond, are attempts not to control or to demand worship, but to show humans how to live well. The biblical commandments then are a user's manual to human life (this is a metaphor which Ben himself uses), and committing fully to these practices will enable one to grow: 'the Creator (Yah) is Himself "life," meaning that one cannot choose life except by choosing obedience to His will' (RJPJ10). Anything which draws one away from God, however, can be justly termed evil in that it is synonymous with destroying one's own health and wellbeing: 'to refuse to follow or obey Yah is to choose death by denying the sovereignty of Yah over your soul' (RJPJ10). Satan has redefined life in terms that 'conceal the fact that what you were/are experiencing is indicative of the dead', and this is the purpose of satan as the ultimate *nihil*, a black hole of chaos, decay, absence. We can also invert the equation: anything which makes us unhealthy, unhappy, less able, is evil and unrighteous. Anything of this nature must be rejected.

Unusually, Ben Ammi thus blends two Jewish approaches to Law, meaning that while there is a metaphysical drawing-close to God (or rather, channelling of God) enacted by following the Law, this is inseparable from the practical benefit of doing so. Ammi demonstrates a clear willingness to probe the commandments and to understand why they have been set down. For him, like Maimonides, the commandments are in no way arbitrary: they are guidelines intended to help us live the best lives. They prevent us from poisoning ourselves; from damaging our relations with each other; from distracting ourselves from the essentialities of living. This is most clear in guidelines relating to food and diet (to be dealt with in Chapter 6), which are commanded in order to encourage the best nourishment, while cutting out the poisonous foodstuffs. But in all the commandments, there is a mechanical correlation between cause and effect: our actions have consequences, and God, caring about us, has provided guidelines for how to go about living.

Ben Ammi's *application* of Mosaic Law, however, differs from rabbinic *halakhah* in many regards. It should first be noted that the AHIJ attempt to take the biblical text as literally as possible, without embellishment or prevarication. In the community's early days they spoke with disdain about the rabbinic reasoning regarding laws such as *kashrut* regulation, and the caveats and exceptions built in by the rabbis. Of course, as the community has evolved and taken on the sophistications required by maturation, they too have developed a unique approach and interpretation of several of the laws, and their interpretations are certainly not self-evident. Most clearly, although the Bible sanctions the eating of meat, they concluded very early on that animal products generally should be avoided, and that this was the will of God as provided to them prophetically and supported by scripture. Likewise, the sacrifice of animals was not to be taken literally anymore – in the new dispensation the community themselves were the sacrifice that was offered to God. Similarly, while the community have endorsed (optional) polygyny as based on biblical example, they seem to have arbitrarily placed an upper limit of seven on the number of wives, and have also arbitrarily made the model one of multiple marriage, rather than concubinage. In order to justify some of these alterations, Ben Ammi wrote that 'Each generation has to interpret and apply the law in accordance with its conditions and exigencies' (MEW93) and that 'The ancient ceremonial regulations were only temporary additions to the law, awaiting the necessary growth of the people in their comprehension of the substance of God's law (instructions)' (GBMT200). He claimed that the people will remain correct so long as the intent remains to follow and worship God. In addition, some passages taken as commanding particular behaviours are better taken as guidelines (MEW92).[30] This approach, of prioritizing the (perceived) spirit of the law over the letter is that usually taken by the Reform Jewish denomination, but the difficulty found by everyone who openly states that the canon of laws can be updated is that it is unclear how far updating should go, and where it is not applicable. In the case of the AHIJ, Ben Ammi claimed prophetic inspiration, and that the present times were a fundamentally new – messianic – dispensation, an approach explicitly rejected in rabbinic Judaism, where the danger inherent in respecting prophetically delivered revisions or annulling of scripture has been taken very seriously.[31]

However, action alone is not enough. Ben Ammi is clear that the correct 'righteous' attitude must also exist behind the performance (in fact, behind everything that one does); without this guiding principle the actions are empty and will not bring about the blessings expected. The same argument is made by the early rabbis, who require each performance to be accompanied by correct intention – however, it was specifically the sixteenth-century Safedian kabbalist Isaac Luria who argued that the reason for the intention is not just to be aware of pleasing God, but because the correct intention was necessary in ensuring the practice attained the redemptive esoteric goal of the commandment.[32] This similarity holds even with regard to the nature of the intention, which must not be simply to receive the benefit: both Ammi and Luria rule that the intention must be to align oneself with righteousness and to aid the process of cosmic redemption.[33]

As already mentioned, it is in the following of the Law that Ben Ammi distinguishes himself from every other (non-Hebrew Israelite) Black religious thinker that went before; because the vast majority have been Christian, they have understood the Mosaic Law as supplanted and therefore inapplicable. Even the radical thinkers who reject much of the European interpretation of Christianity still reject any attempt to maintain the statutes of the Tanakh, despite the pivotal role of those statutes in that text and the gospels. Barashango for example frequently cites biblical references to the Law but interprets these metaphorically: for him 'the law' is 'The laws of nature which are the laws of God', but is not connected with the commandments given to Moses.[34] When Barashango refers to the Ten Commandments he describes them as descending from the '147 Negative Confessions' of the Egyptian Book of the Dead, without reference to the rest of the Torah.[35]

This emphasis on practical matters, on performance and action, also places Ben Ammi in direct opposition to some traditional Christian positions: the central notion of Grace, the will of God in Christian soteriology, is anathema to Ben Ammi, who argues repeatedly that the biblical requirement is on human action. This shift in focus has far-reaching consequences: first, it places a responsibility on the community to demand that its members follow the Law. Second, it creates a direct correlation between action and effect: the theology necessitates that if one wishes to get the rewards – which will come in this life rather than after – then one *must* act according to the plan. The notion that one must rely on God to save one is rejected entirely, and replaced by a conviction that human beings must enact their own redemption, through positive action.

For Ben Ammi, it is the Christian, European, separation of action and belief that has generated societies founded upon a deep ethical rupture: The 'tendency to put their works far from their beliefs instead of equating their works with what they believe' has enabled 'the devout, Christian men [to] produce sick, degenerate, lawless societies' (GBMT98) because when righteousness is wholly determined by thoughts, actions are no longer accountable or even meaningful. People can perform terrible actions as long as they convince themselves that they are good people. Instead, the responsibility that Ben Ammi places upon individuals in managing their actions goes beyond the effects upon themselves, because the whole cosmos is involved: the process of redemption can only occur when the Kingdom of Yah activates itself through the righteousness of its members.

Ben Ammi thus follows a very similar logic to Luria regarding the esoteric effects of the Law. Lawrence Fine writes that the Lurianic iteration of Kabbalah 'served to empower its practitioners by cultivating the theurgic art to an even greater degree than previous kabbalists had done. Each and every halakhic enactment presented one opportunity after another to transform both oneself and the cosmos'.[36] This empowerment of the individual is because of a potent sense of the effects of one's actions, that negative acts cannot simply be forgiven, but impact the future of the world. For Luria, the human must reach out to God and this reaching is effected by performance of *mitzvot*, which enable the flow of divine energy from the Divine to the mundane world. In Ben Ammi's system this is expressed by the divine penumbra of Truth: 'Truth is a creative energy; lies are destructive energy, constituting a harmful influence on mind and behavior' (RJPJn). Therefore, the human can *only* approach God by separating themselves from untruth and unrighteous behaviour, embracing instead the divine Truth of the Law. Particularly potent in this context is the comment, by a kabbalist some centuries prior to Luria, R Azriel of Gerona, who stated that 'All the *mitzvot* are called Truth, as it says, "All your *mitzvot* are truth" [Ps.119.151]'.[37]

In a later text Ammi explains, 'Only Truth can reveal our true nature and create within us an impulse to conform to Divine Law in our daily lifestyles, which is the true worship of Yah' (RHS37). Here Ben creates a neat equation: if we find ourselves, our true nature, it will lead us towards God's Law, the set of guidelines and expectations given in the Torah, and performing these *mitzvot* is identical with worship of God, thereby connecting us with the Divine – a connection which itself will energize our lives and our *realness*. By entering this cycle of growth, Ben Ammi wants humanity to step out of the cycle of destruction, the worship of death which has entranced human beings for so many centuries, and has gradually spread its influence over the globe. Returning to the metaphysical notion of Truth, he explains, 'Truth has the inherent power to produce the promised effects. This observable substance will also be our testimony that He (His idea) is alive and active in us' (RHS4). It is 'Yah's breath of life', that breath that enlivened Adam's inner soul. Truth is therefore 'an essential element in our lives' (RHS205).

There are some important implications herein for the nature of the human mind as mediating force between God and world. These will be explored in detail in Chapter 6.

Heaven and Hell

Just as Ben Ammi seeks to deflate God from the external heavenly being imagined in popular Christian thought, Heaven and Hell are also brought, quite literally, down to earth. These are not places that one is sent after death, but states that one lives in, on earth. It has been traditional in Black America to use the term Hell to indicate the usual life and conditions they experienced (both during slavery and after); in contrast to Heaven, the life and reality of whites.[38] This did not necessarily negate the existence of a Heaven and Hell awaiting us after death, although for some it did. This usage was reappropriated by Elijah Muhammad who confirmed that Blacks were living in Hell in America, but argued that Heaven was within their grasp if they chose to convert – the Nation of Islam thus placed Heavenly life upon earth once again within the reach of Black Americans.[39] Muhammad had no truck with an afterlife or any non-physical existence, his theological thought was resolutely centred in the here and now (indeed, he taught that the idea of a Heavenly afterlife had been invented by the evil Yakub as succour for mothers of the Black children he had killed when creating the white race – indicating its modern role as imaginary compensation to sedate suffering Black Americans).[40]

Ben Ammi thinks similarly, arguing that Heaven and Hell describe states of being that humans experience in their earthly life, and in this case, America is definitely Hell. This Hell of America can be overcome only by entering the Heavenly life of the Kingdom of Yah. Heaven then is 'the reality of the righteous as they live, not a place for spirits after death. [… It] is the manifestation of the Kingdom of God, where life is perpetual. Heaven is the love of one man for his neighbour, the actuality of family as God ordained it and peace for all peoples, harmony between nations' (GMBT63; cf. 230).

Developing Muhammad's thought, Ben Ammi writes that Hell is indeed inhabited by the dead; however, the death that the inhabitants have undergone is not a physical death, but a death of the spirit as they rejected the God of Life. Therefore in Hell, 'the people have the minds of the devil and are dead in God. To escape from hell, you must be resurrected: given a new, living mind, and taught again how to live in God and with God' (GBMT250). This Hell is the world created by 'the heathen nations', a world without God: 'They make these pits to avoid living under the rule and authority of God.'

The Hell of America plays an important role in Ammi's thought, tying into several aspects of his system. As well as emphasizing the immanence of reward and punishment, the Hellish condition of modern America demonstrates his belief in human inadequacy and the necessity of return to the Law: human beings have tried to design the world and they have failed. In quoting Prov.14.12, 'there is a way that seemeth right unto a man but the end thereof are the ways of death,' he comments, 'Man, under satan's system, has been convinced that he has the capacity to order his own steps' (GBMT133). But a world created according to human rather than divine principles is the opposite of Heaven; the only safe way of life is that provided by God.

He continues, 'The entire Euro-gentile political system is an enemy to both man and God. Man, in the genesis, was formed to evidence the creativity of the "God Mind," without which there would always be a lack of knowledge to bring forth what is right'. Humanity now, cut off from God, has descended into madness and sin: 'society has gone morally mad with injustice, greed, prejudice, war, famine, pollution and disease. Then, using his own mental resources to rationalize his evil, man justifies and explains it away' (GBMT134). Utilizing his distaste for much of contemporary American culture, he writes, 'Hell is where laws are passed to protect gays and homosexuals, and where bakeries specialize in making genital-shaped products from dough!'

For Ben Ammi then, Hell was not simply slavery, but was a world where the laws of righteousness are not being followed. Even the slavemasters were living in Hell, unawares; and whatever emancipation the enslaved may lay claim to, to remain in that ungodly world is to stay in Hell, because in an oft-cited saying, the prophets demanded that the faithful 'come out of her', (Rev.18:4) meaning to leave that world physically and mentally. Thus, although Heaven and Hell are mental constructs, they are also social, determined and developed by the shared consciousness of the social world.

On the other hand, in the Messianic Age this will be reversed:

> Those of the earth's destroyers that remain alive will be compelled to live in an atmosphere which is contrary to their composition, with men of God. [...] the earth's destroyers [will] suffer in a heavenly abode. A seal will be put upon them so that all that pass by may know them as the former destroyers of the habitation of men. Their wings of deception shall be clipped. [...] They shall exist in a realm called Everlasting Torment according to the spirit of the Sons of Light. They will bear witness to the rise of African Americans and others of their so-called Third World.
>
> (MEW 142)

Ammi's immanence of salvation is echoed most potently in the Black liberation theologian James Cone, who notes that there is no scriptural basis for a heavenly afterlife in the Hebrew canon; what soteriology there is, is overwhelmingly earthly. It is 'grounded in history and is identical with God's righteousness in delivering the oppressed from political bondage. Salvation is a historical event of rescue. It is God delivering the people from their enemies and bestowing upon Israel new possibilities within the historical context of its existence.'[41] Concentration on the afterlife can function as simply a means of accepting rather than combatting the sufferings of the present, and indeed, this is what Ben Ammi – following Elijah Muhammad – argues Christian soteriology was intended to do. Instead we should be working to change the present, and if this expectation is true of humans then it is even more true of God: 'What good are golden crowns, slippers, white robes, or even eternal life,' Cone asks, 'if it means that we have to turn our backs on the pain and suffering of our own children?'[42] This is to say that a Heaven that comes without requiring any change in the desperate earthly conditions of one's loved ones can offer little meaningful peace.[43]

Anthony Pinn notes that Black and womanist theologies have overwhelmingly sought to replace the 'anaemic soteriology' of otherworldly salvation:

> [B]ecause of its inability to carry the full weight of African American hopes for transformation in the form of a radically improved existence. ... efforts to overly spiritualize the gospel of Christ and the interpretation of this message involve an oppressive posture that does damage to human dignity and integrity by avoiding struggle against modalities of misconduct *in* this world.[44]

And in a passage that could have come straight from Ben, Pinn affirms that:

> Redemption has to do with a new vision of proper relationship between God and humanity, between humans, and between humans and the larger world of nature. It involves an appreciation for and motivation premised on the deep intersections

between all forms of life, all of which hold vitality, significance, and intensity. It is an effort [...] to create a healthy synergy between body and spirit. This desired but unfulfilled synergy exposes the human to the comforting weight of connection to all that is within the range of the individual's life meaning (body) and within the scope of connection to all that is (spirit).[45]

This rejection of otherworldly compensation for suffering is absent also from Jewish post-Holocaust theology, a similarity which will be furthered in the following chapter.[46]

Pinn recognizes a difficulty however, as there is still an elision of the body in these Black and Womanist theologies; they are protected rather than negated in salvation, but they are hardly celebrated in their day-to-day functioning. We might say, life is not of the body, which is still at most a vehicle for the realization of the spirit:

> Lurking behind their large claims regarding liberation, with few exceptions, is a troubled relationship to human flesh, to black bodies: Salvation may entail alteration of the space occupied by these bodies, but this arrangement does little to celebrate the texture, the feel and functions, of these bodies. Theological effort to counter the damage done by discriminatory ideologies and socio-political structures tends to circumvent these same black bodies. This is because [...] liberation theologies in black communities draw from a Christian tradition that has a troubled relationship with the body, in spite of its theology of the incarnation.[47]

Ben Ammi's para-Jewish theology provides much more space for the material: a theology vivified by the Hebrew Bible rather than the New Testament and Greek philosophy is one in which embodiment is central, one which prioritizes physical health, which embraces our material being and sees care for the body as a necessary part of living. Many of the commandments concern physical self-care: it matters what we put in and on our bodies; it matters if we are sick and might pass that on to others; it matters if we are menstruating or not; etc. A return to the Law then is precisely not 'salvation as a form of disembodiment',[48] but salvation as re-embodiment, as accepting one's place within society, within history and with God. So, where Pinn claims that Black and Womanist theologies that do not return to embodiment offer liberation from objectification without fully embracing the gamut of subjectivity, Ben Ammi's avoids this trap.

Ben Ammi also offers designated roles and responsibilities depending on one's place in society. This is not the complete freedom of spirits, but the location of beings embodied in particularity, a particularity which changes as we grow: the rights and responsibilities of the parent or grandparent are different than those of the child. This is not a symmetry of all souls; this is a striated society, yes. But Ben is clear that there are good freedoms and bad freedoms; the freedoms offered by the west, based as they are on a philosophical notion of identicality of all individuals, do not actually liberate us, rather they destroy us by abstracting us from the natural implications of our embodied reality. There are criticisms of this view that need to be addressed, and will be taken up when we explore these ideas further and discuss the conservative nature of Ben Ammi's thought in Chapter 7.

Proactivity

A necessary but perhaps surprising corollary of the emphasis on Law, embodiment and the non-interventionist deity is a heightened sense of human agency. If following the Law is necessary as part of redemption, it is because human actions matter; in fact, the key to redemption is not through Grace, which has no place in Ben Ammi's thought, but through humans making the decision to live and act in ways conducive to their salvation. Therefore, rather than waiting for the divinely ordained time, 'when it is time we must MAKE it happen. We must make a serious and vigorous effort to convince God that we are ready for change before that Change will come' (GLR18). While change is impossible without God's help, it is human beings that must prove their readiness for change, which God will effect by ensuring *their* ability to effect change. Here we can perceive an echo of David Walker, who demanded 'a willingness on our part for God to do these things for us'.[49] This is a similar expectation for the will to change, though Walker still believed the causative agent of that change was God rather than human.

This emphasis on human agency is critical. The very setting of laws and guidelines for humans to follow necessitates the pivotal role of willed human action. For Ben Ammi, the apparent Christian emphasis on Grace and God's Will inculcates the kind of quietist helplessness that has been so rigorously dismissed in theodical terms. What Ben advocates for is a more traditionally Jewish vision, of God and human working in partnership to perfect the world. Thus, it is not submissiveness but assertiveness that is required: 'working, laboring, toiling, worshipping in righteousness, are the qualifications of being a man of God' (GBMT135). God does not answer prayers by performing the request Godself, rather one prays for the strength to do things oneself: 'God instills skill and understanding … if one prays that a huge that a huge mountain be moved, then, after praying, he rolls up his sleeves and takes a pick and shovel and begins moving the mountain' (GBMT135).

Throughout their history, the community have taken matters into their own hands. They did not remain in America, requesting equal rights, but removed themselves to another nation where they could live as the Bible commanded. They did not passively wait for acceptance in Israel, but established themselves there and began creating their institutions. Ben Ammi's proactive stance can perhaps be traced back to the failed hope for transport from Chicago on Passover of 1967: From this he (and other members of the AHIJ) seems to have learnt that change will not come through miraculous events, but must be actioned by human beings; however, if those humans are righteous in intention, God will be on their side and enable them to overcome any difficulties. This conviction appears to be what motivated the community to stand firm against many odds and finally achieve their aim of acceptance and permanent settlement within Israel.

Finally we should say: Ben Ammi may be immanent in persuasion, but he is by no means a materialist; his definition of God as spirit is intended to precisely reject the physical as the ultimate reality. Indeed, before the physical (event) there is always the spiritual/mental thought which causes it. In discussing the modern age's scientism and attempts to disprove the existence of God, Ammi explained that he sees the Kingdom as precisely engaged with the matter of proving God, demonstrating through their own existence and achievements the reality of God, the force outside the material universe which can make the improbable come to pass.[50]

Possible sources and connections with other theologies

This chapter has discussed various aspects of Ben Ammi's theological system: his God-concept has been defined as one of immanent pneumatic vitalism, emphasizing the importance of vitalist terminology – life, growth, etc – as well as that of the indwelling Holy Spirit through which humans are divinized and God embodied. I have shown that the principal practical method through which embodiment and the transmission of divine vitality are achieved is *halakhah*, or Mosaic Law. Because of Ammi's outright rejection of supernaturalism, I have argued that his location of Heaven and Hell as states encountered in the lived experience of *this* world is an expression of his immanence. Tying all of these aspects together, I have suggested that the evident proactive approach of Ben Ammi and the AHIJ is theoretically grounded in his theological deflation, that is to say, his emphasis on immanent understanding provides for a worldview which encourages action rather than prevarication, and the expectation of positive results/reward in the here and now rather than at some later stage.

Ben Ammi's theology is complex and systematic, to the extent that it would be foolish to suggest a single precursor. His concept of God is interwoven into his understanding of ontology, human life and human nature. However, there are some interesting points of resonance and possible influences which can be teased out. It is to these that we will now turn.

The following chapter will investigate in more depth the radical break between Ben Ammi and the field of Black Theology. Black Theology was certainly an interest for members of the community, who have expressed admiration for the work of James Cone and colleagues. However, Ben Ammi did not generally engage with these sources in any explicit manner. As noted, we can find the strongest links between his thought and that of Albert Cleage, who himself was not an academic, and these links relate to history and ideology more than to theology or ontology. The overwhelming and universal emphasis on God as liberator in Black Theology is not reflected in Ben Ammi, although liberation can certainly be named as an integral consequence, perhaps even motivation, for righteousness. Dwight N Hopkins' articulation of God as the 'Spirit of Total Liberation', which is tripartite in its being for, with and in us, is unlikely to be directly influential on Ben Ammi given both his lack of concern for academic theology and for the concept's unrootability in biblical texts, but it can be seen to connect especially in the sense that Ben Ammi's vital God is liberation, although ultimately Ammi collapses God into the latter immanent form: God *in* us.[51]

Having already established the influence of Albert Cleage upon Ben Ammi, it is noteworthy that later in his life Cleage developed a theology similar in its basic principles to Ammi. Jawanza Eric Clark has shown that from 1979 Albert Cleage developed his theology into one of 'cosmic energy and creative intelligence', according to which, God is not separate from the universe but is the energy that constitutes it. According to Clark's restatement of Cleage,

> We are energy beings and if we could open up our energy pathways, we might be able to access more energy at greater levels of intensity. In theological terms, this means the human beings possess an inner divinity, the God incarnate. The point of religion and spirituality is to activate that inner divinity and have it connect with external divinity, the God transcendent.[52]

The process to achieving this is through worship, which serves to connect the community to the divine and 'to increase the community's collective access to divine power, or higher levels of energy and consciousness'. As Clark identifies, this is a pantheistic theology, and one that is qualitatively different from most other Black Theologies. However, the resemblance to Ben Ammi's pneumatic vitalism is obvious. It is unclear what the relationship or dependence might be: Clark utilizes an unpublished 1984 essay of Cleage's to reconstruct his mature theology, and it is uncertain whether or how Ammi, Ben Yehuda or any other AHIJ member would have learnt of this.

A better immediate source can be found internally to the Hebrew Israelite movement, where Divine immanence has been present for a long time. Joseph Crowdy, William Crowdy's nephew and second leader of the main branch of the Church of God and Saints of Christ, apparently held a similar doctrine as well as the belief that Heaven and Hell are worldly rather than afterlife states.[53] Divine immanence was also a central part of his successor William H. Plummer's theology, along with a doctrine of corporate salvation which was very much in line with Ben Ammi's Israelite redemption model.

Indwelling was also integral to Wentworth Matthew's theology, which must be considered in the light of New Thought. New Thought was an American semi-Christian New Age movement of the nineteenth century, initially mostly white, that emphasized monism and extrapolated from this a belief in an indwelling God and the power of creative visualization. Darnise Martin writes that:

> New Thought religions make the audacious, and yet esoteric, statement that human beings are indeed divine beings, made in the image and likeness of their creator, God, because, indeed, there is no other substance. The esoteric and Gnostic truth that New Thought affirms is [...]: There is an inseparable oneness of God and humankind, and the realization of this through mystical or intuitive knowledge is the key to a life of fulfillment and perfection in the human realm.[54]

Ben Ammi's conception of humanity as a functional extension of divinity clearly reflects this view. Ammi's corollary belief in human action as a continuation of Divine creativity is also an explicit claim of New Thought. Based upon these, there is an almost theurgic importance ascribed to human thought, action and ritual in African American New Thought churches which substantially mirrors that of Ben Ammi, and this is expressed through a pneumatic doctrine 'largely informed by Pentecostal understandings of the power of the Holy Spirit', which according to Martin itself displays an affinity with 'the rituals of traditional African religions who regard the Loa or Orisha in much the same way as Holiness and Pentecostal doctrine regard the Holy Spirit'.[55] Indeed, Ammi's own employment of the term 'possession' in regard to spiritual influence upon individuals conjures associations with Voudon, Santeria and other syncretic African/American religious forms.

New Thought was popular in Harlem during the interwar period, and Jacob Dorman has shown that some esoteric aspects of Wentworth Matthew's thought drew on these concepts.[56] In addition, Bishop John Hickerson and George Baker (Father Divine) had developed a theology of immanent, indwelling divine spirit, which came to be closely associated with Hebrew Israelite conceptions of what 'Jewish' belief was. The concept of indwelling could easily have passed from Matthew to Ben Ammi through Matthew's students in Chicago who were Ben Ammi's teachers. New Thought concepts of positive thinking may well have influenced Ben Ammi's insistence on tenacity and self-belief.

Many other aspects discussed in this chapter could be sourced in Matthew. Matthew taught that keeping the commandments was essential for salvation, and held no doctrine of Heaven or Hell.[57] More importantly, he emphasized the significance of the doctrine that 'God is spirit'.[58] A possible precursor to the eventual emergence of his messianism may even be perceivable in Matthew's 'cabalistic' Hebrew amulets (preserved at the Schomburg Center for Research in Black Culture), which Dorman claims display 'not just the idea that God is inside Matthew, but his almost messianic connection with God'.[59] This present-world emphasis was a trend present in the earliest forms of Hebrew Israelite religion, although Ruth Landes noted that this was prioritized most by the Caribbean contingent.[60]

A precursor for Ben Ammi's vitalism might be found in the early twentieth-century Francophone pan-African philosophy of *Négritude*, developed by Aimé Césaire (1913–2008) from Martinique, Léon Gontran Damas (1912–78) from Guiana and Léopold Sédar Senghor (1906–2001) from Senegal (and its president after independence in 1960). In attempting to articulate a philosophy with its basis in African traditions, Senghor claimed that a vital force, the source of all life and being, was the centre of his system.

A passage from Senghor will serve to illustrate some points of similarity with Ben Ammi:

> At the heart of the system, giving it light as the sun lights our world, is existence, that is to say, life. This is the supreme good and all of man's activity is but an attempt at expansion and expression of this vital force. The Negro identifies being with life, or, more precisely, with the vital force. His metaphysics is an existential ontology. [...] But this force is not static. A being is an unstable balance, always capable of reinforcing or weakening itself. In order to exist, man must achieve an expression of his individuality through the expansion and expression of his vital force. And this force, substratum of intellectual and moral life, though immortal, is truly living and capable of growing only by coexisting, within man, with the body and the vital breath.[61]

Here, the centrality of life-force is joined by the necessity of human beings accessing and expressing that force through their own beings, expressed in terms of vital breath.

Of course, *Négritude* explicitly draws on African traditions and concepts, and we might find as much similarity in any of those.[62]

There is in *Négritude* both the acknowledgement of communal existence – that not *I* but *we* is the entity of concern, the natural unit of humanity – and the integration of humanity into the cosmos – an assertion that human beings exist within the cycles of nature, one expression of the rhythmic impulse that dominates and unites African thought according to Senghor.[63] In this there is a profound similarity with Judaism, which asserts both communality and the natural rhythms and cycles as constitutive of human life, and also with Ben Ammi's Hebrew Israelite thought. Both Ammi and rabbinic Judaism can source these impulses in the Tanakh.

Could *Négritude* have influenced Ben Ammi? It is not impossible: the connections made between thinkers of *Négritude* and those of the Harlem Renaissance mean the former's ideas could have found a way into Harlem's Black Jewish communities. The ideas had several decades to percolate through Black American culture, so that they could have found a way into Ben Ammi's thought through many sources. On the other hand, we might consider that for the *Négritude* school, these concepts were essentially African – the re-emergence of them in 1960s Chicago could also be explained by their persistent influence within Africana thought.[64] Certainly the concept of a natural, universal order which must be adhered to, and if transgressed will lead to misfortune and perhaps destruction, is one found in several African systems.[65]

Another possible source of Ben Ammi's vitalist pneumatology is the Afrocentric scholar Ishakamusa Barashango. Barashango's claim that the Hebrew *Ruach haQodesh* means 'a vital stimulating force – especially upon the mind, a motivating power', appears to be Ben's pneumatology in *nuce*.[66] That Barashango developed this idea within a Black Nationalist framework indicates the appeal of vitalist pneumatology within Afrocentrism.

A similar, although more traditionally vitalist, concept can also be seen in the early twentieth-century Christian mystic, Howard Thurman, who understood all of life – human, animal and plant – as united through its source in God. He writes,

> To me, God is the Creator of life and the living substance that out of which all particular expressions of life arise [...] the ground of being out of which all individual manifestations of vitality emerge in the first place. And a commonplace way to express that is that life itself is alive [...] So that the religious experience, then, is the experience in which I become conscious of what I'm calling now the givenness of God in me. It is private. It is personal. It is intimate. It is unique and universal.[67]

There is one question where the source is clear, however: the quote that opened this chapter, that accused satan of lying about God. This can surely be traced back to the time of slavery, when the slavemasters and the priests would claim that Blacks were created by God to serve whites.[68] This fallacy was obvious to many at the time, and became a part of the racist 'White Theology' that would be challenged by the slaves' own religious experience and understanding of biblical theology wherein God was not on the side of the enslaver but on the side of the enslaved.

Finally, the influence of Elijah Muhammad is palpable, particularly in their shared worldly emphasis. Muhammad's identical doctrine of Heaven and Hell has been discussed, and he also rejected any supernatural conceptions of God. However, he directly contradicted Ammi in claiming that God as a spirit was part of the European 'spook' theology; for him God was a physical human: Wallace D Fard. This difference in their basic God-concept is perhaps the most stark difference between Muhammad and Ammi and it should be noted that it is Muhammad who made the radical innovation here; Ammi's God removes the mythical and visual aspects of popular Christian thought, but is still theologically recognizable.

5

Divine Justice/Deserved Liberation: Suffering, agency and chosenness

For every pain, sickness or disease, or for that matter, any problem, there is a cause. Violating the cycles of God brings on these troubles [...] The sad state of Black people's affairs was brought about by their violation of God's laws and cycles. Black people were initially chosen by God to guide the world out of its state of ignorance, but instead they chose to join the world of iniquity. Because of their provocation of God, Black people are not only abhorred by all nations, but are foolishly out of step with the rhythms and patterns established by God for perfection in each of their lives.

(GBMT181)

But it shall come to pass, if thou wilt not hearken unto the voice of the LORD thy God, to observe to do all his commandments and his statutes which I command thee this day; that all these curses shall come upon thee, and overtake thee: [...] The fruit of thy land, and all thy labours, shall a nation which thou knowest not eat up; and thou shalt be only oppressed and crushed always: [...] The LORD shall bring thee, and thy king which thou shalt set over thee, unto a nation which neither thou nor thy fathers have known; and there shalt thou serve other gods, wood and stone. And thou shalt become an astonishment, a proverb, and a byword, among all nations whither the LORD shall lead thee. [...] Thou shalt beget sons and daughters, but thou shalt not enjoy them; for they shall go into captivity. [...] Because thou servedst not the LORD thy God with joyfulness, and with gladness of heart, for the abundance of all things; Therefore shalt thou serve thine enemies which the LORD shall send against thee, in hunger, and in thirst, and in nakedness, and in want of all things: and he shall put a yoke of iron upon thy neck, until he have destroyed thee. The LORD shall bring a nation against thee from far, from the end of the earth, as swift as the eagle flieth; a nation whose tongue thou shalt not understand; A nation of fierce countenance, which shall not regard the person of the old, nor shew favour to the young: [...] And the LORD shall bring thee into Egypt again with ships, by the way whereof I spake unto thee, Thou shalt see it no more again: and there ye shall be sold unto your enemies for bondmen and bondwomen, and no man shall buy you.

(Deut.28.15-68)

The question of theodicy, of explaining how evil and suffering exist in a world created by a God who is good, has taken a primary role in Black Theology, motivated as it is by the need to understand American enslavement.[1] James Cone wrote that 'The point of departure for Black theology is the question, How do we dare to speak of God in a suffering world … in which blacks are humiliated because they are black? This question … occupies the central place in our theological perspective.'[2]

Traditionally in Christian thought Christ's crucifixion has been taken as the archetype of suffering: the pain of a deity who has sacrificed himself by his injection into mortal human life, his rejection and murder as a means of compensating the sins of an otherwise-irredeemable humanity. In Christian Black Theology, the crucifixion is recast as the archetype of suffering under an unjust oppressive social system, which debases, dehumanizes, defaces, and destroys, the freedom, the dignity, the possibilities and finally the lives of its subjects through its many facets, all of which are expressions of one agenda and principle: white supremacy, at all costs and in all situations. This was the reality of the enslaved Africans, and it was that of most of those Blacks living in America until at least 1965 (and still is very present if not all-encompassing today). As all theologies are an attempt to understand the world, to make it comprehensible, and to imbue it with meaning (i.e. to ameliorate it), so African American theologians took the principal tools of the religion they possessed – in this case the crucifixion – and used them to make sense of a situation which otherwise was purely destructive. In this way, suffering was made not a simple brute fact, but something to be wrangled with. And, as in (white) Christianity, where the theo-logic of Divine Self-sacrifice still does not efface the paradoxical suffering of God and even succeeds, most potently, in placing a God who can suffer alongside humanity in our darkest moments, so in Black Theology the suffering of African Americans under a racist, oppressive, violent system can be, not *explained,* but refocused in a way that connects the oppressed with God, placing them clearly on the side of right, and suggesting that God is active both in compassion and in bringing their suffering ultimately to an end. In fact, the suffering could even offer some remediation of humanity: As Black Americans have suffered to the extremes of human endurance, they can play some role in alleviating the suffering which is endemic to human life, and not incidentally, even the guilt of those who imposed that suffering. In this way, the experience of Black Americans – once theologically understood – can function as a means to better the entirety of humanity.

We must recognize that, in contrast to *Christian* Black Theology, Ben Ammi's approach is shockingly simple: Israel offended God, and so God punished them. This 'theodicy of deserved punishment', in the words of William Jones, enacts a surprising (to those versed in modern theology and theodicy) flattening of the ethical plane.

It has been argued that a theology which concretely explains Black suffering as 'deserved punishment' risks ascribing blame to blacks for their own suffering. Indeed, this theodicy explains suffering as, simply, *just.* Their incarceration and murder are deserved because they didn't keep their end of the covenant with God. It is thus their suffering and not their liberation which is sanctified. This could incur a 'quietist' attitude of shameful acceptance of suffering, an unwillingness to struggle for liberation. On the other hand, it also offers the opportunity to write God off as a white racist, one who imposes punishment on Blacks more than any other peoples, for crimes which everyone has committed. If suffering is Divine punishment, meted out via other nations, then God seems to enjoy harming Black people.[3]

Very similar questions are being wrangled with in Jewish theology, most potently in the decades since the Holocaust which saw 5 to 6 million of the world's Jewish population – two thirds of Europe's – systematically wrenched from society, imprisoned, enslaved and finally annihilated. Jewish attempts to explain and understand the Holocaust have ranged from the atheistic to the biblical, thinkers from different schools emphasizing either the purely destructive power of the Holocaust to argue against the value of the covenant and even the existence of God, or forsaking the image of a merciful God for those passages of the Bible which promise powerful punishment for God's Chosen People should they not live up to Divine expectations. The latter may be symbolized by Amos' plaintive cry placed into God's mouth: 'You alone have I singled out, of all the families of the earth – That is why I will call you to account for all your iniquities' (3:2). Simply, God cares more for Israel so his higher expectations engender more unforgiving punishments.

This chapter will look in detail at these concepts, interrogating Ben Ammi's theodicy in terms of theological responses from both Black and Jewish thinkers, from within and beyond the academy. It should be noted that there is much more that could be said about this than I attempt; this chapter is intended as an overview of Ammi's thought, contextualized and placed in dialogue with certain prominent strands, not as an extensive analysis of theodicy.[4]

Black Chosenness, agency and Ben Ammi's theodicy of Divine Justice and Deserved Liberation

Just as African Americans often perceived their suffering in America as replicating that of Israel in Egypt and Babylon, so there has been a frequent logical jump to a concept of 'Black Chosenness', the idea that Black Americans are or have become a world-historical people, selected by God for some special role.[5] This concept, which in its initial form stemmed from the belief in the *similarity* of the Black experience in America with that of the Israelites, appears to be based both in a belief in the similar response of God to this situation and to a literal identification of Black with Israelite which has culminated in the Hebrew Israelite movement (although it is not limited to that). The latter most likely came later: one only needs to search for references to Israel and Israelites in compendia of historical Black protest literature to see that the writers took the biblical stories as a type of their own people's experiences, rather than claiming a linear descent. Ironically, many of these metaphorical uses of the biblical tropes of Egypt, Babylon, and Exodus, have later informed Hebrew Israelite thought.

An implication of Black Chosenness is present already in Robert Young's 1829 *Ethiopian Manifesto*,[6] itself influential on the Ethiopianist movement. Some five decades later Rev. Alexander Crummell wrote that the fact Black people survived slavery and were not destroyed by it indicated, 'There is, so to speak, a covenant relation which God has established between Himself and them.'[7] That is, God chose them for a special relationship.

In some forms of Black Chosenness, slavery was understood as a divine honing process wherein the Black American experience would produce a world-historical people with a special role to fulfil. Even whites have sometimes assigned a messianic role to Black Americans. For some, the special role of Blacks was not only because of their suffering, but depended on special racial characteristics: Du Bois wrote of 'the beauty of [the Black race's] genius, the sweetness of its soul, and its strength in that meekness which shall yet inherit this turbulent earth'.[8] Here, Blacks have been chosen because of their nature to lead the world out of the modern dark ages. This belief was often articulated via Ps.68.31, 'Princes shall come out of Egypt; Ethiopia shall soon stretch out her hands unto God,' Wilson Moses noting that some 'have insisted that the real meaning of the verse is that some day the black man will rule the world. Such a belief is still common among older black folk today'.[9] Thus, Black Chosenness has an intimate relationship with Black messianism.

However, concepts of chosenness and a special collective destiny are imbedded in the American self-concept generally.[10] Therefore a paradoxical duality informs Black Chosenness, which shares in the very values of the system that oppresses it. As Wilson Moses puts it, 'Ironically, it represents both a rejection of white America and a participation in one of its most sacred traditions.'[11]

Many African American religious thinkers prior to the mid-twentieth century held that their suffering was ordained by God, not as punishment but because of some value that it brought; i.e. that it was in some sense 'redemptive'. Bishop Henry McNeal Turner held that slavery had been instigated for the good of Africans, although whites had overstepped the mark by trying to make slavery permanent instead of a limited period of 'training'. Others – among them Martin Luther King – saw undeserved suffering as redemptive in the sense that a non-violent response could potentially provide the perpetrator with cause to reassess their actions, but also be formative for the victim.[12] Thereby, God could bring good out of a human evil. While some Black Christian thinkers have seen enslavement as God's will, as a method of bringing about a state of affairs through which Black people would influence and improve the world, the ethical problem of God causing human suffering was not seen as a damning critique. Albert Raboteau writes that in this time, 'Few questioned why it was necessary for Africans to learn these arts and sciences at the price of so much suffering. God chastises those he chooses. Through suffering, God was purifying Ethiopia's sons in America in order to make them a chosen generation, a royal priesthood, and an holy nation, a peculiar people.'[13] Indeed, Anthony Pinn has concluded that 'redemptive suffering' has been the most common explanation for black oppression within African American religion.[14]

The 1960s saw a decisive shift: for the last sixty years, post-Black Power academic thinkers, trained in philosophy and theology, have taken the stance that enslavement was an affront to God, who abhorred any human suffering. This has been a paradigmatic claim of the *Black Theologians*. Thus, James Cone vigorously rejects 'any concept of God which makes black suffering the will of God. Black people should not accept slavery, lynching, or any form of injustice as tending to good'.[15] Simply put, a God who sneaks in the kind and extent of brutalization experienced by Black Americans under the explanation of effecting a 'greater good' is not one that can be accepted. This argument is one near-universally presumed by contemporary theologians, but I have provided the excerpts above in an attempt to show that this has not always been the case. My reason for doing so is that Ben Ammi evinces something like the arguments given above, by prior generations of Black religious thinkers, and we should recognize that the outright rejection of such belief is not a foundation of African American religious thought, even if it is one of academia.

Ben Ammi expresses it succinctly: 'The Sons and Daughters of God violated the universal law, therefore they were sorely oppressed by God in the house of their enemy so that they would swiftly seek Him with prayer and repentance for their salvation' (GBMT188).[16] In this characteristically frank diagnosis of the situation, Ammi does not seek to engage with philosophical dilemmas, such as the Problem of Evil. This chapter will suggest that in fact Ammi demonstrates an important (though unrecognized due to the biases inherent in academic theology) way of resolving the Problem, however first we must look in detail at his theodicy.

Ben Ammi's own explanation for the suffering of Blacks in America is heavily influenced by Deut.28, according to which the return of the Israelites to slavery is a deserved punishment, one of many negative results of their sinful disobedience. This theodicy of deserved punishment is common throughout the Hebrew Israelite movement, ever since the use of Deut.28 became a central pillar, from the 1920s onward.[17] Throughout the Hebrew Bible, misfortune is understood to be a result of sin; this worldview, that humans are punished in this life for our crimes is only partially challenged in Qohelet (Ecclesiastes); even Job, the classical biblical example of a sophisticated approach to theodicy which centralizes the inexplicability of human suffering, never rejects the persistent human expectation that God will deal justly with us, and our rewards will reflect our actions, God seeming in the end to admit Job's accuracy in holding himself unjustly treated. In this context it is important to note that although Deut.28 promises a return to slavery as punishment for sin, the entry of the Israelites into Egyptian slavery was not punishment – it happened almost by accident, and yet its outcome was one of a small family becoming a great people (in fact the Egyptian bondage presents an important argument for a kind of redemptive suffering, as it was formative upon the Israelites and led to the Mosaic covenant). Deuteronomy's threat of punishment is in actuality little more than that of a *return* to the condition that God had found them in, and liberated them from. The narrative of the Bible tells of a people enslaved without reason and saved by God's compassion, but then threatened with a worse outcome if they should not accept the terms of the salvation. In effect God tells them, 'I just saved your life, now you belong to me. If you refuse, I'll let you die.' This transaction logic is commonplace throughout the Bible, with only a few exemplars of different approaches.

In this model, freedom comes at a price: liberation depends upon following the rules. God enters into a covenant of responsibility only so long as the people keep their half of the deal. But following the rules is a guarantee of liberation (as we will see, they may be metaphysically identical): 'When a people truly seek to be free, and struggle in God's name, God is bound by His nature to help them succeed. God will never leave a people oppressed by His adversary if the people desire to be free to serve Him' (GBMT170). Phrased in a different way, 'except that you desire to be free to worship

God, then there is no benefit to His freeing you' (ibid). This much could be said of any people, it is not particular to Israel, but it does highlight an important part of Ben Ammi's thought: While God has compassion for humans, this does not override other aspects of God's moral makeup.

These questions of agency are important and deserve to be worked through. How do other nations, free will and responsibility fit into Ben Ammi's theodicy? Essentially, as with the Hebrew Bible, Ben Ammi cares about justice universally, but his focus is entirely on the experience and agency of one people – the Israelites. In general, neither the Bible nor Ammi discusses the fates or experiences of other nations, because Israel is the centre of their worlds. Other nations are not mentioned at all except when they interact with Israelites, and for this reason the Europeans are given special place in his schema.

The Europeans, Euro-gentiles, are a paradigm of unrighteousness, and their role in the slave trade is a fundamental expression of this. However, it is difficult to fully untangle the process of agency in Ben Ammi's thought: is Israel's suffering caused by their withdrawal from God? Or is it a punishment willed by God? Are the Euro-gentiles tormenting them because of their own evil, or are they an agent of God, or even an agent of satan? Ben Ammi poses his own question, 'When we look closely and evaluate the predicament of the Euro-gentile race, to what do we attribute their evil, corrupt nature?' (GLRxi) The question might appear to be rhetorical, indeed an explicit answer is not given; but Ben Ammi's intention is made clear in the very same paragraph when he follows up with two questions which *are* rhetorical: 'Racism and greed are on the rise in their world. Has this imbroglio occurred by chance or by plan? Is the fate of the African and African American on an unaltered course of destruction, as pre-destined by the death-obsessed Euro-gentile?' Here, it is made clear: there is a guiding hand behind all of this. The Euro-gentile's evil, corrupt nature is *part* of the divine plan, at the centre of which are the Israelites. However, it is clear that the Israelites bear responsibility for their own unrighteousness, as do the Europeans.

This vacillation between four different causative agents continues throughout his body of work, wherein sometimes he blames the Euro-gentiles for their unrighteousness, their rejection of and opposition to God (e.g. GBMT78), and sometimes presents them as merely tools, enacting God's punishment. It is left up to the reader to find a resolution between any two, three or four agents. For example, we might presume that it is precisely *because* 'generations of the Euro-gentiles despise the Most High God and refuse to accept His established order' (MEW26) that they were able to become 'our rod of correction in the Plan of Redemption of God Almighty' (GBMT164). However, as mentioned previously, an intrinsic part of the Euro-gentiles' unrighteousness is that they have been captivated by an evil spirit. Their own sinful nature seemingly had brought them within satan's sphere of influence, allowing them to be led further astray. So, while it was God that motivated them to enslave the Israelites, the force of evil *also* utilized their susceptibility in order to realize a more substantial goal: 'satan wasn't satisfied with just inflicting hardship upon the Blacks. He went on to bring tremendous suffering to the slave captors as well' (GBMT128). Thus, while Ammi is unrelenting in his description of 'the insidiously evil minds of the captors', as well as that of satan, Ammi still recognizes that 'the suffering, endurance and perseverance of the slaves … was required because of their sins against the Living God' (ibid.).

There is in fact a deep sense of co-responsibility, reciprocal failure and karmic comeuppance in Ben Ammi's narrative. He writes, 'The multiplicity of curses that befell the Children of Israel was God's way of chastising them because of their trespasses and refusal to be a righteous, model nation which the world could emulate' (MEW17). Here the Israelites were supposed to provide a model of holiness for all of humanity, to show the way that humans should live and what they could achieve by doing so. When they failed to live up to this expectation, they were punished; but the extent to which they were punished reflected their betrayal not only of themselves and God, but of all humanity: 'God's chastisements were devastating and sure. That erroneous decision not only negatively affected the Children of Israel, but by shirking their Divine charge, they caused all nations and peoples' dreams of living in a utopian paradise, where harmony, justice and love prevailed to be deferred' (ibid.). This means that although the Euro-gentiles, in their sinfulness, were used to punish Israel, Europeans themselves have been victims of Israel's error. If Israel had lived up to their responsibilities, then the Euro-gentiles too could have been saved (from themselves): 'Because the Children of Israel dodged their responsibility to be Godly leaders and pacesetters, and failed to show others the benefits of righteous living, all men were denied the glory of a world where governments were headed by men governed by God' (MEW17). Thus, it seems that all bear responsibility, and all are guilty: the Euro-gentiles' refusal to follow God, the spiritual force of satan, the Israelite failure to live righteously and God's punishment of the Israelites are all factors in the collapsing *Hell on earth* that we currently inhabit. Each factor has exacerbated the others.

This is not the only point in Ammi's work where a duality or triplicity of intention and causality manifest: while Israel forgot who they were, there is also 'suppression of this fact' on the part of European society. One passage makes clear the intertwined agency of God, satan and the Europeans: after a long passage arguing that satan's 'characteristics and situations manifest themselves in the actions and thoughts of men', he moves swiftly to claim that the Euro-gentiles' actions are 'a manifestation of the anger of God Almighty at our forefathers' disobedience to His laws and instructions'. However, 'it was the *intention of the Euro-gentiles* (as a manifestation of the anger of God Almighty at our forefathers' disobedience to His laws and instructions) to destroy the remembrance and historical connection between African Americans and Solomon, David, Cush and Yeshua (Jesus)' (MEW66–68, emphasis added). This complex of causative intention and agency cannot easily be resolved, other than by the reassessing of what God (and satan) are, as we suggested in the previous chapter.

In a later text Ammi suggests that there is an apotropaic element to righteousness, that the Israelites' abandoning of God rendered them exposed and vulnerable to the pagans who would feast on them. However even here, it is the curses of Deut.28 which provide the model: 'Like bounty hunters anxious for a reward their objective was to maliciously subject you to the prescribed punishment (for violation of the Law) and curses (consequence of walking contrary to the Creator)' (RHS78). What is important for us to recognize is that this argument is being used not in terms of *blame*, but in terms of *power*: 'Europeans did not conquer us they simply took advantage of our vulnerability!' (RHS77) This description is poignant, because for so long in America vulnerability was precisely the lot for the African diaspora: without legal protection, no kind of assault was unthinkable. This is not the intention here, however. Ben Ammi provides a two-pronged assault on traditional modes of understanding the Transatlantic Slave Trade: on the one hand, he affirms that this was not due to the might of the Europeans or weakness of Africans, but because the latter had lost the protective force that they were accustomed to. On the other hand, Ben Ammi is also suggesting that the only way to ensure safety is to return to the one God who will protect them. This is because, 'Without the worship of and accountability to Yah (God) you are left unshielded, unprotected and subject to the curses (consequences) prescribed for such a transgression' (RHS78). This is one of several ways that Ben Ammi defuses traditional conceptions of European power and African weakness, and these form an important implicit part of his theological project: in casting the Slave Trade as not a European victory over the African victims, Ammi rewrites the roles of agency and power such that Africans are the agents of their own demise and hold the keys to their liberation; European power on the other hand is revealed to be nothing but functionality within the arc of God's plan, in which the African is always centred.

At times Ben Ammi suggests that the Europeans' theft and appropriation of the scriptures was not just part of a ploy to destroy the Israelites but partly an expression of jealousy; they envied the (theurgic?) power that the Israelites held.[18] It is in fact because of Euro-gentiles' theft of Israelite scripture and their attempt to make themselves a new Chosen People that they were able to attain world-domination:

> Satan, through deception, created them[19] in his evil image, giving them enormous power and deceptive skills with which to transform the world. They have made *everything* and *everyone* in their image and after their likeness. The Euro-gentile seized the initiative from the fallen African race, who once ruled the world. They accepted the responsibility of becoming the agents of transformation.
>
> (GLR46)

Here there seems to be an innate power, one that can be called upon by whoever 'possesses' the divine tools of Israelite religion, whoever follows them to some degree rather than not at all, and even if they do this while hating God and righteousness. The Europeans stole this power and utilized it for evil, as we can see from the world they have made.

Ben Ammi doesn't state it explicitly, but it is possible to perceive here an inversion of their spiritual Edomite heritage: Esau's spirit wishes to take back what Jacob stole from him, the birth-right which would have (tragically) been Esau's. There would be a poetic logic in God returning the mandate to Esau, once the Israelites proved their unworthiness.

Because of the unrighteous agenda of the Euro-gentiles, however, their use of this power would not lead to a beneficial outcome. When the Euro-gentiles distorted the meaning of the scriptures and concealed the truths of Hebrew religion, not only did they prevent Israel from finding their way back to God, but also themselves: meaning that they too are suffering as a result of their misuse of the powerful concepts contained in the Tanakh. Now, 'the sowers must inevitably reap their harvest. Their imaginations are vain and their glory deceitful by which they themselves are deluded. The infallible Word of God has determined that the web they weaved for others has ensnared them' (MEW26). Here, God appears to be punishing the Euro-gentiles for their overzealous punishment of Israel.[20] And again, 'The lowering of the level of God consciousness was part and parcel of the Euro-gentiles' wickedness, by all means, but it is important to understand that this was merely part of God's Divine and Holy Plan' (MEW79).

As has already been discussed, Ben Ammi's identification of God with Life leads to the corollary presumption that the closer one comes to God, and aligns to the structures of righteousness that God has provided, the better one's life, health and happiness will be. However, the further one draws away from the Divine source of nourishment, the less healthy, happy and productive one will be; which is to say, suffering is created by distance from God; they are inextricably linked. This suffering may not be obvious – indeed, it seems that the pagan Euro-gentiles have increasingly drawn away from righteousness in ways that were very damaging for themselves and others, without realizing that they were enmeshing themselves into short and harsh lives filled with violence. The Israelites too have found themselves drawn into this world of suffering, principally because they chose to stray from God's commandments. Thus, in a simple sense, the evil which one experiences is a direct result of one's own choices, and one can always choose to end that suffering.

The key element here is that God causes neither Black suffering, nor its cessation; indeed, not those of any peoples. These eventualities are in the hands of the people alone, who can choose to follow God's advice or not, and thus receive either the benefits of alignment with life-giving forces, or the consequences of non-alignment. In this sense, Ben Ammi's biblical theology does not depend upon Divine favour, but is simply a mechanical system in which either life or death is chosen.

To return to a comment given at the outset, liberation comes at the price of accepting the commandments: 'When a people truly seek to be free, and struggle in God's name, God is bound by His nature to help them succeed. God will never leave a people oppressed by His adversary if the people desire to be free to serve Him' (GBMT170). The key term here is 'to serve Him'. It is only if the people wish to be free *so that they can worship God*, that God will aid them on their way out of oppression. Of course, as we have already discussed, worshipping or serving God is identical with doing right. In his rephrasing, 'except that you desire to be free to worship God, then there is no benefit to His freeing you' (ibid.), Ben Ammi does not state what benefit God might gain from being worshipped, because there is none. I suggest that until we read it as allegory, where God is non-personal but identified wholly as freedom and life and growth, all of which will be actively spread upon the freeing of a people who live by those principles, we do not fully understand the value or radical import of Ben Ammi's theodicy.

For these reasons, I have termed Ben Ammi's theodicy one not of 'deserved punishment', but one of Divine Justice and *Deserved Liberation*.

Theodicy and Black theology

Here we must ask the question, is Ben Ammi's theodicy completely alien from Black Theology, or could it offer some important elements that have not before been considered? Even if Ben Ammi's theodicy is rejected by academic theologians (as it surely will be), a deep consideration and engagement with the theory might help to further the discussion. It is also important, if we wish to understand the religious thought of Ben Ammi and other Hebrew Israelites, to appreciate their concepts without judging them based upon a straw man construction. In this section, we will apply the arguments developed in Black Theology, attempting to show why Ben Ammi does not share them, and what he perhaps even gains theologically by pursuing a justification that academic theologians reject.

The theodicy of deserved punishment has faced some harsh criticism in terms of Black Theology – ever since James Cone rejected it outright, the appearance of justifying Black suffering by appeal to punishment or greater good has been viewed as inadmissible. Still, the ability to assimilate the trans-Atlantic experience – the shattering effects of the Middle Passage, enslavement, Jim Crow and American racism – is usually viewed as the critical criterion on which Black Theology must be evaluated. If this is the criterion, then Ben Ammi deserves a hearing at least.

This section will consider Ben Ammi's thought mostly in dialogue with that of William Jones, whose pivotal text *Is God a White Racist?* is still considered a crucial analysis of theodicy in Black Theology. Jones writes that 'the initial task of the black theologian is to liberate the black mind from the destructive ideas and submissive attitudes that checkmate any movement toward authentic emancipation.'[21] For Jones, 'the object of the theologian's analysis should be what his black sisters and brothers believe to be true about themselves and the universe of nature and society, for it is this knowledge that regulates their actions.' This is the 'Gnosiological conversion of the Black psyche' which is necessary for redemption: a breaking of the chains of mental slavery. Jones, like all Black Theologians, rejects those forms of theodicy which lead to quietism, to the acceptance of suffering – a state reached when we believe that the suffering is justified, either by our past actions or by the good that might result. In these cases, leaving the ultimate ethical resolution in the hands of God leads us to neither protest nor attempt to end our suffering ourselves. Jones typifies this approach as being 'counterrevolutionary'.[22] This is intuitively correct, but no one could label Hebrew Israelites as quietist: they have been among the most vocal against black oppression. For them, recognizing that enslavement was the will of God entails the necessity of discovering what this punishment was in response to, and changing that causative factor. In Ben Ammi's case, the disobedience to God's Law was cause, and the re-uptake of the Law is the step necessary to end the suffering.[23]

It may be countered that such a severity of Divine punishment is simply not compatible with traditional concepts of a God who prioritizes love. There are two possible responses to this.

The first is that reading the Hebrew Bible on its own terms *can* provide a concept of God who loves, but is also jealous; who rewards but also punishes viciously. It is no secret that the Tanakh contains descriptions of extreme cruelty and violence, oftentimes at God's initiative. Both Christian and Jewish interpretation have sought to soften and de-emphasize these aspects, but they are still there for any reader to find, especially those who read not from a tradition of interpretation which tells them these are not to be taken seriously. The challenge to the theologian then could be phrased, admittedly slightly provocatively, as whether to prioritize theological tradition and modern conceptions of God, or the Bible as read on its own terms.

The second is that this argument supposes a traditionally personalist concept of God. This is to say that a concept of God which does not place God as having a personhood whereby responsibility or agency can be ascribed does not encounter a moral problem with the Divine allowing suffering. In the contemporary period, there are some concepts of God which remove personhood or agency, and thus present God-talk as metaphorical, as describing some of the ineffable mechanisms of reality which are experienced in human life. This is not to say that we must reject a personalist *image* of God, but we must realize that such an image is only a useful way for humans to talk about, and relate to, these processes. To reach conclusions grounded upon the personalist image is then to mistake the representation for the reality – a form of idolatry.[24]

We should consider both of these arguments when analysing Ben Ammi's theology. It is certainly the case that the Hebrew Israelite use of Deut.28 presents a God who could punish with extreme anger the wrongs of God's Chosen People, and one who would reverse that suffering upon the correction of their iniquity. It is also the case that Hebrew Israelites have tended to read the Hebrew Scriptures without recourse to any tradition of interpretation, at least other than a nod towards that developed within the African American community. While the religious expression of slaves seems to have emphasized the immediate and personal saving power of Christ over explaining the problem of slavery (a trend followed in Christian Black Theology), Hebrew Israelite thought seems to have emphasized the latter, explicating the causative reason for Black suffering over personal salvation. If these two factors are linked, as it seems they could be, it is unclear which came first: the de-emphasizing of Christ, leading to a more-keen focus on explanation, or an interest in causation and explanation over imminent *spiritual* salvation which then led to a lessening of the importance placed on Christ. However, it is clear that explaining the mechanism whereby slavery came about will lead naturally to a consideration of the possibility of reversing that cause, and this is what will lead to *communal* salvation.

Whatever the process, and whatever the initial condition, it is clear that this approach is less necessarily Christian in nature. This helps to introduce a concept which has been discussed, to a degree, by Jones and more so by Pinn: that the traditional Christian theology is not the only one through which the material and interest of Black Theology can be approached. While Jones suggests a 'humanocentric theology' and Pinn a 'weak humanistic theology', Ben Ammi provides us with a biblically based Israelite theology.

Ben Ammi takes seriously the biblical notion of a Chosen People – while Christianity and Islam took the Abrahamic faith tradition into a (more or less) universalist direction, where all peoples were of the same nature and responsibility, and were equally open to redemption, Judaism has remained with the biblical idea that there is a single people who are designated with a special responsibility. Ben Ammi's Hebrew Israelite theology likewise presumes that African Americans have a distinct role in Creation, one that they must live up to.

One of the corollaries of this, as seen throughout the Hebrew Bible, is that when God's expectations of God's people are not met, they will be punished. Thus, Ben Ammi demonstrates an implicit problem with the argument advanced by Jones and others. The implicit claim that Divine favour and Divine *disfavour* are incompatible, manifesting also in Jones's notion that Divine racism is a subset of the latter, is shown to be far from watertight by the text of the Bible itself, which demonstrates that Divine disfavour can come as a result of Divine favour. This is how Ben Ammi also conceptualizes it: that the punishment of Black Americans was as a direct result of their favoured status. Indeed, the Bible repeatedly shows that the Israelites suffer not just despite but often because of their status as God's chosen people; they arouse God's disfavour because they inspire his favour.[25]

Jones's argument would only be correct if we presume suffering to be entirely negative. Jones himself has argued that suffering in the Bible is 'multi-evidentiary', which is to say it can signify God's wrath, God's grace or neither. A large part of the second element – that suffering can signify Divine favour or closeness to God – is due to the New Testament. However, even when this is stripped away and we approach only the Hebrew Bible, there are still Job, Isaiah's 'suffering servant' passages and a few others to account for. Therefore, it is difficult to see suffering as entirely negative. However, if we did, then we would have to explain why God would allow God's favoured people to suffer *at all*. Given that God apparently has the power and desire to reduce suffering, why would those whom God loved have to experience any of it? The African Hebrew Israelite response to Jones would be that: 1. All are suffering; in white society all are in Hell, whether they know it or not. All are being destroyed, although the suffering is more obvious for Blacks. 2. If we take the Hebrew Bible seriously, then God explicitly says that Israel, God's beloved, will also be the most punished (Amos). Ben makes the argument is that all of the world has suffered because of Israel's abnegation of its responsibility; this flipping of the narrative thus makes not white Europeans those responsible for Black suffering, but Black Israelites – *to an extent* – responsible for the world's suffering. While this consequence is indirect and unintentional, they still relinquished the role prescribed to them, and punishment was necessary in order to bring them back to the point at which they were able to save the world from the evils committed by other humans (and especially Europeans) without Israel there to guide them.

Admittedly, this is a difficult doctrine to swallow. That African Americans, who have experienced some of the worst imaginable communal suffering over the last four hundred years, might be cast as guilty, not only of their own suffering but of the rest of the world's, goes beyond victim-blaming into a realm similar to the accusations of satanic power which were levelled against Jews at the same time as Jews were being violently persecuted around the world. That a Black thinker could suggest such a concept will undoubtedly be painful for some to hear. Why then has this theory been promoted and, to some extent, accepted by a whole community?[26] Partly, I believe we must explain this with reference to the shift in fundamental dynamics that the narrative imposes: reframing agency, as being primarily the possession of Black America, articulates a firm rejection of passivity and victimhood; it also creates a sense of significance, of the importance of one's actions, the value of which should not be underestimated. There is an inherent dignity in knowing that the choices one makes affect the world, even the cosmos. The next stage, the logical conclusion of this, is an acceptance of responsibility: that the correct-or-otherwise performance of actions is not simply a matter of individual will, but one on which reality depends. This teleological import is one which, as we shall see, brings Ben Ammi's theology into intimate contact with the Jewish tradition, especially of Kabbalah.

A key desideratum proposed by Jones is what he calls the 'exaltation' or 'liberation event'. Based on Is.52.13-16, which predicts that 'My [suffering] servant shall prosper, Be exalted and raised to great heights', this term signifies a point of release from suffering which, as well as establishing the undeserved nature of that suffering, would prove the status of African Americans as the suffering servant/chosen people (and indeed is critical to establishing the idea that it is in God's nature to care about the liberation of Blacks). Without such an event, Jones argues that there is yet no evidence to support divine compassion for Blacks, and a plausibly better case could be made for the opposite. Such an event would be considered by Ben Ammi to have occurred in 1967–9, with their successful exodus from the United States and entry into the Promised Land of Israel. Indeed, the progressive victories of the AHIJ against massive odds have served to prove to many members that God is with them in their struggle.

The reason this works in the case of the AHIJ is that Jones's argument depends on suffering being proved, in some certain way, to be in the past: ongoing suffering with no sign of change appears to contradict the claim that God cares. The AHIJ have, according to their own narrative and from external appearances, passed this event, thereby adding legitimacy to their claim to divine providence *despite or perhaps even because* the rest of Black America, who have not made the same transition as the AHIJ, have not seen their persecution end.

Their success against Jones's test highlights one of the key elements of Ben Ammi's theodicy which challenges traditional Christian Liberation Theologies: while God *does* certainly care about human beings, God will not liberate people simply because they are oppressed. The humans in question must make the initial decisions, and only then will God help them in bringing their goal of freedom to fruition. Ben Ammi does not follow the traditional progressive theology of God as ultimate liberator; at most we could say that what God wants is for people to liberate themselves, which they can only do by following the guidelines given by God.[27]

Here, there is again a very subtle nod in the direction of concepts developed by a Womanist Theologian: Delores Williams challenged the fundamental liberatory emphasis of Black Theology, demonstrating that there is a non-liberative thread running through the Hebrew Bible.[28] In the Bible peoples other than the Israelites are often treated disdainfully, and subjected to persecution without excuse; they are certainly not unconditionally liberated, even when God feels compassion for them.

It should be repeated here, that while condition-free liberation is not the prerogative of Ben Ammi's biblical God, who is principally covenantal, Ben Ammi shows an inherent flaw in the perspective of Liberation Theologies generally. This is, that they tend to presume that those who are not oppressed by other humans represent the ultimate freedom which is the goal of all. Ben Ammi is clear that the 'freedom' of white America is not the panacea to Black America's woes, but is a terrible illusion, the flipside of the oppression of Blacks. Black oppression is in large part *because* of their integration into the world of white America, with the capitalist, consumerist, unhealthy and unrighteous doctrines upon which it rests.

Therefore, incorporated into Ben Ammi's theodicy of Divine Justice and Deserved Liberation is the necessity of human agency in activating the will of God to assist them; human passivity negates any desire for liberation because liberation must be striven for on the humans' part, in order for it to be possible. In effect, this is the same as what Jones calls humanity's 'functional ultimacy' in that we in-our-freedom bear responsibility: God is not the ultimate recipient of all agency.

Having shown the inapplicability of Jones's critique of Black Theology to Ben Ammi's biblical theology, we must also consider how other Black Theologians might respond. It is immediately clear that Ben Ammi's theodicy would be rejected by Cone and others, because it does not align with their conception of God. The reason for this difference is apparent: Black Theologians have worked from a background of Christian thought, wherein God's love and the redemptive power of the Christ event are at the forefront. The latter is of course not present in non-Christian thought, and the former must be subject to a reconsideration. If the Hebrew Bible is taken seriously, on its own terms, are we faced with a God who is overwhelmingly loving?

According to Jewish tradition, the answer – which may well surprise – is no. The Talmud and other rabbinic writings talk in terms of two primary qualities of God: Justice and Mercy.[29] The former is God's harshness, which applies always a transaction logic, which promises that if the Israelites do not live up to their side of the covenant, they will be punished. However, this quality is always tempered with God's Mercy, God's lovingkindness towards Israel and all of creation. The rabbis pray that God's Mercy will outweigh God's Judgement, and indeed it does, according to one rabbi by a factor of 500 – but it can only be provided to those who love God and keep the commandments (the Mosaic 613 in the case of Jews, the seven Noahide laws in the case of gentiles). The principal idea here is that forgiveness can only be applied to one who repents; to forgive one who has not repented leads to the devaluing of repentance and the unlinking of action and consequence. The kabbalists developed intricate methods of both explaining how the world is filled with so much evil and how Jews can help to tip the balance back towards good. More philosophical thinkers understand these as qualities present in the world and human experience, but not of God, Godself: They are the colours through which an invisible God manifests.

Ben Ammi thus demonstrates a way of taking the Tanakh seriously, without concealing the parts that appear unseemly to us. This is a way in tune more with the rabbinic Jewish reading of the text than the Christian.

When reading the Tanakh, Ben Ammi's approach is not one of 'The apparent meaning of this text contradicts what we know of God, therefore we must search for a deeper meaning to the text', but of 'This text is clearly true, and our concept of God must follow that'. Any theological problems encountered are best explained as consequence of a misunderstanding of God; the dissonance between a false picture provided by the enslaver's religion of Christianity, and the Truth of the Bible. The ethical dilemma of slavery being part of God's Justice is negated by the mechanical element we have already explained: distance from God is brought upon oneself; the people strayed from God and found themselves living in Hell, slowly dying, but they can change this situation as soon as they return to God.

The critical element in Ben Ammi's theodicy is that, while whites are not innocent in the ordeal of slavery, in essential cause it was a self-inflicted harm. The suffering of Blacks in America is not due to God allowing others to harm them to such an extent, but is due to God allowing the full impact of their rejection of God to be felt. This is a subtly different problem, and whether or not it is accepted as a valid response to the problem of black suffering, it deserves to be recognized for what it is.

The ultimate causative power of human actions, which produce a spiritual situation leading back to the suffering of those same humans, is not simply an Abrahamic belief: it can be found within the African traditions that some enslaved brought with them to the Americas. Anthony Pinn notes that in many African-based traditions, 'moral evil is the result of an imbalance of cosmic energy – *ashé* – resulting from human misdeeds',[30] and Lewis Gordon has found specifically in Akan thought that they 'took their lot as indication of being off course from their promised purpose in relation to the originating Deity'.[31] This tradition, precisely the kind of theodical explanation that Ben Ammi attempts, could therefore be partly inherited from African sources, if these traditions became incorporated into the religious thought of enslaved members and descendants of that group. Remarkably, both these traditions also presume the kind of less-personal God that I have argued is part of Ben Ammi's theology.

In considering Cleage's position that American oppression is ultimately the result of Black acquiescence and God's disappointment in that, Pinn comments that

> If Black suffering is utterly useless, would not a good God who is somewhat powerful work towards liberation as opposed to simply providing strength? Why does not God use God's own strength to help bring about much needed change? Cleage's "cover-up" falters because it leaves substantial questions concerning God's role in human suffering without satisfying answers.[32]

Clearly, Ben Ammi provides some additional material for this debate, as he provides a proactive conception where Blacks will recognize their identity, and simply leave the land of oppression in order to create their own society elsewhere. The fundamental basis of Ammi's doctrine, however, is the non-interventionist deity.

In this way, Ben Ammi's theology may stand in-between those of Cone et al. and Delores Williams et al. This is to say, that God's quality of *power* for Ben Ammi is largely a soft one. As a non-interventionist deity, Ammi's God still exerts control and is still dominant in a moral sense, although acting more from an internal than external position. God is certainly a comforter, but one that makes demands of us.

Theodicy and Jewish theology

As has been noted, the Hebrew Bible operates generally by a theodicy of deserved punishment, explaining evil that befalls people as the result of their sins. Even in the archetype of Jewish rationalism, Moses Maimonides, we find this expressed:

> If man frees his thoughts from worldly matters, obtains a knowledge of God in the right way, and rejoices in that knowledge, it is impossible that any kind of evil should befall him while he is with God, and God with him. When he does not meditate on God, when he is separated from God, then God is also separated from him; then he is exposed to any evil that might befall him; for it is only that intellectual link with God that secures the presence of Providence and protection from evil accidents.
>
> (GP3:51)[33]

Discussing Ex.31.17, Maimonides even uses apotropaic terms quite similar to those used by Ben Ammi. He explains that God's protection is only active when the individual or community strengthens the connection between them and God: 'the cause of our being exposed to chance, and abandoned to destruction like cattle, is to be found in our separation from God. Those who have their God dwelling in their hearts, are not touched by any evil whatever' (ibid.).

This conception has disappeared from popular and academic Jewish thought since the Holocaust, for the same reason as its disappearance from Black Theology: the extent of suffering was considered unjustifiable. The dominance of the Holocaust and the search for a way to understand its horrors within subsequent decades of Jewish religion mirror the Hebrew Israelite concentration on and attempt to understand the horror of the trans-Atlantic slave trade. In fact, almost every element of the Black American theological approach to understanding and explaining enslavement in America can also be found in Jewish thinkers' attempts to explain and understand the Nazi Holocaust.

Steven Katz divides Jewish approaches to theology after the Holocaust into two forms: (1) those which draw upon the text and traditions to reframe the experience, to think of it in a new way, and (2) those which draw upon the experience and conclude that the traditional interpretations of the texts is flawed and must be reformed.[34] With very few exceptions, the former attempts are to be found within the Haredi (Ultra-Orthodox) thinkers. Haredim have approached the matter within the existing framework of the biblical and rabbinic traditions, which emphasize that 'If a person sees that suffering has befallen him, he should examine his actions'.[35] These have often utilized the promised punishments of Deut.28 and Lev.26, collectively known as *tokhahot* (exhortations), which as Daniel Lasker notes, 'read very much like what happened in the Holocaust [therefore] Those Jews who believe that the Holocaust was divine retributive justice argue that what befell European Jewry is a fulfillment of these biblical threats.'[36] This has presented no small challenge to more liberal Jewish thinkers, who have very often concluded that the Holocaust presented such a qualitative rupture with previous

Jewish history that it could not be subsumed within covenantal theology. To quote Richard Rubenstein:

> Traditional Jewish theology maintains that God is the ultimate, omnipotent actor in the historical drama. It has interpreted every major catastrophe in Jewish history as God's punishment of a sinful Israel. I fail to see how this position can be maintained without regarding Hitler and the SS as instruments of God's will. The agony of European Jewry cannot be likened to the testing of Job. To see any purpose in the death camps, the traditional believer is forced to regard the most demonic, antihuman explosion in all history as a meaningful expression of God's purposes. The idea is simply too obscene for me to accept.[37]

This is to say that, while the Holocaust certainly followed from the previous history of antisemitic rhetoric and violence, it magnified it to the extent that Jewish tradition had to now change, and the concept of an omnipotent God who tested and punished Israel, but ultimately cared for and protected them, was no longer viable. According to this position, a God who loved and could protect Israel would be incompatible with a tragedy of this magnitude.

In a sense then, Black Theology reflects this second stream of Jewish post-Holocaust theology, and Hebrew Israelite thought is the African American counterpart to the first. The Hebrew Israelite approach, like the Haredi, is one which takes the text at face value and extremely seriously, and in the process arguably jettisons even our *modern* common-sense notions of God, justice and love (I highlight 'modern' here because it was evidently no problem prior to the modern age for most to believe that their God could be equally loving and jealous, even if they did not predict American slavery or the Holocaust). Indeed, Katz shows that the Haredi thinkers favour in particular the subdivision of *mipneim chatateinu* (for our sins [we are punished]) which Hebrew Israelism (HI) has also increasingly adopted over the course of the twentieth century. This is only one of several ways in which we find the heightened conservatism of Black Judaism as a religious phenomenon manifested (this will explored further in Chapter 7). In accepting the punitive and contractual aspects of the Hebrew Bible alongside those of forgiveness and lovingkindness, these theologies reject 'traditional' western conceptions of God which elevate God's kindness above all else – conceptions which are arguably overwhelmingly Christian.[38] The HI thinkers appear to have operated a syllogistic method of proof: (1) We know that we have suffered. (2) The Bible says that our suffering is punishment. (3) Therefore we must have transgressed, in the way that the Bible predicts. In this argument, the fact that so many African Americans do not even recognize themselves as Israelites is taken as further proof of the depth of spiritual amnesia effected by their fall from grace.

In comparison it is worth quoting at length a passage from Moshe Avigdor Amiel, the Lithuanian-trained Chief Rabbi of Tel Aviv during the time of the Holocaust, in which he cites Deut.28 specifically with reference to the horrors of those times:

> And if your actions are so evil, then you should plead at such times as Moses, "Why have these evils come upon this nation?" [Midrash Shemot Rabbah, Parashah 5,

Siman 22]. The words "So that thou shalt be mad for the sight of thine eyes which thou shalt see" [Deuteronomy 28:34] were realized. This is the most terrible and horrifying curse. And the question is asked in every era: Why did God do so? And why this great fury? If we go a bit deeper, we will see that to a certain extent we can say: "The foolishness of man perverteth his way; and his heart fretteth against the Lord" [Proverbs 19:3]. In truth, the catastrophe (*Hurban*) did not begin in the present, when the foundation for everything is already ruined and destroyed and the entire area of our settlement in Europe is transformed into a cemetery. Rather, our catastrophe began with the movement for equal rights itself. Equal rights itself has wounded us, and in a shocking and terrible way [...] this is the mistake that the assimilationists made. They based our mission only on the diaspora. Our "final goal" was assimilation among the nations. They completely forgot how all our prophets emphasized that the mission for which we were most qualified was to fill the Land of Israel. The blessings "And in thee shall all the families of the earth be blessed" [Genesis 12:3], "And thou shalt be the father of a multitude of nations" [Genesis 17:4] related specifically to our return to the Land of Israel.[39]

Amiel here traces the sufficient cause for the Holocaust back to Jewish actions. For Amiel, just like Ben, the struggle for equal rights within a fundamentally unrighteous society was a blasphemous red herring. Assimilation was always against the divine plan: Israel should not go after the ways and gods of the nations, rather they should function as a light to the gentiles, showing them the way to holiness. The separation of Israel is thus essential. This is indeed a challenging idea: that equality and assimilation are two sides of the same coin. Both Amiel and Ammi pose the question of whether one can be granted equality in a state without being fully integrated into it; and to what extent can one truly be integrated without being assimilated? However, Amiel explicitly blames not just *Haskalah* (the Jewish enlightenment which saw an increased interest in secular European thought) but also Zionism, to the extent that both were secular movements which posited human agency above dependence on God and the ways of Torah. He is not the only one to think this – such was common currency in the Haredi sphere until quite recently, leading one rabbi to proclaim that '*only* Zionism bears the responsibility and is to blame for all the disasters ... which befell the nation during the Holocaust and afterwards'.[40] Here, suggesting a worldview where agency is the sole preserve of Israelites.

Interpreting the word 'Hebrew' according to rabbinic tradition as 'other/different', Amiel argues that the continued existence of the Jewish people in exile was only possible to the extent that they remained other, and did not try to assimilate. Evidencing a similar concern for self-shaming – that the seeking of approval and acceptance is an admission of submissiveness, the antithesis of pride – as Ben Ammi, Amiel writes that previously, 'We never asked ourselves whether or not the gentiles recognized us as a nation. We did not exist in their terms. But when we began to dream in terms of nationalistic equal rights, we also became perplexed about [our existing on our own terms]'.[41] And so the ultimate conclusion reached by Amiel is that it is Israel's own actions which have brought about the punishment threatened by God. Again, this theologian does not care for the sophistications (intending here the etymological derivation from sophistry) of academic theology which demands an ethical component to God which matches that of humans; his reading of the biblical tradition permits a God who punishes betrayal with furious anger.

To many versed in twentieth-century theologies grounded in Christianity which have prioritized love, forgiveness and mystery, these ideas will seem horrifyingly flat, even cosmically amoral. These readers are advised to recognize that despite this, there is in these vernacular responses a ground for creating strength of belief that is based not on grace, nor on a frequently invisible love, but on a motivation to achieve divine favour once again, by following the rules set out in the Bible; which is to say, to meet God's requirements rather than forcing God to meet ours. This is not a liberal theology. Daniel Lasker demonstrates poignantly the principal difficulty when he concludes his assessment of retributive justice by stating: 'A God Who caused the Holocaust may not be a proper object of love and reverence, and His actions may be inconsistent with every standard of morality with which we are familiar. That does not necessarily make the theory of divine retributive justice false, irrational, or beyond serious consideration.'[42]

If God transcends our morality, our response to that is still our own choice, and the Haredi response is one of persistence. The divine perception of what is morally acceptable does not necessarily align with the human, and to think otherwise is hubris; it may become difficult to understand how, through that, God loves us, but the attempt to know God's love through our own lenses always leads to distortion. Perhaps most importantly then, this approach removes God from the limitations of human thought, and I argue that this offers one view of a possible humanist theodicy, because what is emphasized most often in Haredi responses to the Holocaust is not God's love for us, but the necessity of human (Jewish) love for God; because, while God's love is at times not obvious, it is never right for Israel to remove their love or commitment to God. Therefore, the *primary* responsibility lies with human beings.

In a way this is a reintroduction of a response previously dismissed by Jones. The notion that suffering is an inexplicable mystery, impossible to be comprehended by finite humans, Jones argued, was not an answer but merely an epistemological postponing: the explanation has not been given and would still need to exist, simply at a higher epistemological level. This is correct, but that fact alone does not mean the reasons of God must be understandable by humans: the fact that God's understanding, and therefore justification, of the process may transcend us does not negate that justification. However, this also presents a serious challenge to humanity if we are expected to subsume our moral understanding about the limits of justifiable suffering to something we can never know. Proponents of both Black Theology and Jewish post-Holocaust Theology have rejected this approach outright, and such has become the standard of academic theodicy. But we can now see that such a rejection is not the only possibility.

A tradition from the earliest point of Israelite and Judaic religion might help us here: at times it becomes necessary for the human to petition God, even to the extent of convincing God that God is taking an immoral course of action – one that goes against God's nature.[43] Abraham performed this in his intervention concerning the righteous in Sodom (Gen.18.23-33), as did Moses in petitioning God to remember God's promises to the patriarchs and 'renounce the plan to punish your People'

(Ex.32:12-14), and Job in demanding an explanation or change or course from God. In more recent times, Kalonymus Kalman Shapira, a Hasidic Rabbi of the Warsaw Ghetto, also exercised this right. Shapira, whose sermons up until his transportation to the death camp in 1943 were hidden and preserved, sought to call God's attention to the purely destructive extent of suffering which God was allowing in the Holocaust.[44] In doing this he attempted to change God's mind via direct appeal to God's ethical nature, in a way which preserved the relationship between human and God, without in any way questioning God's reality or nature, or lessening his own commitment to God. Here, there is ground for accepting that there is a gap between the Divine and human perception of acceptable suffering, and that it is human responsibility to call out when the difference becomes palpable. In effect, the demand is that the people of Israel must find in suffering the strength to renew their commitment to God, and if suffering becomes torturous, then to call out to God that the opacity of God's love indicates a problem that can only be solved by God.

Kalonymus Shapira goes further than most, in calling for a repentance on God's part – not merely of the suffering which was heaped upon Israel during the Second World War, but a repentance which would lift them up beyond the unenviable position they held even before. This divine repentance which lifted the faithful Israel up from their centuries-long oppression can be seen to be similar to the dialectical predictions of Holly and Steward, that the Japhetic oppression of Hamitic Africana people would be followed by their ascension as the final representatives of the realization of God's Word on earth.

In the quote presented at the beginning of this section, Maimonides utilized God's own words to establish that God's face is hidden from us as a result of our own sins; and therefore the way to benefit from God's protection once again is to return to the Law (GP3:51). This has also been an important aspect of traditionalist interpretation of the Holocaust, reading it in line with the need for *teshuva* or penitent return. Orthodox Rabbi Bernard Maza explained the Holocaust in terms of the growing secular trend among Jewry in the early twentieth century, arguing that the millions of pious Jews who died with the praise of God on their lips were martyrs whose deaths have somehow led to a renewal of Jewish religiosity around the globe in decades following.[45] Stopping short of speculating about the process, or the degree to which God intervened, Maza claimed simply that a comparison of what was before and what was after led him to believe that the sacrifice was necessary to save Judaism. This too is a highly discomfiting position: accepting it requires that we abnegate our own right to moral judgement. Yet, for one who wishes to maintain the traditional concept of a God who works through history, who designs in ways that are opaque to us, yet always righteous, this appears to be not only necessary but workable. According to this interpretation, God intervenes not to stop the suffering of individuals, but to prevent an exponentially larger tragedy: the extinction of human righteousness. In order to prevent the latter, God may even judge it most worthwhile to use a method which causes the former. In our limited perspective this is incomprehensible, but perhaps we cannot know how terrible would be the outcome of a world minus the righteousness of Israel.

Punishment, then, is sometimes necessary in order to facilitate a change in behaviour. Or, to switch the emphasis, human action is consequential: it actually produces changes in our situation. How we live and whether we are righteous or not actually matters to the broader world, and cannot be simply ignored by a God who wants righteous humans.

Ben Ammi also emphasizes penitent return – this in fact is the core of his programme, believing that the Israelites have so lost their status that they no longer remember who they are. It took hundreds of years for them to realize their responsibility and the requirement to return. The 'resurrection' of Israel, the 'Salvation' that 'would come in the revival of the values and moral codes established by God Almighty' (GBMT94) is one that required, for reasons we cannot comprehend, the suffering of four hundred years to bring about – and yet, the *teshuva* now under way by means of Ben Ammi's leadership is proving it effective.

Still, we must remember that while the results are framed in the language of punishment, Ben Ammi explains well how immoral behaviour is actually a self-inflicted isolation from God-as-source-of-life; God then cannot save us without expressly going against our wishes, short of performing a sort of spiritual rape, or some logical impossibility. This is a somewhat stronger argument than that given by Randolph C Miller, who writes with regard to Process Theology and Black Theology, that 'suffering per se is not a punishment from God through the agency of men, but is the result of anti-God forces at work, which God does not stop except as men respond to His power of persuasion'.[46] In this model, the necessity of wishing to receive what God offers is paramount; it cannot be provided without active human agency to obtain.

What Ben Ammi has managed to do is to establish a covenant-based theodicy of deserved punishment and deserved liberation, while combining it effectively with a biblically sourced vitalist theology in which God, as source of life and truth, can be adhered to or rejected, via lifestyle choices which lead inexorably towards growth, health and life, or malnutrition, decay and death, respectively. This is not a theology which dwells on the long-standing and exceedingly problematic questions of God's omnipotence or human free will. Rather, Ben Ammi, a thinker not bound by the western theological tradition of the seminaries and academies, returns to the texts to take them at face value and as an inspiration for living wherein abstract logical concerns about the contradiction between finite free will and divine omniscience, etc., have far less power than do immediate concerns of forging a viable future for one's people in the midst of oppression. In removing the concerns over humanity's freedom to impose evil on others, Ben Ammi creates a remarkably consistent practical theology, embracing concepts undiscoverable within the confines of academic theology.

Ben Ammi then locates central responsibility on Israel. The western world, the Euro-gentile nations, has been God's rod of correction; but still they exerted their own agency, for their wickedness is conditioned by and informed from their pagan nature. Their cultural ungodliness has taken them away from righteousness into a heathen death-cult, and for this reason they seek to spread death around the world, most especially to the House of Israel who represent the direct manifestation/instantiation of God's Holy, life-giving Spirit, on the earth. Just as the spirit of God seeks to extinguish death and darkness, so the anti-Yah spirit seeks to extinguish light and life. In this assertion of primal opposition between the gentile nations and the people of Israel, as well as the prominent use of the Jacob-Esau typology (in the rabbinic tradition

Rome – and therefore Christendom – is understood as descended from Esau, and sometimes evoked in the literature as Amalek, Esau's grandson), Ben Ammi is firmly akin to the Haredi thinkers. We can also find a distinct similarity in the emphasis on *teshuvah* (repentance) as the correct response, returning to and strengthening righteous action as a means of changing fortunes rather than petitioning heaven to change their circumstances.

I have shown that Ben Ammi's key idea – that God will not save us from ourselves – is also a part of Orthodox Jewish thought, and it is worth considering the application of this to our current precipitous situation on a rapidly degrading planet. We need to put in the hard work to convince the Divine – which if we reject a personalist conception of God might be read as the cosmos, the reality that surrounds us – that we are worth saving, and we might add, especially at this late stage. If we are unable to convince God to change the consequences of our own actions, and yet we consistently murder, rape and pollute the earth, slaughter animals needlessly, all against God's advice, then we have dug our own grave (these specific environmental aspects will be considered in Chapter 6).[47] We have chosen not to put ourselves in line for salvation, by acting in a way that causes our own demise. This is a concept which is not of use to academic theology, but in Ben Ammi's covenantal theology it makes for a surprising yet inspiring realization: we are responsible for ourselves, and considering the state of the human world in the twenty-first century, we as a species are reaping what we have sown. In order not to suffer much worse consequences we must change our actions immediately.

Conclusion

Since the emergence of Black Theology, some commentators have suggested that the best resolution of the problems it presents would be through refining the nature of the God-concept. Jones's conclusion is that only a 'humanocentric theism' will pass the test he creates. This phrase describes a limited God, who does not act in the world, except in the capacity of helping to persuade humans to act; humans thus bear responsibility for the effects of their actions, and God alone is not responsible for what comes about. This builds some additional leeway into the biblical picture of God's omnipotence, but as Jones says, it preserves human free will and defuses the charge of divine racism. Pinn meanwhile proposes a humanist theology – one which does not depend on a personified deity at all but emphasizes the role of humans – as the best candidate.[48] I would suggest that both of these approaches could be satisfied by Ben Ammi's theology, which foregrounds human agency and responsibility, while admitting a deity as cosmic life-source, the principles of adherence to which are preserved in the Hebrew Bible.

William Jones clarified his own critique of Black Theology, writing: 'A primary reason for asking the question Is God a white racist, is to force the black theologian to consider *every* theological category in his arsenal, and in the whole biblical and Christian tradition, in terms of its support for oppression.'[49] Ben Ammi does not assume the goodness of God; he takes the biblical narrative at face value, that God both loves and hates, both rewards and punishes; but he builds in the concept of vitalism so that God is the source of all that is good, and must be adhered to in order to find benefit. This is an assertion of goodness as the basis of God's identity, without requiring the question of why evil happens – simply, when we move away from the source of goodness, we receive less of it. When Rubenstein says, 'We stand in a cold, silent, unfeeling cosmos, unaided by any powerful power beyond our own resources. What else can a Jew say about God after Auschwitz?'[50] We may perceive in Ben Ammi's resolution a similar refusal to accept the traditional Christian God-concept. God 'loves' us but only in such a way that we must behave how God wants in order to receive the love.

The essentiality of God as liberator – in Cone and Black Theology generally – is not reflected in Ben Ammi. Ben Ammi does not seek to essentialize God beyond what is in the Hebrew Bible: while Cone et al. read the Hebrew Bible through Christian thought which prioritizes God's goodness over all else, and thereby ignore or reinterpret God's anger as well as God's particular interest in Israel even after their liberation, Ammi takes these aspects as seriously as Jewish thinkers throughout history have, up to the orthodox rabbinate of the twentieth and twenty-first centuries. The Hebrew Bible does not overwhelmingly present God as merciful or forgiving, but rather as just – this is the plea made to God by Abraham and Job, who appeal to God not to forgive, but simply to act with justice. To the extent that God liberates, this is effected only through aiding the self-liberation of humans who seek liberation through cleaving to God and righteousness. Jones and Buhring, in pursuing a humanocentric theism, have both queried the assumption of essential goodness to the God concept; Ammi shows that, outside of a Christian framework, this can be replaced with an assertion of goodness (where good is identified with health, broadly defined) which is moderated by an equal justice, and which foregrounds human agency.

Even given the above, there are still problems, of course, in Ben Ammi's theodicy: in some areas it does not seem fully thought through. Setbacks against the community, for instance, have been interpreted not as correctives or punishments for their own failings, but have been seen as 'spiritual warfare' of the force of evil against the resurrection of the House of Israel. In a minor, temporarily downloadable text titled *The Restoration Village* (2008) he seems to announce this contradiction himself when, in the midst of asserting that the northern industrialized nations are responsible for the suffering of all humanity (and all sentient life on earth), he quotes his own previous text, saying, 'The truth is, blessings or curses are each the fruit (results) of the works of those upon whom they fall' (GLR; RV8). Did the rest of humanity deserve this fate at the hand of the Euro-gentiles? While it is tempting to simply blame humanity for our own plight, there are vast swathes of humanity who have had no input into the ecological crisis currently engulfing us. It is not stated, but the logic of deserved punishment can only go so far if we are also seeking global social justice.

This perhaps is indicative of an important consideration we should make of Ben's thought: he is not a trained, academic theologian. He is not trying to be intellectually or logically rigorous. Like Albert Cleage, Amiel and Kalonymus Shapiro, he is a theologian in the real world, making a practical theology which affects peoples' lives. In fact, HI is an entirely vernacular religious model: it has been developed by the laity and the important reference points, scriptural passages, symbols, etc. have all been created by unlettered, self-designated ministers outside of conventional religious and academic structures.[51]

Approaching the biblical text without recourse to philosophy or the disputes of philosophers, Ben Ammi does not engage with the 'problem of evil' as such. The Hebrew Bible describes human suffering without apology, at the hands of other humans, and of God. Even the evil actions of other humans – when they are not Israel's own – are taken to ultimately be *either* caused by God (as punishment to Israel), or due to be punished by God.

There are therefore three parallel aspects, or layers to Ben's theodicy, from which we may perceive the influence of three distinct arenas of thought. The first is the vitalist tradition which he inherited from early twentieth-century African American religious thinkers; the second is a cosmic binarism which may be informed by Elijah Muhammad's writing; and the third is a strong dependence on the Hebrew Bible. The former asserts a very humanistic motion whereby humans simply can choose to move closer to the source of life or away from it; the last is the biblical theology of God designing history and punishing humans, especially Israel, for their disobedience. Ben Ammi manages to very skilfully weave these together with the binary aspect, emphasizing those passages in the Bible that describe God as the source of life, that counterpose death and life, and encourage humans to choose life over death. In this way Ben offers a conceptually new reading of the Bible along binary/vitalist lines. The dynamic tension between these concepts, and especially the inherent uncertainty of God as a personal or impersonal force, gives Ben Ammi's theology a power of originality.[52]

What Ben doesn't do is explain away suffering as part of the greater good. It's punishment, yes, but it's God's right to punish, and the intention is (apparently) to bring humans back to a better course of action. Kenneth Seeskin writes that 'If a solution to the problem of evil means we must convince ourselves that Job's pain serves a religious purpose and is good when viewed from the long run, then, I submit, *a solution cannot and should not be found.*'[53] Yet, if the religious reader wants to take seriously the Tanakh, what can one do with Job, or with many other passages that present God acting according to values that do not match our own, or are incomprehensible to us? The answer can only be: to follow the example of Job, and engage with God, demand an explanation or change of course, *while maintaining our own adherence to righteousness.* This committal of Job to God *even when God is wrong* is ultimately recognized and rewarded by God, in the final chapter, when God commends Job as the only one who 'spoke the truth about Me' (Job 42.7-8).

In these ways, Ben Ammi's theodicy – at least in terms of Black suffering – presents an unusually deflationary response, one that finds a high degree of utility precisely because of its down-to-earth explanation. Through explaining African American history in this way, it succeeds in recognizing the suffering, and accounting for it, while not depicting Black Americans as essentially agency-less victims. Ben Ammi's narrative in fact places Blacks Americans in the fundamental role, responsible for their own fate. It also does not negate white responsibility – white society needs to change too, unquestionably so – but it does help to defuse some of the bitterness and the sense of disempowerment that can come from perceiving one's people as victims.

Some, I expect especially those from Christian theological backgrounds, but also those from liberal Jewish backgrounds, will be appalled at these concepts. They fly in the face of the overwhelming social narrative of our time, as well as the most cherished concepts of academic theology. But we should also respectfully be able to accept that many religious leaders, thinkers and lay people have no use for or interest in academic theology. Hebrew Israelites in particular approach the Bible in this way, and the punitive aspect of their theological innovations may be a key aspect of their attractiveness.[54] We should also attempt to look past a reaction of disgust at the initial appearance of such concepts, and really examine whether the red flags they raise are indicative of true danger or merely warning-by-association. The best argument for the latter is the fact that, despite all odds, Ben Ammi succeeded in taking thousands of Black men and women out of America, into (arguably) Africa, where they have established a successful, autonomous community that is respected in the nation and by the state, and has for several decades been reaching out to improve the lives, health, and relations of people in Africa, the Americas and around the globe. In the final analysis, Ben Ammi has succeeded in creating a theology which accounts for and explains Black suffering, and utilizes this suffering to imbue African Americans with a sense of agency and responsibility that has enabled the community *not only* to overcome their resentment towards white society (for this is not so difficult) but also to energize them to take on the role of changing the world, of *mending* it. In this way, Ammi also follows the path set out by post-Holocaust theologian Emil Fackenheim, centring the adherence of Israel to the covenant and their role in *tikkun olam*.

At least – at the very least – if it is not possible for academic theology to incorporate a strand of thought which is so successful, so powerfully motivating, at the vernacular level that it keeps on and on appearing, then the academy should, must, at least recognize and understand the power of this theodicy in generating passion, in creating a fervour for righteousness that retains people within religious structures, even creating new ones, because it feeds a primal human need – to be rewarded for our goodness. Because ultimately the theodicy of deserved punishment is not simply used to explain suffering and to masochistically punish ourselves and each other; it is used most often as a call towards righteousness, towards being better, towards living with more awareness and more compassion towards others. It is used to motivate people towards goodness.[55]

6

The vital self: Body, soul, spirit, world

And God said, Behold, I have given you every herb bearing seed, which is upon the face of all the earth, and every tree, in the which is the fruit of a tree yielding seed; to you it shall be for food.

(Gen.1.29)

Eating in harmony with the B'ray-sheet (Genesis) idea (the vegan diet prescribed in Genesis 1.29), is Yah's preferred mode of consumption and implies your preference for perfect health and life.

(RHS106)

Many of them that sleep in the dust of the earth shall awake, some to everlasting life, some to reproaches and everlasting abhorrence.

(Dan.12.2-3)

I call heaven and earth to witness against you this day, that I have set before thee life and death, the blessing and the curse; therefore choose life, that thou mayest live, thou and thy seed.

(Deut.30.19)

Stephen Finely has argued that the significance of physical suffering and oppression has 'required that the body become the central locus of religious meaning for African Americans'.[1] Physical wellbeing has long been a hallmark of the Nation of Islam, expressed through diet and physical discipline as well as strict dress requirements. This chapter will look at Ben Ammi's approach to the self, foregrounding the body in terms of diet, the immortal persistence of the body and the ecological concern for the natural world.

The Edenic diet

One of the most famous aspects of the African Hebrew Israelites is their dietary regulation. The community have been vegan since roughly 1971,[2] and they ran a string of vegan eateries (the first in Israel), which helped to popularize the plant-based diet.

Slightly less well-known are the metaphysical explanations of why the vegan diet is preferable for the human being, as well as the critical theological element of human immortality as the end result.

Ben Ammi explained the significance of the vegan diet at length, drawing on both biblical and scientific sources, arguing that an 'Edenic diet' of plants is best suited to human beings as they were designed by God. This notion of an 'Edenic diet' alludes to the first chapter of Genesis, wherein Adam and Eve are told, 'I give you every seed-bearing plant that is upon all the earth, and every tree that has seed-bearing fruit; they shall be yours for food' (Gen. 1.29). No mention is here made of eating animals or anything other than plants; in fact, it is not until God instructs Noah, post-flood, how he and his offspring should conduct themselves, that meat-eating is officially sanctioned. Although Ammi does not explicitly cite this passage, it is clearly in his mind when he writes that '[t]o seek and serve a Living God, a man must maintain a living body and mind, fed with the life-giving "live" foods: the fresh fruit, green vegetables and "herbs of the field" diet which God gave to original man' (GBMT44). The biblical passage is often quoted by other community members in relation to their diet.[3]

In his typical style of close analysis and unpacking of scripture in the light of external authorities which serve to justify his insights, Ammi offers further explanation of why such a diet is suited to humanity: in Genesis 1 Man (*Adam*) was taken from the earth (*Adamah*), meaning that we are constituted from the material of the soil. Ammi claims that modern science has shown that precisely the same minerals are present in the soil as are found in human bodies.[4] Therefore, in order to replenish our bodies, we need only consume the direct product of the soil: plants constitute the perfect delivery system for nutrients otherwise locked in indigestible earth. In contrast, '[t]he minerals absorbed through the consumption of animal flesh have been predigested by those animals and are [...] grossly inferior' (PI61).

Ammi consistently valorizes plant sources over animal sources as beneficial, nutritious and correct. In his logic, '[t]he blood and organs of the flesh of dead animals can only produce its counterpart [i.e., death]. The calf livers, dog cutlets, and bear paws you eat today will also be your blood, organs and thoughts of tomorrow' (GBMT45). Plants are a part of harmonious living not just nutritionally, but also because farming and harvesting them connects humans to the life cycles of the planet (EL141-44). Consuming animals, however, has the opposite effect: 'The bond between the soil, the food and the soul should not be broken by the consumption of animal flesh. If we are to ascend into the higher realms of the living/life-experience promised by Yah through His inspired prophets, we must give our mind, body and soul a healthy chance to evolve through a corresponding nutritional/dietary standard' (PI59).

Therefore:

> [Veganism is] us going back to live in harmony with the will of the creator, to move from the transient to the eternal. And I am simply saying to our people that animal consumption has nothing to do with your beginnings but it does have to do with your endings, because when you consume animal flesh you move from the eternal to the transient. So I am a vegan, I am a vegan because I am consuming from

the source of my creation, the soil from which I was taken, from that same soil I receive all of my nutrition.[5]

Ammi's rejection of animal flesh is predicated largely without reference to the lives of animals, but rather with reference to the effects of their consumption upon humans. As he expounds that 'all master teachers know that veganism once was the proper diet of humanity', he explains this and argues for it solely with reference to nutrition: even though 'steak is actually a portion of a dead animal that has begun to decay', it is because '[a]ny nutrients that may have been living in the animal begin to dissipate the longer the cut of meat sits' that this is a problem (MEW70); it is the logical consequence that consuming death leads to death which engenders the conclusion that meat should be avoided.[6]

In this, as in all his other discussions of diet, there is no mention of animals as subjects who might bear rights. Ben Ammi is not without concern for animal welfare, as evidenced when he discusses the plight of chickens wrenched from their natural cycle in order to maximize egg production, and that 'dogs, cats, birds and fish were naturally equipped by God to thrive outdoors, not indoors. Animals locked in the house and in zoos can be equated to man being imprisoned in the worst kind of dungeon or maximum security prison' (GBMT213).[7] He talks with great compassion of seals, elephants, rhinoceros, dolphins and whales killed for various human-centric purposes, as well as condemning hunting for sport (GBMT184). It is curious that he rarely relates this concern to diet; it may be that he simply thought it was obvious, although he was usually very careful to spell out the reasons and implications he perceived in order to leave the reader in no doubt about his agenda. In fact, his concern for global ecology was more often raised than his concern for the suffering of animals.[8] In part, we may explain this as Ben Ammi's concern for the system over its constituents – his anthropo-holistic outlook, with humanity at the centre, means that he is far more concerned about the extinction of species than the death of individual animals; after all, many humans are dying terrible deaths but he is concerned with the future of the human race, not of individuals; of death writ large, not martyrs. Even in his express concern for his own people, it is the Israelites (African Americans) as a people he cares about, over and above any members of that group.[9] This we might easily relate to his grounding in the Hebrew Bible which is overwhelmingly concerned with the national fate of the Israelites.

Ben Ammi did not hold that veganism alone could protect one from illness or death; it is a necessary but not sufficient criterion, and must be taken as part of a righteous lifestyle that includes other physical self-care actions as well as one's thoughts, relations and even the ideas that one imbibes. Everything in individual lives must be oriented towards God, and through this will draw sustenance from the Divine, life-giving, Truth (EL43, 132ff). The incorporation of God in order to get the full results from healthy eating is as essential as vitamin C is for absorbing iron: 'there is a bond between what you eat and the state of mind when you are eating. All of your inner organs are calibrated to respond to a certain code of consciousness. Just to be a vegan is superficial. It is the spirit of the vegan that is vital in releasing the relative response' (PI77).[10] Even eliminating meat from one's diet only to replace it with meat substitutes can be just as harmful – if one subconsciously craves flesh and experiences the substitute as it, 'you're still eating meat; it's just made of something else!' (GLR53)[11] – because the body is working *as if* it were processing meat, the harm is the same.

Health is a fundamental component of the community's message. As John Jackson notes, the 'health message is central to the community's larger cosmological and spiritual goals, but it is also somewhat detachable from those concerns. Saints consider their health mission one of the Kingdom's most important, practical, and immediate interventions.'[12] If the world cannot be saved outright, then preventing people from killing themselves is a good start. However, it is not health itself which is presented as ultimate desideratum in Ammi's theology, but rather righteousness. Ammi consistently argues that the reason for poor health is humanity's unrighteousness, because of our rebellious refusal to follow the guidelines given by God for best-practice living. We are killing ourselves and the world by engaging in practices we have been warned against.

In Ben Ammi's binary system, every action leads towards either life or death; in his opinion it is surely not by accident that a lifestyle that requires the killing of others ultimately kills oneself. Because evil is anti-life, it will always end up trying to justify death:

> In some way, fashion or form it will justify killing. If it establishes a dietary standard, it will require killing. [...] If it establishes a political system, the security component will be centered on killing. As its industry is developed, in some manner its major entities will supply devices and armaments for killing. With a mind/knowledge that cannot sustain life, there can be no comprehension for conveyance of the value of life.
>
> (GLR63)

Therefore, returning to plant-based eating will aid not only ourselves but all of creation: 'This dietary formula (biological nutrition from the soil) [...] will guide the world's inhabitants in a new direction, away from hospitals and pharmaceuticals while playing a major role in restoring the planet's ecological balance' (PI26).

These explanations given by Ben Ammi are mostly shared by the community. Yadah Baht Israel's description of their diet talks only of its role '[a]s part of their system of preventive health care',[13] and Markowitz and Avieli report that they 'have never heard a Hebrew mentioning animal suffering (or animal rights) as the reason for their veganism'.[14] In my conversations with members on this topic, some have mentioned compassion for animals among the reasons for the community's veganism, although this was always third after the prime motives of personal health and living in harmony with the world (both through non-violence and through the connection with the soil and agricultural cycles). One member claimed that the health and the ethical were 'hand in glove' and went on to say that the crucial thing was conceiving dominion as different from domination – that is, the giving of dominion to humans was a duty of care, not one of freedom to abuse. The establishment of the community's four subsequent restaurants in Tel Aviv was apparently intended to spread the idea of eating healthily and preserving one's life to Israelis, as the AHIJ's Soul Veg restaurants were spreading that message in the United States. The single notable exception to this avoidance of ethical justification may be Shaleak Ben Yehuda, who in one early interview presented the principal reason for their vegetarianism as the avoidance of taking life.[15]

If the Edenic diet is cited as the theological reason for veganism, it is clear that there were precursors to this discovery. There is the famous incident of the goat, procured for sacrifice during the second Passover in Liberia, but which rendered itself unkosher by accidentally strangling itself. It was this incident which solidified Ben Ammi's position as leader, as he provided the necessary theological explanation – that God no longer required sacrifices as *the community* were now offering themselves to God – to the distressed community. Asiel Ben Israel has said that it was only after this revelation that further study provided a scriptural basis for the community to transition. It is unclear when Ben Ammi himself stopped eating meat, but it was apparently before the journey to Liberia.[16] He would not be the only one, as at least one other member of A-Beta, Naphtali Israel, had by 1965 become vegetarian in order to meet kashrut requirements.[17] Vegetarianism seems to have gained ground in Liberia, Shaleak Ben Yehuda recounting that it was the free-range given to the community's chickens which convinced many, although not in the expected manner: 'In the beginning few of the people were devout vegetarians, and the majority ate flesh. Soon after the release of [the chickens], many were abruptly changed to vegetarians. After seeing these vultures eating snakes, rodents, lizards, spiders, etc., they swiftly converted.'[18]

The rabbinic tradition's respect for vegetarianism (although usually pushed out of the present, as an ideal state reserved for the Garden of Eden and the Messianic Age) has been discussed at length in several texts;[19] the central biblical passages are the same as those used by the AHIJ and Ben Ammi: Gen.1.29 and Is.65.25. Notably, the rabbinic tradition locates vegetarianism under an ethical rubric, taking little interest in supposed health benefits (in fact some kabbalists conversely interpret meat-eating as ethical because it offers a path for salvation of the animal's soul[20]). There is unlikely to be any direct influence from rabbinic Judaism on the thought of Ben Ammi or the AHIJ. However, there is clear influence from traditions that existed within twentieth-century Black America, including the ethical/health-based vegetarianism of Dick Gregory, the pioneering health and diet work of Alvenia Fulton, and the religious principles of Elijah Muhammad, all of which were popular in 1960s Black Chicago. Each of these certainly contributed to the concern of Ben Ammi, Shaleak Ben Yehuda, and others in the community but most potent is Muhammad's Nation of Islam, with its strict approach to diet, to clean and healthy living, and to longevity which substantially prefigures the thought of Ben Ammi. It has been shown that Black Islam and Black Judaism have some shared roots, in the preachers and groups of the early twentieth century, and the social and physiological importance of abstinence has long been a characteristic of both groups: Elijah Muhammad claims to have received the advice regarding diet from WD Fard, but even before him, Noble Drew Ali taught vegetarianism to his Islamizing followers in the Moorish Science Temple,[21] and even prior to the adoption of biblical kashrut rules by the second generation of Hebrew Israelites, drink and tobacco were demonized by many Black religious leaders including William Christian and William Crowdy.[22] A detailed argument regarding these influences has already been made elsewhere.[23]

The strongest similarity between Ammi and rabbinic Judaism occurs, again, with regard to kabbalistic thought. While Maimonides emphasized the compassionate nature of the kosher restrictions on meat, repeating the Talmud's arguments that we must always consider the feelings of animals we use for food, he maintained the unusual position that all non-kosher food, including the animal products, were prohibited because they caused illness (GP48). It was this conclusion that was adapted and transformed by kabbalists such as the thirteenth-century Spanish colleague of Rabbis Ezra and Azriel, Yaakov ben Sheshet. Specifically, ben Sheshet claimed that one who was in the presence of God (i.e. in mystical contemplation) would need neither food nor drink (or anything else), as the divine energy sustains them; however, upon returning to the normal state, the presence of non-kosher food in the body could be physically dangerous.[24]

Putting aside the issue of meat for a moment, early kabbalists saw eating in general as participating in the circulation of divine energy or *shefa*, that was discussed in Chapter 4. The kabbalists, like Ben Ammi, argued that the correct conscious framing of gastronomy was necessary to facilitate the spiritual effects. As Jonathan Brumberg-Kraus notes, this is eating as theurgy.

For Ben Ammi, the end result of all this is a vision of humanity that lives in harmony with the natural world – immortal, regenerating and with a hint – although not fleshed out – of perpetual progress.[25] Ben Ammi doesn't talk much about the future, other than suggesting its glory, so there is no way for us to provide answers for questions such as the mortality/immortality of other animals and plants; of the problems of infinite, exponential growth of the human populace over an already crowded planet (although Ben has claimed that overpopulation is a myth – following in the footsteps of Elijah Muhammad, who saw this as part of the American plot to stem the Black birth rate, along with the aggressive promotion of abortion).

Immortality: Body, soul and spirit

There is a tradition in rabbinic Judaism – subsequently developed by philosophers and kabbalists – that the human individual was composed of five parts: *nefesh, ruach, neshamah, chayah* and *yechidah*.[26] These here represent, respectively, the blood, the spirit, the breath, the eternal aspect and the divine aspect, although many of the words have broad, overlapping meanings in the Bible. While Ben Ammi does not divide the human in the same way, he consistently articulates three aspects constituting each person: mind, body and soul. These are not as we might intuitively imagine them however, because the 'soul' is in fact the internal organs of the body. This is an innovation which he does not explain, but it appears to be related to Gen.2.7, where God breathes the 'breath of life' (*nishmat chaim*) into Adam, and he becomes a 'living being/soul' (*nefesh chaim*), the same term already used of animals. Accordingly, Ben Ammi believes that the internal parts of the body which maintain the functions necessary to life are what is intended by the term *nefesh*. This demonstrates a proximity to the rabbinic tradition which associates *nefesh* with the blood because of Deut.12.23, 'the blood is the life (*nefesh*)'; in both cases, *nefesh* is interpreted as an interior physical element which animates our external bodies. It may be worth noting that it is the internal organs – from the heart downwards – which were conceived as the seat of emotion in the biblical world; even in the case of God.[27]

If the soul is the internal parts, the body then is the external form, and the mind is the conscious intellect. We will return to these in more detail soon, but first we should note that there is a further aspect to Ben Ammi's constitution of the human. This is a part that does not belong individually to us, but is the divine aspect that was breathed into Adam, and can be accessed by us all: the Holy Spirit or *ruach ha-qodesh* which is identified as the ability of humans to do right, to follow God's Law, and to approach divinity ourselves. This is effectively the same as the rabbinic *yechidah*.

Although the Spirit was breathed into our soul, it is our mind that must choose to follow what our soul knows to be right, and thereby do good. In *Everlasting Life* he explains this relationship, and suggests that the Spirit not only acts through our conscious will but also through our instincts, manifest in our soul:

> The soul is the inner organisms of the physical body of man. Its relationship to the spirit is inseparable; it was created as the dwelling place of the Holy Spirit, the manifestor [sic] and perpetuator of its existence. The soul without the Spirit of God will die/is dead. The Spirit of God is accompanied by the natural law of instinct [...] It exists infinitely within the cycles of life and is manifested by the spirit. Instinct guides and directs by Divine intellect and inclination. It protects and shields against dangers unknown or unseen. Without pre-instruction or teachers, it directs men to walk in the proper direction, eat the correct foods, and speak the right words.
>
> (EL80)

Here Ammi reads instinct as a natural implanted urge to do right; that which guides us without our even recognizing it. It is presumably present also in animals, and is what makes them *nefesh chaim*, enabling them to live as God intended. For more refined functions, those involved in keeping humans on the straight and narrow, revealed Law is necessary; and it is by following this, living the way we should, that we retain our connection with God, articulated as the Holy Spirit remaining within us. The soul is the temple in which worship/work for God occurs; this is the place where the motivation to do right, the conviction of righteousness, exists, and hence it is here that dies once that motivation is lost.

However, when 'The spirit is nourished by Divine and Holy thoughts [and] The soul is nourished by Divine and Holy diet [...] The Living Spirit (resurrected) will then resurrect the body's perfect worship of God (labouring for, toiling for, all actions for and in harmony with God's creation [...] This is the second resurrection' (EL81). This combination of spiritual and physical discipline will then precipitate a third resurrection: bodily immortality.

Immortality is one of the crucial consequences of righteousness:[28] According to Gen.3.19, death was a punishment imposed upon Adam and Eve, one not originally intended and not necessary for humanity; according to Ammi, once humanity returns to righteous obedience to God, then the punishment will be lifted. Then, the curse of death will disappear as our bodies begin to function as they were intended, perpetually regenerating themselves without decay. Veganism is a necessary (though not sufficient) component: The fact that the vegan diet is one that causes no (or at least, minimal) harm to other living creatures is not separable from the fact that it also causes no harm to us: This is the way that the holistically designed world we live in works, and the diffusion of negative effects is a necessary part of the entry of unrighteousness into this world: Our actions would never affect only ourselves.

Ben Ammi's doctrine of immortality and how it will be achieved is set out most explicitly in his fourth text, 1994's *Everlasting Life*, and returned to in 2010's *Physical Immortality* (his penultimate text). Eternal life should not be conceived as something belonging to the realm of 'medical, scientific or technological' achievement; rather it belongs to the realm of Truth, where Truth inculcates righteousness (recalling Ben's specific pneumatic use of this term, discussed in Chapter 2). It cannot be achieved by any other means: 'To enjoy these benefits you will have to be born again into this world of truth' (EL2). The present world, by contrast, is untrue and will be shattered by the coming revelation of Truth; it is in the thrall of 'an anti-life mentality which has been/is being disseminated by the anti-life force on this earth'. A force so imbedded in society it is within our own minds and 'has succeeded in processing the lie into your cells, tissues and organs'. Mortality is not only *untrue* but is obviously unrighteous: 'To think that [God] would create a man to live a short lifetime, during the course of which he is to worry each day about dying (consciously or unconsciously), is a gross misconception. The founder of such an obviously evil lie or concept has to be the devil' (EL44).

Everything around us now convinces us that sickness and death are normal parts of life, meaning that we anticipate and prepare for them, forming a self-fulfilling prophecy. We lead lives that invite death: 'Without access to life's central guiding light (the Holy Spirit) you become incoherent, unable to perform with the logical consistency required of a "living soul". This loss of cohesiveness causes you to decompose and vanish back into the dust' (RHS42). When Ben talks of incoherence here, he means our actions which contradict life. Only those which promote life, and are therefore righteous/True, are compatible with continuing to live; anything else goes against the grain and imposes cumulative damage on the organism, both through leading us towards actions that directly harm us, and through constricting our access to the spiritual lifeforce. The poison that leads to this is not just what we eat; it is also the ideas, concepts and philosophies that we imbibe from society which poison us and prevent our *entire* organism from functioning as it should.

To achieve immortality, these anti-life thoughts must be replaced by life-giving thoughts, those that the community is trying to spread throughout the world. In addition to ingesting wholesome and nourishing food, spiritual Truth must be absorbed through the ears, by hearing and understanding words of righteousness, God's Word. Then, 'The ingestion of Truth will effect a chemical change in the living cells through which energy is provided for vital processes and activities, and spiritually invigorated material will be assimilated to repair and restore normalcy to organ function that was disrupted by the ingestion of lies' (RJPJ108). God's presence within us, the Holy Spirit manifested by us through righteous actions and thoughts, will heal and protect us from all dangers: 'It is the very presence of God in our daily affairs which assures your God-identity and thereby protects your living soul (physical organism)' (RHS42). Immortality is necessarily linked with the absorption of God's Truth, and therefore the embodying and manifesting of the Holy Spirit.

Critical to this process is a return to nature, to the cycles, laws and ways that were built into the natural world, our God-given sustaining environment: 'Man's life [...] is similar to that of all God's creatures and creations. The criterion for becoming eligible to receive everlasting life is the same – remain within the universal cycles of righteousness' (EL3). It is through returning to the natural processes that we can begin to eliminate the negativity in the beliefs, emotions and patterns of thought that slowly kill us.

While one who indulges in such behaviours as drinking and smoking is leading their body towards malfunction, one who does not but is atheist will still ultimately become ill because of their subliminal rejection of the Living God. There is a very subtle implication here that faith in God is how our spirit should work, and we will malfunction without that; indeed, the equation God=Truth=Life requires that we believe in Life and Truth and abide by them in order to not disintegrate. Therefore, 'Good health is the result of a righteous lifestyle within a suitable environment' (EL4).[29]

These arguments lead to another expression of anti-individualism:

[W]e must broaden our scope of our struggle against the anti-life force and confront it from an international/universal aspect. The forces of err continuously instill the subtle impression that each person should be personally satisfied with setting his/herself in order, as if we are a disconnected, individualistic self-contained entity.

(EL4)

It is only when we work together, loving and respecting each other, that we will stop spreading and stop receiving from others these negative energies.

It is apparent that Ben Ammi prioritizes a holistic conception of the self. For him, although the self is divisible into three parts, these parts must be seen as an inseparable whole. What holds these three elements together is the Holy Spirit, which is 'the catalyst and bonding force between them that causes them to synergize (combine their efforts) to sustain life' (PI20). Ben Ammi's defining of the human as the unity of mind (spirit), body (external) and soul (internal organs) is very similar to the common rabbinic tradition, which posits the human as the unity of two elements, body and soul.[30]

While God's Intellect is at times stated as that divine part that was breathed into Adam (in contrast to the above passages which emphasize the soul as the seat of Law), the individual consciousness is never conceived as the be-all end-all of the individual; often it seems to be principally the *mediator* which transmits the righteous way-of-life into the physical body and allows the person *in toto* to go on doing its stuff in the world; Ammi is clear that all three aspects are a necessary united whole (when enlivened by the Holy Spirit): 'If we are to achieve immortality we must begin to see our mind, body and soul as an absolute eternal whole. Truth (the Holy Spirit) is the catalyst and bonding force between them that causes them to synergize (combine their efforts) to sustain life' (PI20).

It is the mind which, by guiding our actions according to the Spirit which inhabits our soul, facilitates God becoming manifest in the world; and it is God's presence in the world and in the human that can revivify us: 'Yah reveal[ed] Himself on earth through Adam, who after receiving the breath (spirit) of Yah became a living soul. The life in his physical body was made dependent upon the active mind (spirit) of Yah guiding him in all of his endeavors' (IL87). The breath God breathed into Adam's soul were the instructions and sense which Adam used to live right, and it is only through living right (according to the Spirit) that we continue to be a Living Soul. To return to our previous terminology, this is the power of Truth as an energy that heals and 'enlivens and sustains the human body and all of its functions'. It is Truth that sustains the Adamic image of God, because 'Truth is a creative energy; lies are destructive energy, constituting a harmful influence on mind and behavior' (RJPJn).

This healing will spread out to the rest of the world, drawing all people towards it, because Good and Evil cannot coexist: 'application of the Holy Spirit would, by its nature (power), restrict all negative occurrences, situations and effects. Thereafter, the subordinate body, soul and environment would reciprocate, manifesting a heaven on earth' (RJPJ8). It is implied here that even accidental deaths will be prevented by the beneficence of the Holy Spirit.[31]

Thus, 'Redemption is holistic' (RJPJ67): We must utilize our minds to refine our actions according to the pull towards God that we feel in our soul. Once we do this, the eco-system will begin to heal; it will provide us with higher quality food to nourish our soul and body, which will enable us to greater manifest the Holy Spirit within us, further sanctifying and nourishing the world.

This stage, obviously, has not yet been reached; even Ben Ammi did not achieve physical immortality. A decade before his death, he perceived that immortality was still an ideal to be reached in the future, one we must strive towards:

> In a coming season of our elevated consciousness, this will result in our ingestion once again of the Genesis 'whole' minerals, and we shall become the observable testimonies of the effects of a true, holistic diet. Thereafter, we shall soon find ourselves capable of extending our life spans beyond what is conceivable in scientific circles.
>
> (RJPJ115)

The twin poles of strict concentration on this-world to the exclusion of discussion of any afterlife, and a belief in (potential/future) immortality have both been seen in previous generations of African American religion. The most obvious may be in the Nation of Islam, which promised vastly extended lifespans as a result of correct dietary discipline, while denying any afterlife. Even in the realm of Hebrew Israelite groups, William Roberson's Ever Live, Never Die society of 1920s New York preached immortality based on acceptance of him as Christ, the Messiah; and the Commandment Keepers held 'Everlasting Life' as the seventh of twelve key principles, based on a number of biblical passages (the health dangers of non-Kosher food were likely related to this).[32]

Jewish views on life and death have covered all possible concepts, although the rabbinic tradition is that the body and soul will be reunited in the Messianic Age at the

Resurrection. From here, physical life for the righteous will be eternal. A concept of immortality can possibly be traced back to the Tanakh, Aron Segal noting 'intimations of immortality' in Dan.12.2 (the resurrected will have 'everlasting life'), Is.25.8 (God will 'destroy death forever'), Ps.125.1 (the faithful will 'endure forever').[33] Even more appealing in terms of Ben Ammi's system is Prov.12.28, 'In the way of righteousness is life, And in the pathway thereof there is no death.' However, the consensus of scholars is that the Hebrew Bible has no doctrine of persistence after death.

The kabbalists however present a doctrine somewhat similar to Ben Ammi's. The thirteenth-century R Ezra of Gerona taught that as a result of performing the *mitzvot* the soul, once separated from the body, is destined to be drawn upwards into the light of (the second highest sefirah) Chokhmah.[34] Whereas this happens after death for Ezra, for Ben it happens immediately during life, and is more of a descending of the Divine than ascent of the human.

Ezra's contemporary R Azriel taught that performance of commandments was a means of drawing down the Divine energy of the Shekhina, and there is an early midrash which teaches that observance of the commandments precipitates blessing from the Angel of Life, while the Angel of Death brings judgement upon those who do not.[35] According to Ezra, the performance of *mitzvot* actually strengthens/brings divine energy onto the individual in the present, rather than simply lifting the soul after death; a notion very much in line with Ben Ammi. Seidenberg notes that in Cordovero's kabbalah, sin (transgressing the Commandments) can cause the soul to deteriorate and even depart from the body, leaving it dead: 'serious sins can impinge first on the lower soul, and then even on the upper soul, which is "in the secret of *tselem*", forcing both of them down and out of a person's body, to be cut off in Gehinom [Hell]'.[36]

We can also find a resonance, perhaps, with the fourteenth-century French Jewish philosopher Levi Ben Gershon (Gersonides), who held a Platonic concept of personal immortality via alignment with truth: because we, as intellectual beings, are constituted by what we know, when we know *truths* then that part of us will last beyond our physical death.[37] Ben Ammi is not as propositional in his understanding of truth, but there is a similarity in his concept of Truth as the connector to God and immortality. Nonetheless, the objection made by Gersonides's Spanish contemporary Hasdai Crescas is similar to one that Ben might make: that life is not about intellectual contemplation but devotion to God, and this is how the afterlife must be spent. Crescas' own orthodox perspective on immortality falls neatly into line with Ben Ammi's: he argues that devotion to God and the Commandments are the critical requirements for attaining 'life in the world to come'.[38]

This perhaps indicates a central divergence between Ben Ammi and much medieval Jewish thought: that, to the extent Ben Ammi believes in a 'divine science', it is not understanding God that is crucial but loving and living by God's rules; thus aligning one's will rather than one's intellect with God's. The eternal afterlife of contemplation of God/union with God is in many ways a self-ish goal, one which indeed imagines the self without any social relations; Ben Ammi imagines a future of harmony with other people, working to manifest the will of God on earth, and so is more in line with the early rabbinic concept of bodily resurrection.

What of those who, prior to the attaining of immortality, have died? Ben Ammi did not deny that the self continues after death, only that a heavenly afterlife was part of the scriptures. He simply claimed we cannot know what happens next. The community do not use the term 'death', preferring the word 'transition'. This could be an ontological transition, from a conscious self into a 'spirit' which is merely an invocable set of behaviours, or a personality-type that can be imbued onto a person but does not have its own independent animating force. On the other hand, it may be the conscious mind of the individual, simply disembodied. Physical immortality is thus not the only kind; even when a body dies, the spirit may stay alive. There are a few passages where he hints at this, relating eternal life to the cyclical process of tree and fruit, whereby a perpetual continuity is achieved. Explaining that the Hebrew word *chaim* (life) is plural in form, he concludes, 'For those that believe in God, there seems to be a gift of God that sanctifies them even as they depart from the detection of the carnal eye' (EL94). The fact that they only depart *carnal detection* suggests that they are still in some way present. He later confirms this when he states, 'that which giveth life does not get buried in the graveyard. The flesh that is buried is not the determinant that the individual is dead' (EL98). However, this is only the case for the righteous: 'All men of God that become spirit are like the wind; they lose image, shape and form.' Thus, 'There are those that we know that have been made eternal spirits.' He specifically includes David, Enoch, Elijah and Yeshua in this category (EL99).[39] The spirits, of course, do not inhabit another world or plane of existence: just like God, they dwell invisibly in *this* world. If we are to ask what Ben means by the idea of a spirit, we find little explanation, other than comparison to the wind. Whatever the case, these spirits can be called upon, for their assistance in times of need: 'These Holy Spirits can be activated according to the Will of God by men in God's service through prayer, meditation, abstention and the need to carry out His instructions' (EL109). There also seems to be provision for reincarnation, where the spirit moves to inhabit a new body, either newborn 'or already in existence' (EL45) – a suggestion which evokes the possibility of spiritual possession.

None of this is true for those who let their spiritual connection with God die even while their body struggles on; they will simply cease. Spirits which are outright evil, however, will persist in a different way: They will 'justly inherit an unrighteous state of existence; reaping continuously all of the ramifications of the evil they have sown. The hell which such a spirit creates shall in turn be its perpetual habitation' (EL45).[40]

This doctrine of a persistent spirit seems a little confused; in the first place, it is entirely detached from the Hebrew Bible, wherein there is no grounds therein for a spiritual essence which is separable from the body (indeed, most of the passages cited in this regard are from the New Testament).[41] Second, it does not sit well with Ben Ammi's overwhelmingly embodied approach, and third it appears only in a few passages where it is not completely consistent. It may be that Ben inherited the concept of a post-partum spirit from his teachers, without having a clearly defined idea of its nature. The presence and honouring of spirits is of course a part of many African religions that may have survived the Middle Passage.

After this discussion of diet and the immortal body, it is worth noting that Ben Ammi clearly rejects what Anthony Pinn calls 'the troubled relationship to human flesh', of Black Theology.[42] Theology generally is not a discipline which has a historically warm relationship with the body; it has too often been seen as the temporary housing of the more important soul (at best; at worst it was a prison). At least, that is true of Christian theology; rabbinic Judaism has always been a religion *of* the body, one which emphasizes the spatio-temporal nature of human life, which is weaved into a fabric of rituals to be performed manually, at specific times, with specific motions, and of course specific words.[43] This tradition is one carried over from the Hebrew Bible but it finds particular emphasis in rabbinic Judaism, in which the body and soul complement each other rather than tussle with each other. For Ben Ammi, as the rabbis, the human is something for which the body is crucial, and whose bodily needs and pleasures should neither be indulged excessively nor chastised or ignored.

Ben thus offers a way out of the frequent disregard for the body, by connecting religion once again with performance: commandments bind human beings to time, space and place, necessitating that we consider carefully what we put into our bodies, how we clothe and present our bodies, and how we relate to others via our bodies. He centres the person in the body and in action, rather than in abstract thought. This affirms the *embodied self* as the core part of African American theology that Pinn has argued for, in contrast to the postmodern Death of God-led disappearance of the self which has been emphasized by some contemporary white theologians. Ben carefully and fundamentally places the subject in charge of itself, able to exercise the executive faculty and make decisions; the right decision is to align with God's will, anything else will lead to decay. There are many non-god forces which pull us away from the correct path, but we must use our will to come back to it. We must overrule our other desires by exercising self-mastery.

However, what Ben Ammi does not offer is a specific consideration of black physicality, of what *black* embodiment means, and here we must recognize that in all of his work there is no ontological distinction made between Blacks, whites or any other races; ultimately all are human and all have the same presence in the world, all have the same requirements of righteousness (even if they are more firm for the Chosen). In this, he is decisively different to Elijah Muhammad, who pitted white against Black as part of white nature, while Ammi views at most white skin as a regrettable consequence of sin, although intermingling of the bloodlines occurred very soon after the Flood. This unified ontology is due in part to his particular approach to theodicy, which actively negates the traditional interrogation of blackness as a problem within the white world, as this would require the double-consciousness of incorporating white perception. Ben Ammi has no intention of doing this; rather, he explains why blackness is not a problem, but in fact the solution: African Americans must go free, 'come out of her [America]' and take their position as world leaders, thereby destroying the (false) white perspective entirely.

Some of the unusual characteristics of Ben Ammi's psychology can likely be traced back to one specific Hebrew Israelite text, Clark Jenkins's *The Black Hebrews* (1969). This book was published in Detroit but came into the possession of Shaleak Ben Yehuda, who recommended it to John Henrik Clark as highly esteemed.[44] The influence upon Ben Ammi's concept of the God-mind is apparent when Jenkins argues via exegesis of several passages acquiring the mind that was present in Jesus is a desideratum, attained through obedience to scripture.[45]

Ecology

Not just the individual human body but the planetary environment too is subject to the effects of human lifestyles. Ecology was a concern that Ben Ammi returned to with increasing urgency as the extent of the environmental crisis became apparent. For him, the destruction of the habitat that we and other inhabitants of earth require was another manifestation of the Euro-gentile death fixation – one especially obvious in the popular Christian focus on death and afterlife. This lack of concern for the present has brought us to the point of global destruction: 'Man, through deceptive education, has been given the impression that the earth is not his ultimate dwelling place. Therefore, he is complacent in watching all things around him being destroyed' (MEW136). The AHIJ's environmental concern has only grown since Ammi's death. In recent conversation with the author, Sar Ahmadiel Ben Yehuda stated that 'We have to understand that our existence on this planet is ultimately at stake here … and the superficial racial issue is a distraction from our collectively addressing that reality.'[46]

The world, for Ben Ammi, is not ours to use and do with as we please. The dominion given to humans is a unique and specially defined relationship with the world – one of stewardship and responsibility.[47] The planet was intimately designed prior to the creation of humans, and humans were created from it; it was subsequently gifted to us by God, as a sustaining home, which would help us regenerate ourselves forever, but it is not our property: 'the "earth" (all of God's Holy Creation) was not made for man, but man was made for the earth. For at his coming it was already in existence. He neither consented to nor advised in its creation' (GBMT47). This means that it has value in itself; Ben Ammi doesn't believe we should interfere with nature or disrupt natural ecosystems unless it is necessary, and he is particularly concerned with natural cycles – whether these be of the seasons, plant and animal life, or the human body.[48]

It is past time for humanity to realize that we must adapt ourselves to the planet, not bend the planet to meet our needs: 'It is not man's task to impose order upon the Creation, but to maintain, reflect and harmonize with this Divine order [that God built into it]' (GBMT43). Therefore, we must consider everything and prioritize the ethical nature of every component in our societies: 'In our quest for our true God, everything in our societies must be ethical and righteous. We must have ethical education, ethical music, ethical eating habits, ethical politics, ethical clothing, economics, etc. We must keep God living in the midst of us' (GBMT43).

Ben Ammi's concern for the suicidal nature of our ecological destruction sometimes prompts a Gaia-like hypothesis which restates again the mechanical nature of the forces at play. Here, it is not God who will punish humanity but nature who will defend itself against us: 'To continuously destroy the balance of the eco-system while simultaneously subjugating nature for the sake of profit or material greed, leads all of mankind down the path of self-destruction. Because nature's ultimate resilience has but one recourse, and that is to preserve itself' (MEW7). In a later minor text, he states this idea in a way that recalls his apocalyptic predictions:

The planet – as evidenced by the unprecedented occurrences of earthquakes, floods, hurricanes and other phenomenon – has utterly rejected contemporary man's position. Actually, the great majority of ecological crises threatening the continent and the globe, stem from the same underlying cause: the undisciplined, Euro-American contemporary society which is guilty of polluting and wantonly destroying the planet's eco-systems.

(RV5)[49]

This reciprocal process, of humans maltreating the environment, which causes the environment to maltreat humans, is true too of conventional agriculture which requires destabilizing the soil with chemicals which travel back into our bodies: 'This abusive treatment of the soil is done under the guise of increasing the yield while, truthfully, it is destroying the "whole" mineral content and killing the spirit of the produce' (RJPJ114). In a critical and oft-repeated motif, Ammi explains that the relationship between the Hebrew *adam* (Man) and *adamah* (soil) 'reveals the direct synergy between man and the soil' (RJPJ114).[50]

It is because, 'the organisms of the human body are an inextricable part of the soil and subsequently, respond appropriately only to whole minerals found in the soil [...] that our organs are renewable: the soil used in their creation can also be used in their regeneration' (RJPJ61). Not only do we come from the soil and depend on it for our sustenance, sharing its nature and chemical composition, the basis of human life must be agricultural; it is through agriculture that we integrate ourselves into the supporting web of natural seasons and cycles. Yet, while human evil has succeeded in pulling nature off-course, the solution also begins with us: restoring the *bereshit* idea in the mind of man will 'cause it to be restored in the soil' (RJPJ108). So, as we regenerate our minds, we will renew the soil which will renew our soul (inner organs) and our bodies will become immortal. The connection spreads to our lifestyle as well, because 'Perhaps shelling peas, snapping beans, picking greens and shucking com are spiritually important acts with benefits far beyond essential nutrition' (EL141). Here Ben Ammi suggests that a return to past lifestyle where the whole community are involved in agriculture will deepen our sense of ourselves as fundamentally living through a harmony with the earth and its natural cycles. At another point he suggests that the wondrous site of a field of vegetables growing can offer unexpected psychological benefits: the experience 'will provide essential God knowledge for your mind even before it provides the nourishment for your soul. Maybe one day soon, through the grace of God you will realize that plants are an inextricable part of the authentic life designed for all who honor and give reverence to God' (EL144).[51]

Ecology functions as a practical gauge of righteousness: because of the interconnectedness of the world we inhabit, the earth's response to our actions can confirm their validity: 'Everything created in the righteous order of God Almighty is recycled into the earth ... The perfect gauge to measure the righteousness of man's creations is simply the earth's acceptance or rejection of that organism. Evil creations – poisonous gases, synthetic materials, radioactive particles, plastic etc. – are not readily recycled' (GBMT182).

The model that Ben Ammi takes for ecological life in the Messianic Age is that of a traditional African village – everything that can be locally sourced must be, so that each community lives in harmony with its own environment. Using this idea, he inverts western stereotypes about Africa: 'We should not see Africa as being under-developed, but as being miraculously preserved by God to become the center for producing sound leadership of the human family, providing the light for a new, ecologically-sound social order' (RV4).[52]

Many of these concepts are easily discoverable in the Tanakh, and most of them are reflected in rabbinic Judaism too.[53] As Arthur Waskow explains, the cycles of shabbat, sabbatical year and jubilee impart a temporal system whereby the individual, the society and the natural world are given periods in which they rest, resume their equilibrium and can approach the next active phase refreshed.[54] The Bible, and rabbinic Judaism, is inherently temporal and while the present world is bookended by the Edenic and Messianic Ages, the reality we inhabit is cyclical and repetitive, imbedding us into a world that we are required to sustain. The emphasis on 'divine cycles' is thus no innovation of Ben Ammi, but simply an acceptance of the Hebrew Bible's system.

Ben Ammi's agricultural emphasis is also clearly predicted in the Bible, which emphasizes in many places the superiority of agriculture over hunter-gatherer lifestyles, most potently in the archetypal conflicts between Cain (hunter) and Abel (farmer), and Esau (hunter) and Jacob (farmer).

The Bible is likewise clear that land is never the property of humans: we are only tenants of God's, and therefore we have responsibility to the land itself.[55] Although individual gain is tolerated in the short term, the possibility for generational gains to accumulate into a deeply stratified society is removed, principally through the implementation of shabbat and jubilee years, which constitute ecological and social reset-points. This is reflected in the rabbinic doctrine of *bal tashchit*, 'do not destroy': based upon the biblical injunction against destroying fruit-bearing trees during wartime (Deut.20.19-20), the rabbis argued that one should never destroy or wastefully use natural resources. This has been interpreted as providing rabbinic grounding for ecological concern in the modern day.[56]

Mari Joerstad has argued that the Hebrew Bible contains an inherent ground for environmental ethics, because of the – almost animist – way it personifies parts of the natural world: trees, the sun, the wind, all engage with God and humanity and relate to them as if they are persons. In one intriguing passage that is perhaps related to this animist perception, Ben Ammi informs us that the Garden of Eden was populated with talking trees:

> These Edenic trees represented those whose attributes were placed in the service of God at the creation of Adam. We could say that they were angels of paradise. After close perusal of the message of Genesis, we ascertain that we are not to visualize these 'trees' as having trunks and branches of wood and leaves. We must envisage trees with tongues for talking and knowledge for consumption. This is evident from the wrathful response of God to the strange behavior of Adam and Eve upon His return to the garden. 'Who told you that you were naked ...' (or with whom have you been conversing)? These trees were to provide all of the required assistance to Adam's intuitive understanding to perfectly fulfill the will of God.
>
> (EL164)[57]

Even this tradition has a rabbinic precursor: the eight- to ninth-century midrash, Avot de Rabbi Natan describes the serpent demonstrating the harmlessness of the Tree by shaking it until its fruit fell to the ground; to which the text adds, 'But there are those who say it did not touch the tree at all; for when the tree saw the serpent coming it shrieked, "Evil One! Evil One! Do not touch me!" As it is said, "May the foot of pride not approach me, nor the hand of the wicked drive me out"' (Ps.36.12).

What may be missing in the Hebrew Bible and the rabbinic tradition is Ben Ammi's closeness to pantheistic ideas. These are expressed in his adoption of Gaia-like emphasis in his later texts, and more generally in his intimate integration of God into the human being as sanctifier of the natural world. Some kabbalistic texts come close to this kind of emphasis, as shown by Elliot Wolfson. Wolfson has written on the kabbalistic interest in the natural world as a mirror and expression of divinity, concluding that the Zohar in particular conceives the created world as reflecting the Divine in order that the two are conjoined and God's omnipresence spreads over both; in some texts, the world as manifestation of God approaches pantheism. Here, there is 'a continuous ontological chain that not only leads back to the Infinite but guarantees that the spirit/breath/light of the Infinite permeates through every aspect of the universe'.[58]

However, the kabbalists were not filled with adoration for nature, viewing it largely as something to be overcome; for them it was little more than a glass through which we might perceive the Divine. Despite this it should be clear that the kabbalists and especially the Zohar connect with Ben Ammi in how they construct nature as *itself* divine, shot through with a concealed divinity, rather than being merely an animate environment for our satisfaction. Ariel Mayse writes that the 'classical Jewish mystical sources ... assert the centrality of humanity while upsetting hubris and underscoring our fundamental, even pre-ontological, obligation to ensure the flourishing of the nonhuman world'.[59] Suggestively, Mayse locates several passages wherein the stemming of the divine flow caused by human evil is represented via images of ecological collapse.

***

It is the first few chapters of Genesis, the how and why of which we were created, which particularly fascinate Ben Ammi, indicating that it is the nature of humanity that is his core interest. He wants to take us back to the original design, to return to the Genesis idea, because he thinks that is where we went wrong. On the one hand this indicates a belief that in the twentieth to twenty-first centuries we are doing the task of being human incorrectly; we have got something about our nature essentiality wrong, having distanced ourselves from divinity and from the godly concepts and ways of being. But also it demonstrates a general dissatisfaction with humanity, that our deviance has been from the very beginning; and that we can undo this and reclaim a missed utopian opportunity only by erasing our history of mistakes and beginning again. This is a true utopianism, then; Ben Ammi wants to collapse the entirety of recorded human history into *an error*: that was the time of the fall, but now we are entering the time of the ascent. While Adam and Eve's previous mistake introduced the spirit of err into human life, Ben Ammi can now show us the way to eliminate that erroneous spirit.

What is truly interesting about Ben's messianic utopianism, however, is that this is not imagined as a static, perfect life. Instead, the future of the Messianic Age is one of ever more, increasing growth and vitality: human beings would first extend their lifespans and soon would become immortal. In addition, he hints that the capacities of human beings would likewise extend and grow beyond anything we can now imagine, as we first reclaim and then transcend the miraculous capabilities of Moses and other Israelites. He does not try to describe the possibilities, although some community members have shared with me their expectations (or hopes), of the increased potency of human will and a growing harmony/community with other animals. The miraculous achievements of the Israelites may represent some of the abilities we will acquire, but Ben was clear that we have no way of knowing the full possibilities before us in the future.

In this way, the entirety of recorded human history is elided/concatenated as a cosmic false start; the Messianic Age is the true natural successor to creation, when we were intended to live on in the garden of Eden. This fascination with Eden and the nature/consequences of the first humans' disobedience is not common in rabbinic Judaism, although it has been dwelt upon by some thinkers, more usually of the mystical tradition.

Ben doesn't use the Catholic term 'original sin' for Adam and Eve's disobedience – it was unlikely to be used in the Black Baptist Church he and most other members grew up in, which was of the Protestant tradition – but the concept of Adam's primordial sin is still very present in all forms of Christian biblical interpretation. What is also different, missing in Ben, is an idea of an ontological change: there is not really an inherited flaw which took supernatural means to ameliorate; in fact it was the power of the evil spirit which had concealed the divine spirit necessary for correct interpretation of the Torah. Only when this was broken by the appearance of Yah's anointed, Ben Ammi, could humans really understand Torah and find their way back to God.

The power to define: Words, ideas, names and scripture

What you say (the words you speak) carry the effect and force of a powerful machine. Words are interpreted as having spirit: they thusly convey life ... positively or negatively. You must understand, as we move along the course charted by the prophets of God, that certain words create or destroy. Some words make you laugh, others make you cry; some words give you strength, others weaken. The adversary of God has a problem with the African, African American using terms like "Savior," "Lord," Messiah," and "Kingdom of God." He is aware that all things begin with a word. You can use a term so often until it will inspire and invoke a similar spirit.

(GLR39)

The Euro-gentiles have used the "Power to Define" to halt the process of conscious human development. The Euro-gentile, anti-Yah civilization proceeded to blot out Truth, to define darkness as light ... paganism as worship of Yah, a faith without works ... and our captivity as our freedom.

(IL161)

And God said, Let there be light: and there was light.

(Gen.1.3)

Words have an inherent power: as a means of communication they express concepts and locate them within certain contexts. The way we use words can make new things seem possible, or impossible; they can change the way we feel about our existing reality. Studies have shown that simply seeing or hearing certain words can influence the way we interpret data that follows. As such they should be used carefully, and wisely. A century after philosophy's 'linguistic turn' these ideas have become something like truisms. Ben Ammi understood well the power of words, and the essentiality of using words in the right way as part of influencing thought, and the reality that thought creates. This chapter will look at various aspects of Ben Ammi's thinking concerning language, including his approach to Hebrew language and scripture.

The power to define

In a speech in London, in July 1967, Stokely Carmichael cited a famous passage from Lewis Carroll's *Alice in Wonderland*:

> "When I use a word," Humpty Dumpty said in a rather scornful tone, "I mean just what I choose it to mean, neither more nor less." "The question is," said Alice, "whether you can make words mean so many different things." "The question is," said Humpty Dumpty, "who is to be master." That is all.

He commented,

> And I think Lewis Carroll is right: those who can define are the masters. White Western society has been able to define, and that's why she has been the master. The white youth of my generation in the West today starts off with subconscious racism because he accepts the writings of the West, which have either destroyed, distorted, lied about history. He starts off with a basic assumption of superiority that he doesn't even recognize. The people of the Third World are going to have to stop accepting the definitions imposed upon them by the West.[1]

Huey P Newton likewise stated in 1970 that Blacks must,

> no longer define the omnipotent administrator as "the Man" ... or the authority as 'the MAN'. Matter of fact the omnipotent administrator along with his security agents are less than a man because WE define them as pigs! I think that this is a revolutionary thing in itself. That's political power. That's power itself. Matter of fact what is power other than the ability to define phenomenon and then make it act in a desired manner? When black people start defining things and making it act in a desired manner, then we call this Black Power![2]

Here, two leading proponents of Black Power articulate that there is a deep power in being able to determine what words and concepts mean. The social capital to do this is what we call authority.

Following a very similar line of reasoning, Ben Ammi argued that not only was language a critical tool of oppression or liberation, but that the 'Power to Define' was now passing into African Hebrew Israelite hands, having been in the possession of Euro-gentiles for two millennia. This, for Ben Ammi, was a key element of the spiritual warfare currently ongoing as satan attempted to retain control over people's hearts and minds.

Anyone spending time with the community will be familiar with the phrase, the 'Power to Define'; it is repeated regularly as part of their agenda and also their right. Now that the Kingdom of Yah has been established, they are 'seizing the Power to Define' in their approach to the world and their reality. One classic example of this is their confident insistence that Israel is not part of the Middle East or Asia, but is Northeast Africa. This simple example – nothing more than a redrawing of continental dividers on a world map – for them signifies an important recognition: that the Hebrew Bible talks constantly of Africa, its people and civilizations, while Europe languished in underdevelopment for millennia. Europe is barely mentioned in the Tanakh, becoming a presence in the New Testament only because of Rome's brutal imperial rule. Attempts to reframe the Bible as not a product of western civilization, but one of ancient Africa, abounded throughout the twentieth century, alongside early attempts to recognize that the Israelites were not white in the modern sense, but dark-skinned.[3] The European who often presumes their centrality to world history then appears as something of a latecomer, emerging only in the last 2500 years or thereabouts (and in the case of Anglo-Saxons much later). And yet the European claims the invention even of what they decisively appropriated: Christianity, a religion based upon the teachings of an anti-Imperial Judean from the country next door to Egypt.

The Power to Define is a functional term, meaning that it is not a Divinely ordained right of the Israelites, but simply describes the position of authority which confers the *ability* to impose one's meanings upon discourse. The Power to Define means inscribing one's own narratives and one's own perspectives into culture in a way that these are no longer questioned even by those who would not naturally share those perspectives. The authority to do this has finally, after many centuries, slipped from Euro-gentile hands. Now, 'We who have freed ourselves from the Euro-gentile's power to define, define for ourselves, speak for ourselves and name ourselves and thereby control our destiny. History has proven that that which is relevant to white America is evil unto the Sons of God' (GBMT56).

Clearly witnessable for Ben Ammi is the failure of the protest movement in America, which did not succeed in liberating his people. This was because, 'our enemies monopolized and manipulated our struggle and determined those results they deemed desirable for us' (GBMT60). Just as the adversary had defined salvation in a way that led *away* from the people's redemption, so the adversary managed to define the goals of the protestors as merely achieving material gains and economic parity with whites, rather than finding the truth that worked for them. So, they got legal rights, 'tokens that would symbolize freedom' instead of true freedom (which would be spiritual) (GBMT65); they got integration into America instead of recognition of who they were. This then achieved the incredible feat of making the Euro-gentile system their saviour rather than their enemy. So, while the situation of Black Americans may *appear* to have got better, it is actually worse than ever, because they have simply progressed further into the conceptual world of the Euro-gentile. Now, they are even blind to the fact they are oppressed.

The deception of the adversary has manipulated Black Americans into the Euro-gentile outlook even to the extent of them favouring those conditions which harm them: 'The devil has deceived the people of God by using the Power to Define. He has caused you to look upon your curse as a blessing, your ignorance as intelligence, and your death as life' (GBMT242). Thereby, 'You have made the destiny of your enemy your destiny also' (GBMT243). For Ben Ammi, it is demolishing hospitals rather than building them which should be a sign of progress, as this indicates the growing health of the population.

The simple fact, which many now perceive, is that America has been built by and for white supremacy. Educational institutions inculcate the natural superiority of white values and the inferiority of African values. Therefore, every presumption must be challenged: 'We must question every facet of existence under Euro-gentile domination. All things must be brought to the Sons of God as they were brought to Adam, for naming and renaming' (GBMT61). As he poignantly states later, oppression is a given in America, but it is most humiliating when one is oppressed even while trying to integrate into the society that oppresses:

> If people of African descent are to be persecuted by the Euro-gentiles, then Abba let us not be persecuted trying to get an education in his school system, nor trying to be accepted in his societies. But rather let us be persecuted, with his batons and police dogs placed upon us (as they were during the civil rights protests of the 1960's), in search of Heaven, and trying to acquire the wealth of God.
>
> (GBMT79)

The principled 'equality' of America is something which comes in for particular criticism from Ammi: as well as an example of a definition which works for some but not all, the concept of equality at the point of birth is one example of the beautiful things *said* by Euro-gentiles which conceal the hideous things they do. Ammi remarks that men are not *created* equal but must be *made* equal by righteous systems (GBMT72). There are all kinds of differences built into individuals, but it is the responsibility of *society* to ensure that these differences do not confer an exponential advantage to anyone. The present order actively works against this: 'the present order is not conducive for the creation of family stability, harmony, mutual trust, love, dedication, good health, and certainly not peace of mind, body, society, neighbourhood or home [...] this world's order is not ideal for perpetuating these principles, virtues or effects' (GBMT59).

Among this talk of particular perspectives, we must remember that the perspective Ben Ammi seeks to centralize is not intended to be theirs alone, but rather God's. Centralizing God and righteousness will not be of benefit merely to those already righteous, but will make the world better for everyone, aligning us all with Truth: 'Let it be clear that we have taken the Power to Define into our own hands and the results will be freedom for all men' (GBMT68).

As will be discussed in the next chapter, part of Ben Ammi's redefining is the nature of the Good and the Good Life; while the west has taken individual liberty as an unsurmountable ideal, Ben remarks simply that this is not necessarily the case. Not only the people in a larger sense are connected, the individual having little value without their family or community, also all of humanity is part of the natural world which exists on planet earth. If any part of this richly interdependent world begins to harm more than help the whole, there is no future for any of it.

There is something more going on than this of course, as the ability of the Israelites to seize the Power to Define is produced by the shifting of the eras. In Ben Ammi's metaphysics, the AHIJ's activation of prophecy, releasing again the Word of God, is causing the friction which destroys the untrue values of the Euro-gentile world:

> The return of the Children of Israel and the subsequent establishing of the Kingdom of God signalled the end of Euro-gentile dominion over God's creation

and people. [...] The Word of God and the entire planetary force have combined forces to bring about instability, hostility, anxiety and fear in all countries of the world. The Word of God is the major destabilizer, bringing all evil doctrine into judgement.

(GBMT56)

The Kingdom indicates the shifting era, and now the opening of scripture is bringing the evil elements to destruction. The 'Universal Corrective Force' is behind the manifold challenges – environmental, etc. – to the Euro-gentile world, as the Kingdom is becoming established and the Age of Deception coming to an end (GBMT57).

We can find parallels in Black Power's sense of autonomy and refusal to accept the existing order; its recognition that gaining equality within society was not true freedom if that society was structured according to the needs, perspectives and wishes of their historical oppressors. Following the passage quoted at the start of this section, Carmichael went on to contrast the media's framing of Black protests against their treatment in the United States as 'violent', in contrast to centuries of colonial expansion and destructive plundering which were not considered as such. The many brutal conquests, injustices and cultural vandalisms committed by the west have been defined as the heroic bringing of 'civilization' to barbarians, but they are better understood as destroyers of earlier, more peaceful and usually more egalitarian civilizations.[4] These conversations have become increasingly recognized in the half century since Carmichael's speech, especially in recent years when the removal of statues and names of historically important individuals who engaged in and profited from highly unethical practices has been discussed and implemented as a means of challenging the common narrative around such figures. The frame of what is ethical and what is acceptable is indeed in the process of changing. This represents the 'revolutionary' element of Ben Ammi's 'revolutionary conservatism': he is committed to overturning and replacing the present order.

The Hebrew Language

[T]hese [Ben Ammi's] writings in their entirety encompass Hebrew thought. Since culture lives by language my objective is to convey meanings from the Hebrew mind, not the Greek or Latin. Language also transmits instructions that have been long forgotten that can assist us in finding our way back. Language subsequently is not only crucial for reading, writing and speaking, but also for thinking and understanding.

(RJPJ6)

Hebrew and its reclamation were very important for Ben Ammi and the community from its inception. Learning, becoming fluent, and not just speaking but living in Hebrew was viewed as a necessary part of reclaiming the spirituality and heritage of Israel. Some early members of the community, once fluent, refused to speak anything but Hebrew, and while some adult arrivals have not yet achieved mastery the large majority are functionally bilingual, the children learning Hebrew and English as first languages. Much communication, even internally, still happens in English due to the presence of more recent members (and guests) from the United States who have not fully mastered Hebrew. However, this is changing as, now, the third and fourth generation of adults mature into positions of power.

Ben Ammi was fluent in Hebrew, often addressing officials and other residents in the native tongue. This Hebrew is the modern *Ivrit* that is spoken in Israel, and the community make little distinction between that and Biblical Hebrew; Ben Ammi does not hold with the alternative reconstruction of Hebrew developed by One West's Abba Bivens, known as *Lashawan Qadash*.[5]

He mentioned frequently the importance of thinking in Hebrew, claiming that the language provides a different sense of ontology, metaphysics and value than English – as would be expected, the holy tongue has special qualities. This is no different than longstanding Jewish tradition which elevates Hebrew above all other languages as the language through which God created, and the only tongue that angels understand. According to generations of kabbalists, Hebrew can provide insight into the ontological structure of objects, people and actions, displaying their essential nature and relationships to each other. Ben Ammi expresses a similar notion of the special qualities of the Hebrew language when he writes, 'Although my writings are in English, the thought is in Hebrew because they are written according to the understanding revealed in the original Hebrew text' (GBMT82).

Ben Ammi discussed often the significance of God's Word, although this is not the Christianized *logos* but the Hebrew *davar*: 'The Word will be a doctrine, a living doctrine so it will give life. The Word will have life within itself, and when you hear it and follow its instructions, you will pass from death into life' (GBMT92). Ammi emphasizes the importance of *hearing* rather than *reading* the word, picking up on a strange irony in Jewish culture: despite the overwhelming centrality of the written text, the Torah, the Word of God is something that must be heard, not seen (crucially, this is so in Ezekiel's vision of the dry bone which must *hear* the Word in order to be resurrected). Aural reception is supremely important *within* the Torah, even though the Torah has become the medium for transmitting that message. Prophets usually receive God's Word aurally, and even when God delivers scrolls to his elect these are bizarrely not read but *eaten*. Of course, the Torah is written to be read out-loud by the religious leaders, rather than consumed silently through the eyes.

Ben Ammi often analyses Hebrew words, showing their connections to other words and offering interpretations based on their structure. Already mentioned is his exposition of *avad* as equating work and worship, and the deep meaning he draws from this, as well as the unavoidable relationship between *adam* (human) and *adamah* (earth), whereby 'The Hebrew language reveals the direct synergy between man and the soil' (RJPJ114). Other examples peppered through his texts include an extensive explication of *amen* (faith) and its various verb, noun and adjective constructions which demonstrate the relationship of faith with training, education and society.

As he often offers analysis of Hebrew words to explicate a deeper meaning than a simple translation can provide, he sometimes provides improved translations of

specific biblical passages. However, it is in these that we can see the cracks in his
Hebrew knowledge. For instance when discussing Exod.20.12, 'Honor your father and
your mother, so that you may live long in the land the LORD your God is giving you'
(GLR65), he reads *yarkhon* as being a transitive verb, mistaking it for saying effectively
'they, your parents, will stretch your days' where it actually means 'your days will
stretch'. The transitive would require an '*et*' (the untranslatable word indicating a verb's
object), and would also likely be plural – i.e. *yarkhru* (as it is more sensible to read the
singular form as indicating 'days', meaning the remaining lifespan of a person rather
than their parents).

And while he enjoyed displaying his knowledge of Hebrew to the reader, weaving
a story of meaning around one word or verbal root, it is not uncommon to find Ben
Ammi advancing interpretations which are difficult to uphold in the Hebrew. It is
clear that Ben Ammi did not typically read the Bible in Hebrew: He was, despite often
criticizing its failings and its status as a product of the Euro-gentile world, enamoured
of the King James translation, as are many Hebrew Israelites. This can be confidently
stated because he misinterprets the 'standard' of Is.62.10's phrase 'lift up standards for
the people' as being standard of living, so that 'The coming of the Kingdom of Yah
sets in motion the initiating of new standards from Jerusalem' (RJPJ111). The Hebrew
nes in fact means banner or flag; only in the KJV's English is it translated with the
homograph 'standard'.

The AHIJ share with many of their Africana contemporaries a fascination with the
creative manipulation of language. Words are reformulated, spelt in new ways, given
new etymologies, in order both to highlight the colonial-oppressive past of certain
concepts, and to present a new, liberatory meaning of others. This can be seen in their
rebranding of their diet as a 'live-it', raw food as 'live food', and (related) the Dead
Sea as the Live Sea. Rastafarians are famed for such linguistic creativity,[6] and Susan
Palmer has described such practices forming an integral part of the preaching style
of the eclectic Afrocentric/Islamic/Hebrew group known as both Ansaaru Allah and
Nuwaubian Nation.[7] Such may even be witnessed in Elijah Muhammad's coining of
the portmanteau 'tricknology' to describe the subtle influence of Christianity upon
Black consciousness. Perhaps this creative reconfiguring of language should be seen
via Fred Moten's claim that all black performance is improvisation: the desire to
create connections which demonstrate an immediately felt significance, one with an
explicatory power far greater than historical etymological accuracy.[8]

Scripture

The Bible from Genesis to Malachi is a recorded history of Africa and Africans,
Black men and women in transition after their fall from God's graces.

(MEWix-x)[9]

What is the primary source of life-sustaining information? It is the Bible from
Genesis to Malachi. The secondary source is Matthew to Revelation.

(MEW104)

As the above quotation shows, Ben is clear that the Hebrew Bible is not just a religious text, but a historical one. The Bible tells the story of the people who would become African Americans. The Bible is more than this, of course: it forms a guide to life, the exoteric text which must be mined for its secrets.

That there are 'secrets' to the Bible is common Jewish tradition, but what Ammi means here is that the common translations of the Bible have obscured the original meaning which can only be brought out by African Hebrew scholars. The last 2000 years of the Dominion of Deception have been a time of concealment, when scripture became opaque and the true mention was inaccessible to people. The Tanakh forms something of a portal whereby Truth can re-enter the world; for two millennia they have been lying dormant, awaiting one who could open them again: 'The Hebrew scriptures or Biblical verses written in Hebrew carry with them a living spirit whenever they are significant or true (not distorted). They come alive and meet whoever is of Truth and confuse those who are not of Truth' (MEW77-8).

In his introduction to *Revival of the Holy Spirit*, Sar Ahmadiel writes:

> The 'rise' of Europe meant the rise of an accompanying Eurocentric theology. Various concepts which they acquired upon our fall were reinterpreted in a manner complementary to their mythical roots. Though familiar to the Greco-Roman, Anglo-Saxon or Celtic mind, these newly formed conceptualizations couldn't help but 'miss the mark' in relating to the original African Hebrew idea or thought.
>
> (RHS9)

The Euro-gentile interpretation of the Bible is wrong – Hebrews need to return to the text and read it free of pagan concepts to hear what it actually says (GBMT107). Ben Ammi has done this and provided the key to correct interpretation.

The KJV was always Ben's favoured translation, and his favoured Bible was the Scofield Reference Bible. It is the Hebrew Bible which is Ben Ammi's focus, but he quotes frequently from the New Testament, especially the Gospels and Revelation. While the Hebrew Bible is unequivocally a text with divine origins, recording the words of the inspired prophets sent by God, the New Testament is more problematic. This is a human text, one whose authors simply tried their best to record what they saw, but were often led astray by their Hellenic preconceptions. Explaining the community's approach to the New Testament, he suggested that there was often, though not always, a resolution to discrepancies but if one could not be found the Hebrew canon must be prioritized: 'If the words [of the NT] conflict with or appear to contradict the words of the Prophets, seek clarification and explanation. If that is not possible, then hold fast to the words of the inspired prophets of God' (EL123). The same might be said of other Judean writings: the apocrypha are cited on occasion, as are the Dead Sea Scrolls.

Despite his ambivalence about the New Testament, it has indisputably informed and conditioned Ammi's theology from its inception. This is most clear in his reading of satan as *God's* arch-adversary. This is fundamentally a New Testament reading, not a biblical one: it emerged at the end of the Second Temple Period along with the hosts of angels which are present in the apocalyptic and pseudepigraphic literature of that time; these texts, the Dead Sea Scrolls and the New Testament all came very much from the same worldview, but it is one that is difficult to find in the Tanakh, which contains only two explicit references to satan (Job1-2; Zech.3), the former of which has him as a figure within the heavenly hierarchy, who interacts, works with but also challenges God.

As has been noted, Ammi is suspicious of Paul and quotes sparingly from his letters. It is only in one of his last texts, *Revival of the Holy Spirit,* that Ben Ammi introduces the idea of a deception *within* the gospels. Describing the Greek concept of *logos* as an imposter designed to simulate and replace the Hebrew *ruach,* he claims that the scribes hereby smuggled a pagan concept into the theology. In this reading, even the gospels are no longer trustworthy, their authors 'Hellenists'. He explains: 'By way of the *logos,* the Hellenists showcase their intellectual power and skilfully cause you to transfer your allegiance to another while withdrawing your affections from the Holy One of Israel' (RHS58).[10] These writers 'skilfully w[ove] into the fabric of the NT writings only certain aspects of the life and dynamic ministry of Yeshua,' (RHS62) which if correctly understood would demonstrate the absolute consistency of his teachings with the Mosaic Law. All of this was to separate from the Hebrew teachings and from the God of the Bible. Similarly to the rabbis, he links Christianity with the emergence of the Septuagint as the first stage in devaluation and integration of Greek concepts into Hebrew scripture. This 'caused a significant devaluation and distortion of the contents of the Hebrew canon … transplanting the Greek character into the core of the plan of salvation' (RHS62). It was from this beginning that the essentially pagan Greek concepts of Grace, *logos* and Original Sin entered.

This revision to his previous teachings represents a significant shift: while he had previously spoken of the deceptive creation of Christianity, he had not challenged the authenticity of the Gospels.

Referring to the early Christian dependence on the Septuagint over the earlier Hebrew versions of the biblical texts, as well as to the Greek composition of the New Testament documents, he suggests that this actively defuses their sacred power, and allows for the manipulation of the concepts:

> The sentiments, feelings and ideas of Christian culture have been conveyed primarily by the Greek language and thought, not the Hebrew. Without key mistranslations of the Hebrew writings into Greek there would have been no misunderstanding or scriptural support from the text of the Hebrew canon, hence no Christian culture.
>
> (RJPJ205)

However, as with his occasional misuse of Hebrew, he sometimes seems confused about the writing of the New Testament – or at least, to hold an unlikely belief about its history. After offering his own translation of Ps.97.7 – 'Confused be those who worship [work for, labor for] graven images [vain materialism] and praise themselves of their idols [materialistic gods]. Bow down to him all gods.' – he applies the same ideas to the Gospel of Matthew as if it were written in Hebrew. But Matthew was written in Greek, and it is unlikely that the intent behind the Greek would have been the same as in the Hebrew, when most Jews did not speak Hebrew as a daily language by then

(GBMT115). At another point he presumes that Jesus spoke in Hebrew, rather than the contemporary Judean *lingua franca* of Aramaic (EL12).

Revelation seems to be the one book of the New Testament which Ammi views as completely trustworthy – the epistles are unsound, and the gospels are open to a small degree of doubt regarding the authors' Hellenized misconceptions.

This concept of scriptural deception is similar, although not identical, to that found in Elijah Muhammad. Muhammad claimed that 'from the first day that the white race received the Divine Scripture they started tampering with its truth to make it to suit themselves and blind the black man'.[11] this was a two-stage process, where the Jews 'altered' their Bible and the Christians 'poisoned' the gospel.[12] While Ammi shares the concern about Christian manipulations, he is unable to argue that the Tanakh was altered for two reasons: first, he disagrees with Muhammad's typification of the receivers of the Tanakh as white and therefore negative – the Israelites were and are essentially righteous people; secondly, where Muhammad is able to hold the Tanakh in suspicion because it strengthens his argument for dependence on the Qur'an, Ammi requires the truth of the Tanakh for the basis of his faith. Therefore, Ben Ammi makes a more subtle claim: that the *meaning* of the Bible was manipulated, its spiritual truth entering a period of occultation wherein correct interpretation became impossible. Ben Ammi supports this by the use of Dan.12.4, which claims that the book will be sealed until the eschatological period.

Names

When the names of the master were instilled into the minds of the slave, his life-style took on the spirit of the master. All his habits mimicked his oppressor's.

(GBMT145)

The changing of name, or adoption of a second one for religious purposes, has been a part of African American religion since Noble Drew Ali instructed his followers to replace their surnames with 'Moorish' ones such as El and Bey. Continued in both the Nation of Islam and almost all Black Jewish/Hebrew Israelite congregations, this renaming represents both the removal of the western names imposed by enslavers, and also a return to (allegedly) authentic identity; it is pursued even outside of these circles, Albert Cleage and Stokeley Carmichael respectively taking the African names Jaramogi Abebe Agyeman and Kwame Ture. Renaming in general has a powerful significance that can represent taking on a new role, a new identity, even being born again as a new person.[13] However, an aspect that has not been mentioned by scholars is that all Jews who live in the diaspora also have an alternative, Hebraic name, for religious purposes, something which serves to align this practice particularly with Judaism. While the first generation of Hebrew Israelites do not appear to have taken Hebrew names, this trend emerged in Harlem in the 1920s, Howard Brotz noting that several Black Rabbis took Jewish names.[14]

These attempts to rename and reject the terminology imposed on them by slavemasters have persisted, visible in the popular disavowal of the term Negro, replaced by Colored, Black, Ethiopian, Afro-American or African American, reflecting the appeal to terms such as Moor, Muslim, Israelite or Ethiopian by religious groups. As Weisenfeld notes, these latter constituted a rejection of the white capacity to define and impose racial categories;[15] but for Ben Ammi, the ongoing series of new terms seemed to be symptomatic of the confused searching for lost identity which can only be satisfied by embracing the truth of Israelite identity.

Ben notes that even in the Bible, Daniel is renamed when captured, suggesting that this is a timeworn procedure based on the power of names: 'Gentiles have used this procedure in grooming slaves for thousands of years and have not changed' (GBMT147). Applying European names to Africans has been one way of inculcating them with European ideals and outlooks – part of the process of distancing them from their true identity and from God. The American Black today 'is only African in body', his spirit and mind having been changed, reformed in the satanic European image (GBMT156).

Names are important not just culturally; they also have a spiritual import: they connect the individual to their family and nation, and also to God, as is evident in the many theophoric names of the Bible: 'The changing of one's name directly leads to the praise and worship of another deity. The Black world is not conscious of the far-reaching consequences of Euro-American names because Blacks have been taught to believe that whatever Europeans give them is acceptable' (GBMT148). For this reason, 'The slave owners took caution not to give names of any positive spiritual prowess or significance' (GBMT139). Because of this 'genocide of the mind', African Americans feel no allegiance to African nations or to their religious heritage: 'The plan was to totally destroy your African heritage and former African mentality. Everything that was inherent to the African slave was uprooted, and replaced with a foreign culture and nature' (GBMT159).

The same manipulative agenda is present in several areas already discussed: the renaming of Yeshua, the days of the week named after Roman gods, etc. Here, we return to the importance of holding the Power to Define: for Ben Ammi, only once African Americans were capable of determining their own names according to Hebrew principles, would they truly be free of western Eurocentric dominance. Now, members of the community are named with Hebrew names (while original members took biblical names, subsequent generations have been given neological Hebrew first names, the surname following the pattern of Baht or Ben Israel, Shaleak, Yehuda, etc.

8

Revolutionary conservatism: Social theory, human life and gender

There is no parallel between the state of deviancy of contemporary society and the sins of our fathers only a generation ago. If you recall, the trends defined as normal during your childhood and those of the present day are worlds apart.

(EL177)

It is an irony that has been not infrequently noted, that the Black forms of Judaism known as Hebrew Israelite are markedly more conservative than precisely those versions of American Judaism which are most willing to accept them as Jews. Reform Jewish congregations, being the most liberal of the major denominations, have been accommodating of non-traditional modes of claiming Jewish identity where Orthodox and Conservative congregations have defined the matter simply in terms of *halakhah*: the Talmud requires birth from a Jewish mother or conversion, and without proof of either of these, no one of any background is accepted as Jewish. The Reform movement has generally seen *halakhah* as an evolving body of doctrine, not all precepts of which are applicable to the present day. Because of this, they have accepted patrilineal descent as equal to matrilineal, they were the first to permit female, queer and transgender rabbis, and likewise have been more willing to accept the Jewishness of individuals who believe themselves Jewish without any documentation, such as Hebrew Israelites. However, the latter often find themselves dismayed by the relaxed observance of Reform congregations, as well as their willingness to accept into the rabbinate those other identities which *halakhah* excludes.

This is the case generally in America as well as for African groups who have followed a self-directed path towards Judaism. One of the issues may be that Reform Judaism is one which could correctly be categorized as American in form and nature, ergo it expresses a kind of American value system. In the contemporary period the values and priorities of the Reform school are almost entirely progressive and left wing, whereas arguably one of the principal motivating factors behind the African American[1] interest in Hebrew religion is a return to a more authentic, tradition-centred and *less* westernized way of life: one which demands more than Christianity, in terms of behaviour (*halakhah*) as well as identity. The issues involved are complex and not in tune with academic discourse on the matter, especially in a time when liberation is perceived as a one-size-fits-all drive to complete individual freedom. For the Hebrew Israelite movement, it may be tempting to think that the individualism that drives the liberal project of personal freedom is something essentially western, European and, perhaps, gentile.

This chapter will address the social conservatism of Ben Ammi's thought, in terms of individualism-communalism, tradition and nationalism, and gender/sexuality. But it will also highlight that Ben Ammi evokes a complex doctrine, because while he advocates in many ways a return to older 'traditional' social forms, he advocates this in a revolutionary manner: the current society must be uprooted and destroyed completely. As he writes, 'the system *itself* is our curse' (GLR33).

Ben Ammi was clear that the present world must be overturned. In discussing the current age he cites often the time of Noah and the flood, suggesting that contemporary society is irredeemably corrupt and must be washed away, to be replaced in its entirety by a fresh creation according with God's will. Ben expresses a revolutionary spirit when he argues that everything in the present order must be challenged and overthrown: 'As we start the journey back, we will find our people clothed with ungodly lifestyles, symbols and perverted Euro-gentile wisdom. There has to be an undressing piece by piece until we arrive in Genesis naked (innocent) and pristine before God, that He may redress us in Holiness' (GBMT31). The interrogation of modern society must be total: it is

> an infrastructure clandestinely designed to maintain Black subordination whereby the leaders could forever rely upon it to uphold the injustices of bigotry and racism [...] The religious system, the educational system, the economic system, the political system and the social system are all active parts of a racist system of government.
>
> (GBMT163).

The replacement, likewise, will be a total system: Ammi's project is one of totally transforming the outlook of a culture, of refining value because the things that we're taught to value are not the valuable things. Thus, '[i]n our quest for our true God, everything in our societies must be ethical and righteous. We must have ethical education, ethical music, ethical eating habits, ethical politics, ethical clothing, economics, etc. we must keep God living in the midst of us' (GBMT43).

On the other hand, in case there is any doubt that Ben Ammi is fundamentally a conservative, it is instructive to compare Ben Ammi's points of concern with those of another American-Israeli conservative – Yoram Hazony – who cites, 'God and Scripture, nation and congregation, marriage and family, man and woman, honor and loyalty, the sabbath and the sacred', as among 'the most important ideas and institutions around which life in Britain and America had been built'.[2] That Hazony is entirely supportive of the endeavour of America and western society in general, and cites exactly those elements which make up Ben Ammi's putative revolutionary desiderata as the foundation of these societies is an irony whose implication – that there is a deep conflict in Ben Ammi's thought – will be addressed below. However, we note Wilson Moses' recognition that messianism has always been 'politically revolutionary but culturally reactionary'.[3]

First however a moment should be taken to address the different approach taken here to that of earlier chapters. In previously discussing some positions of Ben Ammi, most notably his stance on theodicy, I have argued for the value of his taking the Bible seriously, without trying to force it to fit into an existing modern sense of decency.

In this chapter, especially with regard to gender, it may appear that I am arguing the opposite, indeed that I am criticizing Ben Ammi precisely for his subsuming of contemporary concepts of gender equality and the deconstruction of gender norms, under those depicted in scripture. The reason is that my principal concern is not the defence of the Hebrew Bible, but the explication of Ben Ammi's thought, with a view to placing it in the context of Black Theology, and demonstrating that it deserves to be taken seriously for its contributions to the discussion. Therefore, I have sought to demonstrate that Ammi's theodicy succeeds in developing from scripture a working and successful theodicy; however now, I will argue that Ammi's own approach to gender not only simplifies the evidence of scripture in service of a reactionary cultural agenda, but also incorporates a lot of tertiary prejudices and presumptions into that agenda, which make it neither biblical nor, arguably, workable in the long-term; and even the lived practice of the AHIJ is not as clear-cut as it may seem from Ammi's work. Previous chapters argued for the taking of the Bible seriously as a theological source; the benefits of doing this, and of allowing for a more fully rounded God-concept including the faculties of divine anger and punishment, might serve to help us resolve the problem of evil in a new and more balanced way. However, the Hebrew Bible does present a biased picture of human nature, such that it should match specific cultural practices far removed from modern-day culture. Those practices now require rethinking, whereas it is the transcendental God of classical theology which I, and Ben Ammi, have argued requires removal.

Individualism

Ben is resolutely critical of the liberalism which presents individuals as the basic unit of society, and which permits them to act in ways he considers obviously evil. He argues that the liberal democratic idea, that ideology which founds itself upon personal freedom, actually forms a kind of prison, because within it human beings are liberated from not just any coercion but from any responsibility. It is very difficult to *resume* taking the burden of responsibility with all the limitations on our freedom that requires. Yet, society is better and everyone is healthier and happier when we understand that we are not isolated individuals but a holistic network where each person's actions affect everyone else. Therefore:

> You must focus on the vital eco-systems that exist between Yah, His creation and the families of the earth and realize that individualism poses a major threat to your existence on this planet. The reckless promotion of individual rights and 'free choice' can, and has been used to justify anything and every behavior.
>
> (RJPJp)

In fact, '[t]he ultimate satanic sin is to allow you the "freedom" to do the things that are known (to the "God Mind") as destructive and wrong' (RJPJ87). Humans now 'are under the hypnotic effects of a world called "freedom"', which is actually 'liberal undisciplined godlessness' (GLR53-4). It is this 'purposeless freedom' that 'is the problem. Man needs urgent restraints placed upon his destructive habits of freedom. [...] for true freedom begins with discipline' (MEW136-7). The idea of liberalism that Ben promotes here is one of a soft and flabby, uncontrolled submission to all base appetites without the necessary refiner of self-discipline. Certainly, the discipline necessary to not follow every impulse is an important part of maturity and of self-realization. The gains found by the development of such self-control by converts to strict lifestyles, such as those of the Nation of Islam or Hebrew Israelite groups can be considered as engendering a new kind of freedom: the freedom from one's own urges. Similar to Elijah Muhammad's rejection of overeating and sport spectatorship, Ben Ammi opposes any sign of decadence: 'The healthy desires for pleasure and inspirational public performance will provide the basis for life-supporting creativity instead of the insidious, frivolous and destructive entertainment which now has the world out of balance' (RV8).

The pull away from American liberalism and an enforcing of strict behavioural norms has been seen as one of the primary attractors of the NOI. The adoption of rigid personal discipline by individuals used to unstructured freedom and unsure how to harness and direct one's energies can have a powerful effect, creating a new understanding of one's capabilities and the possibility of utilizing this discipline in other realms of one's life. The sense of existing as part of a community, and connecting with the cosmos or deity, is what motivates ritual generally, and is evidenced not only within religion (although this is what many consider its natural home). Cultural conservatism replicates this by creating a sense of connecting with our ancestors and contemporaries, of following in their footsteps, living by values they would recognize, and performing the same daily, weekly or yearly rites that ordered their lives.

This is certainly the case for Ben Ammi who, like Albert Cleage, perceives the urge to individual freedom as bound up with the pagan nature of Europe.[4] Ben Ammi goes slightly further, in claiming that these pagan freedoms are increasingly emphasized within twentieth-century America as part of the mechanism/agenda of preventing African Americans from returning to their God and righteousness. In this case, the freedom to wear clothing which would contravene previous generations' moral code, to engage in sexual practices frowned on by the conservative moral majority, and the freedom to choose who and how we worship are understood as a concerted effort to deconstruct the innate sense of morality and sense of 'how things should be' within the community.

There is here an important sense that the individual is not the primary unit of society; men and women do not live their lives alone and their choices, whatever they are, always impact others because they take place within an organic society. This is to say that, while the dream of liberalism may seem beautiful, once it becomes realized, the atomization of society into autonomous individuals who feel no responsibility towards each other is extremely dangerous. This was also the background realization of Black Power: the Civil Rights movement attained individual rights which had been lacking under Jim Crow legislation, but it very quickly became clear that individuality could only offer so much to a minority such as Black Americans – there was also a need to achieve communal power, and maintain communal integrity. The sense of self that group belonging bestows and the support that such a group can offer to individuals are important especially for minority communities, from which it may be difficult to completely enter the mainstream of society.

There is, however, more than simply this to Ben's argument. He makes a very acute point when he writes, 'man today has been imprisoned by the forces of evil that make up his environment and determine his every thought. Unknown to you, your entire life has been subtly predestined for you though you may subconsciously be led to feel that you are freely selecting and determining for yourself.' This analysis of how free will is so easily manipulated by the society around us, by its subtle presentation of the options available to us in order to point us towards one in particular is very important in any discussion of freedom. Liberty is compromised if others are free to manipulate us and take advantage of our weaknesses. In this case our freedom becomes something that others can use for their own advantage. In the current era we are aware of Google, YouTube and Facebook algorithms which subtly manipulate our actions while never *forcing* us to do anything; they simply manipulate our desires and our natures. Ben makes the case that much of liberal democratic social norms are the same: they are not the free choices of individuals, but are being manipulated by some concealed force which doesn't have the interests of people at heart.

He provides an example, where the 'Euro-gentile' system tells us that speed kills, sells us a car designed to break the speed limit and then issues speeding tickets for using that capacity (MEW138). For Ben Ammi, this contradiction is intolerable, and while he is incorrect that there is a single system responsible (rather many systems working alongside and within each other with different purposes), for him the fact that these contradictions emerge indicates the flawed nature of the current social order. The fact that we well know the best limit for safe driving and yet still allow cars that go much faster to be produced suggests that the system doesn't care at all about human lives. The same is true of (Ben Ammi's favourite subject of attack) the tobacco industry – viewed by him as simply a slow means of suicide, working in direct opposition to the health services. This flaw epitomizes the biblical quote he uses often, that 'If a house is divided against itself it cannot stand' (Mk.3.25).

One of the sad realizations that the twentieth century forced upon us is just how easily humans can be led into evil – many psychological studies since the Second World War, which initially sought to understand how members of society could commit such atrocities to their fellows and neighbours, have shown how generally this is true. If Ben Ammi argues that musicians (demonstrating his era, he highlights LL Cool J and Madonna) influence their listeners, and make certain behaviours seem acceptable or even attractive, he is surely not wrong – we might question whether sexuality should be more or less free, but in terms of the question whether we are influenced by our environment there is no debate. We absorb very easily the mores and attitudes of our immediate environment, and our ethical sense is no less malleable than our tastes in food and music. Ammi's quick pivot into the fast-food industry and how it actively promotes foods which are unhealthy is poignant especially in terms of the Black community, where such commercial interests have often aggressively attached themselves to neighbourhoods already blighted by poverty. Here too, arguments supporting liberty seem to protect the liberty of businesses at the expense of individuals – businesses which are driven only by their loyalty to shareholders who demand ever more profit regardless of the effects of the business's practice upon human beings or the environment. Indeed, where is the freedom when only the unhealthiest products are advertised or promoted? The amount of work required to find a healthy alternative makes it a much less likely choice; in this case, freedom, again, seems to be provided to business to a greater degree than to people.

The idea that Ben returns to repeatedly is that people should be free *in God*; they should not be free to do wrong. If the rulers are ruled by God, and intent on ruling in accordance with righteousness, then it is their responsibility to prevent people from doing wrong, and not abdicate their right to judge others' preferences.[5] It goes without saying that this outlook flies in the face of modern western values, which emphasize personal freedom over almost everything; this is a sacred right in liberal democracy, although it is one being challenged more rigorously in the present moment (not least because in practice the extreme form – libertarianism – often aptly demonstrates the need to temper personal appetites with an appreciation of social good). In a sense Ben Ammi is not making a very different claim than present reformers who argue that free speech does not permit the promotion of violent racism, or self-defence the right for anyone to buy guns, because of the evils that we know ultimately come from these; so, public good trumps individual liberty. However, it would be a different kind of reformer who, like Ben Ammi, suggested that immodest clothing could be a factor in social dissolution.[6] In this case, the common progressive argument is that it is the responsibility of those provoked by such clothing to contain themselves, and of society to educate people (particularly men) against objectification. Here, the freedom of one to dress as they choose is prioritized over the effect that may have on others. The structure of the argument is different however, as the reformers argue that we have the prerogative to curtail freedoms because of how some might abuse them, while Ben Ammi believes that some things are wrong in themselves because they debase us, they distort our natures and take us into places that are dangerous.

This concept of an innate ethical nature to all actions is related to Ben Ammi's theological near-dualism: there are simply good and evil actions – behavioural patterns which nourish us and bring us closer to God, and behaviours which are destructive, taking us further away. Furthermore, any faith which structures itself according to ancient texts such as the Hebrew Bible are more than likely to adhere to a conservative form of morality – simply, if we honour the ancients and the revelation given to them, then we will try to mimic their lives and follow the rules they set down for themselves.

Tradition

As with many evangelists, Ben does not strictly define, he simply says we have strayed from God and must return: but the vision of what it means to return to God, of how the Bible should be interpreted, which parts jettisoned and which retained, are always necessarily personal. However, Ben Ammi is clear that we are currently heading in the wrong direction: 'There has never been a time in history when we were weaker, sicker, and more fragmented. The men are in jail, the women are in lib, and the children are in confusion. We must *swiftly* reorder our lives, change our priorities and restructure our families. This process begins with a return to God' (GBMT52).

The corruption and anti-Life / anti-Yah nature of modern society is not limited to obvious evil, but is present in the many ways that life is subtly inhibited: 'a social system that derides or subtly limits the desire to walk, run and play, alienates you from sunshine, moonlight and fresh air and places you in a state of deactivation, is leading you to decadence and degeneracy' (EL78). Sexual deviancy stems 'from a lack of understanding, not intelligence. They literally don't know what to do with themselves', and so they develop strange habits/desires. 'This is illustrated in the expressions of disco, punk rock and drug cultures, bikini bathing suits, mini dresses and see-through blouses' (EL79). His description of modern life, saturated by technological convenience and the mundanity of TV, computer, ready-meals and cars can seem luddite, but Ammi does not totally condemn technology. New inventions can have their place but they must be designed and used to serve existing needs, rather than exacerbate our negative traits or create unnatural desires: 'Even modern medicine, radio and television, transportation and education were good at their conception, but were made evil by stagnant minds' (EL79). Many inventions have been used as a temporary reprieve, to help those whose time has been consumed by society and don't know how to slow down to enjoy life or company. They actually help to convince us that we are legitimately busy, and therefore we willingly sacrifice our ability to relaxedly enjoy taking a walk, etc., in order to rush from one thing to another. For Ben Ammi, many of the jobs which are necessary in capitalist society are simply there to keep the system afloat: they add nothing to human life and therefore cannot be considered as divinely sanctioned.

Ben's conservatism sometimes seems to conflict with his other views. He complains that progressive doctrine has evolution taught in schools while 'God and prayer were legislated out', (GLR87; GBMT95) without acknowledging that the religious elements in question were Christian ones, which must have been part of the conspiracy to seduce and constrain Black Americans. Indeed, it is because contemporary religion is 'a diabolical universal plot to destroy the true God-presence from among men', that he wishes us to return to 'the fundamental (pre-European) concepts concerning spirituality, the human family and truth' (EL14).

Ben also, predictably, opposes the separation of church and state. Instead we need – and the Kingdom of Yah will implement – 'separation of satan and government' (RHS45). In the replacement for the present world order, the Divine system, everything is divinely ordained: 'He has created all things and set them in Divine order. To obey that order is to worship He that set the order' (GBMT27). The fundamental problem is that human beings have believed themselves capable of designing a system that would work, but the only system that can provide wholeness and growth is that which brings us closer to God. This is the only way of going with the grain of reality.

When Ben consistently places God at the forefront of every human endeavour, he echoes the conservative religious paradigm of many societies and many ages. His attacks on the human arrogance of attempting to design the world by our own echoes that of contemporary Jewish 'national conservative' Yoram Hazony, who writes, 'When one believes he has no need of God to make his system of universal political and moral thought work, the system he is proposing has confused his own local perspective for the universal, and the pronouncements of human reason for God's thoughts'.[7] The transcendent knowledge of God is far above what humans can achieve. Quoting Prov.14.12, 'there is a way that seemeth right unto a man but the end thereof are the ways of death', Ammi comments, 'Man, under satan's system, has been convinced that he has the capacity to order his own steps.' But 'there is an "enemy structure" that has to be totally dismantled' (GBMT133). And just like Hazony, Ben Ammi emphasizes pragmatic evaluation of outcomes as the best demonstration of validity: 'The Bible teaches that we will know if we are doing things right by the fruit, or results' (GBMT52).

The West's hypocrisy is a frequent target. Ben cites the example of 'all men are created equal' as a beautiful statement that the west makes, serving as a smokescreen for the evil actions it commits. The 'equality' cited here ends immediately after birth, as society stratifies people by all kinds of divisions. For Ben Ammi, the inverse should be the case: there is no equality at birth, rather society must intervene and create equality (MEW97). Satan creates an impression of competition within the system and the appearance of choice (including the choice between communism and capitalism) but all the choices are equally evil. It is only by stepping outside the system that one can find God.

However, Ben Ammi is also damning of the global moral order and the tendency to hegemonically apply principles designed in the west. He claims that discourse of 'humanitarian needs' is one technique used to attempt to destabilize traditional African culture and begin replacing it: The championing of 'children's rights, women's rights' is a lever where 'the real target is African or Yah-centric culture which is still too dominant in African countries' (RJPJ26).

As he complains about 'easy divorces and abortion rights', (RJPJ31-2) (although the latter not for the reason one would expect)[8] similar is his reactionary take on contemporary attempts to highlight 'micro-aggressions', leading to the adoption of another conservative talking point: 'The sequence of behavioral adjustments required to keep you within the "status quo" framework of being "non-discriminatory" to keep your job, manage your business of not offending anyone), has led you into the domain of satan' (RJPJ31-2). It is possible to see this also at the root of his frequent reliance on 'common sense', itself a conservative trait: common sense being (according to Hazony) the received wisdom that we acquire from our culture.[9]

If Ben's distaste for progressive western liberalism is in line with many conservatives, his dislike for capitalist economics is not.[10] For him, the entire spectrum of political options from Marxism to capitalism 'are merely flip sides of European culture tradition' and so unrighteous, ungodly (MEW95). The free market and economic growth are no less secular in nature than human rights legislation: these are all systems designed by humans, and so cannot help but be corrupt (IL58; RHS35; RJPJ74); any alternative that is not the Bible will not provide stable, healthy societies, because only God is the source of life. Ben Ammi prioritizes human life, and the ecology that support that, over any other value or social system, so he has no qualms in stating that 'the individualistic ambitions of the over-developed nations to attain more wealth must be resisted and subordinated for the benefit of the whole' (RV6). Ben Ammi accuses capitalism of forsaking human lives in the service of its own god, profit. We now exist in a world where there are 'too many machines ... taking the jobs once done by people. What benefit is it to develop a social system that employs unlimited machinery and leaves people idle and homeless?' (RV15) The political vision proposed by Ammi requires a new system that is holistic and integrated, and that therefore can be determined top-down to act in the best interests of humans and the other life on this planet. So, 'Governments must accept the responsibility to emphasize to the individual (via education) and the corporation (via standards of accountability) that employment and business are functions of national service, and exist not just for their personal gain' (RV15). The restriction of individual and business liberties should not be considered off-limits if these will lead to a better world for all.

In discussing the apparent collapse of value systems in the developed world, he interprets this as part of an intentional 'undertaking to refashion all of the inhabitants (Adamic civilization) into a new image with an impious, implacable type of nature' (RJPJ74). However, the specificity of his take is demonstrated when he continues that 'the knowledge being implanted will not be able to sustain life' because modern consumerism is not conducive to life and regeneration, in the way that previous value systems/social ordering *have* been able to foster and support the life and growth of human communities. He has previously derided materialism as the 'King's meat' with which Nebuchadnezzar tempted Daniel (GBMT142). He is, of course, completely correct that materialist consumerism is destroying the viability of human life and society continuing in the future; if this was not obvious to everyone when he was writing in 2005, it is now. However, he makes an important connection between this idea and spirituality, when he argues that the problem is not the objects but the lust with which people approach objects: 'The covetousness and lust for these gadgets far supercedes the spiritual love for one's neighbor and relatives' (GBMT113). Thus, it is not technology as such which Ammi rejects, but the place it has in our lives. This should come as no surprise, because the AHIJ have consistently embraced new media technology in spreading their message.

Nationalism

Ben stands in the tradition of Black Nationalism, although this is quite distinct from traditional conservative nationalism. Where the latter promotes a competitive identity – and birthplace-based nationalism, the former has sought to carve out a national identity for African Americans, with the possibility of self-determination for that people either within the United States, within a breakaway republic of a proportional number of states or within an emigrationist framework. Ben Ammi chose the latter, supported by the biblical predictions of the return of the Israelites to their land. The competitive aspect, wherein different nations favour themselves over others and attempt to gain more in their own interest at the expense of others, is not a part of Black Nationalism generally, nor of Ben Ammi's iteration of it. Ben is concerned that the duty upon everyone is to help each other, and in particular it is the ordained responsibility of the people of Israel to help to improve the practices and the lot of all nations by setting a positive example.

The critical factor in Ben Ammi's nationalism is, as always, God. The hierarchy he envisions is of nations ruled by righteous men (and yes, it will be men), who are ruled by God: 'it is absurd to think that one can separate God from government or righteousness from authority' (GBMT21). Therefore, the culture, politics and economy must all be systems that are given by God. America in particular offers the example of what happens when this principle is not followed: 'Mankind, using its own mind, has failed dismally.' In fact, because it has followed its own path instead of God's, 'The entire Euro-gentile world is characterized by corruption, immorality and greed; it is plagued by terrorism and other forms of violence, and is beset by confusion and chaos' (GBMT24).

In critiquing the concept/doctrine of 'human rights', Ben takes the argument further than other conservatives: his group-based preference to individualism prioritizes both the family and the nation above the person, and it is to them that their loyalty lies, although all (individual, family and nation) must principally devote themselves to God, which means living righteously. Thus, responsibilities are more important than rights. However, Ben takes the additional step of critiquing religion, politics and economics as similar distractions from the ultimate desideratum of righteousness:

> [T]he present notion of human rights does not denote or cause one to expect human righteousness. The objective of western nations championing human rights was to open the doors of societies to all manner of evil lifestyles which in itself is the denial of human dignity and the root of human suffering and anguish.
>
> (IL24)

And so in the end, Ben Ammi's nationalism actually devours itself: because the purpose of the Israelite nation separating themselves from the unrighteous, in order to practise their righteousness, is actually to serve as a light to the nations and encourage all others to adopt these practices and so dissolve the distinction between themselves and Israelites. This universalism is one posited in the Bible, where several prophets predict a point where all will join themselves to Israel and worship God by God's Hebrew Name YHWH.[11] This messianic prediction is the biblical reversal of the confusion of tongues which took place after the monolingual humanity endeavoured to build a tower which would reach up to heaven – in Ben Ammi's reading the emergence of discrete nations is inseparable from the divine punishment of multiple languages. Ben explicitly links all of these ideas, concluding that 'We must be released from the bounds of competition to enjoy the freedom of complementing' (EL20-21). For him, the diversity of tongues also represents a diversity of worldviews which make it impossible for humanity to unite – until the predestined time.

This coming-together of humanity across nations is correlated with the coming-together within nations, so that division in general ends: Ben Ammi is critical of the diversity of opinions that flourish in the modern age, and of the tolerated freedoms which may have given us temporary glories, but ultimately constitute the cacophony of voices which question everything, including climate science and the need for greener living. The lack of certainty engendered by constant debate leads to a future where we all die; the decomposition of society makes us weaker not stronger, and less likely to survive. This of course is in contrast to rabbinic tradition, which prioritizes the multiplicity of voices and opinions by preserving less popular opinions which lost the debate in the historical literature, but may be necessary at some unforeseen point in the future. This provides a flexibility to the tradition which allows it to adapt to new circumstances, even while having a set mode for the usual conditions.

The singularity of opinion and outlook however is an important part of Ben Ammi's anti-liberal agenda. Just as there is only one God and one Truth, from which any deviation necessarily means a descent into falsehood, so there is only one good way of living which everyone must keep to. Any tolerance of otherhood would mean tolerance of evil, and this is not possible in the Kingdom of Yah. The absolute, total system must spread over the world and consume everything, even if it is acknowledged that human beings are imperfect and cannot keep the will of God in every action. In *Imitation of Life*, Ben Ammi answers Cain's rhetorical question – 'Am I my brother's keeper?' – with a firm 'Yes' (IL39). Because society and the world are holistic, we will be affected by what happens anywhere in the world, and therefore we must take an interest in it, and help everyone else to progress towards righteousness. Ben Ammi frames it in theological language, but the core point is clear: the actions of our neighbour, and their neighbour, impact upon us. The world is interconnected in a holistic framework.

Ammi relates 'evil' to the progresses of the modern world. Present world institutions have promoted unrighteousness through technology that kills (weapons), entertainment that destroys the family (porn), the loss of nature and wildlife and polluting of the environment and of society. Complementing his reliance on God as well as the previously mentioned 'common sense' arguments is a recourse to 'nature' arguments. According to these, society has become demonstrably unnatural, but the 'natural' way is God's design and therefore correct.[12] This is found is various forms, including reproductive/contraceptive technology, nutrient-free processed food and that made from animal parts, drugs and sexual immorality. The flaw in Ben Ammi's logic is obvious: many of these things are present in nature, and where they are not there is no necessary reason to condemn them for that, any more than there would be to stop eating broccoli, a product of millennia of agricultural manipulation of the mustard leaf plant. In reality, nature and civilization are a blurry dichotomy and there is no way to clearly distinguish their products.

However, while KOY have acknowledged and live as a part of the modern Israeli state, the centrality of it to their lives is marred by a complete absence of it from Ben's written writings.[13] Whenever he discusses nationhood, he is clear that he means African Americans/Israelites. Modern nation states are not of interest to him, and in the grand scheme, the present state of Israel is transitory and ultimately irrelevant. It seems that while the AHI are not (any longer) working to overthrow the system, they are content to wait patiently for it to fall, at the set time, at which point they will become the authority, the representative of the holy land.

Gender and sexuality

The perspective of Ben Ammi, and the HI in general, on sexuality and associated issues of gender, transgenderism, etc., is proudly and uncompromisingly patriarchal, traditional and homophobic.[14] Ben Ammi often criticizes feminism and other modern liberation movements as designed to break up families (an all-too-common perception) and deny the fundamental nature of both female and male, while homosexuality is an unacceptable evil comparable with murder. I cannot ignore this, and neither can I condone it: it goes against my own values and instincts, which are overwhelmingly progressive. However what I can here try to do is explain the reasoning and particular points of focus in Ben Ammi's work, illustrating where I think the internal logic is flawed, and try to explicate some of the reasons why this kind of conservative construction has become important within the movement, while highlighting how it relates to parallel movements/thinkers and to discussions currently taking place in academia.

The construction of gender in the writing of Ben Ammi, and in the community generally, draws on traditional western/American Christian tropes of male and female, arguing that gender is strictly binary and that men should rule their families, be authoritative and strong, while women should be submissive to their husband. Ben Ammi's mandate that 'Man must accept God's authority over him, woman must accept man's authority over her, and children must be returned to childhood by their parents' (GLR29)[15] reflects to some degree the Rastafarian belief that Man is to Woman as God is to Man, and the prevalence of male supremacy in Abrahamic religions and societies indicates the extent to which those who interpret the scriptures are likely to reach such conclusions. The Hebrew Bible is certainly a text grounded in patriarchy, and while the Talmud offered a more complicated conception of gender which admitted the possibility of in-between or indistinct individuals, they were acknowledged only in order to facilitate their placement into the existing binary system.[16] Some, perhaps many, other cultures have accepted a more nuanced understanding of gender and individual expression, as have an increasing proportion of groups within the modern world.

One aspect of the AHIJ's lifestyle that is hotly debated is that of polygyny: men are permitted to take up to seven wives (though relatively few men take more than one and more than two or three is usually the preserve of high-status males, because they must prove ability to support each new wife plus children). Curiously, Ben Ammi does not actually discuss this in any of his writings, although one member of the community has penned a book on the subject. It is worth noting that the institution of 'Divine Marriage' has been largely accepted by AHIJ women, and some even sing its praises: Dr Haraymiel Ben Shaleahk's book on Divine Marriage[17] includes forewords by two of his wives, possibly a deliberate move to indicate the support that the institution has from female members. Gheliyah cites her own negative experiences of monogamy in the United States, including being the 'other woman' in several relationships, as evidence of the brokenness of that approach. Indeed, the extent to which monogamy is compromised by concealed relations with others is often cited including by Ben Ammi as one of the major flaws. Ben Ammi himself took his second wife before the move, but the general practice of Divine Marriage was instituted in Liberia, apparently with the explanation that the females outnumbered the males quite heavily, and that without making some provision for this the community would face a destabilizing situation of many unmarried women and a struggle over the few men. This issue of gender balance is an important one, because it is a problem faced in the African American community in particular where males have a high rate of incarceration and early death, as well as twice the rate of out-marriage, leaving many eligible females without viable spouses (and some males the ability to therefore pursue multiple relationships without censure).[18] But it raises the opposite problem of that which it intends to solve, because without the American situation which produced the imbalance the Israeli community would soon reach a natural gender balance, meaning that if even a fraction of males took several wives there would soon be a surfeit of single men, unless a higher number of women were consistently 'imported' from the United States.

Marriage and nuclear families generally have decreased to an alarming degree among African Americans (with whites following the same pattern, with a delay).[19] This trend is frequently highlighted by Ben Ammi, and he sees multiple problems stemming from the lack of stability and strong male presence for children. Unlike Hazony he does not explicitly mention the importance of raising children for the development of men, though he is surely aware of this also.

Haraymiel's position is more radical than that adopted by the community, claiming that 'a man is *supposed* to take more than one wife'.[20] He argues that because multiplication is a principal command of God, and male and female productivity differs, it is God's intention that men should be breeding with multiple women at once.[21] Haraymiel is also more willing than Ben Ammi to publish claims without fact-checking, for instance writing that 'In any given period there are at least twice as many female births as there are male births'.[22] This is demonstrably not the case, and it is difficult to know how anyone would believe it to be true – nowhere in the world are there twice as many women as men.[23] References to animal species which organize by means of male-led harems also ignore the fact that such 'societies' involve constant and fatal battles between males for control of such harems – because there are necessarily less multi-female harems than there are males. Such is not a desirable model for human society, and in any case the variety of sex-roles, sex-natures and social organization of the sexes among animals mean any model can be successfully evidenced: a large number of examples of animal species which complicate and even invert conservative notions of gender essentialism can be produced.[24]

However, polygyny is certainly practised successfully in many African communities, and is noted without condemnation of several biblical patriarchs and heroes. These are the examples often provided as the cultural background for Divine Marriage, leading to the argument that Divine Marriage is simply a return to the traditions which were disallowed by colonial forces.

In comparison to this, it is noteworthy that Ben Ammi does not spend much time defending – or even explaining – his views on polygyny. Clearly he was not against it, being a practitioner and promoter of it himself, but it is difficult to find any direct mention of it in his body of work. My own sense from my interactions with the community has been that while it is an accepted practice, there is a certain defensiveness which comes from an awareness of its negative reception in the western world. My impression is also that it is on the decline, as the community adjusts itself to the norms of Israeli society and endeavours to not court negative publicity.

Divine Marriage has also not been without its discontents from within. Several ex-members have critiqued the practice, including the apparent inability of existing wives to refuse a new partner. When an Israeli team filmed a documentary called *Sister Wife* in 1997 about Atur Khazriel's upcoming second marriage, his first wife Tsiporah soon after left the community but remained in Israel where she advocates against the community and that practice in particular.[25] Despite this, most female members of the community, whether in a multiple wife marriage or not, do not see it as problematic. Indeed, some have welcomed the companionship of their 'sister wife', and the bonds between these women have sometimes survived even the departure of the husband.

Given these facts, it is worth addressing the question of why and how the gender balance since the early days of the community was so skewed towards women.[26] Some of the obvious answers – that Black women have sought out such religious expression more, or that the imbalance reflects the incarceration or early death rates for Black men – may be challenged by the fact that parallel movements such as the Nation of Islam always had a much stronger male bias. However, several researchers have noted that Black nationalist movements tended to attract women in high numbers, Paulette Pierce writing that whereas 'women usually represented a major, if not the majority share of the participants' in such groups, including in leadership positions, their contributions have systematically been ignored.'[27] Pierce notes that polygyny was a not-uncommon suggestion in regard to the frequent over-representation of women in contemporaneous Black nationalist movements, and therefore 'demographics and nationalist definitions of acceptable gender behavior made it easy for men to reap the fruits of women's domestic labor ... while freely indulging their sexual appetites – all in the name of nation-building!'[28] Similarly, ex-member Mahaleyah Goodman observed that 'The sisters were the glue that held the KOG together [...] But much of their hard work and sacrifices often went without notice or appreciation.'[29]

Markowitz tells the narrative of four women, demonstrating the reasons that two of them had for joining and remaining in the community, including the ability to raise children in safety, to fulfil feminine roles and to attain stability in their emotional/romantic lives. She writes,

> By emphasizing spirituality over materialism, by tending to household duties and placing their husbands and children first, they hope to strengthen their families and develop feminine self-esteem. But beyond these personal pleasures, as sisters in the Kingdom reasserting God's plan, the women rest assured that they are contributing to the salvation of the black race and bettering the general condition of humankind.[30]

The second two women left the community, Markowitz noting that what for some is desirable for others is not, and that '[t]he community places demands upon its women to be a particular kind of woman, and it mandates a particular kind of relationship between a woman and her children.'[31] For those who stay, however, '[t]he protected "second place" of women in this community is not nearly as objectionable as the "no place" in which many had felt themselves to be in America.'[32]

Men likewise have expectations placed upon them. Markowitz writes that the position of 'responsible and righteous men at the helm [of families] is crucial to the

Hebrew Israelites' communal lifestyle and culture'. Responsibility is a key word here – the urge for men to take responsibility is a refusal of stereotypes of African American men, as violent, hyper-sexed, out of work, absent fathers. It is suggested that if men take responsibility and live up to their calling as the head of families in the AHIJ, then they will pull the rest of the community – their wives and children – with them. Women and children must also know their responsibilities, but they are to a much greater degree in submission to the figure of the man, who is the primary agent. Ben Ammi dictates that, in the Kingdom, 'Holy men are not soft, docile or effeminate', but neither will they 'be oppressive and chauvinistic, or insensitive for fear of appearing weak' (RHS94). The hope is that men will indeed live up to this, but it is likely (given human nature) that not all will; reports of child sexual abuse which have emerged from the community especially demonstrate the licence some men have felt able to take.[33] This is of course not to say that the AHIJ is particularly prone to this, or to male misdemeanour; it is not, simply men are, and the AHIJ so far has not been able to completely curtail some of the antisocial behaviours linked with masculinity.

One of the major concerns regarding any kind of patriarchal system – male aggression – is hardly mentioned by Ben Ammi. He does not see it as natural for men to fight or engage in violence; this is understood to be a flaw that occurs because of some incorrect development. Indeed, violence is traditionally seen by twentieth-century African American thinkers as something essentially European: violence is the path the European took in subjugating others in the world, but it is not a part of African culture.

The feeling of a cultural 'hopelessness' regarding men[34] – that men, especially Black American men, were prone to a typology of hypersexuality, and irresponsible detachment (one exacerbated by the destruction of family structures among the enslaved) – is likely what led Ben Ammi et al. to try to reinstate some of the traditional forms of role, and family. Male laxity could also explain the acceptance of polygyny as the lesser of evils, as it provides some leeway for male sexuality while still binding men into patterns of discipline and responsibility towards their partners and children.

The community recognize that there is a crisis in Black masculinity and responsibility is one of the key factors of this – however, in reclaiming masculinity and seeking to reassert the common role of males as fathers and husbands, as responsible family men, they have imagined this in a stereotyped form that provides more agency to family men than to family women. This is not to say that women of the community are oppressed, and Ben Ammi explicitly states that he does not countenance a repressive attitude towards women; the requirement for a degree of submission to their husbands does not equate to a mandate on effeminacy and there is no indication that women must be socially submissive, or that they cannot pursue careers, or must dress or behave in ways pleasing to men.[35] Women are expected to mother, to nurture, but not to be weak or helpless as some male stereotypes would suggest. Modesty is expected of everyone, and revealing or sexualizing clothing is not deemed appropriate for men or women. However, the common statement of the community that 'a woman can be anything she wants to be – except a man' in matters of gender demonstrates some of both the flexibility and the rigidity of their expectations.

If the above provides a conceivable explanation of female acceptance of the structures created by Ben Ammi and other men of the community, it does not justify those structures. It could be that as the community continues to evolve, a fairer and more egalitarian balance will emerge. Equally, it may not.

Another factor must be addressed here: the hypocrisy of the west's stance on such matters, and its use of them to denigrate other cultures.[36] This is acutely analysed by Ben Ammi who argues that while western individualism is served by the ability of every individual to engage in practices as they choose, there are other ways in which people are harmed by this. In regard to polygyny, Haraymiel argues that the sex industry's prevalence in the west is a response to monogamy, and that the west 'reject[s] the multiple wife concept, asserting that it is unfair, chauvinistic and immoral while endorsing and allowing all manner of perversions and inequities to proliferate'.[37] It is worth examining this example in more detail.

However we look at it, the association of monogamy with the western world often conceals the fact that the taking of mistresses by powerful men has for a long time been tolerated, seeming to be part of the 'special deal' package by which the powerful could transcend moral duties placed upon ordinary people. The fact that other societies have accepted this tendency openly, on the one hand, lent legitimacy to the model of male as 'head' of the family (even in monogamous relationships in those societies), but on the other hand enabled the formal assumption of widow's rights to those who would be extra-marital non-entities in legally monogamous societies. It was tempting for early anthropologists to ignore this while claiming that the different cultural approaches indicated a progression through social orderings away from the barbaric practice of polygamy. Current research indicates that polygamy may emerge from a variety of factors. Some of these are the social importance of politics, power and prestige. These principles articulate the bonding function of marriage (its ability to unify relations between different groups), as well as the existence of power differentials which mean higher status males can attain multiple marriages, along with the corollary display of power through the ability to attain and support multiple wives.[38] Secondly, the increased material productivity and reproductivity of such families have been emphasized, although the latter is only true for males; females in such marriages appear to have significantly less children than monogamous females.[39] This last highlights the facts that most of these explanations come from the male point of view, and while it is certainly advantageous to a female to marry a man who has obviously the resources to support her, the splitting of male attention between several partners, and the attendant lowering of status from sole wife to one of several, makes this less attractive to most women than monogamy. The ultimate question, then, is who is society being ordered by and for?

The adoption of polygyny during the AHIJ's time in Liberia can thus be seen as relying two factors: a surfeit of viable females, along with a patriarchal, male-dominated social structure wherein males consolidated their status by the attraction of more wives.

Having dealt initially with this issue in purely ethical terms, it is necessary to advance the following, detailed, caveat. Western society *presents* itself as the pinnacle of ethical practice, but it is still very far from realizing this in terms of the experience of many, maybe most, persons. When we discuss issues such as women's rights, queer and trans rights, and rights of any other minority in other cultures, we should always acknowledge that the battles for such rights in our own nations are yet incomplete. Legal provision does not lead inexorably to practical equality, and the social situation in many parts of western nations is still not what some urban pseudo-intellectuals would believe.

According to Lori G. Beaman,

The fiction of equality in Western democracies can be marked in any number of ways, including a review of domestic violence against women, sexual assault against women, the murder of women, women's inferior rates of pay in the paid labor force, women's overrepresentation in statistics about division of domestic labor, the representation of women in the media, women's self-mutilation through cosmetic surgery, the control of women's reproduction, and so on.[40]

This indeed is another example of Ben Ammi's complaint, that the west makes beautiful speeches about *essential* equality, while somehow still allowing vast inequalities to emerge along society's fault lines (MEW97).

It is worth considering also the process of gender construction in Black America. bell hooks has written that, according to their own testimonies, free and enslaved Black men during American slavery,

did not see themselves as sharing the same stand-point as white men about the nature of masculinity. Transplanted African men, even those coming from communities where sex roles shaped the division of labor, where the status of men was different and most times higher than that of women, had to be taught to equate their higher status as men with the right to dominate women, they had to be taught patriarchal masculinity. They had to be taught that it was acceptable to use violence to establish patriarchal power.[41]

Accordingly, after emancipation the struggle to establish what should be the gender roles for a people who had no valid models, caused tension between the genders. Thus,

Despite the stellar example of W.E.B. Du Bois, who continually supported the rights of women overall, black males seemed to see the necessity of black females participating as co-equals in the struggle for racial uplift with the implicit understanding that once freedom was achieved black females would take their rightful place subordinate to the superior will of men. In keeping with sexist norms, sexist black folks believed that "slavery and racism sought the emasculation of Afro-American men" and that the responsibility of black folks to counter this, that black women were to "encourage and support the manhood of our men."[42]

Ben Ammi indeed follows this logic – the primary target and victim according to Ben Ammi was the Black male, who in many cases was attacked *via* the Black female (GBMT236).[43] Because of this it is principally the Black male's position and role which must be reclaimed. In the AHIJ, women have been expected to commit everything, as fully as men, but they are denied the right to the highest leadership roles or full self-determinacy.[44] Ben narrates this as simply being true to the created nature, as revealed in the Bible, and in the latter he is basically correct: the Bible tells little of women's agency, while not denying it and allowing for certain remarkable individuals to break from the norm, the pattern of male dominance is clearly laid out.

Ben Ammi does not explicitly assert a dominance of men and states clearly that men and women are equal – however, 'equal but different' has a long history of being cover for horrific abuses of those who are judged the less equal among equals. So, when he critiques feminist aspirations to equality as 'suspiciously synonymous with "sameness"', before describing the 'evil element's' endgame as 'a genderless society and completely interchangeable roles', it is difficult to not see in this an urge to put women back in their place (MEW126).[45]

Indeed, Ben suggests that it is feminism or women's liberation that has caused the breakdown of family structure; he asks, 'Did man really abandon his family or has the system compelled the newly independent woman to drive her man out as a statement that she can survive without him?' (RJPJ27) He goes on to present the lyrics of Beyonce's Independent Woman: 'no falling in love / no commitment from me / I'm number one priority' as indicating the logical and selfish outcome. On this note it is worth remarking that love is not ignored by Ben Ammi – it is the foundation of marriage, but he inverts the common conception of 'falling in love' as something unwilled that removes our agency. In a particularly beautiful turn of phrase, he remarks, 'How strange, yet beautiful, it would be to hear: " I think I'm rising in love with ..."' (GLR120).[46] This phrase has become the common expression within the community.

hooks claims that the tendency to worry about rigid gender roles and the emasculation of Black males who are outperformed or out-earned by their wives is only an issue for those who have internalized the patriarchal gender roles of white society. To an extent Ben Ammi has done just this, as many of his beliefs come not from the Bible but from the assumed wisdom of twentieth-century America. This is made clear in the introduction to *God and the Law of Relativity*, where Ben writes,

> There was once a time when the Law of Relativity was an inherent, ingrained principle within the conscious as well as the unconscious mind of man. Therefore, evil behavior and deeds were exceptions to the rule, evildoers did not overtly flaunt themselves as they do in the world today, the old cowboy movies we watched, the bad guys all rode together and when they came to town, the good people scattered to disassociate themselves from these evil men. Today, the "badder" you are, the more popular you are.
>
> (GLRviii)

Here, in summoning the concept of a long-lost golden age when society was as it should be, he uses the unexpected example of early America – and furthermore, a fictional construction of that America. He tells not of utopic African civilizations, but of a time when white Europeans were exterminating Native Americans. The tragedy that western oppression of non-heteronormative lifestyles has now created similar attitudes (and laws) in places where alternatives were previously tolerated, or even accepted, is replicated in Ben Ammi's intolerance.[47]

Slightly later he repeats the error, utilizing a gender-role typology based fundamentally on the United States: 'What is naturally right is that women are the homemakers, wives and mothers of society, not men. However, there is nothing good in promoting the idea of men staying home to cook the meals, clean the house and raise the kids while the wife works driving the Mack truck' (GLR7). This is a principle which one *can* extrapolate from the Bible if one wishes, but there are no commandments regarding such gender roles. These roles are American, not biblical.

A very similar dynamic was present in the NOI, leading two scholars to conclude that 'despite the emancipatory language of racial redemption, the symbolic strategies for the contestation of subordination, in the face of entrenched economic depravation, displaces tyranny onto women rather than confronting its reproduction'. In this case too, 'it structures its protest against Black masculine subordination on the field and within the coordinates fixed by the metaphysics of nature, history, and race in the general configuration of Western nationalism'.[48] The implication is that gender liberation would only become possible in such movements once masculinity became detached from white society's necessarily dominant conception of it. As Markowitz and Avieli have shown, the AHIJ have attempted this in their rescripting of masculinity; however, they have not succeeded in going all the way. It should be noted that despite what the above may suggest, and the absence of women from the top tiers of the AHIJ hierarchy, the women of the community and their contribution have been honoured on numerous occasions including the recent 'Women of Faith, Courage and Vision' iteration of the annual Hebrew History Month. And none of this is to place responsibility at the feet of the AHIJ; as a biblically based community they read God's punishment of Eve as ruled by her husband (Gen.3.16) as defining the created gender order. However, if they are truly succeeding in undoing the first sin, this order too will be overturned.

Particularly disturbing is Ben's attempt to shame women from exercising agency with the withdrawal of male love: 'The truth is no Son of God can manifest the true love of God for a woman who is out of her cycle. In attempting to do so, he would find the greatest opposition in his own human nature. Men, real men, simply don't like being "hen-pecked"; they detest being forced to play a feminine role' (GLR74). This idea of fixed gender natures, of a universal essence to what being a 'man' is, is attractive but also very reductive. It fails to acknowledge that individual personalities can sometimes trump biological norms, and that, to the extent that there is such a thing as 'maleness', some women will have more of it than some men, and therefore common roles do not work for everyone. The erasure of this means that some men will end up trying to dominate more than their personality allows, ending up surely in what Ben terms 'being unreasonably overbearing in projecting one's masculinity (as a bully, which often indicates an inferiority complex)' (GLR75). This idea of 'God-given roles' for men and women refuses to take into account how individuals vary vastly, instead reading a vibrantly complex reality into a simple binary that cannot contain it.

The argument made by Ben is that the re-inscribing of gender roles and functional patriarchy is not oppressive but just the opposite: because males and females have been oppressed by western notions of 'freedom' that advised them to let go of their natural behaviours and preferences, it is only now that they are able to reclaim the only structure in which they can be themselves and find true freedom. However,

Ben Ammi's deconstruction and redefinition of white social norms and values have served to reinscribe some of them by not questioning also the white world's gendered presumptions; in not including women in the decision-making process and in adopting the typical patriarchal structure of a rigid hierarchy, the community have replicated some of the worst features of Europe-America.

Regarding individualism and marriage, western society faces something of an unrecognized dilemma: while sexual relations are increasingly being seen as a domain of personal freedom, where consenting adults can engage in whatever format they desire, yet anyone wishing to engage in a format of more than two people cannot do so legally as a marriage. The contradiction is usually defended by appeal to women's rights and the abuse that could be faced by the condoning of polygyny; this, ironically, has not made any inroads into polygynous practices outside of marriage, to which the law has been seen as inapplicable. While, indeed, the practices of the AHIJ do limit the freedoms of women, in that they are not able to refuse the taking of another wife, and are not themselves able to take more than one husband, there is a plausible argument that in recognizing the possibility of polygynous marriages the AHIJ are solving at least as many problems as they are creating. Lori Beaman has noted one case where 'the range of people and groups who deployed the rhetoric of women's equality to condemn the practice of polygamy' was in fact an exercise in straw-clutching behind which was a 'near-hysterical and moralistic response' to polygamy, and behind which, 'Bluntly put, the lack of availability of women for men is a dominant concern.'[49] This use of 'women's rights' as a tool to defend a patriarchal vision of a community's women as their property which can be shared out in ways fair or unfair *to males* has been used sometimes to conceal sexist agendas: in recent times a defence of monogamy has recently been attempted by right-wing psychologist Jordan Peterson, who saw the provision of a mate and sexual outlet to every male as essential to stabilizing society; *whose* needs were important to fulfil for Peterson here, are obvious, indicating the way that polygyny can be seen as dangerous principally for males. The subtext – that some men would find themselves judged unmarriable unless women had to compete for the single marriage option of each man, and that some women should therefore settle for less-than-desirable, possibly violent, men – is difficult to defend when revealed.

***

Ben Ammi is relatively frank in his discussions of sex, but nowhere near as explicit as the rabbis tend to be. Ben adopts the same sex-positivity as Judaism generally, describing sex as a necessary and beautiful part of marriage – and the physical pleasure 'is an added blessing of the Eternal, blessed be He' (GBMT220). There is no sense of abstinence as a desirable or holy way of life. But he also does not come close to the discussions of the Talmud where explicit details are shared, laughed about, sometimes with a kind of locker room humour; to them sexual relations were no different than eating habits and could be dissected and analysed with equal enthusiasm.[50] Luria's disciples were no different, Vital having apparently quizzed the former's neighbours about his sexual habits, so as best to follow his practices. Ben Ammi does not indulge in such antics, nor does he discuss requirements for female satisfaction as the rabbis did. It seems that western (Christian-influenced) prudence still had a hold over him, so it is difficult to know whether he held any position on such.

However in matters such as modesty and lewdness, they are in agreement. This is not restricted to women's dress: men should also dress modestly and according to biblical principle. Likewise, and somewhat unusually, Ben is equally strict about male and female sexualities, emphasizing biblical regulations regarding both menstrual and seminal emissions; 'established primarily to prevent men from copulating with other women and women from copulating with other men on the same day (as in prostitution), an indulgence which is a prime source of venereal disease' (GBMT209).

Regarding queer sexualities, Ben Ammi writes, 'No matter how forceful or how often they put forth their arguments, a homosexual shall have no place in the New World to come, and shall be labeled a perverted, deceptive worker of iniquity' (GLR36).[51] To my knowledge there has been no challenge to this within the community.[52] The absence of homosexuality is celebrated alongside the absence of drug abuse and crime, and the acceptance of homosexuality within contemporary western societies is marked frequently in Ben Ammi's books as a symptom of decadence. The AHIJ share this feature with the large majority of traditional and orthodox religious communities (of all Abrahamic religions), and the reason for this can be simply stated as Lev.18.22. However, as we have seen, Ben Ammi has not been averse to revising and conditioning the community's practice of the Mosaic commandments; if he wanted to, he could have argued that while homosexuality was banned for the ancient Israelites, in the present dispensation the requirements had changed (or he could, as Daniel Boyarin shows, follow the Talmud and interpret it without recourse to very modern constructions of homo- and hetero-sexuality as simply a ban on anal penetration, not on other same-sex activities[53]). That he did not do so, and that this feature has been proudly presented as a boon of the Kingdom's life may also be explained with reference to the prevalence of such attitudes within the African American religious communities.[54]

I, like many of my readers, cannot support this, although the logic at least deserves to be explained. Essentially, for Ben the public-private divide is different than in the contemporary west. Those areas usually considered private, and therefore enshrined within the realm of personal freedom in liberal democracies, such as religion, sexuality, morality and leisure, are all public for Ben Ammi; all are accountable to God but the individual is accountable *via* the collective; the Hebrew Bible demonstrates this view, that the group are held accountable for the actions of individuals in their midst, and therefore the group is right to enforce controls on these behaviours. Clearly this is a different epistemology than the one in favour around the west, and in the case of sexuality, just like all others, Ben argues that nothing is 'no one else's business'.

***

In this final chapter I have attempted to address Ben Ammi's social thought, admitting and explaining even the parts I find objectionable. It is my concern that even if we disagree with Ammi on some important issues, these should not serve as cause to reject all of his thought. This kind of call-out culture can lead us to condemn almost everyone for some point where we find their belief disagreeable. In my view there is much that we can gain from Ammi even despite disagreements.

In conclusion, it may be worth stepping back from the particular flaws or arguable specifics in Ben Ammi's social programme, in order to see the bigger picture: that what he proposes is a culture where all people exist in a web, bound together, and where the impact of each's actions on others (i.e. their responsibilities) are acknowledged; where the individual is not the basic unit of society. In this, he speaks a value system which many will support. In fact it is notable that Hazony's 'conservative democracy', based on the Bible and inherited tradition, which he designates as the necessary next stage in order to prevent liberal democracy's (putative) inevitable slide into Marxism correlates relatively well with Ben Ammi's project. To the extent that we can learn from Ammi's emphasis on the whole over the individual, and on responsibilities rather than rights *while also protecting the hard-won freedoms of women and sexual (and all other) minorities*, we would do well to.

While Ben Ammi rejects the individual freedom to act according to one's own priorities and interests, one can see that his primary concern is with what is good for humans. To a certain extent, enforcing their good requires removing liberties and compelling people to certain behaviours. Ben Ammi's opposition to liberal democracy comes from a deeply rooted suspicion regarding the capability of human beings to freely do what is right, and is reinforced by his cultural conservatism that is horrified by many of the progressive steps away from what he perceives as 'tradition'. In these ways he is naturally a conservative. However, his replacing of traditional western social structures with a biblical one and his conviction that the western world is evil from its inception and must be eradicated before being replaced make him a revolutionary.

Conclusion: Gnostic and kabbalistic reflections

In the subsequent chapters we have surveyed several central aspects of Ben Ammi's thought. The initial three chapters explored those elements which are most concretely the early part of his thought, demonstrating an attempt to reframe history around African American identity. This attempt displays paranoiac tendencies towards persecution, grandeur and total interconnectedness. As I have shown, these elements became less profound both in their presence and in their formulation as Ammi matured. Later chapters have shown the extent to which Ben Ammi's thought progressed beyond these, with his mature thought exploring detailed concepts of God, ontology, human nature, ecology and society.

James Cone defined Black Theology as 'a theology of survival, because it seeks to interpret the theological significance of the being of a community whose existence is threatened by the power of non-being'.[1] Ben Ammi has created a new mythological foundation for the African diaspora experience in the Americas, one which draws deeply upon the shared foundations of African American religion. It connects Black Americans with Black Africans; it overcomes the problematic of a community existing defined by their oppression, defined by their oppressor; it provides a realistic hope for a future of betterment, making realizing this a responsibility of Black Americans; and it even opens this future up to the rest of the world.

Ben Ammi is particularly interesting to me because of his worldly theology. He does not provide any ultimate meaning for his followers; there is no grand vision or utopic heaven of perfect bliss to be attained. There is not even a mystical union with God, and even the immortal earthly life of the future is unknown, opaque to us. Humans must simply follow Torah, and that will lead us to where we should be. There is no grand scheme, or ultimate experience to be attained. Humanity lives on earth, in community, according to God – that's all there is to it. This vision of simplicity, of living how we always have, and not reaching beyond, not transcending ourselves, not uniting with the divine (except in the simpler sense of manifesting the spirit of God) is highly deflationary and must appeal to those who are uninterested in the faux mysticisms; the *Theological* project in general is of no interest here; the intellectualization of theology is rejected by Ben. Theology instead is lived, it is an orthopraxy. In doing this he places himself outside of the academy and its fancy games which appeal to only certain kinds of people, and locates himself within his own community who definitely needed a practical way of life to save them from their immediate condition of struggle. The lack of grand meaning to life, of significance other than the living of it, also makes his theology very Jewish.

Having mentioned that several scholars of Black Theology have proposed humanocentric or humanistic theisms as the best option, Ben provides an example of what this can look like. He foregrounds human responsibility and agency over that of God; this is the model whereby 'God exhibits power primarily through human freedom and is immanent within humanity'.[2] But in another sense, Ben provides a theological position which decentres the human, which reminds us that we are not the most powerful force in the universe and that we must humble ourselves before forces that can easily destroy us. This is the God encountered in many biblical texts – a God of whom we must have awe rather than judgement. This is the God that we may be facing, regardless of our acceptance of that fact, in the looming environmental crisis.

Perhaps we can now see some of the unique qualities of Ben Ammi's thinking, as well as what the emphases and agenda of his thought were. Ben Ammi was overwhelmingly focused on life, health, growth and abundance. He emphasized repeatedly the necessity of the positive elements, those which create, to replace the overwhelming emphasis on death and destruction – even under the guise of enjoyment – in our societies. His critique of intoxicants, alcohol, tobacco, etc., was not one from a position of distrust towards personal pleasures. He frequently discussed the many pleasures provided to us by God, including those of music, family, sex and nature. But whereas these pleasures help to buoy up life, improving our wellbeing, the negative pleasures are those that shorten our lives, making us weaker, less discerning, physically and mentally sick.

Stokeley Carmichael stated that 'The Negro problem' was not one of individuals, 'but rather of Negroes as a class that is exploited, enslaved, and despised by the colonialist, capitalist society'.[3] In this case we can view Ben Ammi's project as entirely successful in managing to carve out a space in which the African diaspora was allowed to live with its own narrative and autonomy, without being *utilized* by capitalism; and doing this in a way that would, still, be very difficult within America. The AHIJ have succeeded in escaping what Carmichael described as the 'institutionalized racism that keeps the black people locked in dilapidated slums, tenements, where they must live out their daily lives subject to the prey of exploitative slum landlords, merchants, loan sharks and the restrictive practices of real-estate agents'.[4]

Stephen Finely and Biko Mandela Gray have previously argued that there is an essential phenomenological-existential aspect to African American religion;[5] this study supports that and has shown that this is at the forefront of Ben Ammi's theodicean response, which is the ground for his historical reconstruction. It is also present in his pneumatic-vitalist theology. What is most intriguing about Ben Ammi however is that he succeeded in breaking the boundary that circumscribed African American religion, first by relocating it outside of the Americas and second by expanding the influence and membership of his own community into the entirety of the Africana world, but especially within Africa itself.

It is clear how much Ben Ammi was influenced by Elijah Muhammad. This has been shown throughout every chapter, and it is testament to Muhammad's power and influence in Black American culture and especially religion. The abundant doctrinal similarities between the Nation of Islam and the African Hebrew Israelites can be summarized as follows: supra-scriptural dietary restrictions and narcotic abstinence; apocalyptic expectation, leading to a Black-ruled utopia; African American descent from Abraham and their fulfilment of the 430 years prophecy; their fulfilment of Deut.28; immanence (no afterlife); heaven and hell as modes of life; pacifism; resurrection as meaning the resurrection of the Black race; a Manichean racial cosmology; racial separatism expressed as nationalism; self-sufficiency based on an agricultural model; a de-emphasizing of the category religion; a prior national identity of African Americans which was erased during slavery; the historical priority of Black before white; the leadership role of African Americans for Blacks globally; and Christianity as designed for Blacks' enslavement. Some of these similarities are explained by tropes and biblical interpretations that were present in African American religious thought prior to either movement emerging, likely prior even to the twentieth century. Some are explained by the interchange between the two groups and the clear influence of Muhammad's teachings on members of the AHIJ. Some speak to the culture of the black urban 1960s in particular. Muhammad's teachings are markedly more maverick: Blacks originally inhabited the moon, whites were grafted from Blacks by a mad scientist; God is orbiting the earth in a spaceship which will bring the apocalyptic destruction to America, whereas Ben Ammi's thought does not indulge in such speculation because he prefers to base himself solely on what can be biblically founded (whether or not it came from there originally).

Ammi described Muhammad as 'appointed by God', despite the AHIJ publicly disavowing Muhammad in 1974, when he publicly offered the Nation of Islam's thanks to white capitalists who had helped them.[6] The feeling of betrayal behind this reaction itself demonstrates the importance of Muhammad for the nascent community. However, the community have maintained close relations with Louis Farrakhan and his renewed Nation of Islam. Farrakhan's attempted gradual movement towards a form of universalism has roughly been mirrored by the AHIJ's acceptance of the state of Israel, although the latter has been much more successful both internally and externally. For them, the emigration path was surely critical to their success: removed from the pressure of American society, government and racial bias they were able to evolve in a new direction. Farrakhan's other attempted move, towards Sunni Islam, has no parallel – the religious form of Ben Ammi's community has not noticeably moved towards a closer relationship with rabbinic Judaism, even if their political and eschatological outlook has adapted. However as Nathan Saunders comments with regard to Farrakhan's mellowing, 'describing whites as racially degenerate and wicked, and calling African Americans to remove themselves from white society does not resonate quite as much as it did in the mid-twentieth century.'[7] For Ben Ammi, the progressive acceptance and integration in Israel as well as the shifts in American society have provided cause for reassessment and deradicalization.

Ben Ammi's AHIJ clearly fulfils Anthony Pinn's 'quest for complex subjectivity', in that they have redefined the nature of Black America, in a very similar way to that of Elijah Muhammad's Nation of Islam. However, they have gone beyond what Muhammad created by establishing a community outside of America with significant impact globally. They have also succeeded in creating a forward-thinking community who have broken with American capitalism and foreground the most pressing contemporary issues such as ecological degradation. Ben Ammi's agility in transcending old, potentially challenging doctrines of imminent Armageddon demonstrates an adaptable and skilful thinker. These ideas have allowed the AHIJ to create a programme for the future where members are engaged outside of the community in helping disadvantaged communities. In essence, the historical narrative may not be so important, but rather what it does: it offers the African diaspora a grounded identity, stretching back before the incursions of Europeans; it provides a sense of dignity.

Theologically, what Ben Ammi might most powerfully demonstrate is the problematic presumption of Christianity behind Black theology. William Jones wrote that:

> Once it is concluded that Christianity is infected with 'Whitianity,' once it is granted that a racist doctrine of the tradition has been perpetuated, the tradition must be scrutinised in the most radical and comprehensive manner. Like the rotten apples in the barrel of good apples, nothing prior to the examination can be regarded as sacrosanct for black theology be it God, Jesus, or the Bible. Each and every category must be painstakingly inspected, and if it is found to be infected with the virus of racism or oppression, it must be cast aside.[8]

Ben Ammi does quite literally this. And the parts he has found wanting – the Pauline elements of the New Testament, the Caucasian Israelites and the very nature of Christianity as a faith itself – have been jettisoned in pursuit of a new, Tanakh-based religion which is re-read through the lens of the African American experience.

Gnostic resonances

In his classical text on Gnosticism, Hans Jonas noted, 'The cardinal feature of gnostic thought is the radical dualism that governs the relation of God and world, and correspondingly that of man and world.'[9] Stephen Finley has already argued for the Gnostic character of Nation of Islam mythology, and Ammi seems to take up this motif.[10] Jonas divided Gnostic dualism into two types: the Iranian and the Syrian-Egyptian, where the former is a dualism of cosmic principles pitted against each other, and the latter one in which a deficient/evil principle emerges from the primordial and absolute principle of good. Where Ben Ammi, like Elijah Muhammad, differs from the former type is that their dualism operates within the framework of monotheism. The binary is fundamentally present at a lower ontological level than that of divinity, even though it is characterized in terms of God versus satan. This is necessary because both Ammi and Muhammad are committed to the omnipotence of God and the final victory of good according to the divine plan. Thus, while the finite lives of human beings are characterized by an unavoidable and overwhelming struggle between light and darkness, on the infinite level of divinity there is no struggle because God is in complete control. Both thinkers are therefore closer to the model of Syrian-Egyptian

Gnosticism, in which the good-evil struggle is always subsumed under the rulership of God. We can see this in Ben Ammi because, despite the radical destructiveness and ontological opposition of the evil force to the good, God alone is the generative principle; evil by its nature wants to annihilate reality. The essentiality of this articulation of the second pole into a concentrated form to the creation of the world, as we know it, very often engenders an anti-materialist worldview which rejects creation as irredeemably tainted. In Ben Ammi, as in Muhammad, this is expressed through the total rejection of white Eurocentric society, although Ammi (perhaps demonstrating the influence of economic debates within Black Power in the 1960s, which came too late to influence Muhammad) goes further in rejecting also capitalism as an essential evil inseparable from white supremacy.

We can also perceive in Ammi's articulation of the *logos* as a fake-god, who simultaneously deceives humanity into worshipping them while they believe they worship the Creator, and is steadily remaking humanity in their own image, as replicating the Gnostic demiurge. This deceiving deity has bound humanity – and especially the Israelites, who in this schema represent the pneumatics, the Gnostics themselves who bear a direct relation to the true, Alien, God – into a confusing world of chaos, which we know is not right but cannot recognize how to escape from. This-world as a prison is very effectively transformed into the this-world of American Hell as an ongoing captivity. The Gnostic notion of a pre-cosmic fall of some element of divinity, leading to the 'captivity' of this part within material reality can be seen within Ammi's myth of the fall of the Adamic Civilization, leading to the present dispensation of descent, which has culminated in the literal captivity of Israelites in America, representing the lowest possible rung of existence.[11]

Most potent however is the motif of concealment. Often expressed in Gnostic thought as the soul's forgetting of its true (divine) nature and its absorption into the bodily world, this is replicated by Ammi and Muhammad in the forced amnesia of Black Americans' true identity, and the progressive adoption by them of American identity along with the fundamentally corrupt/evil mode of European consciousness. We could apply verbatim to Ben Ammi the famous dictum of Valentinus: 'What liberates is the knowledge of who we were, what we became; where we were, where into we have been thrown; whereto we speed, wherefrom we are redeemed; what birth is, and what rebirth' (*Exc. Theod.* 78. 2). Jonas comments that in the metaphor of a soporific existence, an imposed amnesia, we are dealing 'not with a mythological detail, a mere episode in a narrative, but with a fundamental feature of existence in the world to which the whole redemptional enterprise of the extramundane deity is related. The "world" on its part makes elaborate efforts to create and maintain this state in its victims and to counteract the operation of awakening.' The sleeping pseudo-death of existence in a world which suppresses our access to knowledge is one expressed commonly in twentieth-century Black American culture, as John Jackson has shown; and it is broader than just this: a generalized cultural Gnosticism, which views with suspicion the surface narrative and conspicuous consumption of late twentieth-century America has been expressed several times in popular culture, the most notable examples being the films *They Live*, *The Matrix*, and more recently the aforementioned *Get Out*. These films share the basic imprint of innocent humans asleep and drugged by the overwhelming deception which dominates American culture – a deception based in conspicuous consumption and surface pleasantries which conceals a vampiric agenda, an alien presence manipulating and consuming us.

In addition, there is another icon of twentieth-century popular culture which may be useful in understanding Ben Ammi. The visionary sci-fi writer Philip K Dick wrote of his own work that it told 'a message of one world obscuring or replacing another (real) one, spurious memories, & hallucinated (irreal) worlds, the message reads 'Don't believe what you see; it's an enthralling – & destructive, evil snare. *Under* it is a totally different world, even placed differently along the linear time axis. And your memories are faked to jibe with the fake world.'[12] Dick, born in 1928, wrote the majority of his work during the 1960s and 1970s, admittedly in a very different environment. He was also a keenly religious thinker, fascinated with not just similar concepts, but also similar source texts as Ben Ammi. In considering the gnostic aspects of Ben Ammi's thought, it is worth considering how it relates to Dick.

Dick was generally interested in telling the story of a single person trying to figure out the illusion that entrapped them, trying to realize which of their memories were false, implanted and what the truth was that lay underneath them. But if he had told the story of a people, it would certainly not be unlike Ben Ammi's: a people trying to find their way out of a grand lie that had consumed them for centuries, concealing their past and replacing it with a fictitious one; all constructed by an evil spiritual force that sought only annihilation and recognized the true spiritual potency of this one group, and therefore the necessity of suppressing them first. Furthermore, it would not be at all unusual in his corpus. The epic struggle between truth and falsity, not only of the past but of how to live and how to make it to the future, is a grand narrative worthy of high-end science fiction or fantasy; in this it is perhaps like the esoteric narrative of many religions, demonstrative of the connection between epic fiction and our mythical worlds.

Dick's autobiographical character Horselover Fat describes in *Valis* the reception of a stream of near-infinite information seemingly downloaded from another realm via a beam of pink light (an experience Phil actually had, in March of 1974).[13] His significant realization from this data was that 'the empire never ended': the evolution and collapse of the Roman Empire after New Testament times were an illusion, time had been artificially stretched, but behind the appearance of the twentieth century we were still in the reality of first century Judea, encompassed by the demonic and oppressive force of the Roman Empire. The discovery of the Nag Hammadi texts in 1945, and the Dead Sea Scrolls in 1948 – during the formative years of both Dick and Ammi – indicated the spiritual moment we inhabit, when a rupture in the illusion allowed some crucial message to break through from the invisible 'real' world. It is intriguing to consider the similarity in outlooks and interpretations of these two thinkers who never encountered one another.

The twentieth century has shifted our sense of reality and our certainties in many ways – these historical findings changed our knowledge of the history of Christianity and Judaism, the religions that have shaped and informed western culture, but more broadly we have discovered much about power, human nature and history, empire, gender and many other things. The gnostic veiling/unveiling of a hidden world, one concealed perhaps *by* a cultural hegemony which presumed its own divine status is, as Slavoj Zizek hinted,[14] the popular religious impulse of this era, for good reason: we can see things now, and see in ways now, that humans before us could not, including the relativity of our own myths. Grand narratives have been mortally challenged by the fragmentation of societies. Ben Ammi comes from this era, and speaks powerfully about many aspects of it – he is a prophet for our times.

The connections highlighted herein are obvious and potent, signifying the importance of Gnosticism as an adaptable model which can be applied independently by different groups to understand their diverse worlds. Another system which has been read as a modern iteration of Gnosticism is the Kabbalah of Isaac Luria, and in this we will find an arguably even greater degree of correspondence.

Kabbalistic resonances

The kabbalist Isaac Luria (1534–72) was born in Jerusalem and lived in the Land of Israel for most of his life, although he studied also in Egypt. He was the son of an Ashkenazi father and Sephardic mother, in the generation following the expulsion of the large and ancient Jewish communities from Spain in 1492 and Portugal in 1497. Luria's rich and complex mythology was informed by the Zohar and other kabbalistic writings of previous centuries, but he created a new narrative of creation and meaning which quickly spread and captivated the Jewish world with its potent articulation of a cosmos gone-wrong. He described creation as born of a primordial error due to the flow of divine energy which shattered the intended vessels (the sefirot), leaving reality as a kind of miscarriage hanging limply in the demonic realm, subject to the constant presence of evil forces. The pioneer of scholarship on Jewish mysticism, Gershom Scholem, argued that Lurianic Kabbalah represented an attempt to allegorically explain the dislocation and chaos that the Jews of the sixteenth century found in their world.[15] For Luria and his followers, the impetus was upon the Jews to repair the divine structure, by performing *mitzvot*, hence drawing divine energy down into the phenomenal world, ameliorating and restoring it to its position in direct communion with God. The details of Ben Ammi's system are of course different, but I will argue that some of the most important aspects of Ben Ammi's thought can be found to closely parallel that of Luria.[16]

The initial similarity is obvious: it is the already described Gnostic element of concealment, of yearning for a higher truth and escape from (and explanation of) a corrupt and suffering world. It is what makes Lurianic Kabbalah, in the words of Gershom Scholem, a 'myth of exile and redemption'.[17] It tells the story of creation as one of a cosmic error, in which a flaw generates the apparent universe that we live in. The flawed nature of reality is explained by reference to this primordial error, which is in the process of being worked-out, although creation hangs broken and distant from the Divine source. Humanity (and Israel in particular) is in exile from their Divine source, poetically representing the material condition of Jews living subservient under gentile rule, scattered throughout the nations. Although the biblical creation story is not literally true, it represents key incidents in reality as metaphorical drama. Ben

Ammi's narrative tells of a true story behind the metaphor of Eden, Adam and Eve, and the serpent, where a great flaw was imbued into the world, such that the flawed world we inhabit is one of increasing descent, surrounded by the threatening presence of satan; the exile of the slave trade in particular represents the culmination of the evil force, indicating the necessity of a 'return' to righteousness. The Hebrew Israelite narrative too is a myth of exile and redemption.

There are some deeper resonances, which we might divide into two basic kinds: those of mythology and those of ontology. The first represent similar interpretations of the Edenic narrative, in particular with regard to the emergence of evil and the 'impregnation' of humanity by the serpent. Curiously, both Luria and Ammi articulate this concept: the serpent was responsible not just for convincing humans to disobey God, but actually inseminated the human bloodline with its evil, creating another crypto-genetic lineage *within* humankind, a second 'seed' in conflict with the divine Adamic lineage. Ben Ammi himself writes that:

> God also told the serpent that he would put enmity between the two seeds, thus separating the serpentine seed and the Holy seed, and setting the tone for the struggle between good and evil, the Sons of Light and the sons of darkness. As the plan of God continued to unfold, Adam is used to impregnate Eve, and thus to bring forth in the flesh the substance of the two seeds that she had allowed to be impregnated in her mind in the Garden of Eden. Thus were born Cain and Abel, representing the serpentine seed and the Holy seed. We see from the events that followed (Cain killing Abel) that Cain was the continuity of the serpentine seed.
>
> (MEW51)

This was discussed in Chapter 1, which briefly noted a similar tradition in the Talmud (b.Shab.146a, cf. b.Yeb.103b; b.Abod.Zar.22b). There, the story is told that the serpent inseminated Eve with poison – describing it with a grotesque eroticism as *zohama,* 'slime' – which mixed with her descendants' bloodline. The poison was negated by Israel's encounter with God at Sinai, however gentiles still bear it. While the Talmud does not discuss this further, the Zohar (1.52a–54a) links the serpent's poison with the evil inclination, and claims that the worship of the golden calf reinscribed the Israelites' state of sin. Developing this theme, the core doctrinal section of the Zohar, Idra Rabba (3.143a), explains that the serpent was a manifestation of harsh judgement – the divine energies which act to compress the otherwise overflowing mercy – and after penetrating Eve with these energies, she rid herself of them by producing Cain, and to a lesser extent Abel.[18] Furthermore, the spirits of murderer and murdered persist, from which come the souls of brazen sinners and messenger spirits respectively (while righteous souls come from Adam). Melila Hellner-Eshed notes that Cain and Abel, having been expelled from the primordial body of Adam 'ultimately become the source of evil in the human world'.[19] According to Luria, however, it was through the mixing of the seed from the serpent and from Adam that Cain and Abel (and subsequently all humanity) came out a mixture of good and evil.

The similarity of this obscure rabbinic tradition to that of Ben Ammi is attention-grabbing. Even more so is Luria's use of it to argue that it represents the blending of good and evil in all subsequent humanity. The notion that the serpent channels the force of evil into humanity through its impregnation of Eve and siring of Cain, and Cain's responsibility not just for the inauguration of murder in the world, but Cain's spirit as the literal source of evil in human beings, are readings not found in any Christian tradition, to my knowledge.[20]

It is difficult to know where Ben Ammi might have learnt of this tradition; he could easily have read of it in a number of different sources, however the way it functions within his system bears the strongest resemblance to the Zoharic/kabbalistic view, which Oded Yisraeli reasons to be 'the first version of the legend in Jewish exegetical circles' to locate Cain as the 'nest' and progenitor of all human evil.[21]

The Lurianic myth of the exile of the Shekhina can be seen to be reflected in a more condensed form, in Ammi's notion of the occultation of God and Torah achieved for the last 2000 years – Israel was unable to reconnect with God, was lost in a world of shells, a demonic reality of powerful evil forces. It is only through reawakening and performing *mitzvot*, to connect themselves once again with God and to revivify themselves and the world – to resurrect the dry bones – that they can set the world to rights and re-establish the broken divine unity.[22]

In reading reality as we know it as the product of an error or catastrophe, Ben Ammi constructs significant embellishment to what went before in Luria: for Ammi the reality that was created by mistake is the last 6000 years. This present dispensation however was prefigured by an even longer era of purity, the Edenic civilization which predated Adam, and has now been forgotten. This suggestion of a Golden Age, although only a very minor motif within Ammi's output, differentiates Ben Ammi quite distinctly from Luria and Gnosticism, which *begin* the cosmic drama with catastrophe. Ben Ammi offers a complex reading of Genesis, whereby it provides the instantiating paradigm for our reality, while holding that reality to be preceded by a much longer era of purity.

While Luria does not tie Esau-Jacob into his cosmology, Edom is particularly important to him. According to him, the Edomite Kings of Gen.36.31 represent the vessels which broke under the pressure of the energies of Judgement, and fell into the uncreated and undivine demonic depths. This breaking and descent represents both a first stage in the separation of judgment from compassion and the first stage of manifest reality, as creation is built upon/within these. Therefore, the primordial destruction/error from which creation as we know it emerged could be perceived as itself part of the corrective process. The Kings of Edom represent the separation of evil from good just as Ben Ammi argues Edom represents the concentration of evil, separated from the concentration of good which was present in the descendants of Jacob: Israel. While the presence of evil in reality is a problem addressed and explained by most religions, the articulation of the problem as the *mixing* of good and evil and the need for their separation, rather than simply extinguishing the latter, is highly specific and not to my knowledge evidenced elsewhere. Hence, one of the principle cosmological motifs developed by Ben Ammi – the problematic mingling of good and evil as the flaw of creation which it is the work of humanity now to undo – can be seen as predicted within Lurianic Kabbalah.

Related to this is Ben Ammi's metaphysical conception of Truth, discussed in Chapter 1. Truth in Ammi's system functions somewhat akin to Light in the kabbalists': it is the principal energetic emanation from God, which shares God's divinity without being personified, and it is that which nourishes and sustains manifest reality.[23] Primordial Light for Luria however seems to be a complex entity, admitting the presence of both divine Judgement (*din*) and Compassion (*rakhamim*, not to be confused with *chesed*, Lovingkindness). This primordial admixture of negative and positive means that the need for *tikkun* is, so to speak, baked into creation (creation is in fact an expression of the complex impurity of divinity). It is, then, the human responsibility to perform *mitzvot* in order to separate good from evil in the created realm, which will effect the purification of the divine, resulting in a God who is purged of the potentially dangerous quality of Judgement. Here, then, the disentangling of good and evil is the work of humanity, as it is in Ben Ammi – who likewise reads this entanglement back to Edenic times as the indulgence in the Tree of Good and Evil. While the presence of evil or temptation within Eden is a part of any reading of that narrative, the symbolic reading of the Edenic struggle as representing the earliest stages of a cosmic battle *within* humanity, which must effect the separation of Good and Evil within itself, is specific here.

The overwhelming emphasis on Mosaic Law, and the performance of commandments as a means of *repairing* the world is shared by Ammi and Luria. Lawrence Fine states that it was the unbending commitment to traditional *halakhah* which allowed the huge revisions of Lurianic kabbalah's theology to maintain its position within rabbinic Judaism without the overwhelming condemnation of the establishment.[24] This is simply to reiterate the oft-made claim that Judaism is far more committed to orthopraxy than orthodoxy, but it is worth noting that, when Interior Minister Aryeh Deri, of the Haredi (Ultra-Orthodox) Shas party, visited the Village of Peace in 1990 it was very likely the community's strict adherence to biblical law that convinced him to begin normalizing their status, in spite of their ideological or theological differences. The orthopraxy of Judaism is a central focus of Ben Ammi's Hebrew Israelite thought – not in terms of minutely correct practice of the commandments, as the rabbis are, but in simple terms of keeping to the Torah's laws.

Tikkun is, of course, a central part of Lurianic thought, and one that has become a central pillar of Reform Judaism. The doctrine that human beings have a responsibility to perform right actions imbues a strong sense of human partnership with God in completing and perfecting creation. This concept is present even in non-kabbalistic forms of Judaism.

There is more than a surface similarity between Ammi and Luria's doctrines however. The pneumatic ontology which undergirds them both is striking. Chapters 4 and 6 examined the significance of the Holy Spirit in Ben Ammi's system, where it plays the role of immanent divine presence, which transmits divine energy into the human and the world. Likewise, Adam Afterman has demonstrated that in the Kabbalah of the sixteenth century, the Holy Spirit was understood as not merely the medium of prophetic inspiration, but articulated 'a more ambitious ideal of mystical integration with the divine in daily life'.[25] Afterman describes how for these kabbalists, utilizing pneumatic and phosphoric imagery, 'The cleaving of the human to the divine influx – conceptualized as a pneumatic divine substance – was configured as the height of religious and human existence, ultimately leading to the ontological fusion of the human with the highest powers of the divine.'[26] Critically however, this *devekut* (cleaving) or *unio mystica* was not one of the soul's ascent, but of the *drawing down* of divinity: In the work of (Luria's student) Chaim Vital, 'the goal is to embody the divine essence – overflowing in the form of the holy spirit through the channel formed through the elongated soul – and not to ascend mystically and leave the body'. This is 'self-sanctification – the transformation of one's self into a vessel or chariot for the indwelling of the divine'.[27] The individual draws down light from the supernal root of their soul, the ongoing umbilical cord that attaches them to their source.

Action and the performance of commandments was the central focus of this drawing-down.[28] Moshe Cordovero, a critical influence on Luria, wrote in *Tomer Devorah* that humans must imitate God in righteousness, and by so doing will attain the Divine image and likeness in which they were made.[29] Thereby, they would theurgically open the flow of divine energy on high to flow down to the phenomenal world: 'As he behaves, so will be the affluence from above, and he will cause that quality to shine upon earth.'[30] As Patrick Koch notes, 'The practitioner thus sustains the very existence of the mundane realm by safeguarding the constant flow of divine power from above.'[31]

We have seen Ben Ammi argue for the physical effects of righteousness. Afterman describes a text of Cordovero's disciple, where:

Sanctification occurs on an ontological and substantial level; the entire human being – body, soul, and mind – is understood as undergoing mystical fusion. This holiness is attained by refraining from prohibited behavior and engaging in righteous behavior. Thus, the human being is transformed into a vessel or chariot for the divine influx, which causes the mystical fusion to occur between the divine and human.[32]

Chaim Vital, Luria's most prolific student and popularizer, writes that keeping the commandments is essential to purifying the soul in its structure as it mirrors the body:

The man whose spirit has moved him to be one who comes to be purified and sanctified, to take upon himself the yoke of the heavenly kingdom in its true way, should prepare himself with all of his strength, and he should hurry to fulfill all 613 commandments. For in their fulfillment, the 613 limbs and sinews of his intellective soul will be perfected [or made whole], as was mentioned earlier. For if he lacks even one *mitzvah* from among the 248 positive commandments, then he still lacks one limb of his soul.[33]

That the 'limbs and sinews' of the soul will be repaired and vivified through the transmission of the Holy Spirit, as a result of fulfilling *mitzvot*, replicates in no uncertain terms Ben Ammi's doctrine that performance of the Commandments is necessary for physical health; we must recall that the soul for Ben Ammi is actually the inner organs of the body.[34] Vital says, 'For the human being, through his actions, draws forth life to the heavens and the earth, and it is as though he himself planted them and established them.'[35] Vital expresses this as cultivating 'resemblance to the Creator', that is, reimbuing the image of God in oneself. He writes,

> It is fitting for a person [to cultivate] resemblance to his Creator, and then he will be in the secret of the supernal form, in image and likeness. For if he resembles [his Creator] in his body, but not in actions (then he shames the form), and others will say of him: "a beautiful form and ugly deeds." For the essence of the supernal image and likeness are his actions.[36]

This expression of divinity through the self might be seen in Ben Ammi's assertion that he is embodying the same spirit that animated Yeshua; however, there is another surprising angle which should be highlighted: Ben Ammi spoke favourably of the invoking of ancestor spirits, naming this as an African tradition. Unusually within rabbinic Judaism, Luria also believed in and practised communing with the spirits of ancestors. This practice, which is otherwise unknown as an operative rite, required the communing of live and dead spirits, to the extent that they became bound together. Luria's term for these practices was *yichudim*, or unifications, and the operative term is *devekut* (cleaving), the same term used for the individual's cleaving to God in prayer. Intriguingly, Luria apparently shared something akin to Ammi's belief in satanic 'possession', Lawrence Fine explaining that he believed when one commits idolatry, 'he is filled with a "strange god" whose removal can only be brought about through great acts of repentance'.[37] This 'strange god' is in fact a demonic presence, from the *qlippot*.

This path was one whereby the human became a vessel for the Holy Spirit, which is understood as not a created or semi-divine entity, but is fully identified with God. The kabbalists at this point were therefore describing a 'spirit' which was fully divine, which flowed down from the height of divinity and nourished the world. Individual action – i.e. the keeping of the commandments – was crucial in that this helped to draw down the overflow; this would happen via the individual soul, which was rooted like an umbilical cord into divinity, and so by the performance of *mitzvot* each individual could act as a channel through which divine energy would enter the world, helping to heal the cosmos which had emerged deformed. The parallels here with Ben Ammi's theological system are apparent, and impressive: in both, through performance of *mitzvot*, the divine spirit is embodied by human beings and brought into the world in order to sustain, nourish and heal a creation which went wrong; the suffering of the Israelites signifies a cosmic breach which can only be healed through human agency.

This could be asserted as the principal pragmatic emphasis which the two systems share: The deep sense in which human agency has power even over God; God is effectively passive, at most trying to attract humans to certain behaviours. But good and evil actions manifest and *realize* God or satan in the world, indicating that without these actions the respective spirit would vanish. Thus in a very real sense, God needs humans because human actions make God real. In acting as the final stage in the divine body, human beings are the vessel of communication between physical world and divine spirit. We are called upon to use our choices to deepen that connection, and to *save* God by bringing God into the material world.

Finally I will offer a speculative suggestion as to why these similarities may be present, which will lead to a recommendation for future research. First, to one familiar with both movements, there are some pertinent similarities in historical condition: Ben Ammi wrote as a descendent of enslaved Africans, after centuries of persecution finally attaining some degree of liberty and beginning to consider why such a condition would have ensnared them; he had taken his people back to the Promised Land and was beginning a process of healing. Luria and his colleagues worked as the first generation of Sephardic Jews after the traumatic expulsion from Spain and Portugal, having been uprooted from their own home of many centuries which had become progressively more abusive towards them, finally presenting them with the choice of expulsion, conversion or death. Luria too was back in the Land of Israel. Both had faced severe cultural trauma and were attempting to explain the history via theological myth, creating a new system, based on their inherited traditions of interpretation (for Luria, most important was the Zohar).

Other than simply recreating a surprisingly similar idiosyncratic interpretation of the same source material, Ben Ammi could have absorbed the traditions indirectly from a number of sources. One of his colleagues might have read of these, although this is unlikely given the absence of popularly available texts describing these Kabbalistic doctrines. It is not impossible that Ammi, Shaleak or other members of the AHIJ discussed theology with some kabbalistically knowledgeable Israelis, although it is dubious that ideas gained in this way would have been integrated so fully into Ammi's system. The final option would be learning these doctrines from their own teachers.

As mentioned, the teachers of Ammi were largely students of Wentworth Arthur Matthew. Matthew had described a cabbalistic aspect to his Judaism, one which he claimed marked it out as authentic. An important part of this was the indwelling God doctrine, described in Chapter 4. Coming from the Caribbean, Matthew himself could well have been descended from Jewish slaveholders, part of a community of mixed-race Jews who inherited some parts of the tradition, according to whether they were considered part of the family or not. While slaves generally would only be taught Torah, not Talmud and certainly not Kabbalah, it is not impossible that freed family members would learn some kabbalistic ideas.

Ben Ammi's traditions do not share the esoteric aspects of Lurianic Kabbalah, but most deeply share the concepts based around action and manifestation; the internal divine drama that Luria is most famous for is not reflected at all in Ammi's thought, and neither is any *sefirotic* doctrine. The parts that Ben Ammi evinces are those that were contained in the Safedian *musar* literature, conduct handbooks which became quite popular in the generations after Luria himself, and which sought to boil down Kabbalah to basic rules of conduct for those not interested in the esoteric details.[38] One of these, Isaiah Horowitz's *Two Tablets of the Covenant* (*Shnei Luchot ha-Brit*, 1649, Amsterdam), drew heavily on Lurianic mythology, and explicitly shares virtually all of the features also found in Ammi's theology: the intimate attachment of God and human; the unnaturalness of death, which entered humanity because of sin, i.e. actions through which Adam 'cut himself off from the source of life'; the blending of good and evil as congenital catastrophe in creation; the seminal pollution inherited from the serpent becoming a part of humanity's lineage, condemning them to mortality, and being directly responsible for the ethical struggle of all subsequent history; suffering as purifying; but human action (choosing Good over Evil) can repair the sin and bring the Messianic Age; *devekut* is achieved through performance of *mitzvot*; theurgy is central, worldly reward and punishment is directly related to performance of *mitzvot*, yet God is imbedded in the world and does not intervene supernaturally (i.e. via miracles); Joseph Citron describes the process of God's response to human actions as 'instantaneous' and even 'mechanical' to an extent that compromised divine free will.[39] Could it be that the wisdom of these handbooks filtered into Matthew's thought, and through his ordained rabbis in Chicago, into Ben Ammi? This suggestion is a radical one, and one which depends upon a presumption categorically rejected by most scholars: that Wentworth Matthew came from a family that had some prior Jewish background. I believe this presumption needs to be reassessed.

Notes

Acknowledgements

1   Chapter 2 draws upon 'The African Hebrew Israelites of Jerusalem,' Originally
    published in the *Critical Dictionary of Apocalyptic and Millenarian Movements*
    (www.CDAMM.org) by the Centre for the Critical Study of Apocalyptic and
    Millenarian Movements, part of Panacea Charitable Trust (www.cenSAMM.org);
    Chapter 6 contains a revised version of part of 'Ben Ammi's Adaptation of Veganism
    in the Theology of the African Hebrew Israelites', *Interdisciplinary Journal for Religion
    and Transformation in Contemporary Society* 7.2 (2021).

Introduction

1   On One West, see Sam Kestenbaum, 'I'm an Israelite': Kendrick Lamar's Spiritual
    Search, Hebrew Israelite Religion, and the Politics of a Celebrity Encounter', in
    Kendrick Lamar and the Making of Black Meaning, ed. Christopher M. Driscoll,
    Anthony B. Pinn and Monica R. Miller (Oxon: Routledge, 2020), pp. 16, and
    Saifeldeen Zihiri, 'Ambassadors of Christ and Israel United in Christ: Comparing the
    Preaching Strategies of Black Hebrew Israelite Camps', *UCLA Journal of Religion* 4
    (2020), pp. 30–68.
2   African communities claiming association – either by choice or by descent – with
    Judaism now cover Cameroon, Equatorial Guinea, Gabon, Ghana, Ivory Coast,
    Kenya, Madagascar, Malawi, Mozambique, Nigeria, Rwanda, South Africa, Uganda,
    Zambia and Zimbabwe, and may number several million. On these groups see Edith
    Bruder, *The Black Jews of Africa: History, Identity, Religion* (Oxford: Oxford University
    Press, 2008); Daniel Lis, William F.S. Miles and Tudor Parfitt (eds), *In the Shadow of
    Moses: New Jewish Movements in Africa and the Diaspora* (Loyola: African Academic
    Press, 2016); Tudor Parfitt and Netanel Fisher (eds), *Becoming Jewish: New Jews
    and Emerging Jewish Communities in a Globalized World* (Cambridge: Cambridge
    Scholars Publishing, 2016); Nathan P. Devir, *New Children of Israel: Emerging Jewish
    Communities in an Era of Globalization* (Salt Lake: University of Utah Press, 2017);
    and Marla Brettschneider, Edith Bruder and Magdel Le Roux (eds), *Africana Jewish
    Journeys: Studies in African Judaism* (Cambridge: Cambridge Scholars Press, 2019).
3   Edith Bruder, 'Black Philo-Semitism versus Racial Myths', in *Africana Jewish
    Journeys*, pp. 2–18.
4   Devir, *Children of Israel*, p. xv.
5   In addition to those mentioned above, see Tudor Parfitt, *Black Jews in Africa and the
    Americas* (London: Harvard University Press, 2013) and Edith Bruder and Tudor
    Parfitt (eds), *African Zion: Studies in Black Judaism* (Newcastle: Cambridge Scholars
    Publishing, 2012). The possible explanations, each of which has some merit, for the

respective communities' claims, include: authentic Israelite heritage; adoption of 'Jewish' identity to avoid forced conversion to Islam; the internalization of colonial and missionary assertions of some tribes' Israelite identity; descent from persecuted Iberian Jews who fled into Africa; and the recognition of a greater similarity to tribal traditions in the Old Testament than the New.

6   Howard Brotz, *The Black Jews of Harlem: Negro Nationalism and the Dilemmas of Negro Leadership* (London: Free Press of Glencoe, 1964); Ruth Landes, 'Negro Jews in Harlem', *Jewish Journal of Sociology* 9.2 (1967), pp. 175–89; Graenum Berger, *Black Jews in America: A Documentary with Commentary* (New York: Commission on Synagogue Relations, 1978); James Landing, *Black Judaism: The Story of an American Movement* (Durham: Carolina Academic Press, 2002); Jacob S. Dorman, *Chosen People: The Rise of American Black Israelite Religions* (Oxford: Oxford University Press, 2013); Bruce D. Haynes, *The Soul of Judaism: Jews of African Descent in America* (New York: New York University Press, 2018).

7   Walter Isaac, 'Locating Afro-American Judaism: A Critique of White Normativity', in *The Companion to African American Studies*, ed. Lewis R. Gordon & Jane Anna Gordon (Malden, MA: Blackwell, 2006), pp. 512–42; 'Beyond Ontological Jewishness: A Philosophical Reflection on the Study of African American Jews and the Social Problems of the Jewish and Human Sciences' (Temple University: PhD Diss., 2012).

8   See, e.g., Eli Faber, *Jews, Slaves, and the Slave Trade: Setting the Record Straight* (New York: New York University Press, 1998).

9   See esp. Jonathan Schorsch, *Jews and Blacks in the Early Modern World* (Cambridge: Cambridge University Press, 2004); Aviva Ben-Ur, *Jewish Autonomy in a Slave Society: Suriname in the Atlantic World, 1651–1825* (Philadelphia: University of Pennsylvania Press, 2020); Laura Arnold Leibman, *Once We Were Slaves: The Extraordinary Journey of a Multiracial Jewish Family* (Oxford: Oxfrod University Press, 2021).

10   For a discussion of the 'irony' of diaspora Africans' 'continued involvement and investment in Christianity', see Anthony Reddie, 'Introduction', in *Black Theology, Slavery and Contemporary Christianity* (Oxon: Routledge, 2016), pp. 1–29.

11   Anthony Pinn, *Terror and Triumph: The Nature of Black Religion* (Minneapolis: Fortress Press, 2003), p. 179.

12   The precise meaning of this term will be discussed extensively in Chapter 3.

13   Mark L. Chapman, *Christianity on Trial: African-American Religious Thought before and after Black Power* (Eugene, OR: Wipf & Stock, 1996), p. 70.

14   Author of *We the Black Jews: Witness to the 'White Jewish Race' Myth* (Baltimore, MD: Black Classic Press, 1993 (1983)). Ben-Yochannan's colourful history cannot be repeated here, but he stood in the line of African American individuals whose own assertions about their background – in this case Ethiopian Jewish – as well as advanced qualifications, have been found wanting by others. See the obituary: Sam Kestenbaum, 'Contested Legacy of Dr. Ben, a Father of African Studies', *New York Times*, 27th March 2015.

15   'Deportations by Israel Hit', *The Philadelphia Inquirer*, 12th October 1971, p. 5; 'Black Israelites Hit Israel Immigration Ban', *Philadelphia Jewish Exponent*, 15th October 1971, p. 1; 76.

16   Reprinted as *God, the Bible and the Black Man's Destiny* (Baltimore: Afrikan World Books, 2001 (1970)).

17   John Jackson has already argued the relevance of Ben Ammi to Afrocentrism, see John L. Jackson, 'All Yah's Children: Emigrationism, Afrocentrism, and the Place of Israel in Africa', *Civilisations* 58.1 (2009), pp. 93–112.

18   See their own website, *House of Yahweh: Pillar and Ground of Truth*, https://yahweh.com/.
19   See Dorman, *Chosen People*.
20   Albert Ehrman, 'Black Judaism in New York', *Journal of Ecumenical Studies* 8.1 (1971), pp. 103–14 (108).
21   Albert J. Raboteau, *A Fire in the Bones: Reflections on African-American Religious History* (Boston: Beacon Press, 1995), pp. 17–18.
22   Stephen C. Finley, 'The Secret … of Who the Devil Is': Elijah Muhammad, the Nation of Islam, and Theological Phenomenology', in *New Perspectives on the Nation of Islam*, ed. Dawn-Marie Gibson and Herbert Berg (New York: Routledge, 2017), pp. 154–73 (155).
23   It should be noted that Ben Ammi's AHIJ, as their name suggests, consider themselves fully African – in contrast to the fragmented New York City Hebrew Israelite groups descending from Abba Bivens' One West Camp who reject any association with Africa. These latter perceive Africans as sharing responsibility with Arabs for selling the Israelites into slavery, so while sharing a skin tone they are a completely distinct people: Israelites are Semitic, Africans Hamitic.
24   Lewis Gordon, 'The Problem of History in African American Theology', in *The Oxford Handbook of African American Theology*, ed. Katie G. Cannon and Anthony B. Pinn (Oxford: Oxford University Press, 2014), pp. 363–76.
25   According to all official documentation I have seen, his legal name was Ben not Benjamin.
26   Penny (Dr Yvonne Gillie-Wallace) is Ben's cousin on his maternal side – her father Frank F. Gillie being Rena's brother. Her mother was Lillie Mae Gillie. Frank and Rena's parents were Joseph and Mary Gillie. Penny was instrumental in filling in some details of Ben's biography for this chapter, for which I am very grateful.
27   Prince Gavriel HaGadol and Odehyah Baht Israel, *The Impregnable People: An Exodus of African Americans Back to Africa* (Washington, DC: Communicators Press, 1993), p. 42.
28   Harold's parents, Roy Lee Washington Sr (1897–1953) and Bertha Jones Washington (1898–1980) divorced in 1928. Bertha and her second husband Ernest Oliver Price (1890–1949) had six children: Ernestine, Ernest Jr, Ramon, Gwendolynn, Elaine and Patricia.
29   Allen Alter (UPI), a syndicated article across the United States, e.g., 'Community of Black Hebrews Thriving Illegally in Israeli Desert', *The Brownsville Herald* (Brownsville, Texas) 30th October 1977, p. 45 This was not a tradition that Penny recalled, and the reaction of his family against his new identity seems to contradict this claim.
30   Landing notes possible confusion caused by both Lazarus and his father being named Joseph; it seems to me that Lazarus Sr is he who bore an association with the somewhat disreputable figure of Elder Warien Roberson (including being arrested together); he had apparently been active in New Jersey, closer to Roberson's Black Jews' Harlem location: Arnold Rosenzweig, 'Black Jews of South Side', pt 5, *Chicago Defender*, 2 February 1963, pp. 1–2; cf. Jackson, John L., Jr, *Thin Description: Ethnography and the African Hebrew Israelites of Jerusalem* (Cambridge, MA: Harvard University Press, 2013), p. 43, Landing, *Black Judaism*, p. 111).
31   It is unclear which branch of the UNIA as the movement had fractured after Garvey's arrest. In 1919 an offshoot, the Star Order of Ethiopia and Ethiopian Missionaries to Abyssinia formed, proclaiming that Black Americans were in fact Abyssinians and were thus protected from Jim Crow discrimination under the 1904 treaty; see *Negro in Chicago* p. 121. It was run by RD Jonas.

32 On Ethiopianism see George M. Fredrickson, *Black Liberation: A Comparative History of Black Ideologies in the United States and South Africa* (New York: Oxford University Press, 1995), pp. 57–93, and Wilson Jeremiah Moses, *The Golden Age of Black Nationalism 1850–1925* (Hamden: Archon Books, 1978), pp. 156–69, who defines it as:

> [T]he effort of the English-speaking black or African person to view his past enslavement and present cultural dependency in terms of the broader history of civilization. It serves to remind him that this present scientific technological civilization, dominated by Western Europe for a scant four hundred years, will go under certainly – like all the empires of the past. It expresses the belief that the tragic racial experience has profound historical value, that it has endowed the African with moral superiority and made him a seer. (pp. 160–1).

In one illuminating interview from the early 1920s, a Black Chicago shopkeeper proclaimed:

> I am a radical. I despise and hate the white man. They will always be against the Ethiopian. I do not want to be called Negro, colored, or 'nigger'. Either term is an insult to me or to you. Our rightful name is Ethiopian. White men stole the black man from Africa and counseled with each other as to what to do with him and what to call him, for when the Negro learned that he was the first civilized human on earth he would rise up and rebel against the white man. To keep him from doing this it was decided to call him Negro after the Niger River in Africa. This was to keep him from having that knowledge by the Bible, for his right name was Ethiopian. This was done so we could always be ruled by the white man. I will call your attention to the Bible. There is not one word of evil against the Children of Israel and Ethiopia written in it. Ethiopia came out of Israel and God said they are his people and he will be their God. He also says after the 300 years of punishment he will never go by [desert] Israel again and will be with him for ever and ever. We find by the Bible that he, the Ethiopian, is the only child of God. The three hundred years of punishment are up, and this is the year of deliverance. It started in 1619 when we were stolen from Africa and made slaves. God is taking care of the black man. Some great destruction will take place, but God's chosen people will be alright. (The Chicago Commission on Race Relations, *The Negro in Chicago: A Study of Race Relations and a Race Riot* (Chicago: University of Chicago Press, 1922), p. 480.

Here we can see, via Ethiopianism, an assertion of Israelite identity and heritage where Ethiopia, Israel and Black America are wholly identified. It is useful to compare this with some elements of Arnold Ford's teaching, see Landes, 'Negro Jews in Harlem', p. 183.

33 On Wentworth Matthew see Brotz, *Black Jews of Harlem*; Landing, *Black Judaism*, pp. 137–40; 205–80; Sholomo B. Levy, 'Wentworth Arthur Matthew', in *African American Lives*, ed. Henry Louis Gates Jr and Evelyn Brooks Higginbotham (Oxford: Oxford University Press, 2004), pp. 567–9; Dorman, *Chosen People*, pp. 152–81.

34 'Survey of Chicago's Black Jews II: Congregation Needs Torah and Ark, Reporter Told', *Jewish Post*, 1st October 1965; Azriel Devine, 'Rabbi Robert Devine', blackjews. com, https://www.blackjews.org/rabbi-robert-devine/ (accessed 3rd October 2022).

35 'Survey of Chicago's Black Jews III: Negro "Rabbi" Claims White Jews Not Jews', *Jewish Post*, 8th October 1965, p. 13.

36 The farm still exists today. See Jason George, 'Promised Land. Promise Fading', *Chicago Tribune*, 7th July 2008.

37 See esp. Merrill Charles Singer, 'Saints of the Kingdom: Group Emergence, Individual Affiliation, and Social Change among the Black Hebrews of Israel' (University of Utah: PhD Diss., 1979); Merrill Singer, 'Symbolic Identity Formation in an African American Religious Sect: The Black Hebrew Israelites', in *Black Zion: African American Religious Encounters with Judaism*, ed. Yvonne Chireau and Nathaniel Deutsch (New York: Oxford University Press, 2000), pp. 55–72; Ethan Michaeli, 'Another Exodus: The Hebrew Israelites from Chicago to Dimona'. In Chireau/Deutsch, *Black Zion*, pp. 73–90; Landing, *Black Judaism*, pp. 387–431.

38 Darlene Clark Hine, 'Introduction', in *The Black Chicago Renaissance*, ed. Darlene Clark Hine and John McCluskey Jr (Urbana: University of Illinois Press, 2012), pp. xv–xxxiii.

39 Landing, *Black Judaism*, pp. 315–26.

40 Christopher Robert Reed, *The Rise of Chicago's Black Metropolis: 1920–1929* (Urbana: University of Illinois Press, 2011), pp. 186–200.

41 Wallace D. Best, *Passionately Human, No Less Divine: Religion and Culture in Black Chicago, 1916–1952* (Princeton: Princeton University Press, 2005), p. 2. He continues, 'Black Chicago churches were far less "otherworldly," escapist, quietist, and otherwise socially disengaged than the normal depictions of early-twentieth-century African American religion' (p. 4).

42 Ibid., p. 45.

43 Judith Weisenfeld, *New World A-Coming: Black Religion and Racial Identity during the Great Migration* (New York: New York University Press, 2016), p. 2.

44 On the early MST, see Susan Nance, 'Mystery of the Moorish Science Temple: Southern Blacks and American Alternative Spirituality in 1920s Chicago', *Religion and American Culture: A Journal of Interpretation* 12.2 (2002), pp. 123–66 who writes that 'The Moors' success was due precisely to their ability to speak to African Americans' desire for an innovative alternative spirituality grounded in local religious culture. Highlighting contemporary black investigations of non-Western religions, the Moors were partly a product of and partly further inspiration to the vibrant experimental religious scene of interwar Chicago'. (p. 125). Also see the detailed reconstruction of Noble Drew Ali's background in Jacob S. Dorman, *The Princess and the Prophet: The Secret History of Magic, Race, and Moorish Muslims in America* (Boston, MS: Beacon Press, 2020).

45 See E.U. Essien-Udom, *Black Nationalism: A Search for an Identity in America* (Chicago: University of Chicago Press, 1962), pp. 46–8; and Robert G. Weisbord, *Ebony Kinship: Africa, Africans and the Afro-American* (Westport: Greenwood Press, 1973), esp. pp. 115–53.

46 St Clair Drake and Horace R. Cayton, *Black Metropolis: A Study of Negro Life in a Northern City*, revised & enlarged edition (New York: Harper & Row, 1962).

47 Opposition to integration would have a violent outcome for one Hebrew Israelite, Marcus Wayne Chenault. Chenault learnt some concepts from Hananiah Israel, of Cincinnati's House of Yisrael, and in 1974 assassinated Alberta King, mother of Martin Luther King Jr, in protest against King Jr's assimilative stance. For an in-depth investigation of the House of Yisrael, see Sabyl M. Willis, 'The House of Yisrael Cincinnati: How Normalized Institutional Violence Can Produce a Culture of Unorthodox Resistance 1963 to 2021' (Wright State University: MA Thesis, 2021).

48   On emigration movements prior to Garvey, see Edwin S. Redkey, *Black Exodus: Black Nationalist and Back-to-Africa Movements, 1890–1910* (New Haven: Yale University Press, 1969).

49   See John T. McCartney, *Black Power Ideologies: An Essay in African American Political Thought* (Philadelphia: Temple University Press, 1992), pp. 171–2.

50   In some places he adopts the biblical view that the Israelites' stubbornness is the cause of many of their problems: 'Under the influence of their oppressors, they became stiffnecked and rebellious; they killed the prophets and stoned the messengers of God who were sent unto them'. (MEW28) He is here possibly referring to the assassinations of Malcolm X and Martin Luther King Jr. He goes on to bemoan a lot of such leaders: 'Every sincere messenger of God should be prepared to have his character assassinated by satan's hidden "teachers of righteousness"'.

51   The foreword to the original (1982) edition of GBMT makes this claim: God should have been in charge of the Black Revolution not Martin and Malcolm.

52   'Former Black Panther Takes Aldermanic Post', *Wisconsin State Journal*, 29th April 1983, p. 15.

53   Related to this, see Topher Vollmer, 'What Would King Think?', *Peace News*, 1st May 2008, https://peacenews.info/node/3976/what-would-king-think and the follow-up 'New Humanity?', *Peace News*, 1st June 2008, https://peacenews.info/node/3975/new-humanity.

54   See Marc Dollinger, *Black Power, Jewish Politics: Reinventing the Alliance in the 1960s* (Waltham, MS: Brandeis University Press, 2018); Michael R. Fischbach, *Black Power and Palestine: Transnational Countries of Color* (Stanford: Stanford University Press, 2019).

55   For some insight into the AHIJ position, see Sar Ahmadiel Ben Yehuda, 'Redefining the Israeli-Palestinian Conflict from an African/Edenic (and Truth-Centered) Perspective', *Hebrew Israelite Nation Times*, September 2020, pp. 24–31.

56   Dorman, *Chosen People*, p. 154.

Chapter 1

1   On Deut.28 in particular as a key text in HI exegesis, see Andre Key, 'If thou do not hearken unto the voice of the Lord thy God: A Critique of Theodicy in Black Judaism', *Black Theology* 12.3 (2014), pp. 267–88. The same argument became part of NOI theology, although it is unclear whether this was an original part of their doctrine or one absorbed from HI circles: see Essien-Udom, *Black Nationalism*, p. 129.

2   Cf. the detailed but slightly different accounts given in Cohane Michael Ben Levi, *Israelites and Jews: The Significant Difference* (Kearney, NE: Morris Publishing, 1997), and Rudolph R. Windsor, *From Babylon to Timbuktu: A History of the Ancient Black Races Including the Black Hebrews* (Atlanta: Windsor's Golden Series, 2003 (1969)). Unlike some other HI thinkers, Ben Ammi does not distinguish between Judeans and other 'lost' Israelite tribes; however, the community have generally held that African Americans descend from all tribes, who mingled either during their migrations or in the United States after their captivity from their various locations. Ben stated in 1972 that ever since the biblical conquests of 721 and 581 BCE, the Israelites were dispersed and 'right after that, people moved in and usurped our culture and our land, while we were under the Divine Curse'. (Quoted in Arnold Forster, 'The "Black

Hebrew Nation", *ADL Bulletin*, February 1972. The same narrative is recounted in Aron Manheimer, 'The Black Israelites of Dimona', *Davka* 2.3, May-June 1972.) However, his subsequent work makes clear that he believes the Judeans of the first century CE were Israelites.

3   The teaching of Black Americans to call upon Jesus rather than Yeshua was a sophisticated spiritual technique. Knowing the true name 'would have kept them in the arena of Truth, hope and reality. At the least, it would have kept them in touch somewhat with a God that could help them the God of their fathers – the Almighty, Holy One of Israel' (GBMT24).

4   Ben admits that Christianity was not solely designed to serve the end function of manipulating enslaved Israelites, although this was a large part of the spiritual reason for its development. For example, 'This church, using the name of Jesus, was sanctioned by the Euro-gentiles as a control mechanism for the masses and had nothing to do with the ancient church of salvation' (GBMT103). However, 'Never in the history of the world have the Euro-gentiles accepted the prophetic God of the universe, the God of Israel, as their savior. [...] The world very tacitly uses the name Jesus while continuing to use all of its ancient customs which were and still are an abomination before God' (GBMT194).

5   Ben Ammi mentions African Jewish or Judaizing communities surprisingly little. The one place where he does do so is an addition in the revised 1990 edition of GBMT. The community generally have little to do with the Ethiopian Beta Israel; my impression is that the latter are more interested in courting acceptance from Jews than from the Hebrew Israelites, and the former view the poor state of the Ethiopian community both in Ethiopia and in Israel as indicating their having not adequately kept the commandments.

6   At one point, he argues that it is the promulgation of the false white god who cannot save which has encouraged the growth of atheism (IL44).

7   Ben Ammi repeatedly claims that the Catholic Church banned the Old Testament (e.g. YHM68); this of course is not true, though they did try to control the translation and the possession of the entire canon by laity.

8   Ammi goes on to claim that Adam was the first anointed messiah and his dominion the first messianic kingdom; the Adamic family were in ascension until satan intervened.

9   This is the interpretation of the important twelfth-century French commentator Rashi who, based on linguistic analysis, concluded that the odd construction of the very first word *Bereshit* meant the best interpretation was 'At the beginning of the Creation of heaven and earth when the earth was without form and void and there was darkness, God said, "Let there be light"'. According to an earlier explanation, it should be read as 'By means of *reshit* [the first], God created', where 'the first' is the Torah (BerR1.1). Other exegetes have developed these challenges to the absolute and primordial reading of Gen.1, most notable among whom are the kabbalists, who suggested a series of worlds created then destroyed prior to this one. On the rabbinic and pre-rabbinic fascination with explaining and interpreting the creation account, see Philip S. Alexander, 'Pre-Emptive Exegesis: Genesis Rabba's Reading of the Story of Creation', *Journal of Jewish Studies* 43.2 (1992), pp. 230–45; Norbert M. Samuelson, *Judaism and the Doctrine of Creation* (Cambridge: Cambridge University Press, 1994), pp. 107–35.

10   For two early non-Hebrew Israelite attempts to systematically argue for the blackness of ancient Israelites, see James Morris Webb, *The Black Man: The Father of Civilization*

Proven by Biblical History (Seattle: ACME Press, 1919) and Joel Augustus Rogers, *Sex and Race: Negro-Caucasian Mixing in All Ages and All Lands* (St. Petersburg, FL: Helga M Rogers, 1968 (1940)), vol.1, pp. 91–4. Webb's argument is simple in that the Bible states many times Israelites mixing with Africans; therefore, they had some percentage of African blood. In arguing that modern white Jews' ancestors were Black, Rogers relies on many of the unreliable sources detailed in Tudor Parfitt's *Hybrid Hate: Conflations of Antisemitism & Anti-Black Racism from the Renaissance to the Third Reich* (New York: Oxford University Press, 2020), which offers an extensive analysis of the entanglement of Black and Jewish 'others' which white Christians often imagined as coming from a single source.

11 William L. Van DeBurg, *New Day in Babylon: The Black Power Movement and American Culture, 1965–1975* (London: University of Chicago Press, 1992), p. 27.
12 Muhammad's historical cosmology has been described several times, the most detailed account is in Stephen Carl Finley, 'Re-imagining Race and Representation: The Black Body in the Nation of Islam' (Rice University: PhD Thesis, 2006), pp. 93–117.
13 Malcolm X, *The Autobiography of Malcolm X: As Told to Alex Haley* (New York: Ballantine Books, 1965), p. 143.
14 Finley, *Re-imagining Race and Representation*, pp. 117–39.
15 Note that Muhammad provides two conflicting dates for the end of the present era: while the ordained 400-year period of white rule supposedly began in 1555, ending in 1955 (*Message to the Blackman in America* (Chicago: Muhammad Mosque of Islam No. 2, 1965), p. 3), the devil's civilization had expired in 1914 with the beginning of the First World War (*Message to the Blackman*, p. 142), a date likely taken from the Jehovah's Witnesses (see Stephen C. Finley, 'Hidden away: Esotericism and Gnosticism in Elijah Muhammad's Nation of Islam', in *Histories of the Hidden God: Concealment and Revelation in Western Gnostic, Esoteric and Mystical Traditions*, ed. April D. DeConick and Grant Adamson (Oxon: Routledge, 2013), pp. 259–80).
16 See Parfitt, *Hybrid Hate*.
17 Justine M. Bakker, 'On the Knowledge of Self and Others: Secrecy, Concealment and Revelation in Elijah Muhammad's Nation of Islam (1934–1975)', in *Esotericism in African American Religious Experience*, pp. 138–51.
18 Ishakamusa Barashango, *God, the Bible and the Black Man's Destiny* (Baltimore: Afrikan World Books, 2001 (1970)), p. 76.
19 Ibid., pp. 30–3.
20 Ibid., pp. 152–3.
21 Roi Ottley, *Inside Black America* (London: Eyre & Spottiswoode, 1948), p. 113.
22 Quoted from Howard Brotz, 'Negro Jews in the United States', *Phylon* 13.4 (1952), p. 331.
23 See especially the pamphlet *Get One While the Getting Is Good: Black Jews of the Judean Tribe of Israel: One God, One Aim, One Destiny* (Special Collections: University of Delaware).
24 W. Henry E. Bibins, *The Mark of a Lost Race* (n.d.), p. 7. This text also cites Dan.12.4 but locates the terminus points as the siege of Jerusalem in 70CE and 1914. Ben Ammi could have absorbed the idea directly from this text, from Matthew via his teachers, or from another AHIJ member familiar with the text. On the authorship of this pamphlet, see the reconstruction by internet sleuth 1 West Chronicler 144, 'Abba Bibbins wrote a book "Mark of the Lost Race"', *YouTube*, https://www.youtube.com/watch?v=AlvLZdsmUfE. It is undated but is mentioned in an interview with Howard Brotz in his 1947 MA thesis (p. 17), so clearly predates that time.

25   See Marley Cole, *Jehovah's Witnesses: The New World Society* (Oxon: Routledge, 2019 (1956)), p. 45.
26   On the multifaceted influence on the NOI see Finley, *Re-imagining Race and Representation*, p. 116 n.103 and the references therein.
27   Albert J. Cleage, *The Black Messiah* (New York: Sheed &Ward, 1965), pp. 53–4.
28   Ben Ammi never capitalized the word satan.
29   Much of this is discussed in MEW46-52 and IL100ff. It should be noted that the seeds are not a literal bloodline, but a spiritual one: 'Since Yah is a spirit and they that worship Him or identify His earthly image must do so in spirit and in Truth, then it certainly stands to reason that His seed (image) implanted into someone would be a spirit' (IL90). While Ben Ammi does not interpret the serpentine/satanic 'seed' literally, there is a surprisingly similar tradition in the Talmud which does. b.Shabbat146a (cf. b.Yebam.103b; b.Abod.Zar.22b) tells a story that the serpent inseminated Eve with poison, which mixed with her descendants' bloodline. The poison was negated by Israel's encounter with God at Sinai, meaning, however, that gentiles still bear it. This tradition will be discussed more in the Conclusion.
30   Landing, *Black Judaism*, p. 318.
31   E.g., 'the misnomers "Negro" and "Jew" have thrown the world into a state of ignorance … Jacob and Esau are hid behind these words', in *Black Hebrew Israelites from America to the Promised Land: The Great International Religious Conspiracy against the Children of the Prophets* (New York: Vantage Press, 1975), p. ii, and also 'the Edomite European Jews had come and established themselves in the American mainstream, had become slavemasters and plantation owners … This accounts for the continued fulfilment of the historical event of Esau and Jacob, for Esau's vengeance against his brother Jacob' (ibid., p. 77). According to Ben Yehuda, it was Jews who instructed Europeans on which Africans to take as slaves, as only they knew how to locate and identify Hebrews. Cf. p. 293. Intriguingly, Farrakhan has added his own gloss to the myth of Yakub, identifying him with the biblical Jacob. The heirs of Yakub, the white race, thus have stolen the true mandate of Blacks (Esau).
32   'The entire Euro-gentile political system is an enemy to both man and God. Man, in the genesis, was formed to evidence the creativity of the "God Mind," without which there would always be a lack of knowledge to bring forth what is right' (GBMT134).
33   On this appropriation of the 'virgin' concept, he remarks that all of the important titles have been mimicked and distorted by the church; the holy space of these terms 'has been occupied by the imitation purposefully to prevent the Sons of Light from finding comfort and spiritual advantage by the use of the term' (IL111).
34   This anti-Papal aspect is unusual in Ben Ammi, though it appears also in Elijah Muhammad. It is most likely an inheritance of the African American religious tradition from its American Protestant roots.
35   Evangelist and founder of the Biblical Museum Ken Ham has recently described a near-identical concept, of 'two religions', the true and the false: https://www.answers.tv/world-religions-conference/season:1/videos/two-religions.
36   Thomas Whitfield, *From Night to Sunlight* (Nashville, TN: Broadman Press, 1980), pp. 46–7. Assertions of whites as devils should be seen in the context of R. Laurence Moore's comment, that 'You did not have to live in a black urban neighborhood to see evidence that sustained notions of white demonology, but it was impossible not to if you did'. *Religious Outsiders and the Making of Americans* (New York: Oxford University Press, 1986), p. 192; as well as Stephen C. Finley,

'The Secret of ... Who the Devil is', who writes that 'Elijah Muhammad was merely describing the world within which he found himself – a world marked by the visitation of racialized violence on black communities by white supremacist people, laws, discourses, rituals, and institutions. Upon *religious* reflection, Muhammad found that the only way he could frame the actions and dispositions of white people – both liberal and conservative – was in terms of the demonic or the devilish'(pp. 155–6). For the enslaved, the slave master often appeared as a proxy for Satan simply because of their treatment of Blacks: See Dwight N. Hopkins, 'Slave Theology in the "Invisible Institution"', in *Cut Loose Your Stammering Tongue: Black Theology in the Slave Narrative*, ed. Dwight N. Hopkins and George C.L. Cummings, second edn (Louisville: Westminster John Knox Press, 2003), pp. 1–33, esp. pp. 12–13. Indeed, David Walker in 1829 referred to whites 'acting like devils'. *Appeal.*

37   See, for example, Barashango, *God, the Blackman and the Bible*, pp. 35; 38. Occasional statements by Ben Ammi such as 'He [God] has made the Euro-gentile the cruelest and most ruthless species ever to walk the earth', (GBMT136) are clearly meant rhetorically, as the context shows – in this case the destruction of the environment. Cleage describes a growing popular belief in white inhumanity, that 'White people cannot grasp the meaning of love, music, or religion because they exist on a lower, bestial level of violence, materialism, and individualism'. He perceives Muhammad's myth of Yakub as the clearest expression of this motif, but responds that it must be countered: 'As Black people we are reacting emotionally to the totality of the white man's oppression, brutality, and exploitation.' However, 'The white man is not a beast. He's not a devil. He's just a human being with power [who] demonstrates the effects of power upon any individual who is not protected against it by adequate group controls.' *Black Christian Nationalism: New Directions for the Black Church* (New York: William Morrow, 1972), p. 94, 101.

38   See Jonathan Broder, 'Chicago Blacks Seek Election in Israel', *Chicago Tribune*, 9 January 1977, p. 5.

39   E.g. GLR35.

40   F.S. Cherry, W. Henry E. Bibins (aka Abba Bivens, founder of One West), Clark Jenkins and Rudolph Windsor. Bibins writes that whiteness comes from a combination of Esau's redness with the leprosy inflicted upon Gehazi the Amalekite in 2Ki.5:27, *Mark of a Lost Race*, p. 25. An almost identical doctrine is suggested of Cherry in Arthur Huff Fauset's *Black Gods of the Metropolis: Negro Religious Cults of the Urban North* (New York: Octagon Books, 1970), p. 34. Drawing on Leviticus' descriptions of leprosy Jenkins posits this and the expulsion of infected individuals from the community as the origin of white peoples, *The Black Hebrews*, pp. 64–76. Windsor accepts the traditional genesis of Caucasians from Noah's son Yaphet, but incorporates the biblical examples of leprotic whitening to explain to change of skin colour, *Babylon to Timbuktu*, pp. 18–25.

41   Wentworth Matthew, *The Anthropology of the Ethiopian Hebrews and Their Relationship to the Fairer Jews*, quoted in Brotz, *Black Jews of Harlem*, p. 20.

42   See Morris Lounds, *Israel's Black Hebrews: Black Americans in Search of Identity* (Washington, DC: University Press of America, 1981), pp. 36–8 on reductionist definitions of Blackness and Israelite.

43   MEW97 is one of the few times he names 'Blacks *and non-Europeans*' (my emphasis). It is notable that, while Ben Ammi heavily criticizes the symbolism of black and

white as one artificially created to aid the subjugation of Blacks, he utilizes without problem the same symbolism when referring to the Sons of Light and the Sons of Darkness in the DSS. (e.g. RHS59).

44 He repeats several times the claim that 'amongst the African Americans are descendants of the ancient Biblical Israelites' (MEW28, his emphasis; cf. p. 17 and 43).

45 The audio of this interview was provided to me by the AHIJ.

46 The irony is that, to many of Ben Ammi's and the Hebrew Israelites' critics, he is saying this all in the defence of adopting an identity which is almost certainly not that of his own African ancestors.

47 A final informative source may be in Arnold Ford's assertion that 'A "Negro" is an African or person of African descent whose mind is a by-product of European civilization, but has not traditions of its own', quoted in Landes, 'Negro Jews', p. 185.

48 W.E.B. Du Bois, *The Souls of Black Folk*, ed. Brent Hayes Edwards (Oxford: Oxford University Press, 2007), p. 8. On *Get Out* and Du Bois' Double Consciousness see Mikal J. Gaines, 'Staying Woke in Sunken Places, or the Wages of Double Consciousness', in *Jordan Peele's Get Out: Political Horror,* ed. Dawn Keetley (Columbus: Ohio State University, 2020), pp. 160–73.

49 Victor Anderson, *Beyond Ontological Blackness: An Essay on African American Religious and Cultural Criticism* (London: Bloomsbury, 2016), p. 117.

50 See Essien-Udom, *Black Nationalism*, p. 59.

51 Norman Saul Goodman, 'Mythology of Evil in Judaism', *Journal of Religion and Health* 15.4 (1976), pp. 230–41 (231).

52 Where Shaleak explicitly claimed this, Ben Ammi only hinted at it. In the revised 1990 edition of GBMT he adds a paragraph which lists African Israelite communities, including Sri Lanka and southern India (GBMT102). This is in direct contradiction to Shaleak's previous claim that 'dark-skinned Jewish people from Yemen and India' are all 'Anglo-Saxon transplants ... Europeans ... under the guise of Jews'. Shaleak Ben Yehuda, *Black Hebrew Israelites from America to the Promised Land: The Great International Religious Conspiracy against the Children of the Prophets* (New York: Vantage Press, 1975), p. 242. A subsequent text by Cohane Michael Ben Levi, *Israelites and Jews: The Significant Difference* (1997) weaves a complex and even quite historically informed (although simplistic and unconvincing) explanation for the appearance of the rabbinic movement from Idumean converts who then took their religion to Europe via the Khazars. This is one of a few points where we see a similarity between HI thought and the antisemitism of the far right. On these issues see Miller, 'Between Edom and Ethiopia: The African Hebrew Israelite Construction of "White Jews"', (forthcoming), cf. Michael Barkun, *Religion and the Racist Right: The Origins of the Christian Identity Movement,* revised edn (Chapel Hill: University of North Carolina Press, 1997) pp. 127–30.

53 In a way this could be seen as paralleling the rabbinic tradition that Torah has seventy faces.

54 Pinn, *Terror and Triumph*, p. 178.

55 Finley, 'The Secret ... of Who the Devil Is', p. 169.

56 John L. Jackson Jr, *Real Black: Adventures in Racial Sincerity* (Chicago: University of Chicago Press, 2005), pp. 101–9.

57 Cf. 'Truth is tied directly into the existence of the Eternal.' (MEW32).

58 One Lubavitch Rabbi makes a statement which has surprising resonance with this, linking the adherence to Jewish law with a natural alignment with truth: 'The reasons for rejecting evil, for not doing a sin, is that the sin is not true. To sin, a Jew has to deceive himself. And not about something outside himself but about himself. On the grounds that it's crazy. So he rejects sin because it's a lie. On the grounds that it's crazy, not on the grounds of unnaturalness or inelegance.' See Lynn Davidman, *Tradition in a Rootless World: Women Turn to Orthodox Judaism* (Berkeley: University of California Press, 1993), p. 144.

Chapter 2

1 Amongst them David Walker who proclaimed: 'O Americans! Americans!! I call God – I call angels – I call men, to witness, that your Destruction is at hand, and will be speedily consummated unless you Repent.' *Walker's Appeal, in Four Articles; Together with a Preamble, to the Coloured Citizens of the World*, third edn (Boston: Walker, 1830), p. 49.

2 On the Black Jeremiad tradition see David Howard Pitney, *African American Jeremiad: Appeals for Justice in America*, revised edn (Philadelphia: Temple University Press, 2005).

3 On African American apocalyptic tradition, see Derek S. Hicks, 'Eschatology in African American Theology', in *The Oxford Handbook of African American Theology*, ed. K.G. Cannon and A.B. Pinn (Oxford: Oxford University Press, 2014), pp. 242–52, who notes that eschatology in African American theology tends to centre on justice and the elimination of oppression, rather than punishment. Cf., Samuel Estabrooks, 'The African American Apocalyptic as Prophetic Social Protest' (Arizona State University: PhD Diss., 2016).

4 Martha Lee, *The Nation of Islam: An American Millenarian Movement* (Syracuse, NY: Syracuse University Press, 1996).

5 Moses, *Black Messiahs*, pp. 214–15.

6 Father Divine's Peace Mission, a successful 1930s group based in Harlem, proclaimed a similar awaiting judgement in less opaque terms, in one of their songs called The Mills of God are Grinding On: 'Let them come in dust and ashes, Let them moan and seek God's Face/Let them feel the bitter lashes, And of their own evil get just a taste/ Let their blood help pay the price Of Centuries of sorrow and blinding pain/They dealt to others in their arrogance; Let them feel God's cold disdain.' See Sara Harris, *Father Divine* (New York: Collier, 1971), pp. 185–6.

7 An article from 1969 quotes them proclaiming 'America's ultimate destruction in 1970', Era Bell Thomson, 'Are Black Americans Welcome in Africa?', *Ebony*, January 1969, pp. 44–50. A Monrovian newspaper clipping of unknown provenance, from January 1969 in the Israel State Archive notes that they 'believe that a Messiah will come sometime in 1970 and this time the strangers now living in Israel will have to quit the land for the proper sons of God'. File: 81.d4.47.7b. Cf. Tsiporah, the daughter of a prominent figure close to Ben Ammi, has said that during her childhood, 'They talked to us about the world coming to an end and everyone dying, and we, the chosen tribe, being saved. My father is still waiting for the whole world to be destroyed.' See, 'Mahaleyah interviews Seporah; the star in the original film entitled: "Sister Wife"', *YouTube*, https://www.youtube.com/watch?v=hJerv2nU8u0.

8   Ya'akov HaElyon, "'Moreh ha-Tzedek" Amar "Lo"?' (The 'Righteous Teacher' says 'No!)
     Ma'ariv, 22nd May 1970, p. 70 (my translation).
9   His published work prior to joining the group in Israel state 1975 as the year by
     which anarchy and mass murder will be leading towards 'the complete destruction of
     America', L. A. Bryant, *Know Thyself* (Chicago: One Inc., 1968), p. 60. Ex-members
     have commented that those who joined in this period had a markedly different
     agenda to most of the original members, including the idea that Ben Ammi was the
     Messiah (in one of a series of articles in January 1979, 'Cult's critics charge secrecy,
     strictness and "brainwashing", *Jerusalem Post*, 22nd January 1979 one defector is
     quoted as saying, 'Things started to change a few years before that 1977 deadline,
     which they said was going to mean the end of the world. The place got crowded with
     lots of newcomers, different from us. They started crowning Carter messiah, putting
     his picture up on the wall. They'd tell people to believe in them and what they were
     doing, brainwashing them, getting their minds and controlling them.' My thanks to
     Andrew Esensten for providing this book.
10   Morris Lounds, *Israel's Black Hebrews: Black Americans in Search of Identity*
     (Washington, DC: University Press of America, 1981), pp. 56–7. Similar predictions
     are recounted in Aron Manheimer, 'The Black Israelites of Dimona,' *Davka* 2.3,
     May-June 1972, pp. 6–12, which describes a Middle East war leading to a 'World
     Holocaust' over the next six years – i.e. beginning imminently and ending by
     1977 – after which the Hebrews would be installed as rulers as of Israel according
     to its biblical borders; and in a lengthy 1975 interview with Asiel, who predicted a
     nuclear 'Armageddon' in 1976, Hoyt E. Fuller, 'The Original Hebrew Israelite Nation:
     An Interview,' *Black World*, May 1975, pp. 62–70. Cf. Joan Borsten, 'Sect Problems',
     Jerusalem Post, 3rd December 1976, pp. 7–8. Shaleak Ben Yehuda also notes 1977
     as the year that the 'Kingdom of Heaven is to be established in its glory', following
     3.5 years of tribulation (*Black Hebrew Israelites*, p. 52; 100). The prediction of the
     Kingdom coming into its 'glory' in 1977 may be what was behind Ben Ammi's
     attempted election bid in 1977. It is unclear exactly what happened, but presumably
     his lack of citizenship scuppered the plan.
11   Noted in 'Another Reason to Fast', *The Sentinel*, 5th February 1976, p. 6.
12   Singer, 'Saints of the Kingdom', p. 137.
13   Perhaps because of the influence of the Hebrew Bible's this-worldly emphasis, HI
     millennialism has almost always foreseen an earthly paradise following the cataclysm.
14   Robert P. Carroll, *When Prophecy Failed: Reactions and Responses to Failure in the
     Old Testament Prophetic Traditions* (London: SCM Press, 1979).
15   John L. Jackson Jr, *Thin Description*, pp. 34–7.
16   See the history and interviews in Jason George, 'Promised Land. Promise Fading',
     Chicago Tribune, 7th July 2008.
17   Brotz, 'Black Jews of Harlem', p. 11 (in the published version p. 23); cf. the similar
     account from 1938 given in Norman N. Glatzer, 'The Synagogue of the Negro Jews
     in New York', p. 128. The groups emerging from Abba Bivens/E. Bibins' Israeli School
     (AKA One West), predicted African American repatriation to Israel upon the return
     of Christ in the year 2000, until it was disproved. See Vocab Malone, *Barack Obama
     vs The Black Hebrew Israelites: Introduction to the History & Beliefs of 1 West Israelism*
     (Phoenix: Thureos Publishing, 2017), and Kestenbaum, "'I'm an Israelite'".
18   Landing, *Black Judaism*, pp. 342–3, cf. Deanne Ruth Shapiro, 'Double Damnation,
     Double Salvation: The Sources and Varieties of Black Judaism in the United States'
     (Columbia University: MA Diss., 1970), p. 122; 126–7.

19 Bishop Allan Wilson Cook, *The Independent Church of God of the Juda Tribe of Israel: The Black Jews* (New York: Cook, 1925), 10. See Michael T. Miller, 'Bishop Allan Wilson Cook (Rabbi Haling Hank Lenht), Queen Malinda Morris and the Independent Church of God: A Missing Piece in the History of Hebrew Israelite Black Judaism', *Black Theology* 21.3 (2023). Rudolph R. Windsor, *Valley of the Dry Bones: The Conditions That Face Black People in America Today* (Atlanta, GA: Windsor's Golden Series, 1986), pp. 129–59 provides a detailed account of the Third World War, which would commence in the Middle East between Israel and Arab states, with the help of Russia.

20 Bibins, *The Mark of a Lost Race*, p. 7. On the authorship of this pamphlet – which was published in the early/mid-'40s, prior to his joining the Commandment Keepers – see the reconstruction by internet sleuth Abu Khamr al-MaseeHee, 'Abba Bibins' Book?' *YouTube*, https://www.youtube.com/watch?v=aOp3G7xcEvY. The use of 1914 is particularly interesting, as it is shared with both Elijah Muhammad and the Adventists.

21 Timothy E. Fulop, '"The Future Golden Day of the Race": Millennialism and Black Americans in the Nadir, 1877–1901', *Harvard Theological Review* 84.1 (1991), pp. 75–99 (92); cf. Albert J. Raboteau, '"Ethiopia Shall Soon Stretch Forth Her Hands": Black Destiny in Nineteenth-Century America', in *African American Religious Thought: An Anthology*, ed. Cornell West and Eddie S. Glaude Jr. (Louisville: Westminster John Knox Press, 2003), 397–413.

22 Theophilus G. Steward, *The End of the World; or, Clearing the Way for the Fullness of the Gentiles* (Philadelphia: AME Church Book Rooms, 1888).

23 James Theodore Holly, 'The Divine Plan of Human Redemption in Its Ethnological Development', *AME Church Review* 1.6 (1884), pp. 79–85, reprinted in Anthony B. Pinn (ed.), *Moral Evil and Redemptive Suffering: A History of Theodicy in African-American Religious Thought* (Gainesville: University Press of Florida, 2002), pp. 131–40. Holly also predicted the Millennium coming at 6000 years after creation – which he calculated to be 1876.

24 *Muhammad Speaks*, 12th February 1965, p. 3.

25 Elijah Muhammad, *The Fall of America* (Phoenix, AR: Secretarius MEMPS Publications, 1973), p. 44.

26 *Muhammad Speaks*, 30th July 1965.

27 Lee, *Nation of Islam*, p. 45.

28 See Nathan Saunders, 'The Evolving Theology of the Nation of Islam', in *New Perspectives on the Nation of Islam*, p. 242.

29 Lee, *Nation of Islam*, p. 48.

30 Muhammad, *Fall of America*, p. 62.

31 In one interesting exegesis, he reads Rev.12.13-17 as predicting their escape from America: 'From the seed of the woman (people) that escaped, a messianic man-child was to be born whose mission it would be to establish the Kingdom of God. Satan attempted to destroy the woman (people) that had escaped to the wilderness of Liberia. But God helped them to survive the great opposition to their upward motion' (MEW146-7). The European Common Market meanwhile is seen as fulfilment of Dan.2.40-43's Kingdom of Iron (MEW159).

32 Landing, *Black Judaism*, p. 233.

33 Singer, 'Saints of the Kingdom', p. 77.

34 Rev.18.4 was regularly read in the early days of A-Beta, as one member recalled to Singer, 'Saints of the Kingdom', p. 79. We may see a similar meaning being gleaned

when he interprets Mal.3.18 as 'we must be able to understand the difference between right and wrong, the Holy and profane, in all areas of life [...]. We cannot fuse two opposing forces together. You cannot make a synthesis between Truth and falsehood' (RJPJ112).

35   See Dorman, *Chosen People*, pp. 113–51; K.J. King, 'Some Notes on Arnold J. Ford and New World Black Attitudes to Ethiopia', *Journal of Ethiopian Studies* 10.1 (1972), pp. 81–7.

36   Generally, the most radical groups have been those most keen to remain in America, a land they believe they will soon inherit.

37   The other being the very small group of Howshua Amariel. A third attempted Aliyah but were unsuccessful: Rabbi Abel Respes' rabbinically oriented Adat Beyt Moshe, originating of Philadelphia before relocating to New Jersey, constituted about fifty people and approached the matter according to all the rules including formal conversion; the disappointment of Israeli officials in rejecting them, who felt that agreeing to their Aliyah at such a sensitive time could lead to an increasing insistence on the part of groups who were less motivated by purely religious concerns, is palpable in the documents held in the Israel State Archive. On the community see Martin Gelman, 'Adat Beyt Moshe: The Colored House of Moses, a Study of The Contemporary Negro Religious Community and Its Leader' (University of Pennsylvania: PhD Thesis, 1965).

Chapter 3

1   Cf. the audio lecture Spiritual Warfare (n.d., audio recording supplied by the AHIJ).

2   See, e.g., Joseph Klausner, *The Messianic Idea in Israel* (London: Allen & Unwin, 1956); Gregory H. Dix, 'The Messiah Ben Joseph', *The Journal of Theological Studies* 27.106 (1926), pp. 130–43.

3   Tziona Yisrael, personal communication, 2021.

4   Singer, 'Saints of the Kingdom', p. 137. Singer also quotes him as saying that the mind of Ben Carter was dead, he was only a vehicle of God, and 'Moses and Jesus are being made to live again through me'. Ibid., p. 135. A concept perhaps hinted at when he notes, after discussing the persistent spirits of holy people that 'instead of looking for a return of Yeshua, people should be listening for a return of Yeshua'. (EL16).

5   See, e.g., Andrei Orlov, *The Enoch-Metatron Tradition* (Tubingen: Mohr Siebeck, 2005).

6   Partially, we can see Ben Ammi's Americo- and Anglo-centrism here, as most European languages (especially those around Eastern/Central Europe and Iberia) actually derive their name for Saturday from the Hebrew term Shabbat due to the significance of the day for their Jewish populations; it is only in English that the day is named after Saturn.

7   Cleage had even mused in 1969 that perhaps identification with Judaism would be 'more practical' for Blacks, who could remove Paul's teachings and take Christianity back to its roots. Ehrman, 'Black Judaism in New York,' p. 113.

8   Steward, *End of the World* also wrote that the west was 'a civilization which is called Christian, but which is essentially Saxon'.

9   'The Nation Israel was a mixture of Chaldeans, Egyptians, Midianites, Ethiopians, Kushites, Babylonians and other dark peoples, all of whom were already mixed with the black people of Central Africa.' Cleage, Jr, *Black Messiah*, p. 3. Cleage here

considers the Israelites a mixture of 'dark' and Black, not as coterminous with 'the Black people of Central Africa'. But already we see the idea of a dark/Black semi-African people struggling against a 'white' European nation. Cleage did not hold any belief in the descent of Black Americans from Israelites, but he asserted repeatedly the descent of 'Black' Mizrachi Jews from them, as well as some amongst Arab and African populations: p. 72, p. 111, etc. Interestingly, his second text, *Black Christian Nationalism*, contains contributions from a Hebrew Israelite rabbi – Moshe Hailu Paris – and the aforementioned Afrocentric researcher and author of *We the Black Jews*, Yosef ben Yochannan.

10 Cleage, *Black Messiah*, p. 37.
11 Arnold Forster, 'The "Black Hebrew Nation"', *ADL Bulletin*, Feburary 1972.
12 Bruce Rosenstock, z"l, who engaged with the community because of his own research on Goldberg, told me he was unable to locate any source for this quote among Goldberg's writings. For his take on Goldberg, see Bruce Rosenstock, *Transfinite Life: Oskar Goldberg and the Vitalist Imagination* (Bloomington: Indiana University Press, 2017).
13 Jawanza Eric Clark, 'Introduction', in Clark (ed.), *Albert Cleage*, p. 3.
14 Van Deburg, *New Day in Babylon*, pp. 237–8.
15 Cleage, *Black Messiah*, p. 4.
16 James H. Cone, *A Black Theology of Liberation* (Philadelphia and New York: J.B. Lippincott Company, 1970), p. 218.
17 William Christian, *Poor Pilgrim's Work in the Name of the Father, Son and Holy Ghost* (Texarkana: Joe Ehrlich, 1896), pp. 4–7. Cf. Landing, *Black Judaism* ref. For some other relevant context, see Charles Price, 'The Cultural Production of a Black Messiah: Ethiopianism and Rastafari', *Journal of Africana Religions* 2.3 (2014), pp. 418–34.
18 On matters of skin colour in the ancient Levant, with a particular view to divinity and the whitening process of European Christianity, see Francesca Stavrakopoulou, *God: An Anatomy* (London: Picador, 2021), pp. 183–9.
19 Ben Ammi cites at least twice the famous FBI memo sent by J. Edgar Hoover, which discusses the importance of preventing a 'Black messiah' from arising who could unite people across America. Ben seems to take this literally, citing it as evidence that the FBI knew that the messianic time was imminent.
20 Cf. Barashango on Israelites as 'the refiners, preservers and guardians of the great religious concepts which they had received of other African people'. *God, the Bible and the Black Man's Destiny*, p. 74. This is also the argument of Yosef A.A. Ben-Jochannan, *African Origins of the Major Western Religions* (Baltimore: Black Classic Press, 1991 (1970)).
21 This motif admittedly appears only in passing, and seems to contradict his insistence on the chosen status of African Americans. Cf. 'After the fall of Adam and confusion of tongues, the merciful God of Creation gave the same pure, fundamental redemptive plan to chosen men around the world. These men passed these ideas of God to their respective nations. Each nation's interpretive application of these fundamentals was an amalgamation of the idea and each nation's respective cultural traits' (EL94-5).
22 Exact calculations as to the beginning and end point of the 400 years have varied. Shaleak claimed 1442 as the beginning of the 400 years, when the first slaves left Africa (*Black Hebrew Israelites* p. 38), although when Lounds interviewed him he stated 1445, when African slaves entered Portugal, and ending with Frederick

Douglass, (Lounds, p. 54; presumably both references referred to the capture of twelve people from Cabo Branco (modern Mauritania) in 1441, who were taken to Portugal). Ben Ammi, following Elijah Muhammad, placed it at 1555, the year of the first African slaves entering America (GBMT29; however, African slaves were taken to the Americas throughout the sixteenth century, with the first arriving in Spanish North America in 1565). More recently Asiel cited 1619 (the now-famous year when African slaves were first brought into English North America), *Voice out of Zion* 2018.

23 On the theme of marginalization and inversion in Ben Ammi's thought see M.T. Miller, 'The African Hebrew Israelites of Jerusalem and Ben Ammi's Theology of Marginalisation and Reorientation', *Religions* 11.2 (2020), pp. 87; M.T. Miller, 'Layers of Liminality and Marginality in the African Hebrew Israelite Community', in *Mind the Gap*, ed. Zohar Hadromi-Allouche and Mike McKay (Lexington: forthcoming).

24 See Allen Dwight Callahan, 'Perspectives for a Study of African American Religion: From the Valley of Dry Bones', *Nova Religio: The Journal of Alternative and Emergent Religions* 7.1 (2003), pp. 44–59.

25 See particularly Windsor, *Valley of the Dry Bones*, pp. 96–128.

26 'To be defined as dead in the spiritual context means: having no knowledge of God; being in a helpless predicament, wherein one no longer hears, sees, discerns or moves. The African American community today is lying helpless in its grave, covered with the dirt of false gods, false doctrines, false worship, false history, envy, strife, disunity, disrespect, hate of one another, and a diet fit for the dead' (GBMT88).

27 This is reminiscent of the rabbinic notion of the exile of the Shekhina, God's presence among the Jews; a midrashic tradition tells that the Shekhina withdrew progressively further from humanity as Adam, Cain, etc., sinned; but was brought back into to the world by righteous individuals (BerR.19).

28 E.g. 'In the Millennial Age, participation in the Kingdom of God is the *natural birthright* of everyone' (GBMT183); 'This [the Kingdom] is for all men, although most do not yet understand its significance' (MEW148). 'We are presently engaged in this relentless spiritual war on behalf of our people in particular, and all of humanity and the Holy creations in general' (IL92); 'The "whole" to which we refer, is the "whole human family," whose quality of life is being adversely affected by incorrect decisions made by the developed nations. The majority of the world's populace are victims by chance, not choice' (RHS7). However, now, judgement will be inverted: 'Our judgment was to be compassed about by the wicked; their judgment will find them compassed about by the righteous. We were tormented by evil; they shall be tormented by Truth and righteousness. At the conclusion of our judgment we must come out of their world; to be saved from their judgment, they must come into our world' (RJPJ70). Windsor, *Valley of the Dry Bones*, p. 159, sources this idea in Is.56.6's claim that in the Messianic Age, 'sons of strangers shall join themselves to YHVH' and keep the sabbath.

29 'The Original Hebrew Israelite Nation of Jerusalem', James Landing Papers box 7 f.50.

30 Little has been written on One West, but a useful overview and introduction is given in the short non-academic text, Malone, *Barack Obama vs the Black Hebrew Israelites*.

31 Muhammad, *Fall of America*, p. 103.

32 In some ways, of course, Israel does admit a fundamental racial binary, although the racialization of the Jewish-Muslim Arab binary is quite a recent phenomenon even if it is growing. It is safe to say that the case in Israel has usually been more complex, and critically not based on skin tone. See M.T. Miller, 'The African Hebrew Israelites of Jerusalem: A Borderline Case', in *The Stranger in Early Modern and Modern Jewish Tradition*, ed. Catherine Bartlett and Joachim Schlor (Leiden: Brill, 2021), pp. 28–46.

Chapter 4

1 Cleage, *Black Messiah*, p. 37.
2 We could see in Ben both the rejection of anthropomorphism and the retaining of intimacy. Cf. the Nation of Islam minister who stated, 'our people have had enough spiritualism from Christianity. ... You can see it in New York. All the nationalists ... in Harlem preach materialism. Our people want to improve their shelter, food and clothing.' Essien-Udom, *Black Nationalism*, p. 193.
3 Miraculous actions will once again be possible to the Israelites as they ascend, just as the Bible shows Israelites causing miracles – according to him it was Noah who brought the rain not God, and Moses that opened the sea. 'These were not always isolated occurrences, nor miracles; these were the ordinary powers of the Sons of God [...] They became rare manifestations only because the people turned away from God, His authority and power [... now] They are weak before their enemies because they do not know the source of their strength, much less how to manifest it.' (GBMT227).
4 It is in this proximity to dualism and the emphasis on satan that Ben Ammi displays his most non-Jewish aspect. While Satan appears in the Bible and rabbinic literature, and is in many cases an enemy of Israel, he is never an enemy of God; at most, he is a servant of God, doing the dirty but necessary work of arguing the case against Israel and other righteous humans in God's court. The classical Jewish tradition would never bestow upon Satan the power to oppose God. The Kabbalah however is a different matter, where a cosmic battle does seem to be taking place between good and evil, order and chaos.
5 In fact, it is the concept of fitting, poetic justice – where the punishment meets the crime – known by the Latin term *talion*, which most reflects Ben Ammi's 'Law of Relativity'. As Patrick Miller has shown, this concept is well represented in the prophetic books of the Hebrew Bible: see *Sin and Judgment in the Prophets: A Stylistic and Theological Analysis* (Chico, CA: Scholars Press, 1982).
6 Lounds, *Israel's Black Hebrews*, p. 56; 72–3.
7 Ammi is a little more detailed than this suggests: as we saw in Chapter 1, evil always requires mixture with good to exist; this miscegenation is one of the complicating factors which can make evil sometimes seem appealing.
8 One of the most explicit ascriptions of will to God relates to God's role in liberation: 'except that you desire to be free to worship God, then there is no benefit to His freeing you' (GBMT170). This statement, repeated in at least one lecture, is odd especially as it follows the claim that 'When a people truly seek to be free, and struggle in God's name, God is bound by His nature to help them succeed. God will never leave a people oppressed by His adversary if the people desire to be free to serve Him.' The former offers a strange kind of transaction logic, where God must get something in exchange for freedom, but the latter makes it clear that the way out from bondage is to truly want to be free, in order to do right (=worship God), not for any other reasons. God does not gain anything from being worshipped, but the moral calculus of being free in order to spread more righteousness into the world makes complete sense. So, until we read the ascription of will to God as allegory, where God is bound by God's nature as freedom and life and growth, it makes no sense.
9 Especially Coleman's Process Theology-inspired notion of a God who has the power of persuasion rather than coercion: Monica A. Coleman, *Making a Way out of No Way: A Womanist Theology* (Minneapolis: Fortress Press, 2008).

10 In one very odd passage, Ben briefly mentions two other apparent deities, both of whom are female: the Queen of Hell who leads women astray from their correct calling into singlehood, careerism, trousers, makeup and cosmetic surgery is joined by 'a Goddess of Heaven/Light who would rise to the occasion, protecting holiness, and cause the Edenic daughters to understand [not to]. But no longer is her voice heard above the hellish din' (RJPJ97-8). I have been unable to locate any explication of this idea, which is perhaps based on Jer.7:18; 44:17–25.

11 Eliezer Berkovits, *God, Man and History*, ed. David Hazony (Jerusalem: Shalem Press, 2004 (1959)), p. 56.

12 Cf. EL145.

13 The intellect is not the only term equated with the Holy Spirit: Chapter 1 mentioned that Truth also was identified as the Holy Spirit, and the Breath of Life is also identified as Truth. By this equation of Holy Spirit=Intellect=Breath of Life=Truth, we can suppose that Truth as the penumbral aspect of the Divine which can enter and enliven human beings does so through consciousness, and it is consciousness accessing the truth of the best way of life, the best way to live healthily and abundantly, that represents the bringing of Godliness into the world, and the consequent sanctification of the world.

14 Not only existence as an expression of divinity, but Truth too, given its divine nature as discussed previously, is under constant attack by satan who tries constantly 'to deceive and mislead without impediment' (GLR51). It is for this reason that everything in the present satanic culture must be interrogated and unmasked as untrue.

15 'For us Yah becomes a mental conception (idea) to be revealed/expressed in our daily lives and the Holy Spirit becomes the same expression in speech.' And therefore, 'the Kingdom becomes the revealed visible environment in which He dwells' (RJPJ4).

16 Cf. 'Inherent in the framework of the promised salvation is the return of the spirit of Elijah the Prophet (Malachi 4:5-6)' (GLR118).

17 On the Five Percenters see Michael Muhammad Knight, *The Five Percenters: Islam, Hip Hop and the Gods of New York* (Oxford: One World, 2007), and Biko Mandela Gray, 'Show and Prove: Five Percenters and the Study of African American Esotericism', in *Esotericism in African American Religious Experience*, ed. Stephen C. Finley, Margarita Simon Guillory, Hugh R. Page, Jr., pp. 177–97.

18 Anthony B. Pinn, *The End of God-Talk: An African American Humanistic Theology* (New York: Oxford University Press, 2012), p. 64. Other aspects include restraint/ self-control, a central role for community; all of which are very much present in Ben Ammi's thought.

19 See Joseph Citron, *Isaiah Horowitz's Shnei Luhot He-Berit and the Pietistic Transformation of Jewish Theology* (Leiden: Brill, 2021), pp. 157–61.

20 Gershom Scholem, *On the Kabbalah and Its Symbolism*, trans. Ralph Manheim (New York: Schocken Books, 1969), p. 117.

21 *Horowitz's Shnei Luhot He-Berit*, p. 111.

22 There are many passages in this chapter which are evocative of American slavery, although slavery is only one part of the curses. Others include inexplicable diseases, suffering, starvation, cannibalism and self-hatred. Parts of the chapter work against Hebrew Israelite interpretation, asserting that these events will happen in the Israelites' own land. As Vocab Malone has noted, there is also a subtle switch from the insistent literalism of 'ships' to the metaphorical interpretation of 'Egypt' when Hebrew Israelites interpret verse 68.

23   This concept of a cosmos perfectly obedient to God's ordained laws (in contrast
      to humans) is one utilized in several Jewish sources. For the rabbinic, see Jacob
      Neusner, *Judaism's Story of Creation: Scripture, Halakhah, Aggadah* (Leiden: Brill,
      2000), pp. 191–7. It is also central to the booklets of 1 Enoch (written between
      the third and first centuries BCE). These booklets argue that the cosmos has been
      pulled out of sync by rebellious angels who have perverted the world's cycles from
      the divine order, apparently with the intention of explaining why the seasons were
      increasingly falling out of alignment with the 364-day calendar that they followed.
      On this see in particular David R. Jackson, *Enochic Judaism: Three Defining Paradigm
      Exemplars* (London: T&T Clark, 2004). It is particularly interesting that temporal/
      calendrical deviation is a focus of this Jewish movement, given the emphasis on
      precisely this in Ben Ammi's theology. The difference of course is that in 1 Enoch it is
      the physical world itself which has been distorted, for example by the angelic powers'
      refusal to bring the sun and moon to their positions on time; in Ben Ammi it is the
      Euro-gentiles' satanically inspired calendar which is leading humans to incorrectly
      appreciate the actual times and cycles of the correct physical world.
24   'God is exemplified by every positive action; to do good is the worship of God;
      helping your brother or sister is the worship of God. Divine dancing, singing,
      laughing or playing is of God and is indeed, the true worship of God. To plant and to
      harvest, to eat, and to be merry is the true worship of God. For truly, life is continued
      action – work and worship. They are inseparable' (GBMT138). Cf., 'the worship of
      God is an ongoing 24-hour-a-day activity that cannot be separated from anything
      you do' (MEW62).
25   Prior to Maimonides, the medieval Jewish philosopher Judah Ben Levi also held that
      the Law served as a point of connection to the Divine Influence, and it was this that
      made Israel a 'living' nation in contrast to those who were not connected to God,
      which were 'dead'. See Judah Halevi, *The Kuzari (Kitab al Khazari): An Argument for
      the Faith of Israel* (New York: Schocken, 1964), 2.33-4. However the resting of the
      Shekhinah on Israel depends on their righteousness (ibid., 2.24).
26   For an overview of the kabbalistic approach to Law, see Daniel C. Matt, 'The Mystic
      and the Mizwot', in *Jewish Spirituality: From the Bible through the Middle Ages*, ed.
      Arthur Green (New York: Crossroad, 1996), pp. 367–404. Matt argues that the
      kabbalists subtly reimagine the Law as benefitting human beings not simply in
      their own beings, but through solidifying the ontological connection with God and
      thereby channelling Divine energy into the world, and thereby, in the words of one
      rabbi, 'to maintain the existence of the world' (ibn Gabbai, quoted p. 394). 'The
      mystic integrates himself into the pattern of the cosmos and stimulates the flow
      of emanation. His ritual act represents the divine and calls it forth. Whereas the
      philosophers had sought to rationalize the mizwot in earthly terms, the Kabbalists
      expand the dimensions. The human actor is now a protagonist in the cosmic drama.
      The mizwot are "literally the essence of life", his life and God's. They are not reducible
      to autonomous reason; nor are they simply imposed heteronomously. As extensions of
      the divine qualities, they permeate the universe and constitute its fabric. The human
      who lives by them is attuned to the rhythm of being. He is imitating God' (395). As
      Matt goes on to describe, not only performance of the mitzvot is necessary, but also an
      understanding of the specific law's sefirotic implications and its role in the unification
      of the divine. Hence, not just action but also the consciousness – *kavvanah*,
      intention – must be attuned to bring about the full results. Nachmanides says those
      who fulfil the mitzvot become 'a dwelling place for the Shekhina' (Matt p. 400).

27   Yakov M. Travis, 'Kabbalistic Foundations of Jewish Spiritual Practice: Rabbi Ezra of Gerona on the Kabbalistic Meaning of the Mitzvot', (Brandeis University: PhD Diss., 2002, p. 118; 125).

28   On this in particular see Moshe Idel, *Kabbalah: New Perspectives* (New Haven: Yale University Press, 1988), pp. 157–66.

29   For the kabbalists, the fulfilling of *mitzvot* was completing the metaphysical unity of God: repairing the broken connections within God that would allow divine energy to flow through into the present reality in which the fallen divine sparks – human souls – were trapped. In doing this, the world and the parts of God that exist in it could be lifted up, once again reconnected with the divine source and revivified. Like Ammi, the kabbalists sought to make even profane action a channel for holiness, effectively sacralizing every act. On the theurgic nature of human action in Kabbalah see Scholem, *Kabbalah and Its Symbolism*, who notes that 'all "upper happening" […] required "stimulation" by a "lower happening" shows clearly to what extent ritual had come […] to be regarded as an action of cosmic import.' p. 125, cf. 132–4.

30   Cf.: 'one should not cloak himself with the letter of the law while strangling the Spirit of the law. The law is as the universe of man. There is an outer law or layer (the letter) and an inner layer (the spirit). Man has been created in like manner, having the outer body (flesh) and the inner (soul). The things you do outwardly must be motivated or inspired by the proper reason. For to be obedient outwardly for the wrong inner reason is to violate the law. Each generation has to interpret and apply the law in accordance with its conditions and exigencies. Yet, it has to always maintain the one original spirit of intention that was and forever shall be.' (MEW93).

31   This is the intent behind the famous case of the Oven of Akhnai (b.BMetz.59a-b), where one rabbi produces a series of miracles to prove divine support for his interpretation; the opponent wins, apparently even against God's pronouncement, simply by citing scripture.

32   On this see Lawrence Fine, *Physician of the Soul: Isaac Luria and His Kabbalistic Fellowship* (Stanford: Stanford University Press, 2003), pp. 187–220.

33   Neither should the motivation be fear of punishment: 'These [Mosaic] laws were to give us insight concerning living and to make us consciously aware that there are certain elements that govern our existence and relationship with our fellow man. You should follow these instructions because you desire to live and be at peace with your Maker, not because of the threat of punishment.' (GLR8).

34   Ishakamusa Barashango, *God, the Bible and the Black Man's Destiny* (Baltimore: Afrikan World Books, 2001 (1970)), p. 88.

35   Ibid., p. 107.

36   Fine, *Physician of the Soul*, p. 219.

37   Azriel ben Menahem of Gerona. Perush ha-Aggadot le-Rabbi Azriel. Edited by Isaiah Tishby. Jerusalem: Mekize Nirdamim, 1945. [Hebrew], pp. 100–1.

38   Indeed, this trend was set in the early times of Antebellum Black Christianity; Yolanda Pierce writes that 'the idea of "hell" is one of the preeminent metaphors for life on earth for enslaved and free African Americans […] the hell presented in black spiritual narratives is not just an otherworldly domain; hell is a metaphor for the time spent on earth in daily physical and psychological suffering.' *Hell Without Fires: Slavery, Christianity, and the Antebellum Spiritual Narrative* (Gainsville: University Press of Florida, 2005), pp. 6–7.

39   Muhammad, *Fall of America* p. 188, *Message to the Blackman*, p. 76. An early precursor could be the forgotten but influential New Jersey Hebrew Israelite Bishop

Allen Wilson Cook who, following the death of his only son, preached that African Americans were living in Hell and the only way to escape was through the following of the commandments.

40   In 1965 he wrote: 'The hereafter means after the destruction of the present world, its power and authority to rule ... My people have been deceived by the archdeceiver with regard to the hereafter. They think the hereafter is a life of spirits up somewhere in the sky, while it is only on the earth, and you won't change to any spirit being. The life in the hereafter is only a continuation of the present life. You will be flesh and blood. You won't see spooks coming up out of graves to meet God. No already physically dead person will be in the hereafter; that is slavery belief, taught to slaves to keep them under control.' Muhammad, *Message to the Blackman in America*, pp. 303–4.

41   James H. Cone, *God of the Oppressed*, revised edn (Maryknoll: Orbis Books, 1997), p. 140.

42   Cone, *Black Theology and Black Power*, p. 126.

43   Cleage saw the Black church as functionally counter-revolutionary because of its doctrines of atonement (salvation of the individual by faith in Christ) and 'individualistic otherworldly salvation' (see *Black Christian Nationalism*, pp. 183–7). To an extent though, the shift in focus to a gospel dealing with life on earth rather than in heaven had already taken place during the twentieth century: Lacey Kirk Williams in the early twentieth century argued that the northern Protestant churches must adapt to the incoming southern migrants and a large part of this would be by altering their outlook from one of the hereafter to concentrating on the here and now and the daily needs of people. Best, *Passionately Human*, p. 19, writes that this change to pragmatic matters was 'a process already in force among many African American churches in Chicago by the late 1920s'.

44   Pinn, *End of God-Talk*, p. 66.

45   Ibid., p. 69.

46   As Dan Cohn-Sherbok, *God and the Holocaust* (Leominster: Fowler Wright, 1996), pp. 120–9 notes.

47   Pinn, *End of God-Talk*, p. 7.

48   Ibid., p. 70.

49   Walker, *Walker's Appeal*, p. 2.

50   'Divine Fundamentalism' (audio recording in the AHIJ archive).

51   Dwight N. Hopkins, *Down, Up, and Over: Slave Religion and Black Theology* (Minneapolis: Fortress Press, 2000).

52   Jawanza Eric Clark, 'Nothing Is More Sacred than the Liberation of Black People: Albert Cleage's Method as Unfulfilled Theological Paradigm Shift', in *Albert Cleage Jr. and the Black Madonna and Child*, ed. Jawanza Eric Clark (New York: Palgrave Macmillan, 2016), pp. 39–58.

53   'Bishop Joseph Wesley Crowdy, Chief of the Pulpits 1875 – 1917', http://www.churchofgodandsaintsofchrist.org/leaders/jwcrowdy.html.

54   Darnise C. Martin, 'The Self Divine: Know Ye Not that Ye Aare Gods?' in *Esotericism in African American Religious Experience: 'There Is a Mystery'* ..., ed. Stephen C. Finley, Margarita Simon Guillory and Hugh R. Page Jr (Leiden: Brill, 2015), pp. 52–69.

55   Ibid., pp. 68; 61. On the centrality of the Holy Spirit in the Black Church, see James H. Evans Jr, 'The Holy Spirit in African American Theology', in *The Oxford Handbook*

of African American Theology, ed. K.G. Cannon and A.B. Pinn (Oxford: Oxford University Press, 2014), pp. 164–73.

56 Dorman, *Chosen People,* pp. 166–7. For more on Father Divine and New Thought see Weisenfeld, *New World A'Coming,* pp. 75–8.

57 Howard Waitzkin, 'Black Judaism in New York', *Harvard Journal of Negro Affairs* 1.3 (1967), pp. 12–44 (33); Howard M. Brotz, 'The Black Jews of Harlem' (University of Chicago: MA Diss., 1947), p. 32.

58 Ibid., p. 41.

59 Ibid., p. 171. Waitzkin described Matthew's seven-part theosophical system, where God is Wind, Water, Fire, Life, Light, Power and Mind, all of which are different elements or processes of the human body also, commenting that 'the black Jews' belief in the hypostatized "elements" has fairly close counterparts in the theosophical system of Jewish cabbala'. Ibid., p. 42; Dorman argued that this cabalistic element may be due to a single Christian cabala text which he utilized often (and copied his amulets from).

60 Landes, 'Negro Jews in Harlem'. She notes that Arnold Ford's BBA also taught the absence of any afterlife.

61 Léopold Sédar Senghor & Elaine P. Halperin, 'African Negro Aesthetics', *Diogenes* 4.16 (1956), pp. 23–38 (24–5). Interestingly, negritude was influenced by the *elan vital* notion, developed by Henri Bergson; himself a thinker of Jewish background. However while the *elan vital* notion has parallels in many earlier systems, it is not necessarily one linked with Judaism in any way.

62 On such concepts in their native form see Henry Paget, *Caliban's Reason: Introducing Afro-Caribbean Philosophy* (New York: Routledge, 2000), p. 25ff.

63 See Senghor's 1939 essay 'Ce que l'homme noir apporte' ('What the Black Man Contributes') which explored the notion of rhythm as constitutive of what he called 'the negro style'.

64 The controversial 'Emotion is Negro, as reason is Hellenic' ('*L'émotion est nègre, comme la raison héllène*', Senghor *Liberté I, Négritude et humanisme* (Paris: Seuil, 1964), p. 288) however has no parallel in Ben. There is virtually zero time or appreciation given to emotion in his writings; in fact some have claimed that he tried to teach everyone to keep a great distance from their emotions which must be controlled at all times. It is difficult to know the reason for this omission, however its absence from criticism in his entire output suggests that this is not a principled rejection but a personal neglect; he did not value emotion. The subjective and personal generally do not appear in his writing but there could be a deeper association of feelings with negative emotionality as was deprecatingly ascribed to blacks during and after slavery.

65 Paget, *Caliban's Reason,* p. 37ff.

66 *God, the Black Man and the Bible,* p. 15. Barashango also expresses a very similar doctrine of spiritual evil, writing that the 'spirit of evil continued to lurk in the atmosphere seeking to find another group of beings through which it could manifest itself' after the destruction of Cain's (white) progeny in the flood, pp. 17–19; 40–1.

67 Howard Thurman, 'Deep Calls Unto Deep, Part 1: The Meaning of Religious Experience, 23 January 1980', *The Howard Thurman Digital Archive,* https://thurman. pitts.emory.edu/items/show/875 (accessed 21st September 2022).

68 Dwight N. Hopkins, 'Slave Theology in the 'Invisible Institution', in *Cut Loose Your Stammering Tongue,* ed. Hopkins and Cummings, pp. 1–33 (21–3).

Chapter 5

1   This formulation of the Problem of Evil, subtly emphasizing God's love rather than God's omnipotence, is characteristically Christian, as demonstrated by John Bowker, *Problems of Suffering in Religions of the World* (London: Cambridge University Press, 1970).

2   Cone, *Black Theology of Liberation*, p. 115.

3   William R. Jones, *Is God a White Racist? A Preamble to Black Theology* (Boston: Beacon Press, 1997).

4   Black and Jewish theodicy have been previously compared in Kurt Buhring, *Conceptions of God, Freedom and Ethics in African American and Jewish Theology* (New York: Palgrave Macmillan, 2008). Buhring, like Jones, argues that the preferable path is humanocentric theism, wherein freedom is maintained, as is God's goodness, but the former is allowed by God even when evil results; that is, God does not step in to prevent humans committing atrocities against each other, because this would limit the fullness of human freedom. He builds into this a necessary element of resistance. Buhring's analysis is worthwhile, but it restricts itself to certain themes of academic theology and does not address the extremely difficult issues raised by thinkers outside the academy, such as Ben Ammi; my own analysis will strive to how they challenge theological and ethical assumptions, and what paths forward these can offer.

5   See Moses, *Black Messiahs*, pp. 1–3; Maurianne Adams and John Bracey (eds), *Strangers & Neighbours: Relations between Blacks and Jews in the United States* (Amherst: University of Massachusetts Press, 1999), pp. 53–104.

6   Robert Alexander Young, 'The Ethiopian Manifesto (1829)', in *Pamphlets of Protest: An Anthology of Early African-American Protest Literature, 1790–1860*, ed. Richard Newman, Patrick Rael and Philip Lapsansky (New York & Oxon: Routledge, 2001), pp. 84–9.

7   Alexander Crummell, 'The Destined Superiority of the Negro', in *The Greatness of Christ and Other Sermons* (New York: Whittaker, 1882), p. 351. On this providential aspect of enslavement see also Anthony Pinn, *Why Lord? Suffering and Evil in Black Theology* (New York: Continuum, 1995).

8   W.E.B. Du Bois, *Darkwater: Voices from within the Veil* (New York: Harcourt, Brace and Company, 1920), p. 1.

9   Moses, *The Golden Age of Black Nationalism, 1850–1925*, p. 157.

10   Ernest Lee Tuveson, *Redeemer Nation: The Idea of America's Millennial Role* (Chicago and London: University of Chicago Press, 1968).

11   Moses, *Black Messiahs*, p. 9.

12   See Pinn, *Why Lord*, pp. 75–9.

13   Raboteau, '"Ethiopia Shall Soon Stretch Forth Her Hands"', pp. 397–413.

14   Pinn (ed.), *Moral Evil and Redemptive Suffering*.

15   Cone, *Black Theology and Black Power*, p. 124.

16   Cf. the video lecture 'The Wonders of Egypt', https://youtu.be/FjUtk3zp1_k.

17   The first examples of this are Cook, *Independent Church of God*, and Fleming Aytes, *The Teaching Black Jew* (New York City: Fleming Aytes, 1927). See Miller, 'Bishop Allan Wilson'. Wentworth Matthew also taught this view, and use of Deut.28 was mentioned by Brotz in 1947: see 'Black Jews of Harlem' p. 73; and cf. Levy, 'Wentworth Arthur Matthew', pp. 567–9 who writes: 'Matthew argued that the

suffering of black people was in large measure God's punishment for having violated the commandments. When black people "returned" to Judaism, he believed, their curse would be lifted and the biblical prophecies of redemption would be fulfilled.' For a critical discussion of Deut.28's place in HI thought, see Key, 'If Thou Do not Hearken unto the Voice of the Lord Thy God', pp. 267–88.

18 Here the Euro-gentiles have agency: 'it was the European realization that they were not chosen by God that prompted their attempt to become an inalienable and accepted imitation as they disguised themselves as angels of light and their people as the teachers of righteousness' (IL44). At another point also, Ammi states that 'His [the white's] problem is strictly his own egocentric race problem', because all the important peoples of history have been black; 'He has authorized book burnings, destruction of manuscripts and interpolation, in his vain attempt to destroy the roots and origins he was born from, trying to conceal all evidence of the fact that in the beginning all people were "colored" – brown or black pigmented. In other words, the Euro-gentiles fear the revelation of their true Black father and mother' (MEW32).

19 Satan did not create Europeans, all humans come from God; but satan created the *image* that Europeans have chosen to emulate in preference to the image of God.

20 This motif of overzealous punishment, already cited by Bishop Henry McNeal Turner, is found also in one early Jewish text: the Animal Apocalypse (1Enoch 85–90, esp. 90.22-24), in which the 'shepherds' (gentile nations) whom God gave dominion over Israel as the latter's punishment treated them even more harshly than was decreed, and whom would then be subject to God's punishment during the endtimes.

21 Jones, *White Racist*, p. 67.

22 Ibid., p. 127.

23 Ammi reflects Jones's concern when, relaxing his usual critique of religion, he asked, 'Isn't the bottom line of every religion the application of its general principles to solve the problems of society and bring us redemption?' (RHS86).

24 On non-personalist theology as a plausible resolution of the Problem of Evil, see John Bishop and Ken Perszyk, 'Concepts of God and Problems of Evil', in *Alternative Concepts of God: Essays on the Metaphysics of the Divine*, ed. Andrei A. Buckareff and Yujin Nagasawa (Oxford: Oxford University Press, 2016), pp. 106–27, who argue that pantheism may lead to quietism in the face of evil; Ben Ammi demonstrates how this consequence can be avoided. The more important problem, of the validity of 'salvation' under pantheism is effectively dismissed by Ammi.

25 See also the discussion in Pinn, *Why Lord*, who notes several assumptions to Jones's argument.

26 The extent to which the community follow the intricacies of Ben Ammi's theology is debatable, but certainly not all members read Ben Ammi as closely as we are in this text.

27 Ben Ammi can thus be said to have engaged with Victor Anderson's critique of Black Theology. Anderson disliked the tendency to essentialize the black experience as one of suffering and oppression; Ben Ammi holds that, to a growing extent for the past several hundred years, the lot of *all* of humanity has been one of suffering, as we became entranced further and further by the Spirit of Err. Ben Ammi also provides grounds for believing that, to the extent this suffering has characterized African Americans, that is now coming to an end, as they awaken to their identity and new role in the world.

28 Delores S. Williams, *Sisters in the Wilderness: The Challenge of Womanist God-Talk* (Marknoll: Orbis Books, 1993). Something Williams highlights, which Ammi never

addresses, are the many acts of brutality (genocide even) committed by the Israelites at God's behest in the Tanakh. One wonders what he made of these events.

29   The best introduction to this concept, which can be summed up in the sentence 'compassion follows only after repentance and acts of atonement', is given in Ephraim E. Urbach, *The Sages: Their Concepts and Beliefs*, trans. Israel Abrahams (Jerusalem: Magnes Press, 1987), pp. 448–61.

30   Anthony B. Pinn, 'Introduction', in Pinn (ed.), *Moral Evil*, pp. 8–9.

31   Lewis R. Gordon, 'The Problem of History in African American Theology', in *Oxford Handbook of African American Theology*, ed. Cannon & Pinn, pp. 363–76 (368).

32   Pinn, *Why Lord?*, p. 80.

33   Moses Maimonides, *The Guide for the Perplexed*, trans. M. Friedländer, second edn (Skokie, IL: Varda Books, 2002), p. 389.

34   Steven T. Katz, Shlomo Biderman and Gershon Greenberg (eds), *Wrestling with God: Jewish Theological Responses during and after the Holocaust* (New York: Oxford University Press, 2007).

35   B.Ber.5a. For the Haredi response see for example, Dina Porat, '"Amalek's Accomplices": Blaming Zionism for the Holocaust: Anti-Zionist Ultra-Orthodoxy in Israel during the 1980s', *Journal of Contemporary History* 27.4 (1992), pp. 695–729; and Daniel J. Lasker, 'Reflection: The Holocaust as Retributive Justice', *Shofar* 15.3 (1997), pp. 97–105.

36   P. 99. Lasker, 'Reflection', p. 101 also notes some Haredi rabbis who argued that the Holocaust was a means of achieving a greater good, cf. the similar mystical approach in Gershon Greenberg, 'Hasidic Thought and the Holocaust (1933–1947): Optimism and Activism', *Jewish History* 27.2 (2013), pp. 353–75.

37   Richard L. Rubenstein, *After Auschwitz: Radical Theology and Contemporary Judaism* (Indianapolis: Macmillan, 1966), p. 153.

38   It is worth noting that the 1985 and 1990 editions of GBMT90 add some paragraphs to emphasize God's love and beneficence amongst the lengthy affirmation of God's anger; prompting the idea that Ammi was concerned he had overemphasized God's wrath. Ben Ammi is not a fire and brimstone preacher, but he is committed to the fundamental concept that humans must return to God in order not to suffer.

39   Moshe Avigdor Amiel, 'To the Perplexed of the Era: A Chapter of Observation about the Essence of Judaism', *Hayesod* 12.388 (1943), pp. 2; trans. Katz, Biderman and Greenberg (eds), *Wrestling with God*, p. 125.

40   Rabbi Benjamin Mendelsohn, quoted in Porat, p. 699.

41   Ibid., p. 127.

42   Lasker, 'Reflections', p. 105.

43   See Anson Laytner, *Arguing with God: A Jewish Tradition* (New York: Jason Aaronson, 1998) and Dov Weiss, *Pious Irreverence: Confronting God in Rabbinic Judaism* (Philadelphia: University of Pennsylvania Press, 2016).

44   See Nehemia Polen, *The Holy Fire: The Teachings of Kalonymus Kalman Shapira, the Rebbe of the Warsaw Ghetto* (Northvale, NJ: Jason Aaronson Inc., 1994), pp. 94–105.

45   Bernard Maza, *With Fury Poured Out: The Power of the Powerless during the Holocaust* (New York: Shapolsky Publishers, 1989).

46   Randolph C. Miller, 'Process Thought and Black Theology', in *Black Theology II: Essays on the Formation and Outreach of Contemporary Black Theology*, ed. Calvin E. Bruce and William R. Jones (Cranbury, NJ: Associated University Press, 1978), pp. 267–86 (p. 277).

47   One of the most concrete challenges to divine personalism comes in 2008's
     Restoration Village when Ammi writes, 'To continuously destroy the balance of the
     eco-system while simultaneously subjugating nature for the sake of profit or material
     greed, leads all of mankind down the path of self-destruction. Because nature's
     ultimate resilience has but one recourse, and that is to preserve itself' (RV7). Here he
     presents a Gaia kind of idea; and it is not God who will punish humanity but simply
     nature who will defend itself against us. See Chapter 6.
48   Most fully developed in *End of God Talk*.
49   Jones, *White Racist*, p. 143.
50   Rubenstein, *After Auschwitz*, p. 152.
51   Admittedly most of the early leaders were Freemasons; it is unclear at this stage how
     much that has influenced HI traditions, an issue which requires further research.
52   It occurs to this author that, just as the biblical J and E sources were brilliantly
     combined to form a single narrative, but there remained a nascent tension between
     the J and E concepts of God (national/passionate, and universal/distant) which
     formed a theological faultline, ultimately prised apart by Shabtai Tzvi in the
     seventeenth century, so there exists a dynamic tension between these two concepts
     in the thought of Ben Ammi which may ultimately come back to haunt this faith
     community.
53   Kenneth Seeskin, *Jewish Philosophy in a Secular Age* (Albany: State University of New
     York Press, 1990).
54   Sam Kestenbaum, in his discussion of Kendrick Lamar's discovery of the movement,
     notes that Lamar was particularly drawn to the notion of a loving and just, yet
     vengeful, God; a depiction he had never encountered in Christianity. Kestenbaum,
     'I'm an Israelite'. In the same collection, also foregrounding the empowering aspects
     of HI thought, is Spencer Dew's 'Hebrew Israelite Covenantal Theology and Kendrick
     Lamar's Constructive Project in DAMN', in *Kendrick Lamar*, ed. Miller and Driscoll,
     p. 18.
55   This author recalls overhearing, at the Village of Peace in 2010, a sermon which
     was also an admonishing for a few schoolchildren who had failed their exams. The
     ear-battering that these children received culminated in the threat that if they did
     not work harder and achieve better than the last year, they would find themselves
     retracing their ancestors' footsteps until they were back in America with a chain
     around their neck. The motivation was, if they did not live up to their responsibilities
     now, they will return to the hell their parents came from. While I cannot comment
     on the psychological benefit or harm of such a childrearing technique, fear can be a
     great motivator.

Chapter 6

1   Finley, 'The Secret … of Who the Devil Is', pp. 158–9.
2   See the reconstruction in Miller, 'Ben Ammi's Adaptation of Veganism in the
    Theology of the African Hebrew Israelites of Jerusalem', *Interdisciplinary Journal for
    Religion and Transformation in Contemporary Society* (2021), pp. 1–29, from which
    the first section of this chapter is condensed. However even in 1970 they refused
    Purim gifts of food brought to them by Israelis, claiming that they did not eat eggs or
    chocolate.

3   Yadah Baht Israel cites this passage as header to the Dietary Habits section of 'The Holistic Lifestyle', in *Hebrew Israelite Community*, ed. A. Paul Hare (Lanham: University Press of America 1998), pp. 27–34.

4   Enumerated as either 102 (PI62), or 112 (In the CD recorded lecture *The Global Crisis: The End Result of Applied Knowledge* (Washington: Communicators Press, 2002).

5   *Global Crisis.*

6   He mentions three times in GBMT the evil of cow's milk, this 'naturally being for calves instead of human babies' (GBMT218, cf. 247); somewhat stronger, he equates formula baby milk with devil worship, because 'The child, filled with animal hormones, becomes more like the beast than the parent' (GBMT118).

7   There is also a brief mention of societies founded to prevent animal cruelty as doing their part of the work showing us the way away from 'the life-destroying, perverted patterns that have become the norm today' (MEW70).

8   E.g. 'Everything suffers under wicked rulers – man, vegetation and beast. Everyday we witness more and more species of natural vegetation and animals added to the list of those facing extinction.' (GBMT184).

9   In 1984 he seems to have shrugged off the death of fifteen of the community's children from malnutrition as unfortunate collateral in the pursuit of a grand objective: 'Just like there are those experimenting with the atomic age we're experimenting with the age of health, the age of love, the age of sharing. But we're paying the price first for the people of Israel, and afterwards for all men.' Elliott, Roberta, *Interview with Ben Ammi*, in *Newsview*, 14 February 1984, p. 17.

10   Cf. Shaleak Ben Yehuda's comments in Lounds, *Israel's Black Hebrews*, p. 59.

11   Meat substitutes such as tofu and seitan are an integral part of the community's restaurant menus, presumably acceptable there because the community have the right mindset and know *how* to eat it.

12   Jackson, *Thin Description*, p. 216ff.

13   Israel, *The Holistic Lifestyle*, p. 13.

14   Markowitz, Fran and Avieli, Nir, 'Food for the Body and Soul: Veganism, Righteous Male Bodies, and Culinary Redemption in the Kingdom of Yah', in *Ethnography* (2020), p. 12.

15   Lounds, *Israel's Black Hebrews*, p. 60.

16   Sister Penny confirmed this to me. He himself stated that 'It was the medical element that initially influenced my dietary transition,' because he wanted to alleviate the suffering – not his own, but that of doctors forced to see sickness all the time (MEW135).

17   Nathan Kaplan, 'Negro "Rabbi" Claims White Jews Not Jews', *Jewish Post*, 8th October 1965, p. 13.

18   Shaleak, *Black Hebrew Israelites*, p. 226.

19   See esp. Jacob Ari Labendz and Shmuly Yanklowitz (eds), *Jewish Veganism and Vegetarianism: Studies and New Directions* (Albany: State University of New York Press, 2019).

20   Jonathan Brumberg-Kraus, 'Meat-Eating and Jewish Identity: Ritualization of the Priestly "Torah of Beast and Fowl" (Lev 11:46) in Rabbinic Judaism and Medieval Kabbalah', *AJS Review* 24.2 (1999), pp. 227–62.

21   Dorman, *The Princess and the Prophet*, p. 213.

22   Christian, *Poor Pilgrim's Work*, pp. 10–14.

23   Miller, 'Ben Ammi's Adaptation of Veganism'.

24   *Sefer Meshiv Devarim Nekhohim,* ed. Georges Vajda (Israel Academy of Science and Humanities, Jerusalem, 1969) pp. 83. [Hebrew].

25   'As we continue to strengthen our relationship with Yah' is a commonly used phrase, denoting the ongoing upward movement. Health and the quality of food, plus its effects, will continue growing.

26   BerR.14.9.

27   Stavrakopoulou, *God: An Anatomy*, pp. 190–205.

28   See Jackson, *Thin Description*, p. 136.

29   Cf. 'there is no injection discovered or yet to be discovered which will allow mankind to continue smoking, polluting and consuming poisons while not being afflicted with cancer. There is no safety in wickedness.' (GBMT202).

30   David Mevorach Seidenberg, *Kabbalah and Ecology: God's Image in the More-Than-Human World* (New York: Cambridge University Press, 2015), cf. Daniel Boyarin, *Carnal Israel: Reading Sex in Talmudic Culture* (Berkeley: University of California Press, 1993), who claims that the rabbis imagine the human as a body which is animated by a soul, in contrast to the Greek conception of a soul which expresses itself temporarily through a body.

31   Maimonides, citing Moses' ability to survive forty days in the presence of God without food or water (Ex.34:28), claims any prophet who approaches so close to God does not need physical sustenance (GP3:51). For Maimonides also the intellect is the aspect whereby the human is connected to God, a bond which can be strengthened or weakened depending on how much one uses it for contemplation of the divine. For him praying, studying scripture and performing mitzvot are the most important ways of maintaining this connection, but one should endeavour to always keep God in mind. As discussed in Chapter 4, Maimonides believed in the providential power of the intellectual connection to God.

32   Brotz, *Black Jews of Harlem*, pp. 40–1. As with most of Matthew's doctrines it is difficult to know how far back this notion went. Cf. Waitzkin, 'Black Judaism', p. 36 on health and kosher food.

33   These of course inspired also the early Christian belief that the resurrection of Jesus foretold the imminent coming of the Kingdom and immortality. Opposing immortality Segal notes as Gen.3.19, 3.22, Ps.49.10, Ps.89.49 and Ecc.9.2.

34   Travis, 'Kabbalistic Foundations', p. 132.

35   Ibid.

36   Seidenberg, *Kabbalah and Ecology*, p. 186.

37   For many medieval Jewish philosophers, the soul was articulated into parts, only some or one of which may survive death. Based on Platonic reasoning some, such as Gersonides, argued that the immaterial 'acquired intellect' is immortal, once formed; it contains those non-material and non-accidental truths realized by the individual. In this way, through a different process, Truth is linked to immortality.

38   This phrase, *olam ha-ba*, 'the world to come', itself is never defined, despite being present throughout the rabbinic literature; it may mean a mediating spiritual afterlife or simply the eventual resurrection.

39   EL110 adds the angels Michael Gabriel and Rafael.

40   In particular he claims the spirit of Antiochus persists (EL46).

41   As Urbach writes, 'In the Bible a monistic view prevails. Man is not composed of two elements – body and soul, or flesh and spirit … [T]he term *nefesh* is not to be understood in the sense of psyche, anima. The whole of man is a living soul … *Nefesh, guf*, and *ruach* [*sic*] form an indivisible entity … This unity finds expression in

a lack of differentiation between the word and the substance in the Hebrew tongue.' *Sages,* pp. 214–5.

42   *Embodiment and the New Shape of Black Theological Thought* (New York: New York University Press, 2010), p. 3.

43   See Boyarin, *Carnal Israel.*

44   Shaleak Ben Yehuda, letter to John Henrik Clarke, 4th June 1973 (JHC Papers, Schomburg, MG571 b41 f1).

45   Clark Jenkins, *The Black Hebrews of the Seed of Abraham – Isaac and Jacob of the Tribe of Judah – Benjamin and Levi after 430 Years in America* (Detroit: Jenkins, 1969), p. 111ff.

46   Personal communication, October 2022.

47   '[A]uthority to oversee the planet was bestowed upon [Adam]. Although God gave Adam dominion over the earth, he was not authorized to exploit it in an evil way, but was to maintain the earth and himself in the God-like, God-preferred manner.' (RJPJ162).

48   See, e.g., 'the use of unnatural products becomes detrimental to life and health … To wear natural products is to be obedient to God's laws and orders, which in turn, enhance the health and longevity of the body […] man's deviation from the right path – his obstruction and deformation of God's righteous cycles, have thrown the entire universe into chaos. The present world state (wars, erratic weather, polluted air, water and food, etc.) is a result of man's violation of God's righteous cycles and seasons.' (GBMT182-3).

49   Ben Ammi draws a correlation between personal diet, and the political/leadership systems which feed the earth a diet of our waste (which is bad for it and which it cannot sustain us from). In this way, 'man's synthetic (imperfect) systems of governing led to his self-engineered annihilation' (GBMT184).

50   That this is in conflict with his previous assertion that it is the 'Universal Corrective Force' of God's Word that is behind the manifold challenges – including the environmental – to the Euro-gentile world (MEW57), should serve to demonstrate the evolution of his thinking.

51   Ben Ammi repeatedly emphasizes the beauty of the natural world, the world created by God. He does not state whether the immortal body will continue to visibly age, but the restoring of vitality to the body as well as to the world suggests a re-beautification. This can easily be related to Elijah Muhammad's emphasis on physical beauty as product of discipline and diet (although neither of them is an admirer of the beauty industry: On the general maltreatment of the female body, he comments, 'no vessel has undergone as much abuse as that of the woman's body'. This includes the loss of understanding what menstruation is and the rules around it, the makeup, chemical ingestions, pills, caesarean sections, abortions, hysterectomies and other surgical procedures. Pinn considers this world-harmonious 'beauty' element a necessary one for living well, and it is an important part of his 'African American non-theistic humanism'. He writes, 'beauty entails an elusive harmony of meaning by which the African American nontheistic humanist is in accord with the world' (*End of God-Talk,* p. 72). In a way, Pinn's discussion seems to propose beauty as an alternative to salvation; beauty constituted by wholeness/fullness and symmetry (where symmetry is the emergence of complex reality from a small number of natural laws; cause and effect beautifully interwoven). This reflects Ben's prioritization of living in harmony with God, nature and society. So, as the Messianic Age spreads across the world, 'There shall be no "deceitfulness of riches," no "rich

get richer; poor get poorer," no "third world" or destruction of the earth's eco-system to satisfy a world of misanthropists. Our true and everlasting wealth – the true and living God, nature and one another – shall be returned in abundance.' (GLR130).

52 Ammi's conception of Africa is (despite the sojourn in Liberia) somewhat idealistic. He upends the traditional western notion that Europeans had brought Christianity and civilization to an Africa which had known only paganism and barbarism, arguing that precisely the opposite is the case. In his construction, Africa is naturally spiritual, and when lead by the continent's spiritual leaders, the monotheistic Israelites, would correctly worship only Yah; whereas Europeans were still essentially pagan, their Christianity merely a glaze applied over the still-dominant polytheistic, mythical, otherworldly faith. There is, of course, something in this – at least, in the latter. Ben Ammi, like many African American thinkers of previous generations, unfortunately shares the European tendency to radically simplify and homogenize Africa, reading onto it a beautiful, simple, peaceful existence at one with nature. This is as idealistic as the Europeans' assumption that Africa was devoid of civilization, sophisticated religions and philosophy.

53 For a detailed argument see Aloys Huttermann, *The Ecological Message of the Torah: Knowledge, Concepts, and Laws Which Made Survival in a Land of 'Milk and Honey' Possible* (Atlanta, GA: Scholars Press, 1999).

54 Arthur Waskow, 'Jewish Environmental Ethics: Intertwining Adam with Adamah', in *The Oxford Handbook of Jewish Ethics and Morality*, ed. Elliot N. Dorff and Jonathan K. Crane (Oxford: Oxford University Press, 2012), pp. 401–17.

55 'The land must never be sold on a permanent basis, for the land belongs to me. You are only foreigners and tenant farmers working for me.' Lev.25:23.

56 Wolff, Keith A., 'Bal Tashchit: The Jewish Prohibition against Needless Destruction' (Leiden University: PhD Thesis, 2009); Tanhum Yoreh, 'The Jewish Prohibition against Wastefulness: The Evolution of an Environmental Ethic' (York University: PhD Thesis, 2014).

57 These trees were not just the two named in the Genesis account: 'We may reasonably conclude that there was an abundance of trees with positive attributes such as: the Tree of Knowledge of Fire, the Tree of Knowledge of Soil, of Air, of Water, of Kindness, of Joy, of Pleasure, of Consumption, of Disposal, of Sharing, of Beauty, of Life's Purpose, etc. Of course, also present was the Tree with the Forked Tongue of Good and Evil.'

58 Elliot R. Wolfson, 'Mirror of Nature Reflected in the Symbolism of Medieval Kabbalah', in *Judaism and Ecology: Created World and Revealed Word*, ed. Hava Tirosh-Samuelson (Cambridge, MA: Harvard University Press, 2002), pp. 305–32 (310).

59 Ariel Evan Mayse, 'Gardens of the Spirit: Land, Text, and Ecological Hermeneutics in Jewish Mystical Sources', *Dibur* 11 (2022), pp. 60–88 (64).

Chapter 7

1 Stokeley Carmichael (Kwame Ture), *Stokely Speaks: From Black Power to Pan-Africanism* (Chicago: Chicago Review Press, 2007 (1965)), p. 79.

2 Philip S. Foner (ed.), *The Black Panthers Speak* (Chicago: Haymarket Books, 2014 (1970)), p. 61.

3   Examples include James Morris Webb, *The Black Man: The Father of Civilization Proven by Biblical History* (Seattle: ACME Press, 1919), and Yosef A.A. Ben-Jochannan, *African Origins of the Major "Western Religions"* (Baltimore, MD: Black Classic Press, 1991 (1970)).

4   In this respect, see the pivotal Afocentric text, Chancellor Williams', *The Destruction of Black Civilization: Great Issues of a Race from 4500BC to 2000AD* (Chicago: Third World Press, 1974).

5   *Lashawan Qadash* teaches that all Hebrew letters are consonantal, and there are no vowel sounds except the long i and long a. As a result, this 'Hebrew' is virtually unusable as a spoken language.

6   See the comparison of Rastafarian and AHIJ linguistic innovations in Martina Könighofer, *The New Ship of Zion: Dynamic Diaspora Dimensions of the African Hebrew Israelites of Jerusalem* (Wein: Lit, 2008), pp. 104–6.

7   Susan Palmer, *The Nuwaubian Nation: Black Spirituality and State Control* (Burlington, VT: Ashgate Publishing Company, 2010).

8   Fred Moten, *In the Break: The Aesthetics of the Black Radical Tradition* (Minneapolis: University of Minnesota Press, 2003), p. 29.

9   Later, this would be revised to 'The Bible, from Genesis to Malachi, is simply the recorded history of a people, and Yah who has shown that He can/has the ability to produce the effect that African Edenic people are in need of all over this planet.' (IL154). Even here, he presumes the Christian sequence of the Hebrew Bible, which ends with Malachi, rather than the Jewish sequence where Malachi is the last of the Prophets, and the final book is Chronicles.

10 In stronger terms: 'the objective of the NT scribes … was to replace the Old Testament making the god of the *logos* superior.' (RHS60).

11 Muhammad, *Message to the Blackman*, p. 87.

12 Ibid., p. 71.

13 See Weisenfeld, *New World A-Coming*, pp. 94–115.

14 He records Mordecai Herman, Ishi Kaufman, Israel Ben Yomen, Israel Ben Herman and Simon Schurz, to which we can add Bishop A.W. Cook aka Rabbi Haling Hank Lenht. Brotz, 'Black Jews of Harlem', p. 5.

15 Weisenfeld, *New World A-Coming*, p. 6; pp. 13–18.

Chapter 8

1   The case is slightly different with African Judaizing movements, whose interested often similarly reflects a desire to de-Christianize, which is to say de-westernize, their communities, while authentically sensing a kinship in the kind of tribal religious practices which call for a subsuming of the individual under communal norms and involve practices common throughout Africa and the Near East such as circumcision and separation of women during menstruation. Ironically, because those groups who have pursued conversion have most often done so via the Conservative rabbinate, they still face difficulty making Aaliyah to Israel due to the Orthodox rabbinate's control over legal definitions of Jewishness.

2   Yoram Hazony, *Conservatism: A Rediscovery* (Washington: Regnery Gateway, 2022), p. 4.

3   Moses, *Black Messiahs*, p. 4.

4   Cleage described individualism as a kind of demonic force that has subdued whites; Blacks could also succumb to it, if they don't adopt a Black Christian Nationalism. *Black Christian Nationalism*, p. 102.

5   'The Law of Relativity [Ben's concept that like attracts like, and should be responded to with like] requires that you express your displeasure with someone that is wrong. Children (or any other wrongdoers, for that matter) must be rebuked *firmly*, for both your sake and theirs.' (GLR69).

6   On this subject it may be worth noting a strange and untrue argument which illustrates that Ben Ammi was not immune to stereotypes: 'We can safely conclude that an individual's personality is relative to the garment being worn. An outlandish woman wears outlandish clothes; a pervert wears an expression of his perversity. Surely you have discerned that the pious and those defined to play roles of wise men dress accordingly. The most aggressively deviant members of society are invariably trussed in boots, tight leather jackets, gloves, something with a low neckline exposing portions or all of the chest, helmets, and other items boding evil. Their clothing is selected to not only let the world know that they exist, but to convince *themselves* that they do. Their clothing defines the roles they play or want to play.' (GLR77).

7   Hazony, *Conservatism,* p. 182.

8   It will be no surprise that Ben Ammi is against abortion, but his reasoning – that 'Abortion violates the natural cycles of the body', (GBMT182), i.e. that it is harmful to the mother rather than to the foetus – is unexpected. The orthodox Jewish perspective on abortion makes it legitimate, mandatory even, if (and only if) the mother's health is at risk. Related to this we should note that in an undated lecture titled Spiritual Warfare (audio recording provided to me by the AHIJ), Ben utilizes Genesis to argue that life is dependent upon the presence of (divine) mind, and is nothing to do with womb or seed. Haraymiel on the other hand argues against abortion because life begins *before* conception, in the sperm and egg, p. 49.

9   Hazony, *Conservatism,* p. 248.

10   Hazony is unusual in arguing that business should be conducted in a way that does not destroy national sovereignty. However, where Hazony prioritizes the example of America as a beacon to the world, Ben Ammi states clearly that the earth cannot afford any more nations to follow its example.

11   E.g., Zech.14; Zeph.3:9.

12   '[T]he Holy Spirit [is] the force behind nature, the natural', whereas 'the unnatural [is] a spirit that is/was unwilling to subordinate itself to Yah, the Creator … a deviant, mutant form of intellect' (RHS34).

13   Perhaps the only mention is in the opening page of *God and the Law of Relativity,* where he lists the overwhelming troubles of modern times as 'the continuous threat of war in the Middle East, the escalation of drug use (cocaine, "crack", "ice", etc.) in our big cities, Black-on-Black killings as seen in South Africa, Liberia and the U.S., the Arab-Israeli hatred which feeds terrorism and a myriad of environmental hazards which threaten nature' (GLR1).

14   For a description of the rigid and binary approach of one other group, see Tad Bollman, 'The Bible and Black Identity: Israel United in Christ and the Hebrew Israelite Movement' (Indiana University: MA Diss., 2018, pp. 16–18).

15   In GBMT he argues that God-Man-Woman-Children is the natural order, which must be abided by, though it doesn't mean men are better than women but that women find their being in their men. Woman derives from man and doesn't exist without him. (GBMT50-51).

16   This is not to say that the Bible or Talmud expresses rigidly fixed gender roles; each engenders the notion that the genders tend towards particular characteristics and roles, but unusual individuals can and do transgress these without difficulty. A good example is Beruriah, a female sage of the Talmud who engages with male rabbis, discussing fine points of *halakhah* and often winning the argument. Similar is the rabbinic designation of prophet status, of which some 10 per cent are women of the Bible.

17   Dr Haraymiel Ben Shaleahk, *Without Pretense: The Final Resolution of the Multiple Wife Controversy* (Dimona: Global Images International Press, 2004).

18   Ralph Richard Banks, *Is Marriage for White People?: How the African American Marriage Decline Affects Everyone* (New York: Dutton, 2011), pp. 29–48.

19   Ibid.

20   Shaleahk, *Without Pretense*, p. 67, my emphasis.

21   Ibid., pp. 59–61.

22   Ibid., p. 62.

23   Likewise his claim that 'many western countries' have lowered the age of consent to eleven or twelve 'so that perverts can have sex with children' (p. 69). Nowhere in Europe or America is it below fourteen, and the trend has actually been to increase the age since the nineteenth century. The one exception was the Netherlands which between 1990 and 2002 experimented with a policy of twelve as the minimum, with parental consent. This misunderstanding of history is a common part of conservative arguments regarding the corruption of modern society, based upon an imagined but unrealistic past of moral uprightness (according to the most-strict modern standards) when the opposite is usually the case – many practices were tolerated and accepted in the past and have only become morally problematic in modernity.

24   See the case studies provided recently in Lucy Cooke, *Bitch: A Revolutionary Guide to Sex, Evolution and the Female Animal* (London: Doubleday, 2022).

25   See the interview with Tsiporah, now Belinda: 'Mahaleyah interviews Seporah; the star in the original film entitled: "Sister Wife"', *YouTube*, https://www.youtube.com/watch?v=hJerv2nU8u0 as well as with the filmmakers at https://andrewesensten.net/blog/2014/11/30/the-feeling-was-that-they-trusted-us/. Markowitz and Avieli, *Food for the Body*, p. 19 n.9 describe the variety of female responses to and degrees of success of the community's polygynous marriages.

26   Fran Markowitz, 'Millenarian Motherhood: Motives, Meanings and Practices among African Hebrew Israelite Women', *Nashim: A Journal of Jewish Women's Studies & Gender Issues*, 3 (2000), pp. 106–38; p. 108. Interestingly, even the Commandment Keepers, in the 1960s, evidenced a 70/30 female to male ratio: Brotz, 'Negro Jews', p. 333.

27   Paulette Pierce, 'Boudoir Politics and the Birthing of the Nation: Sex, Marriage, and Structural Deflection in the National Black Independent Political Party', in *Women Out of Place: The Gender of Agency and the Race of Nationality*, ed. Brackette F. Williams (New York: Routledge, 1997), pp. 216–44 (218). Cf. Rhonda Y. Williams, 'Black Women, Urban Politics and Engendering Black Power', in *The Black Power Movement: Rethinking the Civil Rights–Black Power Era*, ed. Peniel E. Joseph (New York: Routledge, 2006), pp. 79–104 who writes that 'quite often, black women's activism, although central to the sustenance of many grassroots efforts and organizations, has failed to be recognized – not just by scholars but by the very people in the neighborhoods and cities where they struggled' (p. 82).

28   'Boudoir Politics', p. 225. Cf. Banks, *Is Marriage for White People?* pp. 49–67.

29 Mahaleyah Goodman, *Israel's Secret Cult: The Incredible Story of a Former Member of the African Hebrew Israelites of Jerusalem* (Mahaleyah Goodman, 2013), p. 32.

30 Markowitz, 'Millenarian Motherhood', p. 109. In a follow-up article she remarks that these motivations for joining the AHIJ are basically identical with those of men: '(Still) Sacrificing for Salvation: Millenarian Motherhood Reconsidered', *Social Compass* 50.1 (2003), pp. 97–112 (107).

31 Ibid.

32 Ibid., p. 129.

33 See the account given in Goodman, *Israel's Secret Cult*.

34 bell hooks, *We Real Cool: Black Men and Masculinity* (London: Routledge, 2004).

35 However, Ben is disapproving of the beauty industry and lengths that some women go to in perfecting their appearance: 'no vessel has undergone so much abuse as that of the woman's body.' (GBMT204) 'She has waged war against God and lost' (GBMT204; MEW84).

36 Not to ignore the too-common utilization of women as victim-object in intercultural dialogues, as highlighted by Saba Mahmood, who shows how 'women have often been treated as symbolic placeholders for broader struggles over cultural, identitarian, and territorial claims throughout history'. *Religious Difference in the Secular Age: A Minority Report* (Princeton: Princeton University Press, 2016), p. 143.

37 Shaleahk, *Without Pretense*, p. 68.

38 'In most polygamous societies there is a relatively balanced gender ratio; in some polygynous societies males may outnumber females [...] without this fact preventing them from practising polygyny. When skewed gender ratios do occur, for example as a result of armed conflicts, it may lead to higher rates of polygyny, though the increase will probably be temporary as the gender imbalance is an effect of war rather than a cause of polygamy. Typically, in societies with normal gender ratios, men will be able to marry two or more wives only at the expense of other men, who must then marry at a later age than women do.' Mirian Koktvedgaard Zeitzen, *Polygamy: A Cross-Cultural Analysis* (Oxford & New York: Berg, 2008), p. 47ff.

39 'Rich and powerful men clearly enjoy the greatest degree of polygamy cross-culturally, and there is a direct relationship between wealth, multiple mates and reproductive success. Powerful men can successfully take women from less powerful men, especially in connection with violent conflict. Where power differentials are smallest between high and low in society, successful men generally take no more than three or four wives. The concentration of women at the top of social hierarchies implies a relative deprivation at the bottom, resulting in differential reproduction.' Ibid., p. 64.

40 Lori G. Beaman, 'Opposing Polygamy: A Matter of Equality or Patriarchy?' in *The Polygamy Question*, ed. Janet Bennion and Lisa Fishbayn Joffe (Logan: Utah State University Press, 2016), pp. 42–61 (45).

41 hooks, *We Real Cool*, p. 2.

42 Ibid., p. 7.

43 Ben Ammi's lecture at the Sisterhood Conference discussed the idea that the western value system has made a woman 'that is not fit to be a helpmate of man, so the brothers have been marrying strange women. A strange nature has been placed into them. And this nature will not allow the brother to be the head of the family'. And this causes the men to abandon their family into crime, drugs, robbery, looking for something that his home does not provide him. Here, although the male is the ultimate victim and target of persecution, this persecution is effected *via* the

persecution of women; and so male abandonment is the fault of women being led astray. This dynamic and lack of female agency, even while male wrongs are blamed on female influence, is a complete replication of the Adam and Eve story. Here he fulfils what Pierce names, 'the belief that women are naturally more susceptible to cultural corruption (assimilation) and co-optation than are men', and thus are the vessel by which males try to control other males. 'Boudoir Politics', p. 222.

44 Ethan Michaeli, *Twelve Tribes: Promise and Peril in the New Israel* (London: HarperCollins, 2021), p. 187 says that according to Immanuel Ben Yehuda women have 'a much larger role' in decision making since Ben Ammi's death – although it is not clear what relationship there may be between these two facts. Fran Markowitz tells me that 'While no women have been "elevated" to the Holy Council of Princes, some women have served, and are currently serving, in top ministerial and department roles. From 1992-mid 2010s, women were Secretary to Ben Ammi and Director of Public Relations. Prior to my meeting the AHIC, a woman served as Minister of Education, but a mishap occurred during her term, and she was removed from/left that position. Currently two women are Deputy Ministers – of Education and Agriculture. Women have held keys positions in the Community from its inception, even if not in the top leadership positions. This both works to uphold the patriarchy, and to subvert it.' (Private communication, 2022).

45 Interestingly, despite the essential nature of family gender roles, Ben allows that they can be temporarily suspended if temporary circumstances require: 'A situation developing that requires a man to strap the baby on his front or back or grab the stroller is not a sin or a violation of the ordinances of God.' But 'There is a mood, a temperament and behaviors that is essential and has to accompany all role models for both men and women.' (MEW128).

46 While Ben Ammi is reputed to dislike displays of emotion, the reality – particularly in the life of the community – may be different. Even Ben, who wrote that 'This world keeps the human family in opposition to Divine Law, controlled and manipulated by emotions instead of Truth' (RHS37), was recorded crying with joy during one festival.

47 For background on pre- and post-colonial constructions of gender and sexuality in Africa, see Catherine M. Cole, Takyiwaa Manuh and Stephan F. Miescher (eds), *Africa after Gender?* (Bloomington: Indiana University Press, 2007), and Stephen O. Murray and Will Roscoe (eds), *Boy-wives and Female Husbands: Studies of African Homosexualities* (New York: Palgrave, 1998). Ben Ammi, without providing a reason, presumes that African gender roles were fixed (e.g. GBMT160).

48 Paulette Pierce and Brackette F. Williams, 'Insurgent Masculine Redemption and the Nation of Islam', in *Women Out of Place: The Gender of Agency and the Race of Nationality*, ed. Brackette F. Williams (New York: Routledge, 1997), pp. 186–215.

49 Lori G. Beaman, 'Opposing Polygamy: A Matter of Equality or Patriarchy?' in, ed. Bennion and Lisa Fishbayn Joffe *The Polygamy Question* (Logan: Utah State University Press, 2016), pp. 42–61.

50 On the rabbinic approach to sex, see Danya Ruttenberg, 'Jewish Sexual Ethics', in *The Oxford Handbook of Jewish Ethics and Morality*, ed. Elliot N. Dorff and Jonathan K. Crane (Oxford: Oxford University Press, 2012), pp. 383–99. To give one wonderful example, when two rabbis are told by a Roman duchess that they are so fat as to make sex with their wives impossible, they respond that their penises are even bigger than their bellies and the text goes on to provide the reputed measurements (b.BMetz84a).

51   This is just one of many comments. In others homosexuality is placed in the same
      category as disease, drug abuse and even murder.
52   The one apparent example I know of homosexuality in the community had a tragic
      end: three members were expelled at a time when the AHIJ were trying to clean up
      unsavoury elements and become more law-abiding and socially acceptable – one was
      expelled for homosexuality (a crime for the community but not for Israel). He and
      two others (expelled for petty crime and domestic violence) attempted to return to
      Dimona in January 1972 to reclaim some of their belongings but were met by five
      members. A scuffle began which ended in the death of one of the latter two, Cornell
      Kirkpatrick. While the case may have been prejudiced due to the unfavourable
      position the community inhabited in Israel at that time, it ended with a conviction
      for manslaughter, which has always been protested by the community. To my
      knowledge this constitutes one of only three violent deaths for the AHIJ in Israel, the
      others being terrorist victim Aharon Ben-Yisrael Ellis and the alleged suicide of army
      recruit Toveet Radcliffe.
53   Daniel Boyarin, 'Against Rabbinic Sexuality: Textual Reasoning and the Jewish
      Theology of Sex', in *Queer Theology: Rethinking the Western Body*, ed. Gerard
      Loughlin (Oxford: Blackwell, 2007), pp. 131–46.
54   Sana Loue, *Understanding Theology and Homosexuality in African American
      Communities* (New York: Springer, 2014). For a discussion of the absence of
      homosexuality, and sexuality in general, from Black Theology, see Roger A. Sneed,
      Representations of Homosexuality: Black Liberation Theology and Cultural Criticism
      (New York: Palgrave MacMillan, 2010) and Kelly Brown Douglas, *Sexuality and the
      Black Church: A Womanist Perspective* (Maryknoll, NY: Orbis Books, 2003), esp.
      pp. 87–108.

Conclusion

1   Cone, *Black Theology of Liberation*, p. 16.
2   Buhring, *Conceptions of God*, p. 177.
3   Carmichael, *Stokeley Speaks*, p. 78.
4   Ibid., pp. 78–9.
5   Gray, 'Show and Prove'.
6   Ammi made this statement in a lecture in Jacksonville in the early 1990s, titled As in
      the Days of Noah (audio recording provided by the AHIJ). The disavowal was made
      in a letter, which was CC'd to several Black leaders: Letter to Elijah Muhammad, 1st
      April 1974 (John Henrik Clarke Papers, Schomburg, MG571 b41 f1).
7   Nathan Saunders, 'Evolving Theology of the Nation of Islam', in *New Perspectives on
      the Nation of Islam*, p. 247.
8   Jones, *Is God a White Racist*, p. 77.
9   Hans Jonas, *The Gnostic Religion: The Message of the Alien God and the Beginnings of
      Christianity*, third edn (Boston: Beacon Press, 2001), p. 42.
10   Finley, 'Hidden away'.
11   On fall and captivity in Gnosticism see Jonas, *Gnostic Religion*, pp. 62–5.
12   Philip K. Dick, *The Exegesis of Philip K. Dick*, ed. Pamela Jackson and Jonathan
      Lethem (London: Gollancz, 2011), p. 390.
13   Philip K. Dick, *The Valis Trilogy* (New York: Mariner, 2011 (1981)).

14 Slavoj Zizek, *The Parallax View* (Cambridge, MA: MIT Press, 2006).
15 Gershom Scholem, *Major Trends in Jewish Mysticism* (New York: Shocken, 1941), pp. 244–50. This perspective, while influential, has not been universally agreed upon by scholars. Others have argued that Lurianic and Safedian Kabbalah were sometimes heavily influenced by the Christian concepts that Iberian Jews forcibly converted to Christianity had to adopt: Shaul Magid, *From Metaphysics to Midrash: Myth, History, and the Interpretation of Scripture in Lurianic Kabbala* (Bloomington: Indiana University Press, 2008) esp. pp. 34–74. On the emergence of a concept of original sin in Medieval Judaism see also Alan Cooper, 'A Medieval Jewish Version of Original Sin: Ephraim of Luntshits on Leviticus 12', *HTR* 97.4 (2004), pp. 445–59.
16 For the clearest systematic overview of Luria's teachings and life, see Fine, *Physician of the Soul.*
17 Scholem, *Kabbalah and Its Symbolism*, p. 117.
18 The Zohar offers a surprising reading of Cain and Abel whereby Abel is as responsible for his own murder as is Cain; he appears to attract or provoke evil.
19 Melila Hellner-Eshed, *Seekers of the Face: Secrets of the Idra Rabba (The Great Assembly) of the Zohar*, trans. Raphael Dascalu (Stanford: Stanford University Press, 2021), pp. 337–45; On the Gnostic origins of Cain as offspring of Satan and Eve, see Gedaliahu A.G. Stroumsa, *Another Seed: Studies in Gnostic Mythology* (Leiden: Brill, 1984), pp. 38–49, and Oded Yisraeli, 'Cain as the Scion of Satan: The Evolution of a Gnostic Myth in the Zohar', *Harvard Theological Review* 109 (2016), pp. 56–74, who remarks that the kabbalistic interpretation of the tradition 'reveals to us [...] a demonic, deterministic, dualistic framework that divides humanity into the righteous and the wicked, the offspring of Adam and the offspring of Satan, the "sons of light" and the "sons of darkness"' (p. 64).
20 There is however a surprising surface similarity with the thought of the fascist Christian Identity movement. See Barkun, *Religion and the Rise of the Racist Right*, pp. 149–72. The theory that the serpent (in a human form) had impregnated Eve with a second seedline was developed in the nineteenth century and also inherited by some Baptist sects – although these appear to be entirely white groups, the possibility of Shaleak or some other member absorbing it thereby is not impossible.
21 Yisraeli, 'Scion of Satan', p. 70.
22 It might be thought that the Lurianic doctrine of *gilgul*, reincarnation, reflects Ben Ammi's semi-reincarnation compatible theology. However, in Luria *gilgul* occurs because of the primordial flaw in humanity, which means that often souls cannot achieve their purpose in one lifetime and so must return; indeed, if it were not for this flaw, souls would not enter material bodies at all – this realm being demonic in nature. Luria's notion that each soul can be composed of 'sparks' from a variety of earlier souls such as Adam mixed with Cain, etc., resembles Ben's idea of spirits that can be invoked for guidance, as well as his notion of mixing good and evil from the tree of knowledge (though in Luria it is Cain's sin that begins that mixing of Good and Evil). In Lurianic theory the soul of a tzaddik can cohabit a lifetime to aid the development of another soul. On this see Eitan P. Fishbane, 'A Chariot for the Shekhina: Identity and the Ideal Life in Sixteenth-Century Kabbalah', *Journal of Religious Ethics* 37.3 (2009), pp. 385–418.
23 See, e.g., *Zohar* 2:166b, where light is planted as seeds in Eden.
24 Fine, *Physician*, p. 188.
25 Adam Afterman, 'The Rise of the Holy Spirit in Sixteenth-Century Kabbalah', *HTR* 115.2 (2022), pp. 219–42 (220).

26   Ibid., p. 228.
27   Ibid., p. 237.
28   On the commandments as a means of redemption in Luria, see esp. Daphne Freedman, *Man and the Theogony in the Lurianic Cabala* (Piscataway, NJ: Gorgias Press, 2014), pp. 97–117. Freedman explains that the performance of the commandments both restores and reveals the archetypal image of God (as the primordial Adam); in Ben Ammi it also does both, as it manifests God in the world and actively reforms the world along the lines of righteousness, i.e. bringing it closer to God in both proximity and similarity. There is even a suggestion of the undoing of Adam's first disobedience by performing *mitzvot* (p. 108). Luria wanted to repair the vessels that shattered, mythically represented as the sin of Adam and expulsion from Eden, just like Ben Ammi, in order to progress rightly as the cosmos should in the first instance.
29   Patrick B. Koch, *Human Self-Perfection: A Re-Assessment of Kabbalistic Musar-Literature of Sixteenth-Century Safed* (Los Angeles: Cherub, 2015), p. 83.
30   Moshe Cordovero, *Tomer Devorah* (Venice: Cordovero, 1588) [Hebrew], fol. 7a. English translation in *The Palm Tree of Deborah*, ed. L. Jacobs, p. 69.
31   Koch, *Human Self-Perfection*, p. 95.
32   Afterman, 'Holy Spirit', p. 233.
33   Chaim Vital, *Sha'arei Qedushah* (Jerusalem: Eshkol, 2000), [Hebrew], p. 29. Following the translation of Fishbane, 'A Chariot for the Shekhinah'.
34   One area where Ammi and Luria differ is in regard to vegetarianism. Luria's belief that the biblical injunction to send away a mother bird before taking her eggs (Deut.22:6-7) was a situation that one should seek out in order to fulfil, i.e. one should send away a mother bird and then take her eggs even when one would not otherwise want the eggs, is representative of the difference in dietary outlook between him and Ben Ammi. Luria does not see the biblical or rabbinic dietary principles in terms of minimizing harm to animals, but in terms of a much more esoteric cause and effect. This leads him to apparently urge the eating of meat (when this is done with the correct intention) in order to liberate the human souls/divine sparks that have been trapped in these lower bodies.
35   Ibid., p. 128.
36   Ibid., p. 1.
37   Lawrence Fine, 'The Contemplative Practice of Yihudim in Lurianic Kabbalah', in *Jewish Spirituality*, ed. Arthur Green, vol. 2 (New York: Crossroad, 1984), pp. 64–98 (94).
38   See Koch, *Human Self-Perfection*. While these Kabbalah-inspired popular conduct manuals (or *musar* literature) simplified the theological elements and concentrated on conduct, they maintained that it was through right ethical behaviour that each individual could help to sustain and repair the world.
39   Citron, *Horowitz's Shnei Luhot Ha-Berit. Two Tablets*, completed in 1629 a few years after Horowitz left Europe for Palestine, was published frequently, forming a popular and highly regard work; several abridgements and translations were also published in subsequent centuries, and its spread was across the Sephardic and Ashkenazi worlds.

Bibliography

Primary sources

Ben Ammi, *God, the Black Man, and Truth*, revised edn. First published 1982; first revised edn 1986 (Washington, DC: Communicators Press, 1990).

Ben Ammi, *God and the Law of Relativity* (Washington, DC: Communicators Press, 1991a).

Ben Ammi, *The Messiah and the End of This World* (Washington, DC: Communicators Press, 1991b).

Ben Ammi, *Everlasting Life: From Thought to Reality* (Washington, DC: Communicators Press, 1994).

Ben Ammi, *Yeshua the Hebrew Messiah or Jesus the Christian Christ?* (Washington, DC: Communicators Press, 1996a).

Ben Ammi, 'The Prophecy', *Essence* 26.10 (1996b), p. 54.

Ben Ammi, *An Imitation of Life: Redefining What Constitutes True Life and Living in the New World* (Washington, DC: Communicators Press, 1999).

Ben Ammi, *Yeshua the Hebrew Messiah or Jesus the Christian Christ? Part 2: The Final Confrontation* (Washington, DC: Communicators Press, 2002).

Ben Ammi, *Revival of the Holy Spirit* (Washington, DC: Communicators Press, 2004).

Ben Ammi, *The Resurrection: From Judgement to Post-Judgement* (Washington, DC: Communicators Press, 2005).

Ben Ammi, *The Restoration Village: The Restoration of Heaven on Earth through the Revitalization of the African Village Concept* (Washington, DC: Communicators Press (e-text only), 2008).

Ben Ammi, *The Ascension of the New Adam* (e-text only) (2009).

Ben Ammi, *Physical Immortality: Conquering Death* (Washington, DC: Communicators Press, 2010).

Ben Ammi, *Dehumanization: Artificial Intelligence, Technology and the Final Onslaught of the Dominion of Deception* (Washington, DC: Communicators Press, 2011).

Secondary sources

Maurianne Adams and John Bracey (eds), *Strangers & Neighbours: Relations between Blacks & Jews in the United States* (Amherst: University of Massachusetts Press, 1999).

Adam Afterman, 'The Rise of the Holy Spirit in Sixteenth-Century Kabbalah', *Harvard Theological Review* 115.2 (2022), pp. 219–42.

Philip S. Alexander, 'Pre-Emptive Exegesis: Genesis Rabba's Reading of the Story of Creation', *Journal of Jewish Studies* 43.2 (1992), pp. 230–45.

Allen Alter (UPI), 'Community of Black Hebrews Thriving Illegally in Israeli Desert', in *The Brownsville Herald* (Brownsville, Texas, 30th October 1977), p. 45.

Victor Anderson, *Beyond Ontological Blackness: An Essay on African American Religious and Cultural Criticism* (London: Bloomsbury, 2016).

Fleming Aytes, *The Teaching Black Jew* (New York City: Fleming Aytes, 1927).

Justine M. Bakker, 'On the Knowledge of Self and Others: Secrecy, Concealment and Revelation in Elijah Muhammad's Nation of Islam (1934–1975)', in *Esotericism in African American Religious Experience: 'There Is a Mystery'* ..., ed. Stephen C. Finley, Margarita Simon Guillory and Hugh R. Page, Jr (Leiden: Brill, 2015), pp. 138–51.

Ralph Richard Banks, *Is Marriage for White People?: How the African American Marriage Decline Affects Everyone* (New York: Dutton, 2011).

Ishakamusa Barashango, *God, the Bible and the Black Man's Destiny* (Baltimore: Afrikan World Books, 2001 (1970)).

Michael Barkun, *Religion and the Racist Right: The Origins of the Christian Identity Movement*, revised edn (Chapel Hill: University of North Carolina Press, 1997).

Lori G. Beaman, 'Opposing Polygamy: A Matter of Equality or Patriarchy?' in *The Polygamy Question*, ed. Janet Bennion and Lisa Fishbayn Joffe (Logan: Utah State University Press, 2016), pp. 42–61.

Aviva Ben-Ur, *Jewish Autonomy in a Slave Society: Suriname in the Atlantic World, 1651–1825* (Philadelphia: University of Pennsylvania Press, 2020).

Graenum Berger, *Black Jews in America: A Documentary with Commentary* (New York: Commission on Synagogue Relations, 1978).

Eliezer Berkovits, *God, Man and History*, ed. David Hazony (Jerusalem: Shalem Press, 2004 (1959)).

Wallace D. Best, *Passionately Human, No Less Divine: Religion and Culture in Black Chicago, 1916–1952* (Princeton: Princeton University Press, 2005).

W. Henry E. Bibins, *The Mark of a Lost Race* (New York, n.d.).

John Bishop and Ken Perszyk, 'Concepts of God and Problems of Evil', in *Alternative Concepts of God: Essays on the Metaphysics of the Divine*, ed. Andrei A. Buckareff and Yujin Nagasawa (Oxford: Oxford University Press, 2016), pp. 106–27.

W.E.B. Du Bois, *The Souls of Black Folk*, ed. Brent Hayes Edwards (Oxford: Oxford University Press, 2007).

W.E.B. Du Bois, *Darkwater: Voices from within the Veil* (New York: Harcourt, Brace and Company, 1920).

Tad Bollman, 'The Bible and Black Identity: Israel United in Christ and the Hebrew Israelite Movement' (Indiana University: MA Diss., 2018.

Joan Borsten, 'Sect Problems', *Jerusalem Post*, 3rd December 1976, pp. 7–8.

John Bowker, *Problems of Suffering in Religions of the World* (London: Cambridge University Press, 1970).

Daniel Boyarin, *Carnal Israel: Reading Sex in Talmudic Culture* (Berkeley: University of California Press, 1993).

Daniel Boyarin, 'Against Rabbinic Sexuality: Textual Reasoning and the Jewish Theology of Sex', in *Queer Theology: Rethinking the Western Body*, ed. Gerard Loughlin (Oxford: Blackwell, 2007), pp. 131–46.

Marla Brettschneider, Edith Bruder and Magdel Le Roux (eds), *Africana Jewish Journeys: Studies in African Judaism* (Cambridge: Cambridge Scholars Press, 2019).

Jonathan Broder, 'Chicago Blacks Seek Election in Israel', *Chicago Tribune*, 9 January 1977, p. 5.

Howard M. Brotz, 'The Black Jews of Harlem' (University of Chicago: MA Diss., 1947).

Howard M. Brotz, 'Negro Jews in the United States', *Phylon* 13.4 (1952), pp. 324–37.

Howard M. Brotz, *The Black Jews of Harlem: Negro Nationalism and the Dilemmas of Negro Leadership* (London: Free Press of Glencoe, 1964).

Edith Bruder, *The Black Jews of Africa: History, Identity, Religion* (Oxford: Oxford University Press, 2008).

Edith Bruder and Tudor Parfitt (eds), *African Zion: Studies in Black Judaism* (Newcastle: Cambridge Scholars Publishing, 2012).

Jonathan Brumberg-Kraus, 'Meat-Eating and Jewish Identity: Ritualization of the Priestly "Torah of Beast and Fowl" (Lev 11:46) in Rabbinic Judaism and Medieval Kabbalah', *AJS Review* 24.2 (1999), pp. 227–62.

L.A. Bryant, *Know Thyself* (Chicago: One Inc., 1968).

Kurt Buhring, *Conceptions of God, Freedom and Ethics in African American and Jewish Theology* (New York: Palgrave Macmillan, 2008).

Allen Dwight Callahan, 'Perspectives for a Study of African American Religion: From the Valley of Dry Bones', *Nova Religio: The Journal of Alternative and Emergent Religions* 7.1 (2003), pp. 44–59.

Stokeley Carmichael (Kwame Ture), *Stokely Speaks: From Black Power to Pan-Africanism* (Chicago: Chicago Review Press, 2007 (1965)).

Robert P. Carroll, *When Prophecy Failed: Reactions and Responses to Failure in the Old Testament Prophetic Traditions* (London: SCM Press, 1979).

Mark L. Chapman, *Christianity on Trial: African-American Religious Thought before and after Black Power* (Eugene, OR: Wipf & Stock, 1996).

The Chicago Commission on Race Relations, *The Negro in Chicago: A Study of Race Relations and a Race Riot* (Chicago: University of Chicago Press, 1922).

William Christian, *Poor Pilgrim's Work in the Name of the Father, Son and Holy Ghost* (Texarkana: Joe Ehrlich, 1896).

Church of God and Saints of Christ, 'Bishop Joseph Wesley Crowdy, Chief of the Pulpits 1875–1917', http://www.churchofgodandsaintsofchrist.org/leaders/jwcrowdy.html.

Joseph Citron, *Isaiah Horowitz's Shnei Luhot He-Berit and the Pietistic Transformation of Jewish Theology* (Leiden: Brill, 2021).

Jawanza Eric Clark, 'Introduction: Why a White Christ *Continues* to Be Racist: The Legacy of Albert B. Cleage Jr', in *Albert Cleage Jr. and the Black Madonna and Child*, ed. Jawanza Eric Clark (New York: Palgrave Macmillan, 2016), pp. 6–7.

Jawanza Eric Clark, 'Nothing Is More Sacred Than the Liberation of Black People: Albert Cleage's Method as Unfulfilled Theological Paradigm Shift', in *Albert Cleage Jr. and the Black Madonna and Child*, ed. Jawanza Eric Clark (New York: Palgrave Macmillan, 2016), pp. 39–58.

Albert J. Cleage, *The Black Messiah* (New York: Sheed &Ward, 1965).

Albert J. Cleage, *Black Christian Nationalism: New Directions for the Black Church* (New York: William Morrow, 1972).

Dan Cohn-Sherbok, *God and the Holocaust* (Leominster: Fowler Wright, 1996).

Catherine M. Cole, Takyiwaa Manuh and Stephan F. Miescher (eds), *Africa after Gender?* (Bloomington: Indiana University Press, 2007).

Marley Cole, *Jehovah's Witnesses: The New World Society* (Oxon: Routledge, 2019 (1956)).

Monica A. Coleman, *Making a Way out of No Way: A Womanist Theology* (Minneapolis: Fortress Press, 2008).

James H. Cone, *Black Theology and Black Power* (Maryknoll: Orbis Books, 1997 (1969)).

James H. Cone, *A Black Theology of Liberation* (Philadelphia & New York: J.B. Lippincott Company, 1970).

James H. Cone, *God of the Oppressed*, revised edn (Maryknoll: Orbis Books, 1997).

Bishop A.W. Cook, *The Independent Church of God of the Juda Tribe of Israel: The Black Jews* (New York: Cook, 1925).

Bishop A.W. Cook, *Get One While the Getting Is Good: Black Jews of the Judean Tribe of Israel: One God, One Aim, One Destiny* (Special Collections: University of Delaware, n.d.).

Lucy Cooke, *Bitch: A Revolutionary Guide to Sex, Evolution and the Female Animal* (London: Doubleday, 2022).

Alan Cooper, 'A Medieval Jewish Version of Original Sin: Ephraim of Luntshits on Leviticus 12', *HTR* 97.4 (2004), pp. 445–59.

Moshe Cordovero, *Tomer Devorah* (Venice, 1588) [Hebrew].

Alexander Crummell, 'The Destined Superiority of the Negro', in *The Greatness of Christ and Other Sermons* (New York: Whittaker, 1882).

Lynn Davidman, *Tradition in a Rootless World: Women Turn to Orthodox Judaism* (Berkeley: University of California Press, 1993).

William L. Van Deburg, *New Day in Babylon: The Black Power Movement and American Culture, 1965–1975* (London: University of Chicago Press, 1992).

Azriel Devine, 'Rabbi Robert Devine', blackjews.com, https://www.blackjews.org/rabbi-robert-devine/ (accessed 3rd October 2022).

Nathan P. Devir, *New Children of Israel: Emerging Jewish Communities in an Era of Globalization* (Salt Lake: University of Utah Press, 2017).

Spencer Dew, 'Hebrew Israelite Covenantal Theology and Kendrick Lamar's Constructive Project in DAMN', in *Kendrick Lamar and the Making of Black Meaning*, ed. Christopher M. Driscoll, Anthony B. Pinn and Monica R. Miller (Oxon: Routledge, 2020), p. 18.

Diary of A Revolutionary, 'Mahaleyah Interviews Seporah; the Star in the Original Film Entitled: "Sister Wife"', *YouTube*, https://www.youtube.com/watch?v=hJerv2nU8u0.

Philip K. Dick, *The Valis Trilogy* (New York: Mariner, 2011 (1981)).

Philip K. Dick, *The Exegesis of Philip K Dick*, ed. Pamela Jackson and Jonathan Lethem (London: Gollancz, 2011).

G.H. Dix, 'The Messiah Ben Joseph', *The Journal of Theological Studies* 27.106 (1926), pp. 130–43.

Marc Dollinger, *Black Power, Jewish Politics: Reinventing the Alliance in the 1960s* (Waltham, MS: Brandeis University Press, 2018).

Jacob S. Dorman, *Chosen People: The Rise of American Black Israelite Religions* (Oxford: Oxford University Press, 2013).

Jacob S. Dorman, *The Princess and the Prophet: The Secret History of Magic, Race, and Moorish Muslims in America* (Boston, MS: Beacon Press, 2020).

Kelly Brown Douglas, *Sexuality and the Black Church: A Womanist Perspective* (Maryknoll, NY: Orbis Books, 2003).

St. Clair Drake and Horace R. Cayton, *Black Metropolis: A Study of Negro Life in a Northern City*, revised & enlarged edition (New York: Harper & Row, 1962).

Albert Ehrman, 'Black Judaism in New York', *Journal of Ecumenical Studies* 8.1 (1971), pp. 103–14.

Roberta Elliott, 'Interview with Ben Ammi', *Newsview* 14.02 (1984), p. 17.

E.U. Essien-Udom, *Black Nationalism: A Search for an Identity in America* (Chicago: University of Chicago Press, 1962).

Samuel Estabrooks, 'The African American Apocalyptic as Prophetic Social Protest' (Arizona State University: PhD Diss., 2016).

James H. Evans Jr., 'The Holy Spirit in African American Theology', in *The Oxford Handbook of African American Theology*, ed. Katie G. Cannon and Anthony B. Pinn (Oxford: Oxford University Press, 2014), pp. 164–73.

Eli Faber, *Jews, Slaves, and the Slave Trade: Setting the Record Straight* (New York: New York University Press, 1998).

Arthur Huff Fauset, *Black Gods of the Metropolis: Negro Religious Cults of the Urban North* (New York: Octagon Books, 1970).

Lawrence Fine, 'The Contemplative Practice of Yihudim in Lurianic Kabbalah', in *Jewish Spirituality*, ed. Arthur Green, vol. 2 (New York: Crossroad, 1984), pp. 64–98.

Lawrence Fine, *Physician of the Soul: Isaac Luria and His Kabbalistic Fellowship* (Stanford: Stanford University Press, 2003).

Stephen Carl Finley, 'Re-imagining Race and Representation: The Black Body in the Nation of Islam' (Rice University: PhD Thesis, 2006).

Stephen C. Finley, 'Hidden away: Esotericism and Gnosticism in Elijah Muhammad's Nation of Islam', in *Histories of the Hidden God: Concealment and Revelation in Western Gnostic, Esoteric and Mystical Traditions*, ed. April D. DeConick and Grant Adamson (Oxon: Routledge, 2013), pp. 259–80.

Stephen C. Finley, 'The Secret … of Who the Devil Is': Elijah Muhammad, the Nation of Islam, and Theological Phenomenology', in *New Perspectives on the Nation of Islam*, ed. Dawn-Marie Gibson and Herbert Berg (New York: Routledge, 2017), pp. 154–73.

Michael R. Fischbach, *Black Power and Palestine: Transnational Countries of Color* (Stanford: Stanford University Press, 2019).

Eitan P. Fishbane, 'A Chariot for the Shekhina: Identity and the Ideal Life in Sixteenth-Century Kabbalah', *Journal of Religious Ethics* 37.3 (2009), pp. 385–418.

Philip S. Foner (ed.), *The Black Panthers Speak* (Chicago: Haymarket Books, 2014 (1970)).

Arnold Forster, 'The "Black Hebrew Nation"', *ADL Bulletin*, February 1972.

George M. Fredrickson, *Black Liberation: A Comparative History of Black Ideologies in the United States and South Africa* (New York: Oxford University Press, 1995).

Daphne Freedman, *Man and the Theogony in the Lurianic Cabala* (Piscataway, NJ: Gorgias Press, 2014).

Hoyt E. Fuller, 'The Original Hebrew Israelite Nation: An Interview', *Black World* (May 1975), pp. 62–70.

Timothy E. Fulop, '"The Future Golden Day of the Race": Millennialism and Black Americans in the Nadir, 1877–1901', *Harvard Theological Review* 84.1 (1991), pp. 75–99.

Mikal J. Gaines, 'Staying Woke in Sunken Places, or the Wages of Double Consciousness', in *Jordan Peele's* Get Out: *Political Horror*, ed. Dawn Keetley (Columbus: Ohio State University, 2020), pp. 160–73.

Martin Gelman, 'Adat Beyt Moshe: The Colored House of Moses, a Study of the Contemporary Negro Religious Community and Its Leader' (University of Pennsylvania: PhD Thesis, 1965).

Jason George, 'Promised Land. Promise Fading', *Chicago Tribune*, 7th Jul 2008.

Nahum N. Glatzer, 'The Synagogue of the Negro Jews in New York', Almanach des Schocken Verlags (Berlin, 1938/9), pp. 121–9.

Mahaleyah Goodman, *Israel's Secret Cult: The Incredible Story of a Former Member of the African Hebrew Israelites of Jerusalem* (Mahaleyah Goodman, 2013).

Norman Saul Goodman, 'Mythology of Evil in Judaism', *Journal of Religion and Health* 15.4 (1976), pp. 230–41.

Lewis Gordon, 'The Problem of History in African American Theology', in *The Oxford Handbook of African American Theology*, ed. Katie G. Cannon and Anthony B. Pinn (Oxford: Oxford University Press, 2014), pp. 363–76.

Biko Mandela Gray, 'Show and Prove: Five Percenters and the Study of African American Esotericism', in *Esotericism in African American Religious Experience: 'There Is a Mystery'* ..., ed. Stephen C. Finley, Margarita Simon Guillory and Hugh R. Page, Jr (Leiden: Brill, 2015), pp. 177–97.

Gershon Greenberg, 'Hasidic Thought and the Holocaust (1933–1947): Optimism and Activism', *Jewish History* 27.2 (2013), pp. 353–75.

Ya'akov HaElyon, '"*Moreh ha-Tzedek*" Amar "*Lo*"!', (The 'Righteous Teacher' says 'No'!) *Ma'ariv*, 22nd May 1970, p. 70 [Hebrew].

Prince Gavriel HaGadol and Odehyah B. Israel, *The Impregnable People: An Exodus of African Americans Back to Africa* (Washington, DC: Communicators Press, 1993).

Judah Halevi, *The Kuzari (Kitab al Khazari): An Argument for the Faith of Israel* (New York: Schocken, 1964).

Sara Harris, *Father Divine* (New York: Collier, 1971).

Bruce D. Haynes, *The Soul of Judaism: Jews of African Descent in America* (New York: New York University Press, 2018).

Yoram Hazony, *Conservatism: A Rediscovery* (Washington, DC: Regnery Gateway, 2022).

Melila Hellner-Eshed, *Seekers of the Face: Secrets of the Idra Rabba (The Great Assembly) of the Zohar*, trans. Raphael Dascalu (Stanford: Stanford University Press, 2021).

Derek S. Hicks, 'Eschatology in African American Theology', in *The Oxford Handbook of African American Theology*, ed. Katie G. Cannon and Anthony B. Pinn (Oxford: Oxford University Press, 2014), pp. 242–52.

Darlene Clark Hine, 'Introduction', in *The Black Chicago Renaissance*, ed. Darlene Clark Hine and John McCluskey Jr (Urbana: University of Illinois Press, 2012), pp. xv–xxxiii.

James Theodore Holly, 'The Divine Plan of Human Redemption in Its Ethnological Development', *AME Church Review* 1.6 (1884), pp. 79–85, reprinted in A.B. Pinn (ed.) *Moral Evil and Redemptive Suffering: A History of Theodicy in African-American Religious Thought* (Gainesville: University Press of Florida, 2002), 131–40.

bell hooks, *We Real Cool: Black Men and Masculinity* (London: Routledge, 2004).

Dwight N. Hopkins, *Black Theology USA and South Africa* (New York: Orbis, 1989).

Dwight N. Hopkins, *Down, Up, and Over: Slave Religion and Black Theology* (Minneapolis: Fortress Press, 2000).

Dwight N. Hopkins, 'Slave Theology in the "Invisible Institution"', in *Cut Loose Your Stammering Tongue: Black Theology in the Slave Narrative*, ed. Dwight N. Hopkins and George C.L. Cummings, second edn (Louisville: Westminster John Knox Press, 2003), pp. 1–33.

Aloys Huttermann, *The Ecological Message of the Torah: Knowledge, Concepts, and Laws Which Made Survival in a Land of 'Milk and Honey' Possible* (Atlanta, GA: Scholars Press, 1999).

Moshe Idel, *Kabbalah: New Perspectives* (New Haven: Yale University Press, 1988).

Walter Isaac, 'Locating Afro-American Judaism: A Critique of White Normativity', in *The Companion to African American Studies*, ed. Lewis R. Gordon and Jane Anna Gordon (Malden, MA: Blackwell, 2006).

Walter Isaac, 'Beyond Ontological Jewishness: A Philosophical Reflection on the Study of African American Jews and the Social Problems of the Jewish and Human Sciences' (Temple University: PhD Diss., 2012).

Yadah Baht Israel, 'The Holistic Lifestyle', in *The Hebrew Israelite Community*, ed. A. Paul Hare (Lanham: University Press of America, 1998), pp. 27–34.

David R. Jackson, *Enochic Judaism: Three Defining Paradigm Exemplars* (London: T&T Clark, 2004).

John L. Jackson, 'All Yah's Children: Emigrationism, Afrocentrism, and the Place of Israel in Africa', *Civilisations* 58.1 (2009), pp. 93–112.

John L. Jackson Jr., *Real Black: Adventures in Racial Sincerity* (Chicago: University of Chicago Press, 2005).

John L. Jackson, Jr., *Thin Description: Ethnography and the African Hebrew Israelites of Jerusalem* (Cambridge, MA: Harvard University Press, 2013).

'The Original Hebrew Israelite Nation of Jerusalem', James Landing Papers box 7 f.50.

Clark Jenkins, *The Black Hebrews of the Seed of Abraham - Isaac and Jacob of the Tribe of Judah - Benjamin and Levi after 430 Years in America* (Detroit: Jenkins, 1969).

'Cult's Critics Charge Secrecy, Strictness and "Brainwashing"', *Jerusalem Post*, 22nd January 1979.

'Survey of Chicago's Black Jews II: Congregation Needs Torah and Ark, Reporter Told', *Jewish Post*, 1st October 1965.

'Survey of Chicago's Black Jews III: Negro "Rabbi" Claims White Jews Not Jews', *Jewish Post* 8th October 1965, p. 13.

Yosef A.A. Ben-Jochannan, *African Origins of the Major Western Religions* (Baltimore: Black Classic Press, 1991 (1970)).

Yosef A.A. Ben-Jochannan, *We the Black Jews: Witness to the 'White Jewish Race' Myth* (Baltimore, MD: Black Classic Press, 1993 (1983)).

Hans Jonas, *The Gnostic Religion: The Message of the Alien God and the Beginnings of Christianity*, third edn (Boston: Beacon Press, 2001).

William R. Jones, *Is God a White Racist? A Preamble to Black Theology* (Boston: Beacon Press, 1997).

Nathan Kaplan, 'Negro "Rabbi" Claims White Jews Not Jews', *Jewish Post*, 8th October 1965, p. 13.

Steven T. Katz, Shlomo Biderman and Gershon Greenberg (eds), *Wrestling with God: Jewish Theological Responses during and after the Holocaust* (New York: Oxford University Press, 2007).

Sam Kestenbaum, 'Contested Legacy of Dr. Ben, a Father of African Studies', *New York Times*, 27th March 2015.

Sam Kestenbaum, '"I'm an Israelite": Kendrick Lamar's Spiritual Search, Hebrew Israelite Religion, and the Politics of a Celebrity Encounter', in *Kendrick Lamar and the Making of Black Meaning*, ed. Christopher M. Driscoll, Anthony B. Pinn and Monica R. Miller (Oxon: Routledge, 2020), p. 16.

Andre E. Key, 'If thou do not hearken unto the voice of the Lord thy God: A Critique of Theodicy in Black Judaism', *Black Theology* 12.3 (2014), pp. 267–88.

Andre E. Key, 'Toward a Typology of Black Hebrew Religious Thought and Practice', *Journal of Africana Religions* 2.1 (2014), pp. 31–66.

K.J. King, 'Some Notes on Arnold J. Ford and New World Black Attitudes to Ethiopia', *Journal of Ethiopian Studies* 10.1 (1972), pp. 81–7.

J. Klausner, *The Messianic Idea in Israel* (London: Allen & Unwin, 1956).

Michael Muhammad Knight, *The Five Percenters: Islam, Hip Hop and the Gods of New York* (Oxford: One World, 2007).

Patrick B. Koch, *Human Self-Perfection: A Re-Assessment of Kabbalistic Musar-Literature of Sixteenth-Century Safed* (Los Angeles: Cherub, 2015).

Martina Könighofer, *The New Ship of Zion: Dynamic Diaspora Dimensions of the African Hebrew Israelites of Jerusalem* (Wein: Lit, 2008).

Ruth Landes, 'Negro Jews in Harlem', *Jewish Journal of Sociology* 9.2 (1967), pp. 175–89.

James Landing, *Black Judaism: The Story of an American Movement* (Durham: Carolina Academic Press, 2002).

Daniel J. Lasker, 'Reflection: The Holocaust as Retributive Justice', *Shofar* 15.3 (1997), pp. 97–105.

Anson Laytner, *Arguing with God: A Jewish Tradition* (New York: Jason Aaronson, 1998).

Martha Lee, *The Nation of Islam: An American Millenarian Movement* (Syracuse, NY: Syracuse University Press, 1996).

Laura Arnold Leibman, *Once We Were Slaves: The Extraordinary Journey of a Multiracial Jewish Family* (Oxford: Oxford University Press, 2021).

Cohane Michael Ben Levi, *Israelites and Jews: The Significant Difference* (Kearney, NE: Morris Publishing, 1997).

Sholomo B. Levy, 'Wentworth Arthur Matthew', in *African American Lives*, ed. Henry Louis Gates Jr and Evelyn Brooks Higginbotham (Oxford: Oxford University Press, 2004), pp. 567–9.

Daniel Lis, William F.S. Miles and Tudor Parfitt (eds), *In the Shadow of Moses: New Jewish Movements in Africa and the Diaspora* (Loyola: African Academic Press, 2016).

Sana Loue, *Understanding Theology and Homosexuality in African American Communities* (New York: Springer, 2014).

Morris Lounds, *Israel's Black Hebrews: Black Americans in Search of Identity* (Washington, DC: University Press of America 1981).

Shaul Magid, *From Metaphysics to Midrash: Myth, History, and the Interpretation of Scripture in Lurianic Kabbala* (Bloomington: Indiana University Press, 2008).

Saba Mahmood, *Religious Difference in the Secular Age: A Minority Report* (Princeton: Princeton University Press, 2016).

Moses Maimonides, *The Guide for the Perplexed*, trans. M. Friedländer, second edn (Skokie, IL: Varda Books, 2002).

Vocab Malone, *Barack Obama vs The Black Hebrew Israelites: Introduction to the History & Beliefs of 1West Israelism* (Phoenix: Thureos Publishing, 2017).

Aron Manheimer, 'The Black Israelites of Dimona', *Davka* 2.3 (May-June 1972).

Fran Markowitz, 'Millenarian Motherhood: Motives, Meanings and Practices among African Hebrew Israelite Women', *Nashim: A Journal of Jewish Women's Studies & Gender Issues* 3 (2000), pp. 106–38.

Fran Markowitz, '(Still) Sacrificing for Salvation: Millenarian Motherhood Reconsidered', *Social Compass* 50.1 (2003), pp. 97–112.

Fran Markowitz and Nir Avieli, 'Food for the Body and Soul: Veganism, Righteous Male Bodies, and Culinary Redemption in the Kingdom of Yah', *Ethnography* 23.2 (2020), pp. 181–203.

Darnise C. Martin, 'The Self Divine: Know Ye Not That Ye Are Gods?' in *Esotericism in African American Religious Experience: 'There Is a Mystery'* ..., ed. Stephen C. Finley, Margarita Simon Guillory and Hugh R. Page, Jr (Leiden: Brill, 2015), pp. 52–69.

Daniel C. Matt, 'The Mystic and the Mizwot', in *Jewish Spirituality: From the Bible through the Middle Ages*, ed. Arthur Green (New York: Crossroad, 1996), pp. 367–404.

Daniel C. Matt (ed.), *The Zohar (Pritzker Edition)* 12 vols (Stanford: Stanford University Press, 2004–17).

Ariel Evan Mayse, 'Gardens of the Spirit: Land, Text, and Ecological Hermeneutics in Jewish Mystical Sources', *Dibur* 11 (2022), pp. 60–88.

Bernard Maza, *With Fury Poured Out: The Power of the Powerless during the Holocaust* (New York, NY: Shapolsky Publishers, 1989).

John T. McCartney, *Black Power Ideologies: An Essay in African American Political Thought* (Philadelphia: Temple University Press, 1992).

Ethan Michaeli, 'Another Exodus: The Hebrew Israelites from Chicago to Dimona', in *Black Zion: African American Religious Encounters with Judaism*, ed. Yvonne Chireau and Nathaniel Deutsch (New York: Oxford University Press, 2000), pp. 73–90.

Ethan Michaeli, *Twelve Tribes: Promise and Peril in the New Israel* (London: HarperCollins, 2021).

Michael T. Miller, 'The African Hebrew Israelites of Jerusalem and Ben Ammi's Theology of Marginalisation and Reorientation', *Religions* 11.2 (2020), p. 87.

Michael T. Miller, 'The African Hebrew Israelites of Jerusalem', in *Critical Dictionary of Apocalyptic and Millenarian Movements*, ed. James Crossley and Alastair Lockhart (Bedford: Panacea Charitable Trust, 2021), www.cdamm.org/articles/ahij.

Michael T. Miller, 'The African Hebrew Israelites of Jerusalem: A Borderline Case', in *The Stranger in Early Modern and Modern Jewish Tradition*, ed. Catherine Bartlett and Joachim Schlör (Leiden: Brill, 2021), pp. 28–46.

Michael T. Miller, 'Ben Ammi's Adaptation of Veganism in the Theology of the African Hebrew Israelites', *Interdisciplinary Journal for Religion and Transformation in Contemporary Society* 7.2 (2021).

Michael T. Miller, 'Bishop Allan Wilson Cook (Rabbi Haling Hank Lenht), Queen Malinda Morris, and the Independent Church of God: A Missing Piece in the History of Hebrew Israelite Black Judaism', *Black Theology* 21.3 (2023).

Michael T. Miller (Forthcoming), 'Layers of Liminality and Marginality in the African Hebrew Israelite Community', in *Betwixt and Between Liminality and Marginality: Mind the Gap*, ed. Zohar Hadromi-Allouche & Michael Hubbard MacKay (Idaho Falls: Lexington, 2023) pp.15–36.

Patrick Miller, *Sin and Judgment in the Prophets: A Stylistic and Theological Analysis* (Chico, CA: Scholars Press, 1982).

Randolph C. Miller, 'Process Thought and Black Theology', in *Black Theology II: Essays on the Formation and Outreach of Contemporary Black Theology*, ed. Calvin E. Bruce and William R. Jones (Cranbury, NJ: Associated University Press, 1978), pp. 267–86.

R. Laurence Moore, *Religious Outsiders and the Making of Americans* (New York: Oxford University Press, 1986).

Wilson Jeremiah Moses, *The Golden Age of Black Nationalism 1850–1925* (Hamden: Archon Books, 1978).

Wilson Jeremiah Moses, *Black Messiahs and Uncle Toms: Social and Literary Manipulations of a Religious Myth*, revised edn (University Park: Pennsylvania State University Press, 1993).

Fred Moten, *In the Break: The Aesthetics of the Black Radical Tradition* (Minneapolis: University of Minnesota Press, 2003).

Elijah Muhammad, *Message to the Blackman in America* (Chicago: Muhammad Mosque of Islam No. 2, 1965).

Elijah Muhammad, *The Fall of America* (Phoenix, AR: Secretarius MEMPS Publications, 1973).

Stephen O. Murray and Will Roscoe (eds), *Boy-wives and Female Husbands: Studies of African Homosexualities* (New York: Palgrave, 1998).

Susan Nance, 'Mystery of the Moorish Science Temple: Southern Blacks and American Alternative Spirituality in 1920s Chicago', *Religion and American Culture: A Journal of Interpretation* 12.2 (2002), pp. 123–66.

Jacob Neusner, *Judaism's Story of Creation: Scripture, Halakhah, Aggadah* (Leiden: Brill, 2000).

Andrei Orlov, *The Enoch-Metatron Tradition* (Tubingen: Mohr Siebeck, 2005).
Roi Ottley, *Inside Black America* (London: Eyre & Spottiswoode, 1948).
Henry Paget, *Caliban's Reason: Introducing Afro-Caribbean Philosophy* (New York: Routledge, 2000).
Susan Palmer, *The Nuwaubian Nation: Black Spirituality and State Control* (Burlington, VT: Ashgate Publishing Company, 2010).
Tudor Parfitt, *Black Jews in Africa and the Americas* (London: Harvard University Press, 2013).
Tudor Parfitt, *Hybrid Hate: Conflations of Antisemitism & Anti-Black Racism from the Renaissance to the Third Reich* (New York: Oxford University Press, 2020).
Tudor Parfitt and Netanel Fisher (eds), *Becoming Jewish: New Jews and Emerging Jewish Communities in a Globalized World* (Cambridge: Cambridge Scholars Publishing, 2016).
'Deportations by Israel Hit', *The Philadelphia Inquirer*, 12th October 1971, p. 5.
'Black Israelites Hit Israel Immigration Ban', *Philadelphia Jewish Exponent*, 15th October 1971, p. 1; 76.
Paulette Pierce, 'Boudoir Politics and the Birthing of the Nation: Sex, Marriage, and Structural Deflection in the National Black Independent Political Party', in *Women Out of Place: The Gender of Agency and the Race of Nationality*, ed. Brackette F. Williams (New York: Routledge, 1997), pp. 216–44.
Yolanda Pierce, *Hell Without Fires: Slavery, Christianity, and the Antebellum Spiritual Narrative* (Gainsville: University Press of Florida, 2005).
Paulette Pierce and Brackette F. Williams, 'Insurgent Masculine Redemption and the Nation of Islam', in *Women Out of Place: The Gender of Agency and the Race of Nationality*, ed. Brackette F. Williams (New York: Routledge, 1997), pp. 186–215.
Anthony B. Pinn, *Why Lord? Suffering and Evil in Black Theology* (New York: Continuum, 1995).
Anthony B. Pinn (ed), *Moral Evil and Redemptive Suffering: A History of Theodicy in African-American Religious Thought* (Gainesville: University Press of Florida, 2002).
Anthony B. Pinn, *Terror and Triumph: The Nature of Black Religion* (Minneapolis: Fortress Press, 2003).
Anthony B. Pinn, *Embodiment and the New Shape of Black Theological Thought* (New York: New York University Press, 2010).
Anthony B. Pinn, *The End of God-Talk: An African American Humanistic Theology* (New York: Oxford University Press, 2012).
David Howard Pitney, *African American Jeremiad: Appeals for Justice in America*, revised edn (Philadelphia: Temple University Press, 2005).
Nehemia Polen, *The Holy Fire: The Teachings of Kalonymus Kalman Shapira, the Rebbe of the Warsaw Ghetto* (Northvale, NJ: Jason Aaronson Inc., 1994).
Dina Porat, '"Amalek's Accomplices": Blaming Zionism for the Holocaust: Anti-Zionist Ultra-Orthodoxy in Israel during the 1980s', *Journal of Contemporary History* 27.4 (1992), pp. 695–729.
Charles Price, 'The Cultural Production of a Black Messiah: Ethiopianism and Rastafari', *Journal of Africana Religions* 2.3 (2014), pp. 418–33.
Albert J. Raboteau, *A Fire in the Bones: Reflections on African-American Religious History* (Boston: Beacon Press, 1995).
Albert J. Raboteau, '"Ethiopia Shall Soon Stretch Forth Her Hands": Black Destiny in Nineteenth-Century America', in *African American Religious Thought: An Anthology*, ed. Cornell West and Eddie S. Glaude Jr. (Louisville: Westminster John Knox Press, 2003), pp. 397–413.

Anthony Reddie, 'Introduction', in *Black Theology, Slavery and Contemporary Christianity*, ed. Anthony Reddie (Oxon: Routledge, 2016), pp. 1–29.

Edwin S. Redkey, *Black Exodus: Black Nationalist and Back-to-Africa Movements, 1890–1910* (New Haven: Yale University Press, 1969).

Christopher Robert Reed, *The Rise of Chicago's Black Metropolis: 1920–1929* (Urbana: University of Illinois Press, 2011).

Joel Augustus Rogers, *Sex and Race: Negro-Caucasian Mixing in All Ages and All Lands* (St Petersburg, FL: Helga M Rogers, 1968 (1940)).

Bruce Rosenstock, *Transfinite Life: Oskar Goldberg and the Vitalist Imagination* (Bloomington: Indiana University Press, 2017).

Arnold Rosenzweig, 'Black Jews of South Side', pt.5, *Chicago Defender* (2 February 1963), pp. 1–2.

Richard L. Rubenstein, *After Auschwitz: Radical Theology and Contemporary Judaism* (Indianapolis: Macmillan, 1966).

Danya Ruttenberg, 'Jewish Sexual Ethics', in *The Oxford Handbook of Jewish Ethics and Morality*, ed. Elliot N. Dorff and Jonathan K. Crane (Oxford: Oxford University Press, 2012), pp. 383–99.

Norbert M. Samuelson, *Judaism and the Doctrine of Creation* (Cambridge: Cambridge University Press, 1994).

Nathan Saunders, 'The Evolving Theology of the Nation of Islam', in *New Perspectives on the Nation of Islam*, ed. Dawn-Marie Gibson and Herbert Berg (New York: Routledge, 2017).

'Another Reason to Fast', *The Sentinel*, 5th February 1976, p. 6.

Gershom Scholem, *Major Trends in Jewish Mysticism* (New York: Shocken, 1941).

Gershom Scholem, *On the Kabbalah and Its Symbolism*, trans. Ralph Manheim (New York: Schocken Books, 1969).

Jonathan Schorsch, *Jews and Blacks in the Early Modern World* (Cambridge: Cambridge University Press, 2004).

Kenneth Seeskin, *Jewish Philosophy in a Secular Age* (Albany: State University of New York Press, 1990).

David Mevorach Seidenberg, *Kabbalah and Ecology: God's Image in the More-Than-Human World* (New York: Cambridge University Press, 2015).

L.S. Senghor, *Anthologie de la nouvelle poésie nègre et malgache de langue française* (Paris: Presses Universitaires de France, 1948).

L.S. Senghor and E.P. Halperin, 'African Negro Aesthetics', *Diogenes* 4.16 (1956), pp. 23–38.

L.S. Senghor, *Liberté I, Négritude et humanisme* (Paris: Seuil, 1964).

Dr Haraymiel Ben Shaleahk, *Without Pretense: The Final Resolution of the Multiple Wife Controversy* (Global Images International Press, 2004).

Deanne Ruth Shapiro, 'Double Damnation, Double Salvation: The Sources and Varieties of Black Judaism in the United States' (Columbia University: MA Diss., 1970).

Yaakov Ben Sheshet, *Sefer Meshiv Devarim Nekhohim*, ed. Georges Vajda (Jerusalem: Israel Academy of Science and Humanities, 1969), p. 83. [Hebrew].

Merrill Charles Singer, 'Saints of the Kingdom: Group Emergence, Individual Affiliation, and Social Change among the Black Hebrews of Israel' University of Utah: PhD Diss., 1979).

Merrill Singer, 'Symbolic Identity Formation in an African American Religious Sect: The Black Hebrew Israelites', in *Black Zion: African American Religious Encounters with Judaism*, ed. Yvonne Chireau and Nathaniel Deutsch (New York: Oxford University Press, 2000), pp. 55–72.

Roger A. Sneed, *Representations of Homosexuality: Black Liberation Theology and Cultural Criticism* (New York: Palgrave MacMillan, 2010).

Francesca Stavrakopoulou, *God: An Anatomy* (London: Picador, 2021).

T.G. Steward, *The End of the World; or, Clearing the Way for the Fullness of the Gentiles* (Philadelphia: AME Church Book Rooms, 1888).

Gedaliahu A.G. Stroumsa, *Another Seed: Studies in Gnostic Mythology* (Leiden: Brill, 1984).

Era Bell Thomson, 'Are Black Americans Welcome in Africa?', *Ebony* (January 1969), pp. 44–50.

Howard Thurman, 'Deep Calls Unto Deep, Part 1: The Meaning of Religious Experience, 1980 January 23', *The Howard Thurman Digital Archive*, https://thurman.pitts.emory.edu/items/show/875 (accessed 21st September 2022).

Yakov M. Travis, 'Kabbalistic Foundations of Jewish Spiritual Practice: Rabbi Ezra of Gerona on the Kabbalistic Meaning of the Mitzvot' (Brandeis University: PhD diss., 2002).

Ernest Lee Tuveson, *Redeemer Nation: The Idea of America's Millennial Role* (Chicago & London: University of Chicago Press, 1968).

Ephraim E. Urbach, *The Sages: Their Concepts and Beliefs*, trans. Israel Abrahams, 2 vols (Jerusalem: Magnes Press, 1987).

Chaim Vital, *Sha'arei Qedushah* (Jerusalem: Eshkol, 2000) [Hebrew].

Topher Vollmer, 'What Would King Think?', *Peace News*, 1st May 2008, https://peacenews.info/node/3976/what-would-king-think.

Topher Vollmer, 'New Humanity?', *Peace News*, 1st June 2008, https://peacenews.info/node/3975/new-humanity

Howard Waitzkin, 'Black Judaism in New York', *Harvard Journal of Negro Affairs* 1.3 (1967), pp. 12–44.

David Walker, *Walker's Appeal, in Four Articles; Together with a Preamble, to the Coloured Citizens of the World*, third edn (Boston: Walker, 1830).

Arthur Waskow, 'Jewish Environmental Ethics: Intertwining Adam with Adamah', in *The Oxford Handbook of Jewish Ethics and Morality*, ed. Elliot N. Dorff and Jonathan K. Crane (Oxford: Oxford University Press, 2012), pp. 401–17.

James Morris Webb, *The Black Man: The Father of Civilization Proven by Biblical History* (Seattle: ACME Press, 1919).

Robert G. Weisbord, *Ebony Kinship: Africa, Africans and the Afro-American* (Westport: Greenwood Press, 1973).

Judith Weisenfeld, *New World A-Coming: Black Religion and Racial Identity during the Great Migration* (New York: New York University Press, 2016).

Dov Weiss, *Pious Irreverence: Confronting God in Rabbinic Judaism* (Penn: University of Pennsylvania Press, 2016).

Thomas Whitfield, *From Night to Sunlight* (Nashville, TN: Broadman Press, 1980).

Chancellor Williams, *The Destruction of Black Civilization: Great Issues of a Race from 4500BC to 2000AD* (Chicago: Third World Press, 1974).

Delores S. Williams, *Sisters in the Wilderness: The Challenge of Womanist God-Talk* (Marknoll: Orbis Books, 1993).

Rhonda Y. Williams, 'Black Women, Urban Politics and Engendering Black Power', in *The Black Power Movement: Rethinking the Civil Rights–Black Power Era*, ed. Peniel E. Joseph (New York: Routledge, 2006), pp. 79–104.

Sabyl M. Willis, 'The House of Yisrael Cincinnati: How Normalized Institutional Violence Can Produce a Culture of Unorthodox Resistance 1963 to 2021' (Wright State University: MA Thesis, 2021.

Rudolph R. Windsor, *From Babylon to Timbuktu: A History of the Ancient Black Races Including the Black Hebrews* (Atlanta: Windsor's Golden Series, 2003 (1969)).

Rudolph R. Windsor, *Valley of the Dry Bones: The Conditions That Face Black People in America Today* (Atlanta, GA: Windsor's Golden Series, 1986).

'Former Black Panther Takes Aldermanic Post', *Wisconsin State Journal* 29.4 (1983), p. 15.

Keith A. Wolff, 'Bal Tashchit: The Jewish Prohibition against Needless Destruction' (Leiden University: PhD Thesis, 2009).

Elliot R. Wolfson, 'Mirror of Nature Reflected in the Symbolism of Medieval Kabbalah', in *Judaism and Ecology: Created World and Revealed Word*, ed. Hava Tirosh-Samuelson (Cambridge, MA: Harvard University Press, 2002), pp. 305–32.

Malcolm X, *The Autobiography of Malcolm X: As Told to Alex Haley* (New York: Ballantine Books, 1965).

Sar Ahmadiel Ben Yehuda, 'Redefining the Israeli-Palestinian Conflict from an African/Edenic (and Truth-Centered) Perspective', *Hebrew Israelite Nation Times* (September 2020), pp. 24–31.

Shaleak Ben Yehuda, letter to John Henrik Clarke, 4th June 1973 (JHC Papers, Schomburg, MG571 b41 f1).

Shaleak Ben Yehuda, *Black Hebrew Israelites from America to the Promised Land: The Great International Religious Conspiracy against the Children of the Prophets* (New York: Vantage Press, 1975).

Oded Yisraeli, 'Cain as the Scion of Satan: The Evolution of a Gnostic Myth in the *Zohar*', *Harvard Theological Review* 109 (2016), pp. 56–74.

Tanhum Yoreh, 'The Jewish Prohibition against Wastefulness: The Evolution of an Environmental Ethic' (York University: PhD Thesis, 2014).

Robert Alexander Young, 'The Ethiopian Manifesto (1829)', in *Pamphlets of Protest: An Anthology of Early African-American Protest Literature, 1790–1860*, ed. Richard Newman, Patrick Rael and Philip Lapsansky (New York & Oxon: Routledge, 2001), pp. 84–9.

Mirian Koktvedgaard Zeitzen, *Polygamy: A Cross-Cultural Analysis* (Oxford & New York: Berg, 2008).

Saifeldeen Zihiri, 'Ambassadors of Christ and Israel United in Christ: Comparing the Preaching Strategies of Black Hebrew Israelite Camps', *UCLA Journal of Religion* 4 (2020), pp. 30–68.

Slavoj Zizek, *The Parallax View* (Cambridge, MA: MIT Press, 2006).

Index

Printed in the USA
CPSIA information can be obtained
at www.ICGtesting.com
LVHW020406071123
763256LV00007B/216

9 781350 295131